Emergent Issues in Education

SUNY Series
FRONTIERS IN EDUCATION
Philip G. Altbach, Editor

The Frontiers in Education Series draws upon a range of disciplines and approaches in the analysis of contemporary educational issues and concerns. Books in the series help to reinterpret established fields of scholarship in education by encouraging the latest synthesis and research. A special focus highlights educational policy issues from a multidisciplinary perspective. The series is published in cooperation with the Graduate School of Education, State University of New York at Buffalo.

Emergent Issues in Education

Comparative Perspectives

Robert F. Arnove
Philip G. Altbach
Gail P. Kelly
Editors

State University of New York Press

23869367

Published by
State University of New York Press, Albany

© 1992 State University of New York

For information, address State University of New York
Press, State University Plaza, Albany, N.Y., 12246

Production by E. Moore
Marketing by Bernadette LaManna

Library of Congress Cataloging-in-Publication Data

Emergent issues in education : comparative perspectives / Robert F.
   Arnove, Philip G. Altbach, Gail P. Kelly, editors.
        p.   cm. — (SUNY series, frontiers in education)
   Includes index.
   ISBN 0-7914-1031-5 (alk. paper) — ISBN 0-7914-1032-3 (pbk. :
alk. paper)
     1. Comparative education. 2. Education and state. I. Arnove,
Robert F. II. Altbach, Philip G. III. Kelly, Gail Paradise.
IV. Series.
LB43.E46 1992
370.19'5—dc20   91-4328
                                                                                          CIP

10 9 8 7 6 5 4 3 2 1

Dedication

This volume is dedicated to the memory of our friend and colleague, Gail Paradise Kelly, who passed away in January 1991. Gail worked closely with us on this volume. Gail Kelly's contributions to this volume and the field of comparative education were significant. She pioneered the comparative study of women and education and had a lasting impact on the development and shape of the field. She served as the President of the Comparative and International Education Society and, at the time of her death, was General Secretary of the CIES. Her intellect, compassion, activism, and grace will be missed by comparative educators. We will miss her as a cherished friend and colleague.

PHILIP G. ALTBACH AND ROBERT F. ARNOVE

Contents

PART V
ASSESSING THE OUTCOMES OF REFORMS

ROBERT F. ARNOVE
PHILIP G. ALTBACH
GAIL P. KELLY

Introduction

Comparative education as a field of study emerged after World War II. Unlike other fields which delineated themselves by specific discipline-based methodologies and theories, comparative education arose with neither. It was and remains a loosely bounded field which is held together by a fundamental belief that education can be improved and can serve to bring about change for the better in all nations. Scholars in the field consistently have focused on the relationship between school and society. Inquiry often has sought to discover how changes in educational provision, form, and content would contribute to the eradication of poverty or the end of gender, class, and ethnic based inequalities.

While cohesion is found in an underlying belief in the transforming power of education, there is a wide diversity in the approaches comparative educators have taken in their work. A range of theories as disparate as structural functionalism and Marxism guide research. A large number of case studies, historical studies and ethnographies along side of statistical scholarship form the research base of comparative education. Some studies are truly comparative, consisting of research conducted in or on several different nations. A majority, however, are case studies of education in a single country. Comparative education, in short, is a diverse field which most commonly addresses questions about schooling and school/society relations.

This book reflects the field as it has emerged in the 1990s. The essays we include focus on a broad range of issues, many of which have been debated since the field's inception, and some of which have surfaced recently. Many of the long standing issues focus on the importance of education to the state, and whether differences in political systems foster differences in educational prac-

1

tices, contents, and outcomes. The text also reflects the debates over theory that have remained unresolved since they emerged in the 1960s. The debates have centered on whether or not theory should guide research and, if so, which theories would be appropriate to the field. Like events on the world stage, theory undergoes change as scholars and researchers reformulate their concepts and intellectual frameworks to explain more accurately social phenomena and arrive at general propositions about school/society relations.

Beginning in the 1960s, comparative education underwent a major transformation. It moved from a field which by and large described education within the context of a specific country to a discipline which examined the outcomes of education without necessarily taking into account national cultural, political, social, or economic factors. In the 1960s, comparative education endeavored to build a set of "scientific" laws. By 1990, after decades of unsuccessful transference of practices from one national context to another, based on these "scientific laws," many began to reassess the role of culture and national histories in shaping school practices and outcomes. Such developments are covered in this volume.

Between the 1960s and 1990s, there have been other shifts in focus. In the 1960s and 1970s, the field concentrated almost exclusively on assessing the *outcomes* of education. These outcomes, however, seldom were cognitive or pedagogical in nature. Instead, scholars sought to link political attitudes, adult social status, and incomes of individuals to number of years of schooling. In similar fashion, the stability of a political system or the wealth of a country were linked to percentages of students enrolled in different levels of an education system or the average amount of schooling found in the workforce and population at large. By the mid-1980s, research in comparative education recognized that such linkages were difficult, if not impossible, to establish. Research increasingly turned to analyzing schools as educational institutions and focused on assessing how reforms in school practices might change cognitive as well as other outcomes. Recently, studies have emerged on issues like school finance, teacher education, testing practices, curriculum, and textbooks. The input-output studies which hitherto had dominated comparative education were muted. This volume emphasizes these new trends by including chapters on testing, teaching as a profession, school management, finance, and effective schools.

In the ten years since the publication of our first jointly edited text, *Comparative Education*, the issues of the day have changed. At the beginning of the 1980s, for example, the field still assumed that resources for school expansion were abundant. Many researchers in the field also tended to ignore educational questions pertaining to teaching-learning processes. In the 1980s, world-wide recession made issues of educational efficiency and effectiveness central.

Other events on the world stage introduced unexpected situations and new issues. In addition to the economic downturns experienced by major regions of the developing world, there are the remarkable changes that have occurred in recent years in the Soviet Union and Eastern Europe and other one-party states pursuing a socialist path to development. As these countries move toward market economies and parliamentary forms of democracy, what transformations will occur in their education systems and will proposed changes facilitate or hinder reform efforts in the political and economic arenas?

This volume illustrates the dynamism and increasing diversity of comparative education and, as such, can be considered a state of the art volume on the field of comparative education. It reflects the theoretical and pragmatic currents—the concerns of educational scholars as well as policy makers. It further reflects the changing research foci and the increasing desire on the part of comparative educators to contribute to the wider education community—to improving educational practices both nationally and internationally.

ORGANIZATION AND CONTENT

Even more so than our previous text, this volume is comparative in nature. Only two of the chapters involve in-depth analysis of single countries—appropriately China and India, which because of their size, complexity, and significance provide interesting cases for examining propositions concerning the universality of modernization processes and the possibility of altering current patterns of financing schooling. Two of the studies involve the comparison of the United States and the United Kingdom. The remaining studies draw upon data from many countries to examine different issues and reforms.

Following a chapter by Gail Kelly on trends in the field of comparative education, the text is organized into four principal sections: (1) world trends in education, (2) theoretical frameworks, (3) contemporary reform movements and emergent issues, (4) assessing the outcomes of educational movements and reforms.

Trends in Comparative Education

Kelly defines comparative education as a field still in search of a distinct identity. After reviewing four decades of debates in the field over methodology, theory, and specific substantive issues, she concludes that for the foreseeable future comparative education will be characterized by a diversity of theoretical frameworks and a broad range of topics studied from a multiplicity of disciplinary perspectives. As reflected in the content of this text, debates will shift as educational practices and needs change and trust placed in particular theories, social systems, or reforms prove themselves valid or not. For Kelly, the continuous search for an identity is a source of strength rather than weakness.

World Trends in Education

The various chapters in this section provide frameworks for analyzing the worldwide expansion and institutionalization of education from primary through higher education. The chapters indicate that there is increasing convergence across countries with regard to notions of education's contributions to national development; and despite significant divergence in chosen routes to modernization, the organizational form schooling takes, particularly at the higher education level, is remarkably similar. The emergence of a global education system raises concerns about the possibility of increasing stratification within it—just as there is in the global economy, with different countries playing different roles in the creation and dissemination of scientific and technological knowledge.

Boli and Ramirez, in chapter 2, examine the dynamics underlying the establishment of compulsory schooling. They point out that most sociological explanations of schooling as a source of social solidarity and preparation for adult roles, as a mechanism of social control, or as an outcome of status group competition are limited in viewing educational development as the result of internal social processes. Instead, they argue that mass schooling is best understood as the prominent consequence of the development and diffusion of the cultural framework of the West. The rise of compulsory schooling in the nineteenth century is explained as the coalescence of a new model of social organization based on notions of the enhanced individual and the expanded state working jointly to pursue national programs. The authors attempt to track empirically the spread and institutionalization of education in relation to the characteristics of national societies that may hinder or slow down the passage of compulsory schooling.

Boli and Ramirez focus on the lower levels of schooling. Altbach examines the universal expansion of higher education. Like Boli and Ramirez he documents the increasing convergence in the basic organization, patterns of governance, and ethos of universities. He explains the movement toward a common Western academic pattern as a manifestation of the continuing influence of metropolitan centers on their former colonies, a dominance that is buttressed by the centers advanced levels of science and research. Issues underscored by Altbach include the ability of higher education institutions to keep pace with the demand for increased access, the economic difficulties these institutions face, and the need for their curricula to be more closely related to employment prospects and national development plans. In the face of these pressures, there are increasing efforts for higher education institutions to rely on user fees and private sector support, to establish closer ties between universities and industries, to reduce the traditional autonomy of these institutions and make teachers more accountable. These trends are reflected in subsequent chapters of the book that examine various levels of schooling.

Berman builds on and expands Altbach's discussion of convergence in higher education institutions and academic research while also providing a critique of Boli and Ramirez' assumptions concerning the universalistic/integrative nature of educational expansion. He agrees with Boli and Ramirez that an understanding of the global expansion would be incomplete if it failed to assess the impact of outside organizations on national educational development, but he believes they ignore the phenomeon that nation-states in the late twentieth century are part of an interdependent world system in which the actions of the stronger determine to a considerable degree the ability of the weaker to act unilaterally. His chapter documents the role that networks of international and national aid agencies play in influencing the reconceptualization, expansion, and reform of Third World education systems.

Hayhoe's chapter, using the case of China, examines these questions: "Are there a variety of ways of being modern or only one? Are the differences between capitalist and socialist modernity fundamental ones or are they simply two branches of Western modernity?" She examines what kind of theoretical framework might make possible comparison of China's experience with that of other nations and at the same time take into account its unique cultural dynamics. These frameworks are the "problems approach" of Holmes, the structural theory of imperialism and World Order Models Approach of Galtung, the world systems theory of Wallerstein, and the critical theory of Habermas. She points out the strengths and limitations of each approach and concludes that studies of Chinese modernity await forms of thought and analysis that are cognizant of, without being subservient to, those of Western socialism or Western capitalism. As she suggests, perhaps the most exciting discoveries may escape the logic of either Western orthodoxies and open up new possiblities for genuine cultural diversity.

Kozma views events in Eastern Europe and the transition from totalitarianism to democracy in light of the past histories of these societies and the various tensions that lay beneath the surface of Soviet domination of the region. As with the case of China, the efforts of these societies to become more closely integrated into the world system demand an understanding of the contending political forces and ideological debates that have occurred over the path of development to be followed. His thesis is that the transition has gone hand in hand with the revival of conservatism, involving "a shift in paradigms" with regard to what issues are to be debated and in what terms. The new conservative paradigm is manifested most clearly in attempts to reform curricula by engaging in an "ideological housecleaning" of Soviet and Marxist-Leninist content and decreasing emphasis on science education and internationalism, reviving traditional elite secondary education institutes such as the grammar schools while downplaying comprehensive secondary schools, and privatizing the education system. As with the Chinese reform movements of the past, an emphasis on traditional institutions and national values may have the unintended consequences of contributing to separation from rather than integration with Europe and the rest of the world and may impede economic growth and the transition to democracy.

Theoretical Frameworks

The chapters in this section provide ways of conceptualizing equality of educational opportunity, reconceptualizing thinking on the role of education in the economy, and bringing into sharper focus theories of the state. As such, they represent some of the more promising developments in theory building and the formulation of comparative perspectives on educational phenomena derived from the disciplines of sociology, economics, and political economy.

Farrell uses a model to summarize what much of recent comparative data tells us about education's contribution to equalizing the life chances of children in different societies. His model examines equality with regard to access to schooling, participation in different levels of an education system, academic achievement, and the outcomes of education (e.g., occupational attainment, income, power, and status). His analysis also includes ways of interpreting educational and social equality/inequality over time in societies at differing stages of development.

Easton and Klees contend that at present there are no adequate conceptualizations of the role of education in the economy that illuminate such issues as the educational-labor mismatch or fairness in allocation of jobs, income, and other social roles. According to the authors, human capital theory and neoclassical economics offer little useful guidance to policy. Their brief examination of other schools of economic thought, however, foreshadows possible new directions for "reconceptualizing" the multiple relationships between education and the economy. Easton and Klees believe that useful insights must come from other fields—among them, anthropology, literature, religion, and even education.

The chapter by Carnoy contributes to new perspectives on education's role in the economy and society. Whereas Easton and Klees discuss the necessity of looking at the role of government in shaping the nature of schooling and its economic outcomes, Carnoy places that discussion within a broader theoretical framework. As Carnoy notes almost all analyses of educational problems—even if they be only studies of educational costs and benefits—have implicit in them theories of the state. Education's inexorable linkages to politics require a discussion of what the state is and how it relates to the economy and social relations. In his esssay, Carnoy provides a typology to facilitate analysis of how different notions of the state influence educational policy and practice. The different ideal types are the Peripheral State, the Instrumental State, the Contested State, the Institutional State, the State in Transition, and the Redemocratized State (the case of Eastern Europe today).

Contemporary Reform Movements and Emergent Issues

The chapters in this section discuss educational governance and finance, the use of secondary school leaving examinations, the status of teachers as professionals, and effective school reforms. The issues that are reiterated and elaborated upon in these chapters include those of centralization v. decentralization, public v. private education, autonomy v. accountabiltiy, equality v. quality.

McGinn examines decentralization as a possible solution for low levels of participation by communities, teachers, and parents in decision-making that helps to resolve problems of insufficient finances and inefficiencies in management. His historical review of reforms in governance in Europe, the United States, and Latin America indicates there is no simple correspondence between degree of popular participation in State power and the forms of governance or control of a State's education system. He suggests that proposals for reform of governance be evaluated not in terms of labels such as centralization or decentralization but with regard to their impact on the means by which people can participate in decision-making and their commitment to democratic participation.

Using data from India, Tilak questions the validity of prevalent assumptions concerning the possibility of greater contributions of the private sector to the financing and running of schools. These assumptions posit that (a) the opportunity costs of education in underdeveloped countries are insignificant due to large-scale unemployment and (b) the ability of families to pay for education has not been sufficiently tapped. The evidence he has marshalled does not substantiate such claims. Moreover, as Tilak points out, those who advocate privatization often overlook the costs a society has to pay in the long run in the form of increasing socioeconomic inequities that result from the creation of dual structures of education.

In addition to the issues related to the governance and financing of education, a number of countries are attempting to bring about educational change by raising the level of school achievement. Noah and Eckstein examine the various uses of secondary school examinations to effect educational reform. Their study of eight national systems reveals that examinations may prove to be obstacles to change in some countries but levers of change in others.

As the various chapters in this text underscore, the success of reform measures depends upon contextual factors. Judge, in his cross-national study of teachers, follows the tradition of researchers who use the insights furnished by comparative education to identify precisely that which is specific to a particular society. He contrasts this tradition to those who would seek supranational rules or underlying general principles. He selects the United Kingdom and the United States to study how societal perceptions of the status and role of teachers are influenced by the unique context of each society. The specific dimensions of professionalism that he analyzes involve the scope of legislation, collective bargaining, and degree of centralized control over teachers (what he calls "nationality"), the hierarchical differentiation of teachers ("stratification"), syndicalism, autonomy, and unity of teachers.

In a complementary chapter, David provides a contextual framework for viewing educational reforms in the two countries as subsets of the political changes that occurred in the 1980s. With the advent of conservative administrations in the United States and United Kingdom there was, as she notes, a remarkable similarity in the way educational issues were addressed—schools were scapegoated for the economic problems of the societies and emphasis was placed on raising academic standards. However, the process of educational reform in the United States took a different tack from that in Britain: in the United States the approach was to reduce the federal role, rather than to use the central government, as in Britain, to command an increasing role for local communities in educational change while strengthening national control over curricular matters.

In contrast to previous chapters which concentrated on the limitations of proposed reforms, Levin's chapter documents those cases where reforms have brought about more effective schools in both industrialized and industrializing countries. Although the concerns of those involved in establishing effective schools are similar, a variety of strategies work. At base, however, those who wish to create effective schools have a vision or a "central philosophy" concerning what a more ideal education should be. This ideal involves a profound transformation of schools. The set of conditions that facilitates the achievement of this vision includes decentralized approaches and solutions; empowerment of teachers, students, and parents; and a heavy emphasis on community participation, much in line with McGinn's thesis.

Assessing the Outcomes of Reforms

The concern of various authors in this text with the effects of reforms on schools and society and especially on the life chances of minority children and women (see, for example, Farrell and David) is addressed in greater depth in the final section of the text.

Husén examines the effects of the most comprehensive international effort to study school achievement and the factors associated with it. The history of the International Evaluation of Educational Achievement (IEA), the various stages it passed through and its outcomes at two levels—those of national policy and classroom practice—are reviewed with regard to what lessons might be learned for future comparative assessment efforts. He analyzes policy outcomes at three levels: (1) the overall quality and/or performance of a national system of education, including its role in achieving social and economic objectives, such as greater equality of opportunity; (2) the structure of the formal system and its influence on student achievement; and (3) the influence of school resources and methods of instruction on learning.

Kelly studies the extent to which women's gains in access to education have been matched by favorable economic outcomes. Kelly's extensive review of data from a broad range of countries leads her to conlude that economic outcomes have not been the same for women as men. She attributes these differences to the lack of change in the sex role division of labor in the family and the lack of social legislation recognizing family organization and women's role in it. Under these circumstances, women have few options but to enter low-wage "female" occupations. As she argues, achieving gender-based quality in the workforce and in society will take more than opening schools to women.

Arnove and Graff examine the legacies and lessons from four hundred years of literacy campaigns in more than a dozen societies. Among the lessons to be learned are these: there are many paths to literacy; literacy's relation to political, economic, and social development is complex; the quantity and quality of literacy (and the acquisition and use of literacy) are not linearly related; the consequences of literacy are neither direct nor simple; and literacy is never politically neutral. Literacy is potential empowerment, but the extent to which literacy is used for emancipatory purposes depends on the context in which literacy campaigns and activities take place. Their chapter underscores the value of comparative and historical perspectives for an understanding of an educational movement as fundamental as a literacy campaign, a priority on the educational agendas of many countries today.

CONCLUSION

This volume discusses some of the most important themes in comparative education at the beginning of the 1990s—the themes of educational expansion and reform, of equality and quality, of private resources and public responsibility, of autonomy and accountability, of centralization and decentralization in governance, of convergence and divergence in approaches to national development and educational reform. We have attempted to provide not only an overview of a vital and constantly changing field of study but also an introduction to many of the key substantive and methodological debates as well as intellectual currents in comparative education. Although, as editors, we have asked our authors to consider specific themes, we have not imposed any uniformity of viewpoints. In some cases, the authors disagree in their conclusions and interpretations of ways in which educational systems function in society. This diversity of perspectives and analyses, in our judgment, is an accurate representation of the state of the field.

Not unlike other cultural and social foundations of education (the history, philosophy, sociology, and anthropology of education), the field of comparative education contributes to the professional training of educators, to informed policy and practice, and to the creation of knowledge by providing an expanded set of analytical categories and modes for examining the realities of education and society. It is our hope that the content of this book will offer both theory builders and practitioners a variety of concepts, theoretical frameworks, and methodological approaches that will enable them to examine in more realistic, comprehensive, and sophisticated ways the nature of education systems around the world in the decade of the 1990s and beyond.

Part One

Trends in Comparative Education

GAIL P. KELLY

Chapter 1

Debates and Trends in Comparative Education

Comparative education has consistently been a field in search of a distinct identity. Since its inception in the United States academy, the field has agonized over its definition, appropriate methodologies, research paradigms, and theoretical constructs; its relation to the social sciences and, more rarely, to educational studies; and sometimes whether as a field it could justify its own existence.[1] Despite these periodic "crises" the field has flourished. A number of high quality journals disseminate research on the field consistently; encyclopedias and handbooks on comparative education have been prepared; and comparative education as an academic field is well entrenched in schools of education in a number of countries. Despite the continuing debates about whether the field is a field, professional organizations of comparative and international education specialists continue to expand. The United States based Comparative and International Education Society membership has grown as has that of the Canadian and International Education Society, the Chinese Comparative Education Society, and the British Comparative Education Society. The World Council of Comparative Education Societies has become firmly entrenched and holds Congresses every three years. In short, comparative education continues its search for identity but that search seems to be a source of strength rather than weakness.

The debates in comparative education have changed over time. This chapter describes those changes and focuses on the controversies which have emerged recently. Early debates in the field focused on methodology and definition; in the 1960s and 1970s questions of theory became paramount and considerable debate emerged about the role of public schools in fomenting change. In the 1980s the field shifted to different debates about the efficacy of public versus private education, and about school efficiency and pedagogical effectiveness. Old debates have re-emerged in the 1990s about the validity of ahistorical, acontextual social science research, and about theory. This chapter outlines the debates characterizing comparative education since the 1950s and discusses how these debates have changed over time. The major emphases will be on the most recent dialogues since past scholarship has discussed fully the nature of the field up to the 1980s.[2]

THE SEARCH FOR DEFINITION

Histories have been written about comparative education which trace the field's origins to Marco Polo, even to Herodotus. While no doubt these gentlemen traveled extensively and wrote about differences between nations concerning anything from political systems to schools to eating habits, comparative education as an academic field of inquiry, situated in universities, began in the 1930s with Kandel's treatise and expanded greatly in the post-World War II period.[3] The definition of the field was at that point murky. Kandel's and Hans' respective works tended to focus on providing descriptions of national school systems and their social, historical, political, and cultural contexts. Both have been labelled "historicists,"[4] and accurately so, since both, like Brickman, Ulich, and other scholars of their generation who built the field in the United States in the 1950s, strongly believed that school systems and educational practices could not be understood outside of their specific national political and social histories. The field as far as they were concerned was aimed at explanation, not prediction or social engineering, and they argued that the schools both reflected and sustained the "national character" of a country. The field, thus, was quite loosely coupled with policy making and was closely allied to the history of education.

Critiques of the field's mainstream arose in the late 1950s. Scholars like Harold Noah, Max Eckstein, and Andreas Kazamias argued that historical studies were "unscientific" in that they failed to draw causative linkages and provided no basis for school improvement. Further, the field's methodology was shoddy and provided the field with no definition, except that it studied foreign school systems.[5]

In the late 1950s and 1960s the field by and large accepted these critiques and sought to legitimate itself by developing a respectable methodology which placed comparative education among the social sciences while distinguishing comparative education from them. Bereday, for example, developed a methodology that might define the field as one of comparison of a range of school phenomena in different national systems.[6] Noah and Eckstein, proceeding somewhat differently, sought to provide rigor to comparative education by advocating the "scientific method" of hypothesis formation, testing, and validation through *quantitative* data about educational systems and their outcomes.[7] Noah and Eckstein in some ways equated science with statistics. Historical, cultural, and social contextualization were basically abandoned. The field transformed from one which described national school systems and sought to explain how they developed in terms of particular national contexts to one which focused on specific educational phenomena—the number of students attending school, for example—to specific social outcomes like the growth of the economy or the degree of support for the political system.[8] The task of the field was to decontextualize these phenomena so that scientific laws governing school/society relations could be established. The goal had become social engineering.

In the 1960s comparative education in the United States became, for all intents and purposes, an offshoot of the social sciences situated in schools of education. Comparative education adopted almost without question the structural functionalist models in vogue in the social sciences. During this period, there was little debate about the validity of the theories guiding research. The debates characterizing the field were over method and these came to focus on applying even more rigorous "scientific methods" to research and on making the field heavily quantitative relying on statistical techniques.

THEORY AND RESEARCH

While methodology may have been the major debate in comparative education in the 1950s and 1960s, by the 1970s, the use of theory and the field's unquestioning reliance on structural functionalism became the central issue. The challenge to structural functionalism came from a number of quarters, in some instances, paralleling the debates over theory arising in cognate social science disciplines like sociology and political science.

The debate over theory was not an abstracted one—it arose from an increasing realization that policies derived from past research had failed to have their desired ends. The great school expansion in the Third World, paid for by poor governments and financed in part by loans and by foreign aid, was not accompanied by economic development. In fact, most Third World countries economies had begun to stagnate. Educational expansion also failed to democratize Third World countries which were increasingly becoming ruled by military dictatorships. The equality of opportunity schools were supposed to provide was illusory. In most countries, the gap between rich and poor and between rural and urban areas had widened. Many alleged that the theoretical bases of research, particularly that generated by comparative education, were to blame, for structural functionalism inherently favored stability rather than growth and the maintenance of the status quo rather than change.[9] Comparative education as a field refused to acknowledge the role of the state in upholding the interests of the already rich and powerful, which more often than not ran against the interests and needs of the overwhelming majority of people.[10]

A number of dimensions of the theory debate appeared. One focused on the validity of the theory, another criticized its social and political uses while yet another drew attention to how theory led researchers to study some phenomena and not others.[11] The critique of structural functionalism as a theory centered on the theory's bias toward the maintenance of the social order as it currently was. It led scholars to focus their research on questions like whether students hold political attitudes supportive of the current political system, whether education contributed to the nation's economic well-being, or whether schools regulated social statuses in a way that allowed the social system to maintain itself. Such questions denied, according to the critics, that the state or the social structure were contested domains. By so doing, they denied the class structures of most nations and the movements for structural change within these countries. Schooling thus came to reproduce existing inequalities both within and between nations.[12]

Equally as strong a critique was leveled at the theory by those who argued that the application of the theory had served to oppress the poor, build capitalism and enrich the few, and in the case of Third World countries had served to build dependency relations with the United States and western Europe. Andre Gunder Frank maintained that the theory's application had served to further underdevelop Latin America.[13] Philip Altbach's work on higher education in the 1970s, Martin Carnoy, in his work on neo-colonialism, and Robert Arnove's studies using world systems analysis elaborated this theme and called for new theories and new practices.[14]

A third set of critiques focused on how structural functionalism had led the field to focus on the political, social, and economic outcomes of schooling to the exclusion of cognitive outcomes or of educational processes.[15] They argued that because structural functionalism assumed that the content of all social institutions were in harmony with one another and with the state specific studies of educational processes and content were deemed irrelevant. Thus, comparative education ironically focused only on outcomes. It did not study schooling, educational practices, or content. In the 1970s and 1980s it had little to say about *educational* reform.

The challenges to structural functionalism sparked a number of debates. One was whether alternative theories existed which were any better. Marxism and its variants—legitimation theory, dependency theory, world systems analysis, and critical theory—were proffered by a number of scholars—Michael Apple, Robert Arnove, Martin Carnoy, Rolland Paulston, and Hans Weiler among others.[16] While they gave rise to heated controversy, they were not widely accepted. Overt attacks on dependency theory emerged in the 1980s, dismissing that theory as simple-minded.[17] A second set of debates emerged as to whether theory was all that important. Erwin Epstein, for example, in a CIES Presidential Address argued that the theoretical debates were divisive and that the data which emerged from research based on structural functionalist paradigms differed little from those generated by Marxists.[18] Rolland Paulston argued that the diversity of theory was indeed healthy—he proposed Marxist theories be used for analyses of educational problems and structural functionalism guide their solution.[19]

Epstein's and Paulston's respective works underscored the fact that there was no way to resolve the debates about theory. The field found itself split and only limited options were available. One was to adopt a single theory. This clearly was not acceptable to most and would no doubt split the field into warring factions. A second option was to deny that theory in the long run made a difference, which is what Epstein proposed; a third was to agree to disagree and end the debate. By the mid-1980s the debate became an undercurrent in the field, mostly muted but nonetheless there and arising over specific theories like human capital theory.[20]

The debates about theory which emerged in the 1970s left their mark on the field in a number of ways. First, research has shifted somewhat from exclusive focus on the social, economic, and political outcomes of schooling to concern about the cognitive outcomes of schooling and about educational efficiency and effectiveness. The International Educational Assessment Project predated the theoretical debates, but the importance of such work to the field became more apparent in the 1980s as the field shifted more toward the examination of education and schooling. In the 1980s research on curriculum, on language use and choice, on textbooks, teachers, and on tests emerged in the field as well. Most of these studies lacked the kind of theoretical premises underlying the school/society relations literature of the 1960s and 1970s. They tended to be framed by a concern for school efficiency regardless of the social context or social consequences of education. Such studies simply avoided the theory debates of the 1970s and early 1980s but they did heed the critiques leveled at structural functionalism which charged that the theory had oriented the field away from the study of educational processes and educational outcomes.

A second way the theory debates of the 1970s and early 1980s left their mark on the field was by opening new topics for study. Research on women's education and on minorities emerged. Much of the research on women discarded structural functionalist as well as Marxist theories, arguing they are male-centric.[21] A considerable amount of the research was qualitative, rather than quantitative and had as a goal the development of new theories which could explain, for example, the meaning of education to women's lives.

A third result of the theory debates of the 1970s and early 1980s was the search for educational alternatives. For those who adopted a Marxist theory, the *state*, particularly the capitalist state, was seen as an oppressive institution. Schools associated with the capitalist state served only to maintain that state. Thus, research focused on creating educational forms that would serve to empower those struggling for change and who were oppressed by the state. Much of this research was strongly influenced by the writings of Paulo Freire. It insisted that liberatory educational forms could only be created by those who were being educated and that research on alternatives could only proceed through the active participation of those directly involved in educational processes. Participatory research was an outgrowth of the theory debates.[22] Much of it emerged without explicitly Marxist theory; some of it directly acknowledged Marxism.

The debates over theory subsided. By the mid-1980s they took new forms. No longer were they focused on Marxist versus structural functionalism; rather, they began to focus on more narrowly conceived theory, like human capital theory; whether theories based on western experience were relevant to the Third World at all; and whether theory made a difference in research.

DOUBT AND RETHINKING

The field of comparative education has always been influenced by contemporary events. The debates over theory in the 1970s and early 1980s took place in the context of economic stagnation in most of the Third World and increasing frustration world-wide with schools' ability to bring about change for the better. Throughout the 1980s, most Third World nations, continued their economic decline. Tanzania, looked to as a model for socialist development in Africa, changed course as its economy stagnated and the free-market system was reintroduced. By 1989, most Soviet bloc nations had begun to abandon communism, and sought to introduce capitalist economic structures. In the face of these events, Marxism no longer seemed the viable alternative to structural functionalism. The field seemingly was left without any overarching theory and whatever theory was used to guide research was left understated. The one exception here was the debate over human capital theory, which emerged in the late 1970s, first with Irving Sobel's critique that the theory did not work, and later in the 1980s with Steven Klees' article which took the theory to task, questioning its assumptions and the policies to which the theory gave rise.[23] George Psacharopoulos of the World Bank made a spirited defense of human capital theory.[24]

The debate over human capital theory was somewhat different from those which occurred in the 1970s about structural functionalism. For the most part earlier debates posited Marxist theories as alternatives. In the late 1980s the debate was over the validity of human capital theory, and few alternatives were put forth.

The debates on human capital theory in the 1980s indicated to some degree a cleavage in the field between academics and international agencies, particularly the World Bank which, after the United States' withdrawal from UNESCO, became the most powerful international agency involved in planning and financing education in Third World countries. World Bank researchers since the mid-1970s had, on the basis of human capital theory, argued that free, state-supported public education was dysfunctional for development. George Psacharopoulos, currently of the World Bank's Latin American and Caribbean Regional Office, even argued that public education represented a subsidy to the rich and therefore was not in the interests of the poor, who were the ones who needed schooling the most.[25] Increasingly, the Bank, called for the imposition of school fees and for privatization of the school system. In its report on Education in Africa, the Bank argued that priority should be placed on primary education and that funding for secondary and higher education be allowed to stagnate.[26]

The questioning of human capital theory was in large part a questioning of the Bank's policy directives. It also was a debate about public education, for the Bank's policies advocated privatization as a means of making school systems more efficient and effective. The field had in the past questioned the role of the schools in social change, but, for the most part, had not argued that private education was a more desirable alternative. Some like Ivan Illich, argued that the schools were oppressive institutions, seeking to maintain the status quo.[27] However, Illich also called for state funding of alternative schools and state assistance in enhancing an individual's ability to select from among alternatives through voucher systems. The World Bank sought to reduce the state's role in education urging not only that individuals should finance their own education, but that schools, opened for profit and run by private entrepreneurs, would be superior to public schools, simply because they were subject to the demands of the free market. Comparative educators working in the academy, for the most part, rejected such policies mostly on the grounds of equity.[28] A spirited defense of public education on its own terms was set forth which viewed the state's role as potentially protecting the poor from the vicissitudes of the market. Some also argued, in Freirean traditions, that education could be liberatory and therefore that the poor, if provided schooling, could use it to their own advantage. Ignorance and illiteracy left the poor unable to control their lives.

Researchers working for the World Bank denied that privatization implied inequality. Rather, they maintained that the poor would benefit since through privatization or the imposition of user fees, education would become more efficient and effective.[29] Additionally, they believed that should the poor have difficulty in paying tuition or fees, a system of scholarship aid, based on need, could be put in place.

While the field debated the validity of human capital theory and the policy prescriptions which derived from it, some began to question whether educational policies and practices could be transferred from one context to another. Such questioning had a long tradition in comparative education. These kinds of issues were raised, for example, by Sir Michael Sadler in the early twentieth century and concerns about the transferability of educational practices and policies guided the works of scholars like Isaac Kandel and Nicholas Hans.

Can Western Social Sciences Guide Research on the Third World?

Ruth Hayhoe, in the 1988 Eggertson lecture, published in the *Comparative Education Review*, raised the issue once again of whether western social sciences were applicable to research on Third World countries. She questioned the validity of social sciences developed in the United States or Western Europe in either understanding how education developed in a particular country or in planning its future course.[30] In her study of Chinese education, she argued that culture and history conditioned not only the meaning of education and its content, but also the relation of education to the state. She argued that educational development followed nationally and culturally specific logics which defied most theoretical constructs the field had developed. She explicitly rejected both dependency and modernization theories' applicability to the Chinese context.

How Important is Theory?

While Ruth Hayhoe denied the applicability of theories derived in one national context in another, the importance of *theory* in guiding research was denied from another quarter. George Psacharopoulos, in a 1990 forum on theory appearing in the *Comparative Education Review*, argued theory does not matter. He stated: "What matters is your position on a substantive issue"[31] like improving school quality or expanding post-primary education. Such issues, Psacharopoulos maintained, were not the preserve of a particular theory, but rather were value and culture free, particularly if research on them was quantified.

Psacharopoulos' notion that theory does not matter was challenged by a number of comparativists, including Don Adams and Rolland Paulston.[32] Adams, for one, maintained that scholarship without theory led to gross simplifications of any of the issues Psacharopoulos had maintained were free of theory and which were "taken for granted" norms. Adams argued that the "taken for granted norms" stem from theories one adopts about how society should work and the proper role of the schools. He contrasted Psacharopoulos' embedded assumptions which derived from structural functionalism with his own which stemmed from Paulo Freire. Rolland Paulston faulted Psacharopoulos with having a very narrow view of research and of clinging to rationalistic notions of planning espoused in the 1960s which have since been proven without basis in reality.

There is no way to resolve the debate over the use of social science research and the relevance of theory to research and its applications. These issues, as was pointed out earlier, have beset the field since its inception. What is interesting, however, is that the field, having abandoned that debate in earlier years, has returned to it in the 1990s. Perhaps this has occurred because many of the policy prescriptions derived from the field in the heady days of the 1960s and 1970s have not had their intended effects when put into practice. Whether this occurred because research was shoddy, theories guiding them were flawed or just plain wrong, or because the search for policy prescriptions that could be generalized from one country to another was doomed from the start is unknowable. It is, however, a sign of vitality that the field has come to ask again about the cultural, political, historical, and social context in formulating research questions, in the conduct of research, and in the interpretation and application of research findings.

THE FUTURE

This chapter has focused on shifting debates about comparative education as a field. The field, over the years, has sought to define itself either by its method or by the theoretical constructs which guide research, and over the years it has failed to arrive at a singular definition, method, or theory. Comparative education remains an ill-defined field whose parameters are fuzzy. No simple theory or method guides scholarship and the importance of culture and historical specificity continue to be debated. The research in the field has been and will in the future be diverse, focusing on a range of topics which at times seem tenuously connected—like school finance, illiteracy among women, textbook publishing practices, colonial schools in Malawi, academics, student attitudes toward politics, and so forth. The field has no center—rather, it is an amalgam of multidisciplinary studies, informed by a number of different theoretical frameworks. Debates in the field will likely over time shift as educational practices and needs change and the trust placed in particular theories, social systems, or reforms prove themselves valid or lacking in validity. The fact that the field has not resolved the debates about culture, method, and theory may well be a strength, rather than a weakness and point to the viability of the field and its continued growth.

Part Two

World Trends in Education

JOHN BOLI
FRANCISCO O. RAMIREZ

Chapter 2

Compulsory Schooling in the Western Cultural Context

INTRODUCTION

In the nineteenth century, throughout the West, mass schooling systems were constructed and compulsory attendance was introduced. The generality of this educational development calls for a general explanation, and in recent years many theoretical perspectives have been set forth. The compulsory aspect of mass schooling has received less attention than the construction of school systems themselves, but an explanation of compulsion can also be derived from most of these perspectives. We identify four general lines of argument:

1. Schooling as a source of social solidarity and preparation for adult roles (*functionalism*): Durkheim argued that the division of labor in modern society made schooling necessary to fashion a sense of collective identity that was no longer automatic or inherent in social structure.[1] Schooling arose as a functional equivalent of religion in traditional society.[2]

   Parsons and Dreeben elaborate this view by emphasizing the role of schooling in transmitting norms and values.[3] They contend that increased societal differentiation made formal regulated socialization necessary. Higher levels of occupational specialization and the generally greater complexity of modern society made the nuclear family an inadequate socialization agency. Thus, the societal need for more effective socialization led to the establishment of mass schooling.

2. Schooling as *social control*: The functionalist approach views schooling as a "positive" force, keeping society working smoothly. But smooth societal functioning is not a neutral condition; it works to the advantage of the upper strata of society. Hence, Bowles and Gintis, Katz, Isling, and Sandin, among others, locate the origins of schooling in the quest for a means of controlling the lower classes.[4] Schooling emerged to teach labor discipline and patriotism, to legitimate the privileged position of the upper strata, and to transmit skills required of labor in the capitalist system. Schooling arose to help keep society together, but it subjected lower groups to the will and purposes of upper ones.

3. Schooling as a *modernizing force*. Schooling may not be a functional necessity, but it can nonetheless contribute to economic development and social modernization as a central feature of a deliberate modernizing program.[5] This perspective thus argues that nineteenth-century economic and political elites used schooling to hasten industrialization and economic growth. Unless one makes the strong assumption that the lower strata shared the same vision of the future upheld by the upper strata, the modernization argument has the character of a benign version of social control theory. Via schooling workers and peasants are "liberated" from traditional constraints and subjected to the demands of modern society.

4. Schooling as *status group competition*. The functionalist and social control arguments assume that schooling exists solely to socialize children. Collins insists instead on the school's role as a status conferral institution: schools provide credentials that constitute status in themselves and facilitate access to higher-status occupations.[6] Mass schooling therefore developed as the result of status group competition, as social classes, ethnic and religious groups, occupational professions, and so on, demanded schooling and constructed school systems to advance their social position. This is the perspective underlying Archer's analysis as well, though the educational system and educational elites within the educational system enjoy greater autonomy in her theory.[7]

The first three perspectives quite directly purport to explain compulsory attendance. Functionalism claims that social integration had become so problematic in modern society that only compulsory schooling could ensure the common culture necessary to glue society together.[8] For the social control perspective, the key problematic was class dominance or elite legitimacy which was resolved through the introduction of compulsory schooling.[9] Within the modernization perspective, mass schooling solved the problem of traditionalism as a stumbling block to development.[10] The status competition argument does not explain compulsion since competition in and of itself should produce only voluntary schooling. When this perspective does confront the issue of compulsion, it usually follows the logic of the social control argument.[11]

All of these perspectives are based on two implicit assumptions: (a) educational development is the result of internal (domestic) social processes as various groups or strata respond to the problems brought about by economic and social differentiation, especially industrialization and urbanization; and (b) mass schooling developed as a solution to these problems, a deliberate rational program designed to attain such goals as social integration and stability, control of the lower classes or immigrants, or the reorientation of tradition-bound populations to modern attitudes and working situations.

We contend that neither of these underlying assumptions is consistent with the evidence.

On the one hand, compulsory mass schooling was not the result of urbanization, industrialization, or differentiation.[12] Proclamations regarding compulsory schooling appeared in the seventeenth century in societies that were overwhelmingly agrarian and rural—in Weimar (1619) in the Massachusetts colony (1642), in Gotha (1643), in Brunswick (1647), and so on.[13] Further proclamations followed in the eighteenth century, in Prussia (1717 and 1763), and in Austria (1774), among others.[14] While these proclamations described intent more than implementation, by the nineteenth century, we find actual school systems with compulsory attendance rules in several agrarian rural polities—in Norway, in Prussia and several smaller German principalities, in Denmark, and in some northeastern American states.[15] Where urbanization and industrialization came early, compulsory mass schooling often developed relatively late, as in the Netherlands (1902), England (1880), and France (1882).[16]

On the other hand, the efficacy of schooling as a program of indoctrination, control or general socialization has been highly exaggerated.[17] An empirical assessment of the Bowles and Gintis "correspondence theory" of school/work linkages shows little factual support for its strong socialization assumptions.[18] Modern schooling certainly promotes respect for authority, patriotism, orderliness and the like; however, it also promotes respect for self-development, individual worth, equality, justice, and other notions that cause all sorts of trouble for ruling elites.[19] In addition, there is good cause to question how important the skills and knowledge taught in school actually are for social integration or modernization.[20]

More fundamentally, all of these theories neglect the fundamental questions: why was *schooling* seized upon as the solution to social and political problems in the nineteenth century? Why was this solution instituted so widely within a period that by historical standards was so short? We have addressed numerous aspects of these issues in greater detail elsewhere.[21] Here we present a summary of the central features of our argument.

THE WESTERN CULTURAL FRAMEWORK
AND ITS TRANSFORMATION

Mass education is best understood as a prominent consequence of the development of the cultural framework of the West as a whole. The separate territorial states of the West arose as subunits of a larger cultural polity, Latin Christendom, that provided a common set of fundamental definitions of the nature and meaning of social reality for all emerging subunits.[22] Within the transnational Christian framework, the dominant symbolic purposes of society were twofold: the glorification of God, which was expressed through theology, religious art, and monumental architecture; and the salvation of the soul, which led to the incorporation of Western populations in comprehensive religious organizations that were the backbone of social life. Underlying these purposes and organizational forms was the institutional depiction of God as the ultimate source of value and authority in society. Human agencies exercised only derivative authority, not original jurisdiction.[23]

The modern transformation of the Western cultural framework altered human purposes and relocated ultimate sovereignty. Two new purposes came to the fore: the construction of economic progress, expressed in material terms as the expansion of exchange and the increasing efficacy of technology;[24] and, the comprehensive development of the individual as a moral, economic, political, social, and cultural entity. The glorification of God was replaced by the glorification of the autonomous human project, while the salvation of the soul was replaced by the expansion of the capacities and personality of the individual.[25] Correspondingly, the ultimate source of value and authority shifted from God to humanity. "The individual" became "the measure of all things," in essence acquiring the status of a modern deity.[26]

The transformation of the West also involved new conceptions of social structure. In feudal or estate society corporate groups were the primary building blocks of society. The family, the village or local region, the estate, the guild, the Church, the university, the monastery—these collectivities were the basis of social organization, considered as "things" in themselves, not mere aggregates of individual persons. These intermediate corporate groups gave way to two mutually reinforcing social units that previously had been only weakly reified: the individual and the national polity. The individual came to be seen as the fundamental social unit out of which all collectivites were made,[27] while the national polity became the dominant corporate unit with reference to which individuals derived their social identity and status.[28] New intermediate collectivites—voluntary associations, classes, business firms, professions—also emerged, but they derived their value and authority to act primarily from individuals and from the national polity.

The emergence and institutionalization of the modern individual was accompanied by the "discovery" of the child and the development of theories of socialization.[29] Traditional socialization was a largely unreflexive taken-for-granted process; children learned to become adults in the routines of daily life. With the conception of the enhanced individual as a sovereign being expected to have all sorts of expanded capacities (initially, piety and spiritual strength; later, rationality and personal character), socialization became a problematic. Deliberate and rationalized socialization by specialists operating in an evironment clearly separated from the routines of the home—this was the model that came to be seen as the most effective way to create developing individuals committed to progress.

Meanwhile, the state was emerging as both master and agent of the polity, as it was transformed from "territorial bully" to *nation*-state.[30] The nation-state was charged on the one hand with ensuring that the conditions for individual initiative and development were maintained (the Lockeian social contract), and on the other hand with ensuring that all individuals contributed conscientiously to the societal project of constructing progress (Hobbes' version).

This dual role of the state is reflected in the dual nature of citizenship. Citizenship consists of both rights, or claims that citizens can make on the state, and duties, or demands that the state can make on citizens.[31] The state and the individual are thus locked in a mutually reinforcing tension: the state depends on and promotes the enhanced individual, who is seen as the source of progress, while the individual depends on and promotes the expanded state which is seen as the most effective organizer of the national polity. The enhanced individual and the expanded state are thus both crucial to the pursuit of the good society.[32]

We see this modern conception of citizenship as the source of compulsory mass schooling. By the nineteenth century sovereignty was fully transferred from God to humanity, the individual and the state had become the central elements of society, and the pursuit-of rational progress as the primary purpose of autonomous human society was winning the institutional high ground. These developments made schooling seem imperative, the best way to transform children into the new type of enhanced and capable citizen who could create this new progress-oriented society. The compulsory aspect of mass schooling derived from the growing hegemony of the nation-state, for the successful pursuit of progress came to be seen as requiring the active participation of all citizens. The dominant ideology was clear: children who did not attend school would fail both to develop themselves and to contribute to national development.

We maintain, though, that the socialization of children is *not* the essential purpose of schooling. Schools may or may not teach literacy, mathematical skills, scruples, self-discipline, tolerance, or loyalty—there is abundant evidence that they did none of this very well in the nineteenth century, and even in the twentieth century the actual efficacy of schooling is subject to considerable doubt.[33] Further, it is not at all clear that the skills and knowledge taught in the schools are themselves particularly important for later life. Most adults make little use of the arithmetic, rules of grammar, tales of European kings, or descriptions of African geography that were forced on them as children, even if they can remember these things later on; and, coping with or succeeding in adult life hardly requires that one be scrupulous, self-disciplined, tolerant, or loyal. As a socialization agency, then, schooling is neither particularly effective nor particularly relevant to the demands and requirements of the adult world.[34]

Yet there is one thing that schools have always done exceedingly well: *ceremonial induction*. Schooling serves as an extended initiation rite that symbolically transforms unformed children into enhanced individuals authorized to participate in the modern economy, polity, and society, and it does so by definition.[35] Once children leave school, they are chartered as social participants: child labor laws set the minimum age for working at the maximum school attendance age, the minimum age for driving a car tends to follow suit, and so on. Furthermore, only schooling is compulsory for children—neither church attendance nor a two-parent home nor museum visits are demanded or provided, only schooling as the putatively effective means of creating active citizens managed by the active state. Hence, the key to the rise of compulsory schooling is not functionally driven needs for socialization; rather, compulsory schooling involves the symbolic construction of the competent and loyal citizen who is supposed to ensure the success of the national polity.

EDUCATION, SCHOOLING, AND COMPULSION

Compulsory mass schooling came at a late stage in the transformation of the West. Mass education first appeared in the wake of the Reformation and Counter-Reformation as Lutherans, Reformists, and Catholics struggled for dominance of the religious symbol system.[36] At this time the operative model was education through the family under the guidance of the church; formal schooling was highly exceptional, was seldom public, and never organized on a mass scale. The goal pursued was the allegiance of the individual to one or another religious faith, but already the emphasis was shifting from external acquiescence to internal spirituality and moral character.

In the seventeenth century we find *compulsory education* developing, particularly in countries having a national Protestant church (Denmark/Norway, Sweden, various German principalities); the Puritan colonies in North America also took the lead. A purified religious polity was now added to the goal of individual belief, the unified faith of the population representing the attainment of moral virtue at the collective level. Education remained overwhelmingly religious and family-based, but the religiosity involved was increasingly individualized, rationalized, and linked to the emerging national polity.

In the eighteenth century *mass schooling* emerged—in the northern American colonies, Norway, some Swiss cantons, most provinces of the Netherlands, and numerous German states.[37] The curriculum of early mass schooling was heavily religious, but the new schools were premised on a very different model of society. Schooling took socialization out of the home and into a more disciplined and rationalized structure. Schooling stressed abstract individual capacities (literacy and numeracy) while it devalued intermediate corporate identities. Schooling promoted qualities deemed crucial to the new type of citizen in the new rational society: self-discipline, industry, efficiency, loyalty, punctuality, and so on.[38]

Finally, in the nineteenth century *compulsory mass schooling* appeared. The parental obligation to educate children was transformed into the duty to place children in schools authorized and overseen by the state. Compulsory school laws were adopted both in countries with somewhat expanded school systems and in countries with quite limited schooling (e.g., Spain and Portugal). The timing is not coincidental. The nineteenth century was the century *par excellence* of the ideology of progress, the ideology of nationalism, and the definitive spiritualization (privatization) of religion.[39] God was dying, society was retooling for building heaven on earth (progress), the state was assuming an active, expansive role in managing society. It therefore seemed imperative that individuals be processed through a formal, rational, national school system in order to become the kind of citizen that was demanded by the new society.

The link between the state and compulsory schooling has become a truism.[40] Only the state is seen as having the authority to make schooling compulsory, despite the fact that earlier calls for compulsion came from religious authorities. How, though, should this link be interpreted? We find it misleading to see compulsory schooling as primarily a matter of social control (ruling elites using the state to indoctrinate the masses) or class reproduction (upper strata creating mass schooling to maintain their advantaged position). The assumption that European elites were united in their support of compulsory mass schooling, and united during roughly the same time period, is simply inconsistent with the historiographical evidence. This premise is even less plausible when applied to the United States of America, which was characterized by an exceptionally incohesive class structure.[41]

Further, mass schooling is too obdurately universalistic to be interpreted primarily as an instrument of social control. Mass schooling developed to include virtually all children, often in a single type of school, employing an increasingly standardized curriculum, and operating under an egalitarian ideology.[42] Its individualistic emphasis tends to develop and enhance children along a variety of dimensions which made social control more, not less, diffi-

cult. Schooling promotes doctrines of justice, democracy, and individual autonomy; it transmits such basic but powerful skills as literacy, self-expression,
and symbolic competence. The individual mass schooling strives to produce
may indeed be manipulated to comply, but this individual is just as likely to
resist and pursue self-interest.

TYPES OF MODERN SOCIETY AND THE
TIMING OF COMPULSORY SCHOOLING

We have discussed the rise of compulsory schooling as a transnational
phenomenon that is best understood by focusing on the developing cultural
framework of the West. Within this framework the modern model of society,
development, and socialization is broadly institutionalized: putatively competent individuals are incorporated into the national polity through citizenship
rules and they are presumed to engage actively in the construction of progress
under the direction of the state. This model made compulsory mass schooling
commonplace throughout the West, while the global triumph of the Western
frame increasingly makes compulsory schooling a routine feature of most
national societies. Thus, we find that while only one out of three independent
countries had established compulsory schooling rules by 1870, eight out of
ten independent countries by 1990 had created compulsory schooling.[43]

What follows is an attempt to track empirically the spread and institutionalization of compulsory schooling rules. First, we examine regional trends
from the early eighteenth century to the present to ascertain the timing, rapidity,
and extensiveness of compulsory schooling adoption patterns. This assessment
leads us to reflect on the structural characteristics of national societies that
may hinder or slow down the passage of compulsory schooling. We consider
both historical and contemporary obstacles to the institutionalization of compulsory schooling. Next, we reflect on the gap between the date of independence and the date of enacting the rule of compulsory schooling, focusing on
changes over time. We depict these changes both by calculating the average
elapsed time between independence and compulsory schooling for cohorts of
countries and by estimating the degree of variation around the average compulsory schooling date for each cohort. If compulsory schooling is indeed institutionalized, we expect to find decreases in both the average elapsed times
and in the standard deviations.

Figure 2.1 traces the growth of compulsory schooling by region and
decade. Our focus is on the legal establishment of compulsory rules, not on the
organizational development of schools. Countries have been grouped into the
following regions: Africa, the Middle East, Asia and the Pacific, the Americas,
Eastern and Western Europe. In all of these regions the trend is in the direction

of greater proportions of countries adopting compulsory schooling. By 1990 compulsory schooling is the norm in every region of the world. But there are interesting cross-regional differences with respect to the timing, rapidity, and extensiveness of compulsory schooling adoption. Figure 2.1 shows that this process started earlier and developed faster in Western and Eastern Europe and throughout the Americas than in Asia, the Middle East, or Africa. Moreover, the adoption of compulsory schooling is virtually universal in the first three regions and, although the norm in the other three as well, compulsory schooling is less extensively entrenched in these regions.

FIGURE 2.1
Cumulative Proportion of Countries which Passed First Compulsory Rule,
by Decade of Passage, for Major World Regions (base is 1980s count, by region)

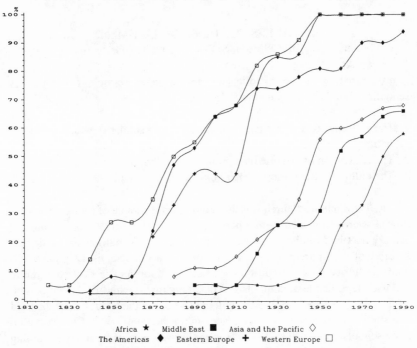

Sources. Data on compulsory rule passage come primarily from the World Survey of Education (UNESCO, 1955-71) augmented by various historical sources (see Ramirez and Ventresca, 1990).

The cross-regional similarities shown in Figure 1 are consistent with the institutionalization of the Western model argument we have advanced. The cross-regional differences suggest that not all regions are equally "at risk" of having their political entities adopt compulsory schooling at the same time.

At first glance one may think that the crucial difference is whether or not a region is made up of independent political entities. We shall later directly address the relationship between the date of political independence and the date of compulsory schooling. For the moment it suffices to emphasize that political independence per se may not be the main issue; note the many independent political entities (civilizational states) that failed to adopt compulsory schooling (e.g., China, India). What appears to be crucial and what may account for the relatively earlier adoption of compulsory schooling in Latin America, for example, is the crystallization of the structure and ideology of the nation-state as an "imagined community."[44] Political entities that are primarily dynastic, imperial, or religious in their symbolic constitution are less likely to institute compulsory schooling.

OBSTACLES TO THE ESTABLISHMENT
OF COMPULSORY SCHOOLING

We turn now to some historical and contemporary obstacles to compulsory schooling, briefly discussing the following:

1. The existence of a strong transnational source of solidarity within a national polity.
2. The reification of intermediate groups.
3. The culture of libertarian associationism.

1. The Catholic Church was the prototypical example of a strong transterritorial source of solidarity that permeated national polities in the eighteenth century and, in diminishing degree, in the nineteenth centuries. From the perspective of the Church, compulsory schooling meant state usurpation of religious authority over the spiritual welfare of children. The Church came to endorse the principle of compulsory education, that is, children should be systematically instructed to develop right character, but the Church often insisted that such instruction should take place within the family or in Church-authorized schools. State efforts to move in the direction of compulsory schooling were often thwarted by coalitions of conservative landowners and Church officials (Spain and Italy are prototypical cases). In Latin America, there are even instances of compulsory schooling legislation being overthrown after the return of a more conservative regime.[45]

All other things being equal, countries were slower to adopt compulsory education if the Catholic Church predominated within their boundaries. The existence of a national Protestant church was not, however, an obstacle. On the contrary, the state was able to use the legitimacy of the traditional teaching authority of such churches to facilitate the adoption of compulsory school-ing.[46] The key difference is that national Protestant churches were usually sub-ordinated formally to the authority of the state, while the Catholic church more persistently maintained its transterritorial autonomy.

Islamic societies in the contemporary world in part resemble the kind of obstacle the Catholic Church once posed. Iran is adamantly opposed to making education compulsory, noting that ". . . to force the people to send their children to school is not a part of educational policy . . . in primary education which lasts for five years between the ages of 6 and 11, the principle of religious purifica-tion takes priority over that of instruction."[47] Compulsory schooling has also not been enacted in Pakistan, Bangladesh, or Malaysia, but it has been established in Indonesia and in many of the Arab states. More research is needed to ascer-tain the conditions under which Islam serves as a transnational solidarity under-mining territorially bounded nation-state solidarity formation.

2. The reification of intermediate groups, what Rousseau called "partial societies," hinders both the development of the ideology of universalistic indi-vidualism that generates compulsory schooling policy and state action to implant this ideology in social structure. When the social order is organized around groups conceived of either as ascriptive sources of value and identity or as functional interests, socialization rituals are likely to be more sharply dif-ferentiated rather than more universalistic. Examples of intermediate groups include groups distinguished by caste or race as well as groups defined by social function, for example, occupation or class. All other things being equal, polities in which individuals were primarily identified as members of partial societies were slower to adopt compulsory schooling rules. Historical examples include the American South (racial reification), England (class reification), and Belgium (ethnic reification); contemporary cases include South Africa (racial reification) and Malaysia (ethnic reification).

3. The culture of libertarian associationism emphasizes the rights of indi-viduals to band together in voluntary associations to pursue progress. A form of negative freedom is enthroned: neither the state nor any other social actor is per-mited to block lawful collective action undertaken by individuals acting in their own interests. This freedom does not obligate the state or any other social actor to assist individuals in their pursuit of progress. Individuals enjoy freedom from external restraints rather than the right to demand entitlements from the state to aid them in the pursuit of their goals. Other things being equal, the culture of liber-tarian associationism hindered the formation of national rules mandating school-ing. The United States and Australia are the best known historical examples of this cultural pattern and their decentralized educational systems are linked more loosely to national state structures than in most other countries. This associational model of society and state does not especially flourish in Third World countries and is not a likely impediment to the formation of compulsory schooling rules.

POLITICAL INDEPENDENCE AND COMPULSORY SCHOOLING

Table 2.1 examines the elapsed time between the date of independence and the date of compulsory schooling enactment for six cohorts of countries. The first cohort refers to countries that became politically independent before 1815 while the last cohort includes countries that became independent between 1961 and 1990. The first column shows that the average elapsed time clearly varies across cohorts and steadily decreases over time. To illustrate, note that the average elapsed time declines from 54.6 years for countries that became independent between 1816 and 1850 to 10.7 years for the 1901-1930 cohort to 2.7 years for the 1981-1990 cohort. The second column shows a decrease in the degree of within cohort variation around the average elapsed time.

TABLE 2.1
Elapsed Time Between Date of Independence and Compulsory Rule Passage,*
By Cohort of Independence

Cohort	Elapsed Time (years)		Cases
	Mean	s.d.	
Overall	21.3	70.1	117
<1815**	111.2	73.3	16
1816-1850	54.6	38.5	18
1851-1900	13.4	18.8	5
1901-1930	10.7	21.6	19
1931-1960	3.8	8.1	36
1961-1990	2.7	5.1	23

*The elapsed time measure was calculated by simple subtraction:

ELAPSE = COMPULS - INDEP

In cases where the first compulsory rule was passed prior to independence, this yields a negative value for ELAPSE; most cases reaffirmed the compulsory rule at independence (in constitutions or education acts), and so we recode ELAPSE for such cases as "0" (that is, compulsory rule at independence) for clarity. The pattern of results is the same.

**Among the countries independent prior to 1815 are several that have been identifiable political entities for a very long historical period; for these cases, INDEP is set to 1740.

Sources. Data on compulsory rule passage come primarily from the World Survey of Education (UNESCO, 1955-71) augmented by various historical sources (see Ramirez and Ventresca, 1990).

A more graphic representation of the same data may be found in Figure 2.2. Within our set of one hundred seventeen known adopters, compulsory schooling for the older countries was both a more contentious innovation and the timing of adoption more subject to historical contingencies. Thus, there was both a greater average lag between the dates of independence and compulsory rule passage and greater variability in the timing of adoption than for

FIGURE 2.2
Elapsed Time Between Date of Independence and Compulsory Rule Passage,*
Plotted Against Date of Independence

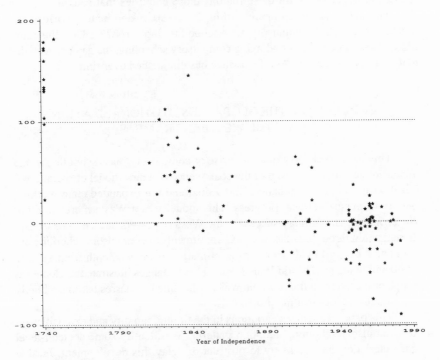

*The elapsed time measure was calculated by simple subtraction:

ELAPSE = COMPULS - INDEP

**For countries that were identifiable political entities prior to the mid-eighteenth century, INDEP is set equal to 1740.

Sources. Data on compulsory rule passage come primarily from the World Survey of Education (UNESCO, 1955-71) augmented by various historical sources (see Ramirez and Ventresca, 1990).

the more recently independent countries. The value of schooling the masses was fiercely debated among some of the older countries and has become a globally taken for granted reality in the world today. Most of the countries that have not made mass schooling compulsory have nonetheless expressed a strong commitment to this educational enterprise. In some cases, Singapore for example, the virtual achievement of universal mass schooling has been cited as the justification for not establising compulsory rules.

To summarize, between 1820 and 1990, compulsory mass schooling has become the norm in every region throughout the world. The movement toward compulsory schooling took place later and less extensively in world regions where the Western model of a national society was less rapidly or less completely embraced. Within these regions those countries that sought to enter into and successfully compete within the Western-dominated world were quicker to establish compulsory mass schooling. Japan (1872-1886) illustrates this process. For countries adopting compulsory schooling, the gap between the dates of independence and rule passage has diminished over time.

CONCLUSION: THE GLOBAL INSTITUTIONALIZATION OF THE WESTERN FRAME

This paper seeks to explain the rise of compulsory mass schooling in the nineteenth century as a result of the coalescence of a new model of social organization based on the enhanced individual and the expanded state working jointly to pursue national progress. This model was a Western creation, but the economic and military success of the Western powers has led to its institutionalization throughout the world. Commitments to compulsory schooling are paralleled by worldwide increases in primary enrollments, both from 1870 to 1940 and in the post World War II era.[48] These changes illustrate the global triumph of the Western frame within which schooling the masses became a highly legitimate and legitimating project.

This paper recognizes variations in the timing, rapidity and extensiveness of compulsory schooling adoption patterns. We identify some societal-level characteristics that are likely to obstruct or delay this development. Further research is needed to clarify the extent to which the probability of adoption of compulsory schooling is contingent on the internal characteristics of national societies, or on the nature and magnitude of their external linkages to the Western world, or whether this event is primarily a function of the time of national entry or incorporation into the Western world. Lastly, further studies need to ascertain whether anti-Western movements have genuinely diluted the cultural authority of the Western frame or merely rearticulated its key assumptions utilizing nominally local dialects.

Chapter 3

Patterns in Higher Education Development: Toward the Year 2000

Universities are singular institutions. They have common historical roots yet are deeply embedded in their societies. Traditionally elite institutions, the modern university has provided social mobility to previously disenfranchised groups. Established in the medieval period to transmit established knowledge and provide training for a few key professions, universities over the centuries have become the most important creators of new knowledge through basic research.[1] The contemporary university stands at the center of its society, an institution which is crucial to every modern society. It is the most important institution in the complex process of knowledge creation and distribution, not only serving as home to most basic science but also to the increasingly complex system of journals, books, and data bases which communicate knowledge worldwide.[2]

Universities are key to providing training in an ever increasing number of specializations that are important for modern societies. Universities have also taken on a political function in society—they often serve as centers of political thought, and sometimes of action, and they train those who become members of the political elite. This essay is concerned with discussing the patterns of higher education development evident in the post World War II period throughout the world and in analyzing some of the reasons for these trends and will point to likely directions for universities in the coming decades. Questions such as autonomy and accountability, the role of research and teaching, reform and the curriculum, and the implications of the massive expansion that has characterized universities in most countries are of primary concern here. Universities are simultaneously international institutions, with common historical roots,

39

and are also embedded in national cultures and circumstances. It is worthwhile to examine the contemporary challenges to higher education in both historical and comparative perspective.

A COMMON HERITAGE

There is only one common academic model worldwide. The basic European university model which was established first in France in the thirteenth century has been significantly modified but remains the universal pattern of higher education. The Paris Model placed the professor at the center of the institution and enshrined autonomy as an important part of the academic ethos. It is significant that the major competing idea of the period, the student-dominated University of Bologna in Italy, did not gain a major foothold in Europe, although it had some impact in Spain and later in Latin America.[3] The university rapidly expanded to other parts of Europe—Oxford and Cambridge in England, Salamanca in Spain, Prague and Krakow in the Slavic areas, and a variety of institutions in Germany were established in the following century.

Later, European imperialist nations brought universities to their colonies along with the other accouterments of colonialism. The British, for example, exported academic models first to the American colonies and later to India, Africa, and Southeast Asia.[4] The French in Vietnam and West Africa, the Spanish and Portuguese throughout Latin America, the Dutch in Indonesia, and other colonial powers also exported academic institutions. Colonial universities were patterned directly on institutions in the metropole, but often without the traditions of autonomy and academic freedom in the mother country.[5]

The university was by no means a static institution. It changed and adapted to new circumstances. With the rise of nationalism and the Protestant Reformation in Europe, the universal language of higher education, Latin, was replaced by national languages. Academic institutions became less international and more local in their student bodies and orientations. Universities were significantly affected by their national circumstances. Protestant Amsterdam differed from Catholic Salamanca. Fledgling Harvard, although patterned on British models slowly developed its own traditions and orientations. Academic institutions have had their ups and downs. Oxford and Cambridge, strongly linked to the Church of England and the aristocracy, played only a minor role in the development of the industrial revolution and the tremendous scientific expansion of the late eighteenth and nineteenth centuries.[6] In France, universities were abolished after the Revolution in 1793. They were gradually reestablished and the Napoleonic model became a powerful force not only in France but also in Latin America.[7] And the German universities were severely

damaged during the Nazi period by the destruction of autonomy and the depar-
ture of many of their professors, permanently losing their scientific preemi-
nence.[8]

For the purposes of this essay, two more recent modifications of the Western academic model are relevant. In the mid-nineteenth century, a newly united
Germany harnessed the university for nation-building. Under the leadership
of Wilhelm von Humboldt, German higher education was given significant
resources by the state, took on the responsibility for research aimed at national
development and industrialization, and played a key role in defining the ideology of the new German nation.[9] The reformed German universities also established graduate education and the doctoral degree as a major focus of the institution. Research became for the first time an integral function of the university.
The university was recognized as a hierarchy based on the newly emerging
scientific disciplines. American reformers took these German innovations and
further transformed higher education by stressing the links between the university and society through the concept of service and direct relationships with
industry and agriculture, democratized the German chair system[10] through the
establishment of academic departments and the development of the "land grant"
concept for both high-level research and expanded access to higher education.[11] Institutions which seem deeply embedded in national soil in fact have
been significantly influenced by international ideas and models.

The world's universities follow institutional patterns which are basically
derivative of these Western models. There are virtually no exceptions. The
one remaining fully non-Western institution, the Al-Azhar University in Cairo,
focuses mainly on traditional Islamic law and theology. Significantly, its science faculties are now organized along European lines.[12] There are many variations, including postsecondary polytechnic institutions in Britain, the Soviet
Union, and other countries, Open Universities in Britain, Israel, Thailand and
elsewhere, and even the two-year community colleges in the United States
and similar institutions, often following the American model, in other countries.[13] While the functions of these institutions may differ from those of traditional universities, their basic organization, patterns of governance and ethos
remain remarkably linked to the basic Western academic ideal.

NETWORKS OF KNOWLEDGE AND HIGHER EDUCATION

There are many explanations for the domination of the Western academic
model and the lack of alternatives in the modern world. The fact that the Western university institutionalized the study of science and later its production is a
key factor. The link between universities and the dominant world economic systems no doubt is a particularly important reason for Western domination. For

significant parts of the world, academic institutions were imposed by colonizers. There were few possibilities to develop independent alternatives. In many cases, traditional indigenous institutional forms were destroyed by the colonizers, as in India when in the nineteenth century the British imposed European patterns and no longer recognized existing traditional institutions.[14]

It is significant that none of the formerly colonized nations have shifted from their basically European academic models. The contemporary Indian university resembles its pre-independence predecessor. Japan, never colonized, recognized after 1868 that it had to develop scientific and industrial capacity and jettisoned its traditional academic institutions in favor of Western university ideas. Japan imported ideas and models from Germany, the United States, and other countries in the development of its universities.[15] Other noncolonized nations, such as China and Thailand, also imported Western models and adapted them to local needs and conditions.[16]

Western universities were seen to be successful in providing advanced education, in fostering research and scientific development and in assisting their societies in the increasingly complex task of development. Universities in both the United States and Germany were active in fostering industrial and agricultural development in the nineteenth century. The harnessing of higher education to the broader needs of national economic and social development was perhaps the most important innovation of the nineteenth century. The idea that higher education should be generously supported from public funds, that the university should participate in the creation as well as the transmission of knowledge and that academic institutions should at the same time be permitted a significant degree of autonomy was behind much of the growth of universities in this century.

Further, Western universities were at the center of a knowledge network that includes research institutions, the means of knowledge dissemination such as journals and scientific publishers, and an "invisible college" of scientists. It is worth noting that the bulk of the world's scientific literature now appears in the English language. Even scholars in such industrialized nations as Sweden and the Netherlands often find it necessary to communicate their research findings in English. The large Dutch multinational publishers, Elsevier and Kluwer, publish virtually all of their scholarly and scientific books and journals in English.

The circulation of scholars and students worldwide and in a sense even the "brain drain" is an element of the international knowledge system, helping to circulate ideas and also maintaining the impact of the major "host" countries and their research hegemony. There are more than one million students studying outside their home countries. The large majority of these students are from Third World nations and they are studying in the industrialized nations, with the United States, Britain, Germany, and the Soviet Union among the major "host" countries.[17] Students learn many things as a result of their sojourns abroad. They gain expertise in their studies. They also learn the norms and values of the academic system in which they are located, often returning home with a zeal to reform their universities in a Western direction. Frequently, foreign graduates have difficulty readjusting to their home countries, in part because the advanced training they learned abroad may not be easily assimilated into less well-developed economies. Such frustrations, along with the blandishments of significantly better remuneration, leads to the brain drain. However, in the contemporary world, the brain drain is often not permanent. For one thing, members of the Third World scientific diaspora often maintain contact with their colleagues at home, contributing advanced knowledge and ideas. They frequently return home for periods of time and work with local academics. And in an increasing number of instances, they return home permanently when academic—and sometimes political—conditions are favorable. They bring with them considerable expertise and often assume leadership positions in the local scientific and academic communities. Without question, the massive circulation of highly educated personnel has a great influence on the transfer of knowledge. With few exceptions, the knowledge and institutional patterns that are transferred are from the major industrialized nations to the Third World—or even to other more peripheral industrial countries with very little traffic in the other direction.[18]

The knowledge network is complex and multifaceted, and there is evidence that while its centers remain extraordinarily powerful, there is a movement toward greater equalization of research production and use. Japan, for example, already has a powerful and increasingly research-oriented university system and some of the newly industrializing countries of East and Southeast Asia are building up research capacity in their universities.[19] While hegemony may be slowly dissipating, inequality will remain endemic to the world knowledge system.

EXPANSION: HALLMARK OF THE POSTWAR ERA

Postsecondary education has dramatically expanded since World War II. Expansion has taken place in virtually every country in the world to differing extents. The growth of postsecondary education has, in fact, been in proportional terms, more dramatic than that of primary and secondary education. Writing in 1975, Martin Trow spoke of the transition from Elite to Mass and then to Universal higher education in the context of the industrialized nations.[20] While the United States enrolled some 30 percent of the relevant age cohort in higher education in the immediate postwar period, European nations generally maintained an elite higher education system with fewer than 5 percent attending postsecondary institutions. By the 1960s, many European nations educated 15 percent or more of the age group—Sweden for example, enrolled 24 percent in 1970, with France at 17 percent. At the same time, the United States increased its proportion to around 50 percent, approaching Universal access.

In the Third World, expansion was even more dramatic. Building on tiny and extraordinarily elitist universities, Third World higher education expanded rapidly in the immediate post-independence period. In India, enrollments grew from approximately one hundred thousand at the time of Independence in 1947 to over three and one-half million in 1986. Expansion in Africa has also been dramatic, with the postsecondary student population growing from 21,000 in 1960 to 437,000 in 1983.[21] Recent economic difficulties in much of sub-Saharan Africa have meant that per-student expenditure has dropped significantly, contributing to a marked deterioration in academic standards.

Similar trends can be seen elsewhere in the Third World. In a few instances, such as the Philippines, where more than one-third of the age cohort enters postsecondary education, Third World enrollment ratios have reached the levels of many of the industrialized nations although in general the Third World lags far behind in terms of proportions of the population attending higher education institutions. For example, despite China's student population of more than two million, only about 1 percent of the age cohort attends postsecondary institutions—about 4 percent of those graduating high school. Expansion in the Third World has, in general, exceeded that in the industrialized nations at least in proportional terms although there are significant variations among Third World nations—some countries maintain small and relatively elitist university systems while others have expanded more rapidly.

Regardless of political system, level of economic development, or educational ideology, the expansion of higher education has been the most important single postwar trend worldwide. Worldwide, about seven percent of the relevant age cohort (twenty to twenty-four years) attend postsecondary educational institutions—a statistic that has shown an increase each decade since World War II. Higher education expanded dramatically first in the United States, then in Europe—currently the main focus of expansion is in the Third World. There are, of course, significant variations in enrollment statistics and ratios. Women, in general, attend less frequently than men although they now constitute approximately 40 percent of university enrollments—with considerable variations by country. The industrialized nations, with a few exceptions, have a higher proportion of the age cohort in postsecondary education than Third World countries. Generalized statistics concerning enrollments in postsecondary education mask many key differences. For example, many industrialized nations have a higher proportion of students in technological and scientific fields rather than in the traditional liberal arts, which tend to predominate in the nonsocialist developing nations.

There are many reasons for the expansion of higher education. A key factor has been the increasing complexity of modern societies and economies, which have demanded more highly trained personnel. Postsecondary institutions have, almost without exception, been called on to provide the needed training. Indeed, training in many fields that had once been imparted "on the job" have become formalized in institutions of higher education. Entirely new fields, such as computer science, have come into existence and rely on universities as a key source of research and training. Nations now developing scientific and industrial capacity, such as Korea and Taiwan, have depended on academic institutions to provide high level training as well as research expertise to a greater extent than was the case during the first industrial revolution in Europe.[22]

Not only do academic institutions provide training, they also test and provide certification for many roles and occupations in contemporary society. These roles have been central to universities from their origins in the medieval period but have been vastly expanded in recent years. A university degree is a prerequisite for an increasing number of occupations in most societies. Indeed, it is fair to say that academic certification is necessary for most positions of power, authority, and prestige in modern societies. This places immense power in the hands of universities. Tests to gain admission to higher education are key *rites de passage* in many societies and are key determinants of future success.[23] Competition within academe varies from country to country, but in most cases there is also much stress on high academic performance and tests in the universities. There are often further examinations to permit entry into specific professions.

The role of the university as an examining body has grown for a number of reasons. As expansion has taken place, it has been necessary to provide increasingly competitive sorting mechanisms to control access to high-prestige occupations. The universities are also seen as meritocratic institutions which can be trusted to provide fair and impartial tests that will honestly measure accomplishment and therefore access. When such mechanisms break down, as they did in China during the Cultural Revolution or where they are perceived to be subject to corrupt influences, as in India, the universities are significantly weakened. The older, more informal and often more ascriptive means of controlling access to prestigious occupations, are no longer able to provide the controls needed nor are they perceived as fair. Entirely new fields have developed where no sorting mechanisms existed and academic institutions have frequently been called upon not only to provide training but also examination and certification.

Expansion has also occurred because the growing segments of the population of modern societies have demanded it. The middle classes, seeing that academic qualifications were increasingly necessary for success, demanded access to higher education. Governments generally responded by providing access.[24] When governments did not move quickly enough, private initiative frequently established academic institutions in order to meet the demand. In countries like India, the Philippines and Bangladesh, a majority of the students are educated in private colleges and universities.[25] At present, there are world-wide trends toward imposing user fees, increasing the stress on private higher education, and raising tuition fees in public institutions. These changes are intended to reduce the cost of postsecondary education for governments while maintaining access, although the long-term implications for quality, access, and control of higher education are unclear.

In most societies, higher education is heavily subsidized by the government and most, if not all, academic institutions are in the public sector. While there is a growing trend toward private initiative and management sharing responsibility with public institutions, there is little doubt that the government will continue to be the main source of funding for postsecondary education.[26] The dramatic expansion of academic institutions in the post-war period has proved very expensive for governments worldwide.[27] Nonetheless, the demand for access has proved to be an extraordinarily powerful one.[28]

There have been significant variations in higher education expansion. For example, many analysts writing in the 1960s assumed that the world, and particularly the Western industrialized nations, would move from elite to mass and finally to universal access to higher education, generally following the American pattern.[29] This has not occurred. In much of Western Europe, the expansion that characterized the 1960s slowed and in some countries came to a complete halt, although there are now signs of renewed expansion. The causes for this situation were in part economic, with a slowdown of the Western economies following the "oil shocks" of the seventies; in part the causes were demographic, resulting from a significant drop in the birth rate and a smaller cohort of young people; and in part philosophical, as countries were less sympathetic to further growth of public institutions, including universities.

Generally, the proportion of the age cohort going on to higher education in Western Europe stabilized at under 20 percent.[30] With the exception of the Soviet Union, most Eastern European countries also enroll under 20 percent of the relevant age group in higher education, thus maintaining relatively elitist academic systems. Similar trends are also evident in the United States, where access is considered to be "universal" and enrollments have stabilized at around 50 percent of the age group.

In sharp contrast to Western industrialized countries, Third World enrollment ratios remain significantly lower, leading to policies for expansion of higher education. This expansion takes place in the context of serious economic problems over the past two decades. This is the case even in countries like India, where there is severe unemployment of graduates and where there is a significant brain drain of university graduates abroad. In sub-Saharan Africa, there has been a slowing of expansion, not so much because demand for higher education has decreased but due to severe economic problems which have limited the ability of governments to pay the costs of continued growth. In many Third World countries, it remains impossible for local universities to absorb all of those qualified to attend, thus creating an exodus of students abroad. This is the case in Malaysia, where about half of the country's enrollments are abroad.[31]

It is necessary to analyze the prospects for continued expansion of higher education from several perspectives. While there are common world-wide trends, such as the increasingly important role of technology, there are also important differences among countries and in different parts of the world. The Third World presents a specific set of circumstances. While it is likely that its pace in some Third World countries will slow in the coming decade, expansion will continue to be a key factor in higher education. Regional variations will be important, with economic factors dominating. Universities will very likely grow more slowly in less successful economies. Rapidly expanding economies, such as those of the newly industrializing countries in East Asia, will have resources to expand higher education and at the same time there will be a demand for graduates. Taiwan and South Korea, for example, can easily absorb university graduates as well as the expenditures needed for larger and better equipped universities. Yet, even where there is evidence that higher educational growth should slow or even stop, it is unlikely that this will take place since popular demand for postsecondary education will remain high and political authorities will find it easier to provide access than to limit it.

The situation in the Western industrialized nations is more difficult to predict. A variety of factors argues for a resumption of growth, although probably not at the levels of the 1960s. There is evidence of a modest upturn in population in some age categories in some Western nations although demographers predict that this will be relatively short lived. The large numbers of graduates trained in the 1960s and now occupying positions in schools and universities, as well as in government and in industrial enterprises, will be retiring in large numbers in the coming years, triggering a significant demand for university-trained personnel. There is also a recognition that university-based research is an important ingredient for scientific and technological strength in an increasingly competitive world economy. Much, however, will depend on broader economic trends. It is also difficult to predict whether resistance to governmental spending in general and for education in particular will continue to be an important political factor in many Western countries.

Despite imponderables, it is likely that in general there will be increased support for higher education spurred by demographic and market factors and continued demand for access by an ever widening segment of the population.

Whether there will be a resumption of the growth of access to wider segments of the population—both of the traditional age group and of "nontraditional" students remains to be seen.[32]

CHANGE AND REFORM: THE LEGACY OF THE SIXTIES

The demands placed on institutions of higher education to accommodate larger numbers of students and expanding functions resulted in significant reforms in higher education in many countries. There was much debate concerning higher education reform in the 1960s—and a significant amount of change did take place.[33] It is possible to identify several important factors which contributed both to the debate and to the changes that took place. Without question, the unprecedented student unrest of the period contributed to a sense of disarray in higher education. Further, the unrest was in part precipitated by deteriorating academic conditions which resulted from rapid expansion. In a few instances, students demanded far-reaching reforms in higher education although generally, they did not propose specific changes.[34] Students frequently demanded an end to the rigidly hierarchical organization of the traditional European university, and significant changes were made in this respect. The "chair" system was weakened and the responsibility for academic decision making, formerly a monopoly of the full professors, was significantly expanded—in some countries to include students. At the same time, the walls of the traditional academic disciplines were broken by various plans for interdisciplinary teaching and research.

Reform was most dramatic in several very traditional Western European academic systems. Sweden's universities were completely transformed in the most far-reaching of the reform movements. Among Sweden's changes were a democratizing of decision making, decentralizing the universities, expanding higher education to previously underserved parts of the country, providing for interdisciplinary teaching and research, and vocationalizing the curriculum.[35] Significant changes also took place in France and in the Netherlands. Reformers in both countries stressed interdisciplinary approaches and a democratizing of academic decision making. In the German Federal Republic, the universities in the states dominated by the Social Democratic Party were also significantly altered, with the traditional structures of the university giving way to more democratic governance patterns.

But in many industrialized nations, structural change was not dramatic and in many instances very limited. In the United States, for example, despite considerable debate during the sixties, there was very limited change in higher education.[36] Japan, site of significant unrest and a large number of reports on university reform, saw virtually no basic change in its higher education system although several "new model" interdisciplinary institutions were established such as the science-oriented Tsukuba University near Tokyo. Britain, less affected by student protest and with an established plan for expansion in operation, also experienced few reforms during the sixties.[37] It is also the case that some of the changes implemented in the 1960s were criticized or abandoned. In the German Federal Republic, for example, reforms in governance that gave students and junior staff a dominant position in some university functions were ruled unconstitutional by the German courts.[38]

Vocationalization has been an important trend in higher education change in the past two decades. Throughout the world, there has been a conviction that the university curriculum should provide relevant training for a variety of increasingly complex jobs. The traditional notion that higher education should consist of liberal nonvocational studies for elites or that it should provide a broad but unfocused curriculum has been widely criticized for lacking "relevance" to the needs of contemporary students. Students, worried about obtaining remunerative employment, have pressed the universities to be more focused. Employers have also demanded that the curriculum be more directly relevant to their needs. Enrollments, at least in the industrialized nations, in the social sciences and humanities, have declined because these fields are not considered vocationally relevant.

Curricular vocationalism links with another key worldwide trend in higher education, the increasingly close relationship between universities and industry.[39] This relationship has implications for the curriculum, as industrial firms have sought to ensure that the skills that they need are incorporated into the curriculum. It also has significant implications for academic research, since many university-industry relationships are focused largely on research. Industries have established formal linkages and research partnerships with universities in order to obtain help with research that they find important. In some countries, such as Sweden, representatives of industry have been added to the governing councils of higher education institutions. In the United States, formal contractual arrangements have been made between universities and major corporations to share research results. In many industrialized nations, corporations are increasingly providing focused educational programs for their employees, sometimes with the assistance of universities.

University-industry relations have significant implications for higher education. Technical arrangements with regard to patents, confidentiality of research findings, and other fiscal matters have assumed importance. Critics also have pointed out that the nature of research in higher education may be altered by these new relationships as industrial firms are not generally interested in basic research. University-based research, which has traditionally been significantly oriented toward basic research, may be increasingly skewed to applied and profit-making topics. There has also been some discussion of the orientation of research, for example, in fields like biotechnology, where broader public policy matters may conflict with the needs of corporations. Specific funding arrangements have also been questioned. Pressure on universities to serve the immediate needs of society and particularly the training and research requirements of industry is currently a key concern for universities, one which has implications for the organization of the curriculum, the nature and scope of research, and the traditional relationship between the university and society.[40] Debates concerning the appropriate relationship between higher education and industry are likely to continue, as pressures grow even stronger on universities to provide direct service to the economy.

Universities have traditionally claimed significant autonomy for themselves. The traditional idea of academic governance stresses autonomy and universities have tried to insulate themselves from direct control by external agencies. However, with the increase in the size, scope, importance, and cost of universities, there has been immense pressure by those providing funds for higher education—mainly governments—to expect accountability from universities. The conflict between autonomy and accountability is one of the flashpoints of controversy in recent years, with the result that there has been an increase in accountability from academic institutions, again with significant implications for the institutions.[41] The issue takes on different implications in different parts of the world. In the Third World, traditions of autonomy have not been strong and demands for accountability, which include both political and economic elements, are especially troublesome.[42] In the industrialized nations, accountability pressures are more fiscal in nature.

Despite the varied pressures on higher educational institutions for change and the significant reforms that have taken place in the past two decades, basic institutional patterns have remained and there have been few structural alterations in universities. One of the few has been in Sweden as part of the dramatic reform that has taken place there. Elsewhere, curricula have been altered, expansion has taken pace, and there have been continuing debates concerning accountability and autonomy, but universities as institutions have not changed significantly. As Edward Shils has argued, the "academic ethic" has been under considerable strain, and in some ways it has been weakened, but it has survived.[43]

TOWARD THE 1990s

The university as an institution in modern society has shown considerable durability. It has maintained key elements of the historical models from which it evolved over many centuries. At the same time, it has successfully evolved to serve the needs of societies.[44] There has been a significant convergence of both ideas and institutional patterns and practices in world higher education. This has been due in part to the implantation of European-style universities in the developing areas during and after the colonial era and because universities have been crucial in the development and then the internationalization of science and research.

Despite remarkable institutional stability over time, universities have significantly changed and have been subjected to immense pressures in the post-World War period. Many of the changes which have been chronicled in this essay have come as the result of great external pressure and despite considerable opposition from within the institution. Some have argued that the university has lost it soul.[45] Others have claimed that the university is irresponsible because it uses public funds and does not always conform to the direct needs of industry and government. Pressure from governmental authorities, militant students, or external constituencies have all placed great strains on academic institutions.

The period since World War II has been one of unprecedented growth—and of the increasingly central role of higher education in virtually all modern societies. While growth may continue, the dramatic expansion of recent decades is at an end. It is unlikely that the place of the university as the most important institution for training personnel for virtually all of the top-level occupations in modern society will be weakened. The role of the university in research will also continue, although as has been noted, there are significant pressures concerning the nature and focus of university-based research and perhaps a weakening of the commitment to basic research.[46]

Internationally, there may well be some further convergence as science becomes even more international and as the circulation of academic elites continues through foreign study. While significant national variations will remain, universities have increasingly similar roles throughout the world and research is increasingly communicated to an international audience.

The challenges are, nonetheless, significant. The following issues, no doubt among others, will be of concern in the coming decade and beyond:

Access and Adaptation. Although in a few countries, access to postsecondary education has been provided to virtually all segments of the population, there is in most countries a continuing demand for higher education. Progress toward broadening the social class base of higher education has slowed and in many industrialized countries stopped in the 1970s. With the emergence of democratic governments in Eastern Europe, the possible reemergence of demand in Western Europe and continuing pressure for expansion in the Third World, it is likely that there will be heightened demand for access and thus expansion of enrollments in many countries. Limited funds and a desire for "efficient" allocation of scarce postsecondary resources will come into direct conflict with demands for access. Demands for access by previously disenfranchised groups will continue to place great pressure on higher education. In many countries, racial, ethnic, or religious minorities play a role in shaping higher education policy. Issues of access will be among the most controversial in debates concerning higher education. This topic may be especially volatile since there is a widespread assumption that all segments of the population should be able to obtain a university education—yet, the realities of higher education in most countries do not permit this level of enrollment.

Administration, Accountability, and Governance. As academic institutions become larger and more complex institutions, there will be increasing pressure for a greater degree of professional administration. At the same time, the traditional forms of academic governance will be under increasing pressure not only because they are unwieldy but because in large and bureaucratic institutions, they are inefficient. The administration of higher education will increasingly become a profession, much as it is in the United States. This means that there will be the growth of an "administrative estate" in many countries where it does not now exist. The demands for accountability will increase and will cause academic institutions considerable difficulty. As academic budgets increase, there will be inevitable demands to monitor and control expenditures. There is, at present, no general agreement concerning the appropriate level of governmental involvement in higher education.The challenge will be to ensure that the traditional—and valuable—patterns of faculty control of governance and the basic academic decisions of universities are maintained in an increasingly complex and bureaucratic environment.

Knowledge Creation and Dissemination. Research is an increasingly important part of the mission of many universities and of the academic system generally. Key decisions concerning the control and funding of research, the relationship of research to broader curricular and teaching issues, the uses made of university-based research and related issues will increasingly be in contention. Further, the system of knowledge dissemination, including journals and books and increasingly computer-based data systems, is rapidly changing and hotly debated. Who should control the new data networks? How will traditional means of communication, such as the journals, survive in this new climate? How will the scientific system avoid being overwhelmed by the proliferation of data?[47] The needs of peripheral scientific systems, including both the Third World and smaller academic systems in the industrialized world, are increasingly important.[48]

While the technological means for rapid knowledge dissemination are available, issues of control and ownership, the appropriate use of data bases, problems of maintaining quality standards in data bases, and related questions are very important. It is possible that the new technologies will lead to increased centralization rather than wider access. It is also possible that libraries and other users of knowledge will be overwhelmed by both the cost of obtaining new material and the flow of knowledge. At present, academic institutions in the United States and other English-speaking nations, along with publishers and the owners of the communications networks, stand to gain. The major Western knowledge producers currently constitute a kind of OPEC of information, dominating not only the creation of knowledge but also most of the major channels of distribution. Simply increasing the amount of research and creating new data bases will not ensure a more equal and accessible knowledge system. Academic institutions are at the center but publishers, copyright authorities, funders of research, and others are also necessarily involved.

The Academic Profession. The professorate has found itself under increasing strain in recent years in most countries. Demands for accountability, increased bureaucratization of institutions, fiscal constraints in many countries, and an increasingly diverse student body have all challenged the professorate. In most industrialized nations, a combination of fiscal problems and demographic factors led to a stagnating profession. Now, demographic factors and a modest upturn in enrollments are beginning to turn surpluses into shortages.[49] In the Newly Industrializing Countries (NICs), the professorate has significantly improved its status, remuneration, and working conditions in recent years. In the poorer nations, however, the situation has, if anything, become more difficult with decreasing resources and ever increasing enrollments. Overall, the professorate will face severe problems as academic institutions change in the coming period. Maintaining autonomy, academic freedom, and a commitment to the traditional goals of the university will prove a challenge.

In the West, there will be difficulties in luring the 'best and brightest' into academe in a period when positions will again be relatively plentiful—in many fields, academic salaries have not kept pace and there has been a deterioration in the traditional academic lifestyle. The pressure on the professorate not only to teach and do research but also to attract external grants, do consulting, and the like, is significant. In Britain and Australia, for example, universities have become "cost centers", and accountability has been pushed to its logical extreme. British academics entering the profession after 1989 will no longer have tenure, but will be periodically evaluated. In the NICs, the challenge will be to create a fully autonomous academic profession where traditions of research and academic freedom are only now developing. The difficulties faced by the poorer Third World countries are perhaps the greatest—to maintain a viable academic culture in deteriorating conditions.

Private Resources and Public Responsibility. In almost every country, there has been a growing emphasis on increasing the role of the private sector in higher education. One of the most direct manifestations of this trend is the growing role of the private sector in funding and in many cases directing university research. In many countries, there has been an expansion of private academic institutions. And there has been an emphasis on students paying an increasing share of the cost of their education, often through loan programs. Governments have tried to limit their expenditures on postsecondary education while at the same time recognizing that the functions of universities are important. Privatization has been the means of achieving this broad policy goal.[50] There are, of course, important implications of these trends. Decisions concerning academic developments may move increasingly to the private sector, with the possibility that broader public goals may be ignored. Whether private interests will support the traditional functions of universities, including academic freedom, fundamental research and a pattern of governance which leaves the professorate in control, is unclear. Some of the most interesting developments in private higher education can be found in such countries as Vietnam, China, and Hungary, where private institutions have recently been established. Inevitably, private initiative in higher education will bring with it a change in values and orientations. It is not clear that these values will be in the long term best interests of the university.

Diversification and Stratification. While diversification, the establishing of new postsecondary institutions to meet new needs, is by no means an entirely new phenomenon, it is a trend that has been of primary importance in recent years and will continue to reshape the academic system. In recent years, the establishment of research institutions, community colleges, polytechnics, and other academic institutions designed to meet specialized needs and serve specific populations has been a primary characteristic of growth. At the same time, the academic system has become more stratified—once individuals are within a segment of the system, it is difficult to move to a different segment. And there is often a high correlation of social class and other variables with selection to a particular segment of the system. To some extent, the reluctance of the traditional universities to change is responsible for some of the diversification. Perhaps more important has been the belief that it is efficient and probably less expensive to establish new limited-function institutions. An element of diversification is the expansion of the student population to include larger numbers of women and other previously disenfranchised segments of the population. Women now constitute 40 percent of the student population worldwide and more than half in fifteen countries.[51] In many countries, students from lower socioeconomic groups, racial, and ethnic minorities are entering postsecondary institutions in significant numbers. This diversification will also be an important challenge for the coming decades.

Economic Disparities. There are substantial inequalities among the world's universities—and it is likely that these inequalities will grow. The major universities in the industrialized nations generally have adequate resources to play a leading role in scientific research—in a context where it is increasingly expensive to keep up with the expansion of knowledge.[52] At the same time, universities in much of the Third World simply cannot cope with the combined challenges of continuing pressure for increased enrollments and budgetary constraints and in some cases fiscal disasters. For example, universities in much of sub-Saharan Africa have seen dramatic budget cuts and find it difficult to function, not to mention improving quality and competing in the international knowledge system.[53] In the middle are academic institutions in the Asian NICs, where there has been significant academic progress and it is likely that these institutions will continue to improve. Thus, the economic prospects for postsecondary education worldwide are mixed, with considerable challenges ahead.

CONCLUSION

Universities worldwide share a common culture and reality. In many basic ways, there is a convergence of institutional models and norms. The key issues identified here will be experienced worldwide. At the same time, there are significant national differences which will continue to be felt. There is little chance that the basic structures of academic institutions will significantly change, although some of the traditional academic ideologies and practices are threatened and alterations are likely, for example, concerning the continuing growth of an administrative cadre in universities. Unanticipated developments are also possible. For example, while conditions for the emergence of significant student movements, at least in the industrialized nations, do not seem likely at the present time, circumstances may change.[54] In the Third World, student movements continue to be an important political and academic force.

This essay has pointed to some key factors that have affected academic institutions worldwide. The past decade has not been an especially favorable one for higher education, yet academic institutions continue to be very important institutions, if anything, expanding their impact on both science and society. The future presents significant challenges but the very centrality of the university in modern society creates a degree of optimism.

EDWARD H. BERMAN

Chapter 4

Donor Agencies and Third World Educational Development, 1945-1985

The increase in school enrollments worldwide has been dramatic in the last forty years or so. Data collected by international and national agencies and by independent researchers attest to the inexorable growth of school places in industrialized and nonindustrialized nations alike. These gains are as notable in nations favoring a market economy as in those championing the principles of state socialism. Educational expenditures—and opportunities—have increased most markedly at the secondary and tertiary levels in the industrialized nations during this period, while the gains made in the poorer countries have been distributed across the primary level as well, reflecting the underdeveloped educational systems that these Third World nations possessed around 1950.[1] What accounts for this unprecedented global expansion of educational systems?

The explanation offered by Ramirez and Boli-Bennett is persuasive, but by itself is insufficient to account for the growth and reform of so many educational systems along such similar lines since 1950. Their earlier analysis identifies the conjunction of two major forces as the causal factors in explaining global educational expansion. The first of these they call the ideology of the state. By this they refer to the power and interest of national governments in organizing increasingly inclusive educational systems which enable the state to use the products of its system—educated students—to insure its maintenance. This is augmented by the ideology of the individual, which refers to the aspirations of individual citizens to gain an education, which they perceive as the most important commodity in assuring them better life chances in states whose economies increasingly demand educational attainment as a prerequisite of mobility.[2]

This analysis ignores the fact that nation-states in the late twentieth century are part of an interdependent world system in which the actions of the stronger determine to a considerable degree the ability of the weaker to act unilaterally. The penetration of the economies of Third World nations by multinational corporations and institutions of finance capital is only one example of the influence that industrialized nations exercise over these dependent countries. The period since the conclusion of World War II has witnessed the appearance of a network of international and national aid agencies linked to and located in the industrialized nations. A major concern of many of these agencies has been to help Third World nations reconceptualize, expand, and reform their educational systems.

The total amount contributed to Third World educational development by these donor agencies has been estimated to be roughly 10 percent of all expenditures on education.[3] This small figure masks the important role they play in helping national governments establish educational agendas while focusing their energies on particular aspects of the system. The way in which this is accomplished and the agencies contributing to this will be noted below in some detail. It will suffice at this juncture to note that these organizations have played pivotal roles in shaping national educational plans by financing certain curricular projects and materials production efforts, encouraging particular directions in teacher education, advocating the introduction of sophisticated technology into schools, helping national universities focus their research interests along particular lines, supporting efforts to strengthen administration and managerial capacities of educational personnel, and, perhaps most importantly, providing unremitting encouragement for educational expansion over an extended period.

During the 1960s UNESCO sponsored a number of Regional Education Conferences; their influence was immense in encouraging educational expansion in third World nations.[4] Also during that decade donor agencies provided important research support that led to numerous studies "proving" the relationships linking education to development and economic growth. This Human Resource Development theory in turn provided powerful inducements for Third World policymakers to devote larger proportions of national budgets to their education ministries. At the same time belief in the efficacy of this theory led the donor agencies to increase their developmental assistance for education.

An understanding of the global expansion of education since 1945 would be incomplete if the analysis were limited, as have been so many in the past, to an examination of a local or national educational system and failed to locate an educational system in the context of the world system and to assess the impact of outside organizations on national educational development. This is not meant to suggest that national educational systems lack considerable autonomy over their goals or activities, or that they are manipulated unwittingly by donor agencies. It is meant to indicate, however. that the presence of donor agencies introduces into national educational planning and implementation a complex interplay of forces over which local policymakers and administrative personnel cannot always exercise control and which frequently limit local options.

DONOR AGENCIES AND THEIR CONCERNS

The reasons accounting for the appearance of the donor agencies concerned with developmental assistance to nations of the Third World after 1945 are numerous, but some of the more important surely include: the issuance of the 1948 United Nations Declaration of Human Rights; the successful independence struggles of former colonial territories in Africa and Asia; heightened Cold War tensions between the eastern and western blocs; an increased awareness in the industrialized nations of the wretched poverty afflicting so large a proportion of the world's population: the belief on the part of western intellectuals and policymakers that Third World underdevelopment could be overcome if the political will and requisite resources could be mobilized and applied in a prescribed manner; and the wide-spread belief that the lack of a schooled citizenry and educated cadre of technical personnel and civil servants represented the main obstacle to overcoming the endemic problems of Third World underdevelopment.

Many donor agencies influenced the direction of Third World development after 1945. For the sake of convenience (if not with total accuracy) they can be grouped into several categories. The first of these includes such multinational agencies as the World Bank and its subsidiaries, for example, the Inter-American Development Bank, the African Development Bank, and the Asian Development Bank; UNESCO and other United Nations' organizations, such as the United Nations Development Program (UNDP), UNICEF, and the World Health Organization, also belong in this category. Included in the second group are the national aid agencies, such as the United States Agency for International Development, the British Ministry of Overseas Development, the Swedish International Development Authority, and the Canadian International Development Agency; Soviet, West German, and French counterparts also belong in this category. The third group includes the major North American foundations—the Carnegie Corporation of New York and the Ford and Rockefeller foundations. The last group of institutions is somewhat more difficult to categorize, both because their funding frequently comes from a variety of sources—including many of the organizations mentioned above—and their contribution to the development process is generally more indirect than that of other agencies. A major concern of the International Council for Educational Development (ICED) and the Canadian International Development Research Centre (IDRC), two representative organizations, is the preparation of reports and studies focusing on particular developmental projects and modalities. Their influence is no less significant for being indirect; their widely disseminated studies provide legitimation for completed programs and for projects contemplated.

The World Bank's involvement with Third World educational development dates from 1962. School construction figured prominently in the early years, but the scope of the Bank's educational activities has expanded significantly since then, as has the financial support for its multifaceted projects. By the mid-1980s the Bank (including its several regional subsidiaries) had approved no fewer than two hundred eighty-four education projects, at a cost of some $12.1 billion. These projects ranged across the spectrum of school and related educational activities, and have included teacher training and curriculum development efforts, examination and textbook development projects, mass media and distance education, technical and general education schemes, and management training programs. The Bank's projects have at one time emphasized secondary and higher education, but more recently greater attention has been directed toward primary education. The reach of these programs has been immense, as evidenced by the fact that Bank projects have been responsible for the creation of some 2.6 million student places in approximately 21,000 educational institutions worldwide. Included in this latter figure are 185 universities, 651 teacher training institutions, 2,903 secondary schools, and 18,000 primary schools.[5]

The World Bank is the most important sponsor of research on the problems of Third World educational development. Some of this is project specific, while some is more general and is undertaken to test particular hypotheses concerning various developmental strategies. Other organizations have sponsored research bearing on Third World educational development, including particularly the Ford Foundation, the International Development Research Centre, and the International Council for Educational Development. The contributions of these latter organizations have unquestionably been significant in determining patterns of Third World educational development, but their efforts have been eclipsed in the last fifteen years or so by those of the Bank. Much of the Bank's extensive research is disseminated in the Staff Working Paper series, some appears in professional journals concerned with developmental issues, and some is published in book form by prestigious university presses receiving a Bank subsidy.[6]

The importance of the research undertaken by the Bank and other organizations on problems of Third World educational development needs to be stressed. This work in the aggregate sets the tone for, and establishes the parameters of, what is considered to be the "significant" educational research on developmental issues. This significant research in turn forms the basis and rationale for the educational loans and grants financed by the Bank and its affiliated International Development Association to underwrite specific projects in the developing nations. The Bank's research tradition from the beginning has been strongly influenced by considerations of the economic return to schooling, efficiency criteria, the importance of macro- and micro-level planning for educational development, and quantifiable outcomes. Numerous commentators have noted that, for all the Bank's investment in research and seemingly rational approach, its studies have produced little evidence to indicate what kind of education really makes a difference to Third World development.[7] At the same time questions have been raised concerning the benefits for Third World people from educational projects growing out of the research traditions subscribed to by the staff of the World Bank, the Ford Foundation, and organizations like IDRC and ICED. To put this another way: critics of much Third World educational assistance charge that it is the adherence by donor agency researchers to a research paradigm drawn from a conservative Western tradition that leads to the funding of so many inappropriate and ineffective field projects that are irrelevant to the needs of recipient nations.[8]

The work of national aid agencies like the United States Agency for International Development (AID) must be understood in the context of the determinants of each nation's foreign policy. Indeed, AID's precursor, the International Cooperation Administration, owes its origins to Washington discussions concerning the role of developmental assistance in American foreign policy considerations after World War II. During its early years AID concentrated its efforts on strengthening the infrastructures of the nations of Africa, Asia, and Latin America. This was accomplished in large part by the provision of developmental loans to facilitate such projects as road building, port expansion, and the extension of telecommunication systems. By the 1960s, AID's concerns shifted from a preoccupation with loans and grants for infrastructure projects, such as those noted above, to the general issue of educational development.

During the next two decades AID projects focusing on education proliferated, for example, involvement with an institute to train administrators in the Congo in the early and mid-1960s, a lengthy commitment to upgrade teacher education programs in Afghanistan in the 1970s, and a program to expand educational opportunities via television programming in El Salvador in the 1970s and early 1980s. Some of AID's work was absorbed into the United States Information Agency during the Reagan years, but the emphasis on aid for education continues. An example of this involves the program that grew out of the 1984 report of the Bi-Partisan Commission on Central America, chaired by former secretary of state Henry Kissinger. The report's recommendations urged the government to offer educational opportunities similar to those made available by eastern bloc countries for talented undergraduate students from Central America to study in United States universities. This represented an unambiguous effort to convince these potential future Central American leaders of the superiority of the gradualist approach to development favored by the United States while simultaneously weaning them from any possible flirtation with socialist paths to societal development—particularly as represented by the Sandinista regime in Nicaragua.[9]

The third set of agencies, the Carnegie Corporation and the Ford and Rockefeller foundations, increased their support for educational programs in the developing world after 1955. Rockefeller personnel had long been involved with developmental aid, especially in the field of medical education, while Carnegie representatives had contributed to the furtherance of educational activities in eastern and southern Africa from the mid-1920s. But as with the other donor agencies it was not until after World War II that the foundations reconceptualized and significantly expanded their educational assistance programs to Third World nations.

Each of the foundations focused on strengthening particular aspects of Third World educational systems in the period from roughly 1955 to 1975. Carnegie programs became identified with teacher education efforts, most notably in former British African colonies. The Ford Foundation concentrated primarily, but not exclusively, on higher education during the 1960s and 1970s and was very active in efforts to strengthen university social science and research departments, while upgrading the administrative structures of these same institutions. Rockefeller efforts were most obvious in its University Development Program, initiated in 1955; the aim of this $100 million, ten-year effort was to strengthen university centers in six countries, a number later expanded. This effort was augmented by concern for upgrading the social science capacities of Third World universities (together with the Ford Foundation) and by the Foundation's continuing support for work in the fields of veterinary science and medical and bio-medical education and research. Fellowship programs designed to enable qualified Africans, Asians, and Latin Americans to study in elite American universities were an integral part of the developmental efforts of all three foundations. The Rockefeller Foundation's fellowship program for foreign students is both the oldest and most extensive of these. Its first grants were made in 1917; within the next fifty years the Foundation provided some $63 million to support the American study of an impressive number of Foreign nationals.[10]

The focus of the educational aid efforts of the Ford and Rockefeller foundations shifted during the 1970s. Their direct aid to Third World universities—and occasionally other nonuniversity educational activities—was reduced.[11] Their support increasingly went to projects designed to strengthen the research and evaluation capacities of numerous Third World research centers, some of which were attached to universities, other of which were not. By 1980 the Ford Foundation had helped to establish ten Latin American educational research centers dedicated to the study of educational problems. In West

Africa the Foundation supported the creation of the Anglophone West African Regional Educational Research Consortium and several research centers in francophone countries, for example, the Ivorian Center for Economic and Social Research. By the 1980s foundation funding had played a catalytic role in establishing a network of Third World universities and research centers that focused considerable attention on the problems of educational development. These efforts were augmented by an increase in fellowship aid for foreign nationals wishing to study at American universities, especially at the graduate level.[12]

The foundations' efforts to create these networks of professional researchers and academics built on their earlier experiences in facilitating cooperation among donor agencies to discuss the issue of developmental aid for education in Third World nations. The Carnegie Corporation organized such a conference in the late 1950s to discuss African education, the Rockefeller Foundation hosted a gathering of donor agency representatives at its northern Italian villa in 1962 to discuss the fortunes of the University of East Africa, and the Ford Foundation brought together members of this same donor agency community in the early 1970s to discuss the broader issue of education and national development and new directions that might be taken.

From this latter meeting came the decision to support nonformal education as the panacea to the seemingly intractable problem of rural development. By the mid-1970s the World Bank, UNICEF, and AID were major supporters of this new direction in development assistance. Much of the foundations' support for this approach was channelled through the International Council for Educational Development, whose major contribution was to undertake research studies demonstrating the efficacy of the new approach. By decade's end the ICED had published an impressive number of monographs examining various aspects of nonformal education in Third World settings. While the ICED studies were providing legitimation for the new nonformal approach to educational development, the International Development Research Centre, with Ford Foundation support, was sponsoring several studies designed to do the same for the evolving "networking" principle that undergirded Ford's decision to establish educational research and evaluation centers around the world. The first of these studies, *Connecting Worlds: a survey of developments in educational research*, appeared in 1981; a second appeared the next year as *Educational Networks in Latin America: their role in the production, diffusion, and use of educational knowledge*. It is clear that organizations like the ICED and the IDRC do not influence the direction of educational development as do other agencies, for example the World Bank, if only because they do not provide financial support for specific projects. At the same time, the importance of these agencies should not be underestimated, especially in view of the facts that (1) they are frequently linked to the more influential agencies that provide direct aid, and

(2) their sponsored studies help to shape the discussion concerning the "appropriate" direction that development aid for Third World education should take.

THE IMPACT OF EXTERNAL AID ON THIRD WORLD EDUCATIONAL DEVELOPMENT

It would be inaccurate to say that Third World educational expansion over the last forty years resulted exclusively or even primarily from the infusion of external financial aid and technical assistance. Clearly the central roles accorded formal education both for national development and individual mobility were important, perhaps the most important, factors accounting for educational expansion in the developing nations. At the same time it would be accurate to note that the extent of this expansion would have been considerably less and the directions taken by some educational systems significantly different had the donor agencies been absent. To be sure, it is difficult to quantify the impact that these agencies have had on Third World educational development, but it is possible to suggest the degree to which their presence and funding priorities have influenced the decisions made by some African, Asian, and Latin American policymakers and the subsequent directions taken by their educational systems.

The degree to which donor agencies can influence the shape of Third World educational systems is suggested by the lament of the Director of Educational Planning of Upper Volta (now Burkina Faso), who noted that 74 percent of his educational budget was dependent on external aid. In such a situation, he continued, "planning becomes meaningless and is reduced to a matter of preparing dossiers for potential donors and participating in a series of negotiations where the money obtained bears no relationship to what is lost in terms of independence and coherent national policy."[13] While this nation's dependence on foreign educational assistance may be extreme, it only differs in degree from numerous other situations in which developing nations find that donor agencies exert inordinate leverage over the local decision-making process. The most cursory review of the literature reveals numerous examples of this, but mention of just a few at this juncture will illustrate the point. Some of these involve fellowship aid which enables foreign nationals to pursue graduate degrees in American universities; others demonstrate how donor agencies influence the implementation of educational projects in the recipient countries.

Beginning in the late 1950s the Carnegie Corporation provided to Columbia University's Teachers College significant financial support to administer a program that made possible the College's involvement in the expansion of teacher education in Britain's former African colonies. Movement of personnel between the African institutes and Teachers College for advanced degree work was an integral part of this Afro-Anglo-American Program. In this way large numbers of influential African educators studied at first hand American educational practices and ideas, while at the same time being exposed to the ideologies undergirding these. The director of the program elaborated on the influence that Teachers College, and indirectly the Carnegie Corporation, had gained in African education in a 1972 report. He noted that of the twenty-seven official African participants at that year's conference of the Association of Teacher Education in Africa—the Carnegie-funded successor to the Afro-Anglo-American Program—one-third had Teachers College connections, primarily through earlier Carnegie funding. At the same time he also noted that Teachers College was associated with all twenty African institutes comprising the Association's membership.[14]

The Carnegie Corporation was not alone in its ability to shape the intellectual perspectives of present and future Third World leaders who would play crucial roles in developing their national educational systems. When discussing the impact of the Rockefeller Foundation on the staff of the University of East Africa in the mid-1970s, a former vice-president noted that "66 percent of all East African faculty have been Rockefeller Foundation scholars and holders of Special Lectureships established with Rockefeller Foundation funding for returning scholars." Rockefeller influence was noticeable as well during this period in Nigeria's University of Ibadan. According to an internal report, the foundation through mid-1975 had supported one hundred fourteen Nigerian fellows, of whom seventy-three were then on the University's staff. It had also provided one hundred seven man-years of teaching for the University by carefully selected expatriates. And the report concluded: "It is evident that the American-trained faculty members—whether provided as visiting faculty or trained in this country under the fellowship program—have had a major impact on the instructional program. [Indeed] the Economics Department . . . is staffed largely by individuals who have received training awards from the Foundation."[15]

Arnove's assessment of the work of the Ford Foundation amplifies on this theme. He notes that Ford staff regularly identified for American graduate study foreign nationals who were attached to universities, research centers, and planning offices that had earlier received foundation grants. These students enrolled for study at one of several elite American universities. In the field of education these "resource bases" were usually Stanford, Harvard, and Chicago, which received large amounts of foundation funding to subvene the cost involved in educating these students. By 1978 the Stanford Program in International Development Education "had trained some 82 Latin American graduate students at the Master's level in the concepts and methods of educational research and planning." There was also a concentration of southeast Asian educators; by the same year some sixty-six of them—primarily from

Thailand, Malaysia, the Phillipines, and Indonesia—had completed the Stanford program. The next year a group of French-speaking educators from West Africa arrived at Stanford to begin a similar program in cooperation with Quebec's Laval University.[16]

The influence exerted by donor agencies on the direction of Third World educational development is, if anything, even greater than that noted above when we examine several efforts at project implementation in the field. The saga of developmental aid for Liberian education in the period after 1972 illustrates the confusion, the dysfunctionality for educational progress, and the degree to which local autonomy can be lost to donor agencies intent on reforming a Third World educational system according to their predetermined prescriptions.

The World Bank was the central player in the Liberian reform efforts. In 1972 it approved a sizeable loan to support two categories of projects; the first to facilitate educational planning and administration, the second designed to focus on secondary education and tertiary level teacher training and the construction of agricultural and vocational/technical education facilities. This loan was in line with the Bank's newly defined emphasis, which had appeared the year before in its first comprehensive educational policy statement. The loan probably would have been enticing whatever its emphases, especially in view of the fact that it equaled approximately 70 percent of the government's expenditures for education.[17]

Four years later another Bank grant was approved, but the projects underwritten then were considerably different from those specified in 1972. Why the lack of continuity? By 1974 the Bank had decided that primary education was *the* key to Third World educational development, reversing its earlier faith in the ability of secondary education to forward societal development. So the second grant emphasized primary education at the expense of continuing support for the secondary school projects already underway.

Two additional World Bank grants followed within the next few years. Primary education continued to be emphasized, again at the expense of secondary and tertiary level projects that had been initiated with the original 1972 grant. Two multilateral high schools emphasizing science and vocational/technical subjects were all but abandoned by Liberian authorities and were among the casualties of the Bank's policy shifts. Local educational policymakers assumed that the good faith they demonstrated by developing and supporting these schools with the Bank's initial loan would be rewarded by subsequent grants. Following a familiar scenario, they decided that the scarce local resources available to the education sector could better be spent on projects not favored by the Bank group—but important in Liberian development plans. This led local policymakers to conclude—understandably enough perhaps, but erroneous in fact—that they could safely leave support for their innovative high schools to the Bank's anticipated second loan, which was approved in 1976.

The problems did not end here. The Bank has a penchant for establishing autonomous units to oversee the various components of its funded projects. In Liberia some twenty new units were established during the term of the four Bank loans. This resulted in a lack of coordination, as many of the newly established units were unfamiliar with the programs of others. More serious, however, at least from the perspective of local decision-making and autonomy, was the fact that the resulting fragmentation and blurred lines of authority made it all but impossible for the person responsible for the system's direction, the Minister of Education, to (1) know what was going on, (2) give coherence to these diffused educational projects, and (3) plan the direction of the educational system qua system.

This situation was made even more confused by the fact that competition developed among the several units for control of the external aid. There might have been hope for reducing the Bank's influence on the direction of the educational system and reestablishing a modicum of local autonomy if Liberian policymakers only had to deal with that agency. But the Bank was only one of many donor agencies involved in Liberia's educational development during this period. The list of the organizations involved reads like a Who's Who of the international aid agencies, and included UNESCO, the International Labor Office, UNDP, AID, the International Development Agency, the Peace Corps, and the United States Information Service. By the mid-1980s it was obvious that Liberia's educational system was merely a pawn in the hands of the donor agencies, each with its particular agenda, most of which were irrelevant to, if not at odds with, Liberian developmental priorities.

A brief recounting of another West African project tells a similar story. In the mid-1970s the government of Sierra Leone entered into an agreement with UNESCO, UNDP, the African Development Bank, and several smaller donor agencies to launch a teacher training scheme for rural primary schools centered in the town of Bunumbu. The project contained the usual elements: provisions for capital construction of a central training institute and outlying schools, fellowship opportunities for indigenous personnel to study the latest appropriate methodologies and theories abroad, the installation of sophisticated technological equipment, and an influx of numerous short-term expatriate advisors.[18]

One problem followed on and compounded others. Members of the original UNESCO/UNDP planning mission spent only limited time at the project site, leading them to misjudge local enthusiasm for the kind of education proposed. Expatriate advisors arrived in Bunumbu just as their local counterparts were leaving for study leave abroad. This poorly-orchestrated scheduling meant that the Sierra Leoneans who studied abroad had almost no interaction with those who had come to help them devise strategies to deal with the practical problems involved in the undertaking. The multimillion dollar Instructional Resource Centre was used only sparingly. This was because of the inappropriateness of its sophisticated technology for the immediate concerns faced by local teachers and the fact that the $6 million power plant required to run it was regularly inoperative, owing to the lack of spare parts and trained personnel to perform routine maintenance.

It would be unfair to say that there were no benefits from this project, just as it would be to make a similar claim drawn from the Liberian case. Although the donor agencies frequently created confusion in the Liberian endeavor, the country did gain many badly-needed primary schools. The Bunumbu project enabled a number of Sierra Leoneans to gain advanced training that otherwise would have been impossible. Also a number of schools were constructed and outfitted. But the price was high, both in financial terms and in loss of local autonomy. This leads to the crucial question of whose interests were/are served by projects such as these. Or to put the question more generally: who benefits from developmental aid for education in the Third World? It is to this concern that we now turn.

IDEOLOGY, DONOR AGENCIES, AND DEVELOPMENTAL AID FOR EDUCATION

The political context that shapes World Bank lending policies has been explicated by others; the activities of the major foundations have also been examined critically. The politicization of developmental aid is, if anything, even more obvious when examining the policies of national donor agencies, for example the United States Agency for International Development. Political considerations clearly play a crucial role, perhaps *the* crucial role, in determining which projects will be funded and which will not. But the political nature of developmental aid is not always overt, and donor agencies regularly deny that their funding decisions are influenced by anything but educational and technical considerations. Can such protestations of political neutrality be taken at face value, or do they merely mask an underlying, but unacknowledged, ideological bias?[19]

As a case in point, the changes in World Bank lending patterns from its first grants in the 1960s to the present have been striking, as suggested by the following table. Noteworthy as well has been the increase in allocations that the Bank has voted for its educational activities over the years. Loans and credits for education and training totalled some $170 million in the period 1970-74, a figure that increased to some $905 million in the 1979-83 period.[20] However, one constant has survived the policy shifts and increased appropriations detailed in Bank documents and subsequently reflected in field projects: the centrality of education in the production of human capital that can contribute to increasing national economic productivity, and the elaboration of sophisticated plans to achieve this.[21] This has been augmented by the belief that a technical approach to the development of educational systems represents the most efficacious way to reach this goal. This belief that educational development was solvable through the application of the apolitical principles of technocratic rationality led to Bank policies emphasizing planning, various input-output measures of school effectiveness, and evaluation procedures to quantify the results.

TABLE 4.1
World Bank Lending for Education, 1963-83*
(percent)

Distribution	1963-69	1970-74	1975-78	1979-83
By Level				
Primary	—	5	14	24
Secondary	84	50	43	34
Higher	12	40	26	18
Nonformal	4	5	17	24
Total	*100*	*100*	*100*	*100*
By Curricula				
General and Diversified	44	42	34	35
Technical/Commercial	25	30	41	33
Agriculture	19	15	11	11
Teacher Training	12	12	12	9
Management	—	—	1	8
Health and Population	—	1	1	4
Total	*100*	*100*	*100*	*100*
By Outlay				
Construction	69	49	48	44
Equipment	28	43	39	35
Technical Assistance	3	8	13	21
Total	*100*	*100*	*100*	*100*

*Source. Education Sector Policy Paper, 1980 (Washington, D.C.: World Bank, 1980), p. 81.

More recently, during the 1980s, Bank statements have advocated a decrease in the amount of government involvement in the education process, an increase in the private sector's role, and greater application of market principles to the organization of Third World educational systems.[22] These pronouncements reflected ideological principles popular among certain Western governments in the 1980s and were strikingly similar to those of the Reagan administration, whose personnel did not disguise their belief that Bank strategies relied too heavily on governments for program implementation. Such sentiments were especially pertinent in view of the considerable leverage that the United States has always exercised over Bank decisions .

The involvement of the donor agencies in Third World educational development has led to the creation of a new professional—the educational planner. Many of these have been trained in economics. Some come from other social science fields that rely heavily on quantification and the conservative economic doctrines associated with the University of Chicago school. This trend is most pronounced at the World Bank, where economists dominate the planning and research offices. From these positions they formulate plans for educational development in a host of Third World countries. These plans range from sophisticated rate-of-return to investment analyses, to studies of the relationship between textbook availability and schooling outcomes, to the role that examinations play in enhancing educational performance, to efforts designed to increase the internal efficiency of existing systems. Whatever the topic currently in favor with Bank planners, the overriding concern remains the production of human resources that can contribute to greater economic productivity. The linkage between the economy and the educational system remains paramount .

The emphasis on educational planning has regularly resulted in efforts at system expansion and/or support for projects designed to incorporate newly identified solutions into existing systems. The planners' mechanical way of looking at the needs of educational systems—be they expansion or curriculum revision—accepts the system as it is and leads to the advocacy of technical answers to problems that may only be amenable to political solutions. At the same time, the work of the planners and their sponsoring agencies provides legitimation for the regimes in power. This is so because their involvement with the educational system signals the belief that the system is basically sound, but in need of changes that can be made without serious societal alterations, be these political, economic, or educational. Such a situation helps to deflect attention from larger political problems that are not responsive to the technical solutions advocated for the educational system, for example, the fact that educational expansion by itself does little to alter inequitable income distribution patterns. While donor agencies and their planners claim that their activities represent only the application of technical solutions to educational problems, Weiler's observation that "planning is an integral part of a political agenda geared towards the maintenance of the status quo" may more accurately reflect reality.[24]

The donor agencies have long subscribed to the belief in the ability of technology and managerial rationality to solve the myriad problems of development. This belief has frequently led to the neglect of social and political factors, whose investigation would reveal that not all problems can be solved by technical means. The consensus among aid agency personnel considers that development that has at its core the acceptance of the efficacy of technology is nonideological, an important factor in insuring the continuance of the developmental process. The emphasis on technique means that moral, social, or political issues raised by policy choices are avoided and are instead transformed into technical problems, to be resolved through the application of the appropriate nonideological, technical procedures. This "technocratic strategy" is a salient characteristic of the policies of the donor agencies; it is considered to be the only rational approach to the seemingly intractable educational development problems. Alternative approaches or development schemes that vary markedly from this technocratic strategy have little currency among the major donor agencies.[25]

But has the dominant paradigm of developmental aid for education worked for the benefit of the Third World nations? After all, it is for them that such aid has ostensibly been institutionalized over the years. Eisemon's recent study suggests not. He notes the donor agencies' penchant for framing educational development issues almost exclusively in ways that elicit quantitative/technical data irrelevant for the betterment of the lives of Third World peoples. Most tellingly, perhaps, is his conclusion that for all their capital expenditures, sophisticated strategies, field projects, and access to data, the agencies do not know what kind of education it is that helps people in the Third World exercise a modicum of control over their daily lives.[26]

ALTERNATIVE STRATEGIES FOR
EDUCATIONAL DEVELOPMENT

Are there viable alternative strategies to the dominant international agency perspective, ones that consider the concerns of Third World peoples before the interests of the donor agencies and the governments supporting them? Is it possible to break the ethnocentric shackles that characterize the dominant paradigm of developmental assistance which too often has strengthened the inequitable status quo?

Klees addresses this latter issue by examining the weaknesses of the neoclassical economics model that undergirds most agency-sponsored research from which educational aid priorities are determined. After some twenty years of micro-level, quantitative studies designed to assess the correlations between various components of schooling inputs and economic growth, there are few precise guidelines concerning what really makes a difference, other than those factors that casual observers of any school system already knew. Since the model currently in vogue has failed to fulfill its promise, Klees suggests other approaches. Specifically, he advocates a participatory, political planning process, one which relies on greater involvement by representative groups of local people and less on the utilization of outside experts who arrive with prepackaged schemes derived from questionable research data, or on local nationals reflecting similar perspectives. The orthodox model that dominates developmental planning has been given a fair trial and it has been found wanting. An alternative model, one whose ideological orientation is better synchronized with the needs of Third World peoples and less with that of the donor agencies, might further meaningful educational development more than has the dominant model.[27]

Ernst Michanek, former Director-General of the Swedish International Development Authority, discusses several alternative paths available to national donor agencies in a wide-ranging discussion of the premises guiding Swedish policy. A priority of the Swedish approach is that it corresponds to "the goals, plans and priorities of the Third World partner countries themselves." This is hardly a striking principle in itself, until it is recalled that donor agencies frequently transfer to Third World nations development schemes and specific projects that are designed without consultation with individuals in the recipient countries, or at best after only token consultation. It has been common practice to transfer to Third World nations educational nostrums which have received only the most cursory field trials. And in some instances donor agencies insist that developing countries institutionalize educational practices that are unacceptable in the home country. One is struck by the incongruity of officials at the United States Agency for International Development insisting that Third World countries produce detailed educational plans when such macro-level planning has never been acceptable in their own system.

One other element of the Swedish approach deserves mention. Swedish developmental assistance actively encourages the growth of locally-controlled nongovernmental organizations to support a host of programs, be they in the social welfare sphere, such as education or libraries, or in the establishment of agricultural cooperatives. Swedish policy holds that these organizations perform valuable developmental functions, both in terms of encouraging citizen participation in democratically-oriented, local organizations and as a third force between the state and the commercial system, both of which take advantage of the majority of their citizens with depressing regularity.[28]

The contrast between the Swedish policy of encouraging and strengthening local groups to participate in the developmental process and the *modi operandi* characterizing the activities of the major donor agencies could hardly be more stark. Rather than encouraging local autonomy, the policies of institutions such as the World Bank and the national aid agencies have steadfastly insisted on working through the existing national political structures. Grassroots movements have only infrequently been encouraged, and their activities have been closely monitored in those rare instances when they have been. An analysis of the direction of developmental aid by the major donor agencies demonstrates unequivocally an effort to domesticate the development process, to channel it into particular directions so that it cannot survive as an autonomous force out-side the control of the established authorities. Donor agencies have attempted to control both the pace and direction of development of their funded programs. This is most commonly accomplished by working through the established political authorities in Third World countries, authorities who, for a variety of reasons—some legitimate, some more venal—frequently identify with the goals and projects of the sponsoring agencies. But, as the following case from southern India illustrates, it is possible for locally-controlled projects to succeed outside the ambit of the usual limitations imposed by donor-sponsored assistance while simultaneously involving large numbers of people usually excluded from more conventional developmental activities.

In his study of the work of the Sastra Sahitya Parishad in Kerala state, Zachariah notes two factors that help account for the rise of such People's Movements dedicated to educational reform, at least in India. First, there is agreement that while development clearly must promote economic growth, this goal can only be embraced if it leads to the equitable distribution of the goods and services created. At the same time this economic growth must be channelled to insure all groups the opportunity to participate meaningfully in society's activities, whatever these might be.

Second, it is felt that the state has failed to insure all children equal access to educational opportunities which will afford them the chance to take control of their lives. The state in short has failed, as Zachariah puts it, "to play a lib-erating or enabling role to justify the hopes of the masses."[29] It is through the state, recall, that donor agencies regularly channel their educational development activities, and in many instances the relationships between the state and the donor agencies are symbiotic.

This issue is so crucial, it seems to me, that it is worth reiterating at this juncture. If indeed the state has not served the best interests of the majority of citizens in Africa, Asia, and Latin America over the last two generations, and if the state is allied with the international donor agencies to provide educational aid, then whose interests are being served by the joint activities of the agencies and the state?[30]

The environment in which the donor agencies operate is one which inex-tricably links them to a system of international finance capitalism that equates development with economic growth and market shares. The outcome of this is that all too frequently funded projects are more concerned with growth per se, to the exclusion of most other concerns that affect people's daily lives. Given this context, it is not surprising that groups advocating autonomy, local control, and a greater opportunity structure regularly receive sympathetic hearings at the local level in dependent societies. Such is the case with the Kerala Science Education Society (KSSP), which has been working to reform local education for more than a quarter century.

The KSSP is unambiguously a revolutionary organization. Its work is posited on the belief that the Indian state, as currently constituted, caters to the rich and influential at the expense of the poor and powerless. The state-sponsored school system reflects the inherent bias favoring the advantaged, a situation which forces the KSSP to work through an alternative, nongovernmental, educational network that it supports through donations, sale of its publications, and membership fees.

Through the teaching of science in a variety of nonschool settings—street demonstrations and theaters, pamphlets—KSSP staff work to raise the consciousness of Kerala's ordinary citizens to the possibilities afforded by science and technology to improve their lives. This can only be achieved, however, if these are harnessed for the people's interest and controlled by them rather than by representatives of the state. KSSP's suspicion of the state's motives are paralleled by its belief that its independence will be compromised if it accepts aid from foreign sources, which invariably are allied with the corrupt state. Underlying its work is the belief that the people's liberation cannot be entrusted to the civil state, which has long since compromised itself at the expense of the majority, and that the state must be captured by an enlightened public which will consider the interests of the majority before those of the few who currently dominate the state apparatus. Paradoxically, KSSP's wariness of the state *qua* state does not prevent it from occasionally accepting modest grants or research funds from state agencies after determining that the products of such cooperation can be used for the peoples' benefit. One example of such state support was a 1986 project designed to improve the open-hearth type stoves used by many rural families in Kerala.[31]

Is this effort by KSSP merely utopian fantasy? Perhaps it is. Some would argue that such groups are oppositional in form only, that they tend to be long on the rhetoric of liberation but noticeably weaker when attempting to move state agencies and bureaucracies toward supporting programs that consider the majority's interests before those of the state (and the bureaucracies themselves). Given the legitimacy crisis affecting so many states, it is possible that popular movements like the KSSP might be tolerated, if not actively supported, by state representatives in order to buttress the state's sagging legitimacy. That is, this might be the case if such groups continually pressure state representatives to support their goals; KSSP members have successfully maintained this pressure for some time now. The result has been that KSSP has been able to enlist state agencies in supporting projects that it (KSSP) has identified as having the potential to better the lot of those it is designed to serve. Furthermore, when viewed from the perspective of the recipients of developmental aid in numerous Third World settings, one can ask if the programs advocated by such organizations are any less realistic than the one put forward over the last forty years by the major donor agencies and their collaborators in the bureaucracies of developing nations.

Chapter 5

Modernization without Westernization: Assessing the Chinese Educational Experience

Are there a variety of ways of being modern or only one? Are the differences between capitalist and socialist modernity fundamental ones or are they simply two branches of Western modernity? In seeking to interpret and understand the educational achievements of different regions and countries, researchers tend either to measure them against the American-European-Soviet experience of modernization or to view them solely within the nexus of their own sociocultural context. Given the increasing economic integration of the world community and the obvious importance of the economic base both to educational consciousness and educational activity, elements of the first approach, whether from Marxist, functionalist, or other perspectives, seem to be essential. At the same time this very economic integration is spawning increasing sociocultural diversity, making the second approach important also.

This chapter focuses on the Chinese experience of education and modernity. I look first at the beginnings of an endogenous modernization in late imperial China before the dual forces of Manchu cultural autocracy and western imperialism brought about the distortions that reduced China to a "poor and blank" nation by the nineteenth century. I then look at China's experiments with both capitalist and socialist forms of Western modernity, its educational efforts under the early republican and Nationalist regimes from 1911 to 1949 and subsequently under Communist rule from 1949 to 1989. An attempt is made to identify problems in the cultural realm created by the imposition of "Western patterns" on the one hand and the urge to create Chinese forms of modernity on the other. In the last section I come back to the question of how to balance forms of comparative analysis that allow some independence to cultural dynamics with those that recognize a certain socioeconomic convergence in global modernization. A few thoughts on some of the frameworks used in comparative education arise from my efforts to make sense of China's experience of education and modernization.

MODERNIZATION POSSIBILITIES IN LATE IMPERIAL CHINA

Hegel's depiction of Chinese society as stagnant and unmoving[1] fitted well with the perception of the nineteenth century missionaries and other western envoys to China who found a civilization that appeared to be crumbling before the onslaught of a series of wars of aggression, fought largely for economic gain. However, Catholic missionaries of the late Ming, less than three hundred years earlier, painted a very different picture. They depicted a society whose patterns of governance and scientific achievements could be upheld as a model in certain regards for European efforts to move out of the Middle Ages.[2] What had happened to China between these two periods? Was China truly a stagnant unchanging society, as Hegel suggested? Or was China's plight entirely due to the forces of Western capitalist expansion, as some Marxist historians would argue?

Some thinkers of the late nineteenth and early twentieth centuries, such as Hu Shi, were so struck by the gap between Chinese and Western science that they came to the conclusion China had had no real scientific tradition, only a highly advanced social scientific heritage which had reached its apogee in the Han learning of the eighteenth century. It took the work of an outsider, Joseph Needham's life-time exploration into the history of science and civilization in China, to demonstrate the remarkable achievements of traditional Chinese science and the many scientific areas in which China had led the world by centuries.[3] Parallel to this, Evelyn Rawski's *Education and Literacy in Ch'ing China* has demonstrated that a considerable level of popular literacy, closer to that of Japan than had been thought, already existed in late imperial China and provided an important basis for the modernization efforts of the nineteenth and twentieth centuries.[4] Far from the early modern schools facing a totally illiterate society, they were themselves partially responsible for the discrediting and final demise of traditional-style local schools that had made possible levels of literacy not achieved again until well into the present century.

Was China then a society moving towards a Chinese form of modernity on its own terms, whose forward movement was rudely interrupted by the aggression of imperialist forces? Were the seeds of modernity already evident in

China's activities in the areas of science and literacy destined to be distorted or trampled upon by the imposition of alien patterns of modernization from outside, including a whole apparatus that called itself "modern schooling?" This is an attractive hypothesis, yet like Hegel's casual dismissal of the Chinese historical process, it is probably too simple. It would be difficult to prove in a definitive way that late imperial China was a society about to produce its own forms of modern consciousness and modern sociopolitical organization. Nevertheless, the well known efforts of Mao's Cultural Revolution to create a viable alternative form of modernity to that of both Western capitalism and Western socialism, also the lesser known yet equally interesting efforts of Liang Shuming to forge a rural-based Confucian modernity in the thirties, indicate that belief in this possibility has been strong among Chinese intellectuals of the twentieth century.

What I will elaborate here is a more complex assessment, one which lies somewhere between the pessimism of a Hegel and the optimism of those who have believed in the possibility of a pure Chinese modernity that could teach the world lessons it needed to learn.

A REVERSION IN CHINA'S HISTORICAL EVOLUTION

In the fifteenth and sixteenth centuries, as Europe was beginning its long transition from medievalism to modernity, a group of Jesuit missionaries, who were traditional in their allegiance to Catholicism yet modern in their determination to use the whole Enlightenment heritage of scientific and humanistic achievements in their battle on behalf of the Catholic faith, introduced their religious beliefs and their scholarly knowledge to China. There they found a considerable receptivity among the ruling literati, especially those who had been influenced by the Ming neo-Confucian theories of Wang Yangming, which emphasized the power of the subjective mind and the latent sagehood of every individual.

In a profoundly thought-provoking analysis of China's attempts to move out of the Middle Ages, the contemporary Chinese historian, Zhu Weizheng, has suggested that this was a historic conjunction of progressive tendencies in both Europe and China, as the necessity of moving out of the Middle Ages pressed upon both societies.[5] Why then did Europe move forward to the creation of modern science and a civilization whose various branches have come to dominate the globe, while China apparently went into reverse, reaching a state of decay by the nineteenth century that left images difficult to erase?

In exploring this question Professor Zhu draws attention to a number of factors, which he sees as part of the randomness of cultural forces in the historical process. On the western side, the openness and rationality of the Jesuit missionaries was gradually challenged by the conservatism of other Catholic orders who finally succeeded in gaining Papal approval for a total repudiation of the respect and tolerance shown by the Jesuits to Chinese thought. This was the famous controversy over whether Confucian rites of ancestor worship were permissible to Christian believers.[6]

On the Chinese side, a new generation of scholars in the early Qing period came to see the collapse of the Ming dynasty as the outcome of the indiscipline and anarchism of Ming neo-Confucianism. In turning away from this philosophy and the openness to Western thought that had been a part of it, however, they did not go back one step to the earlier Song neo-Confucianism, since it had been adopted by the Manchu emperors as the ruling orthodoxy, a "dyke to restrain all thought." Their antagonism to the Manchu rulers inspired an open disdain for Song neo-Confucianism and a studied contempt for the Western scientific gadgetry that was of personal interest to such Manchu emperors as Shunzhi and Kangxi. They went back much farther in Chinese intellectual history, building a whole new approach to scholarship which revived the original classical texts of the Han period and subjected them to rigorous linguistic and textual study.

The Han Learning, as it was called, was modern in its scholarly spirit and had clearly absorbed some of the Western ideas introduced through Ming neo-Confucianism. However it was medieval in content, focusing on ancient texts of a long-gone past and largely oblivious to the new world of scientific interest opening up in Europe. Its demise was followed by an obsessive and fruitless search backward in Chinese history for the purest and most original canons of classical material. Thus China's reversion from the beginnings of modern consciousness back to medievalism was due as much to internal cultural forces, as to external aggression.[7] In the nineteenth century Western imperialism impinged on a society whose movement towards modernity had already been aborted from within.

Without denying the importance of the economic forces of Western capitalist expansion, Professor Zhu explores a complex range of cultural factors internal to the Chinese empire. Both the scientific and educational thought of late Ming China gave evidence of a society on the verge of a potential transition to modern consciousness. The suppression of these emancipatory tendencies had to do partly, at least, with the reaction of the Han scholar-official group, who might have led the way in modernization efforts, to Manchu political and cultural domination. By a strange irony, the very fascination of the Manchu emperors with Western scientific achievements prevented these from becoming a serious topic of research for Han scholar-officials. The educational possibilities of Chinese traditional schools thus played into the hands of an autocratic regime whose minority status within Chinese culture made it determined to suppress all dissent.

In a well argued critique of Rawski's thesis concerning literacy and the potential for modernization in nineteenth century China, Alexander Woodside questions her idea of a continuum of literacy and stresses the importance of distinctions among different levels and types of literacy in relation to modernization possibilities. He argues that the threshold of what might be called "politically empowering literacy" was strictly guarded throughout the Qing period to ensure that political participation was limited to the small gentry elite whose conformity could be ensured through the forms of their participation in bureaucratic rule.[8]

At the higher education level, the independent academies (shuyuan) which had flourished in the late Ming were closed down by the new Qing government in an effort to repress all forms of dissent. When they were revived in the eighteenth century, it was as government-sponsored centers for preparing scholars to pass the civil service examinations. With the flowering of Han scholarship, some independent academies reemerged, but the medievalist content of study and the strict adherence to narrowly defined rules of textual criticism meant they proved little threat to Manchu rule.[9]

If it is true that an emergent Chinese modernity was nipped in the bud as much by these realities of Manchu autocracy as by the force of capitalist expansion, does that mean the only alternative left to China in the early twentieth century, after the overthrow of the Manchus in the 1911 Revolution, was a Western pathway towards modernization, either that of European-American capitalism or of Soviet socialism? Clearly, many Chinese in this century have believed that and have designed modern educational institutions accordingly. Yet there have been others whose faith in the possibilities of a peculiarly Chinese form of modernity has led to a whole series of educational experiments. This may be one of the reasons China's educational history has taken such a tortuous road between 1911 and the 1980s.

EDUCATION AND MODERNITY
IN REPUBLICAN CHINA 1911-1949

The first efforts to form a "modern" set of schools in China actually predated the 1911 Revolution by ten years and represented a long overdue recognition on the part of the Qing imperial rulers that they must adapt to the times. The patterns were those of Japan, which seemed to offer a model for maintaining Confucian familial and state values while effecting economic modernization or national self-strengthening. Thus the classical canons and Confucian moral-political beliefs maintained a central place in the curriculum of the first modern schooling system, legislated for in 1902 and 1903.[10]

The overthrow of the Manchus in 1911 left China in a state of political disunity and economic chaos that made it very difficult for educational efforts to go forward, except those based on local resources. However, two considerations gave the Chinese a stronger reason for rejecting state Confucianism as a pathway to modernity than the Japanese had had: the fact that the Manchus had clearly tried to maintain Confucian educational values to shore up their imperial power and evidence that Japanese imperialist aggression had also found justification in the Confucian notions of state and education which replaced Meiji Enlightenment values with the passing of the Japanese Imperial Rescript of 1890.

Nationalist and republican values were put forward in new educational legislation of 1912 and 1913 and the suggestion was made by the first Minister of Education, the European-educated Cai Yuanpei, that a Chinese aesthetics might replace Confucian beliefs as the bridge between objective knowledge and a new republican morality. While this was difficult to comprehend and act upon, the repudiation of Confucianism reached a climax in the May 4 Movement of 1919. It was largely a critique of the internal constraints of Confucianism over human relations, literature and scholarship. Resistance to Japanese aggression in the twenty-one demands of 1915 and Japan's determination to take over German possessions in China after the First World War was also an important theme.

It is both ironic and interesting to see a more determined rejection of state Confucianism as a road to modernity in China, the home of Confucian thought, than Japan, where it was an imported ideology. Terihusa Horio's study of *Educational Thought and Ideology in Modern Japan* reveals the continuing tensions that have resulted from the preservation of Confucian ideas about education as the right of the state to enlighten from above rather than the right of the people to a knowledge that would enable them to participate in democratic institutions.[11] The other side of this, however, has been a discipline, order and single-minded sense of direction for Japan that has made possible modern economic achievements still elusive to China.

After May 4, Chinese educators and politicians modelled new educational legislation first on the American experience of modernization in 1922 and 1924, later on European patterns, attractive to the Nationalist regime which sought to use education as a tool for the reassertion of state control under a republican form of government. The results of these efforts were a fairly complete set of modern schools spread throughout urban China which represented an eclectic blend of European and North American educational thought and attained remarkable high academic standards, especially in he leading provincial secondary schools located in major cities and preparing students for university study. Universities, for their part, developed new approaches to science and scholarship as well as fostering a new intellectual community with a high level of social consciousness and a determination to support the struggle against Japanese aggression and work to modernize China.

This was, however, exclusively an urban education and one which reflected the economic distortions in China's development of the time. It was largely concentrated in the major East Coast cities, with whole regions and provinces of the hinterland having no higher education and very limited provision at lower levels. Nevertheless, regional loyalty and the impulse to include the hinterland in modern development led many an idealistic young intellectual to return to secondary teaching in remote areas after a period of study in a coastal city or abroad.[12]

With the outbreak of the Sino-Japanese War in 1937 patriotism reached a fever pitch in China's modern universities and a redistribution of resources to the hinterland came about under wartime conditions, as most Chinese universities voluntarily moved to such remote provinces as Yunnan, Sichuan, Shaanxi, and Gansu. They took up practical training tasks relating to wartime needs, contributed to the industrialization of the hinterland, and in a few cases continued to do basic scientific research under difficult conditions.[13]

The dominant model for these urban educational achievements was definitely the capitalist West, although debates over the merits of Deweyan pragmatism, French vitalism and English liberalism, for example, gave evidence of a growing sophistication in Chinese educational scholarship, and an eclecticism that showed considerable independence of thought.[14] However, there was not much success in creating a modern philosophy of education that was characteristically Chinese. The Three People's Principles of Sun Yat Sen were somehow too banal, while attempts to revive Confucian values in the New Life Campaign of the 1930s belie themselves as ill-concealed efforts at Nationalist Party propaganda.

Economically, the Nationalist regime achieved more than it is usually given credit for, and some have even suggested that if it had not been for the Sino-Japanese War, the Communist Party would never have been able to carry out a successful political revolution. Certain cultural dynamics may also have supported the Communist cause in this period of China's historical development. Western educational patterns were very successful in China's cities, but they had little relevance for the Chinese countryside where the majority of the population lived. Rural China thus became the source of two different visions of a modernity distinctively Chinese in character, both of which could be linked back in certain ways to the emancipatory ideas of Wang Yangming and late Ming neo-Confucianism. One vision was predominantly a cultural one, that of Liang Shuming, the other a political one, that of Mao Zedong.

Of the many rural reconstructionists who experimented with attempts at modernizing China during the twenties and thirties, Liang Shuming stands out as the only one who had a total philosophical vision of a Chinese modernity that would not only redeem China but had potential for saving the world from the distortions of Western modernity. In Liang's classic study of Eastern and Western culture, he compared the outward direction of the will in Western culture towards the domination of the environment and the satisfaction of human needs with the inverted direction of the will in Indian thought, which resulted in a sense of the material world being an illusion. He saw Chinese thought as achieving a satisfactory balance between these two extremes in its recognition of the demands of the will for an emotionally satisfying inner life as well as for meeting the outward needs of the environment.[15]

While Liang ultimately phrased his vision for a Chinese rural-based modernity in Confucian terms, it was a consciously cultural Confucianism, enriched by his years of Buddhist scholarship and drawing upon the ideas of the Ming Neo-Confucian scholar Wang Yangming. Liang firmly rejected the notion of education as a tool of state control and refused to have any but the most tenuous links with the ruling Nationalist Party or its modern urban educational system. He worked out an approach to education and rural development that was self-sufficient economically and drew upon the cultural resources of Chinese civilization. His most extensive and sustained experiment, carried out in rural Shandong province between 1931 and 1937, finally ended in disarray with the outbreak of the Sino-Japanese war. Never again able to experiment in the same way, Liang nevertheless clung to his vision of a Chinese rural revitalization that would make irrelevant the heavy industrialism and urbanization he saw as ugly and unnecessary deformations of Western modernity.

Mao Zedong's vision of Chinese modernity was of course both more political and more Westernized. Mao saw revolutionary struggle as the only way forward and wholeheartedly embraced Marxism-Leninism as the main conceptual tool for understanding and transforming China. Nevertheless, from the late 1920s, when an urban-based proletarian strategy for revolution was abandoned in favor of a peasant revolution, he worked to develop a uniquely Chinese approach to modern revolutionary theory and practice, what has come to be known as Mao Zedong Thought. The educational implications of Mao Zedong thought were worked out first in the Jiangxi Soviet and subsequently, after the Long March, in the various liberated border regions of the Northwest. The focus was on basic literacy, education for class struggle and socialist consciousness, and the training of a new generation of Communist leaders able to transform China from a poor exploited society to a prosperous collectivist one.[16]

While Marxist-Leninist thought provided the main contours of analysis in terms of such fundamental concepts as class struggle, Chinese conditions were so different from either those of nineteenth century Europe observed by Marx or those experienced by Lenin in early twentieth century Russia that there was considerable leeway for Maoism to draw upon some of the progressive currents in traditional Chinese thought. One of the characteristics of Mao thought that has often been noted is the tendency to a voluntarism that reflects Wang Yangming's convictions about the power of the subjective mind.

There are fascinating parallels noted by Guy Alitto between Mao's vision of a Chinese modernity based on rural transformation and that of Liang Shuming. These parallels were close enough to cause the all-powerful Mao of the post-revolutionary era to remain somewhat in awe of Liang and surprisingly sensitive to his criticisms.[17] The educational experiences of the forty years since the revolution of 1949 illustrate both the difficulties of fulfilling this vision of a modernization that would make the rural areas its base and the conflicts that arose as a result of the imposition of a second set of Western patterns—those of Soviet socialism.

EDUCATION AND MODERNITY IN
SOCIALIST CHINA 1949-1989

With the success of the 1949 Revolution, a modernity that embraced the countryside and indeed had its foundation in rural reconstruction seemed finally attainable. Land reform was followed by collectivization and finally communization in the Great Leap Forward of 1958. However, parallel to this a very rapid development of the cities and a successful industrialization process focused on heavy industry and took as its model the Soviet Union. The whole urban education system was modified along Soviet lines, with higher education reorganized to ensure both a rational geographical and sectoral distribution. By contrast energetic efforts made to improve rural education were modelled after the educational experiments of Yenan. There thus emerged a two-track educational system, one formal, urban, and precisely modelled after the fundamentally Western patterns of Soviet socialism, the other nonformal, rural, and patterned after Maoist ideas of a Chinese socialist modernity.

The conflict between proponents of these two visions of modernity has largely been analyzed in terms of a political power struggle, which indeed it was. It culminated in Mao's all-out and successful efforts to unseat his Soviet-oriented colleagues in the early Cultural Revolution period and his attempts to implement his own vision of Chinese socialist modernity. However, if this was a mere power struggle at the top, it would be difficult to explain why so many people became involved. Inspired by Mao, they seem to have believed they would be able to create a new form of modernity which would have lessons for a world suffering under the dual shackles of Western capitalist exploitation and Soviet socialist imperialism. No longer would there be two tracks of education, with the Western/Soviet one monopolizing resources and setting the pace, but all education would be integrated with manual labor and organically linked to the countryside. This was the vision. The reality was an anarchism which opened the way for vicious attacks upon all who were thought to have connections with either form of Western modernity.

There is a fascinating parallel between the Nationalist and Communist periods. In both cases, Western patterns provided the dominant shape for urban educational developments, and made possible substantial economic achievements, while rural education became the locale of visionary attempts at creating a Chinese form of modernity. In both cases the rural vision engulfed the cities, first with the political revolution of 1949, then with the cultural revolution of 1966, yet failed in the end to deliver a viable alternative. There seems to have been an attraction in the vision of a uniquely Chinese kind of modernity that went beyond party-political loyalty and drew many into the struggle. Could it be that a cultural need, deeper than political or economic considerations, lay behind these intense struggles?

This is not to suggest that differences between capitalist and socialist versions of Western modernity were not important. However, neither succeeded in eliminating the belief that China could produce a superior version of modernity on its own. Whether this belief is mere self-deception or a real possibility, it has had wide coinage and so constitutes an important cultural phenomenon in China's modernization process.

Since it is intellectuals who have kept this belief alive, a close look at some of the achievements and problems of higher education since 1949 may be worthwhile at this point. Higher education was totally revamped on Soviet lines in 1952 in order to meet the needs of planned socialist construction. All major ministries were authorized to establish their own systems of higher education, resulting in metallurgical universities, railway universities, light industry universities, universities of finance and economics, and so forth, in addition to a small number of comprehensive universities devoted to basic sciences and arts. Care was taken to ensure a balanced geographical distribution of each type of institution among the six major regions of China, and all enrollments and job assignments were carried out in accordance with macro planning for national development. This resulted in a radical redistribution of resources to China's hinterland and the targeted training of qualified personnel for narrowly specific sectors of development. Both institutions and personnel from the major coastal cities were redeployed to developing regions and the idealism of the decade meant that few refused to go where they were sent, even though a newly introduced residential permit system meant that this resulted in a permanent exile from their families and home cities.

During the Great Leap Forward of 1958-60, there were many criticisms of the elitism and unsuitability to China of these patterns of Western socialism. Efforts were made at a dramatic expansion of enrollments which would bring more workers and peasants into higher education and a large number of provincial and local level institutions were established. Also curricular content was adapted to the Chinese context. Severe economic problems, however, resulted in a return to Soviet patterns in the early sixties. The slogans of the Cultural Revolution were similar to those of the Great Leap Forward, calling for the popularization of higher education, and the reform of curricula towards integrating theory and practice and broadening specializations to suit Chinese conditions. The outcome, however, was the total destruction of the system. For several years there were no enrollments in higher education, as young people roamed the country making revolution and large numbers of urban youth were permanently resettled in remote rural areas where they were to learn from the peasants as well as serving local development.

Once the Cultural Revolution decade was repudiated and the patterns of the fifties revived, a process that took place between 1977 and the early eighties, most of these urban youth found their way back to the cities either through restored entrance examinations to higher education or the efforts of their parents to find them urban jobs. The main difference between the post-Cultural Revolution period and the fifties has been a loss of idealism, and a reluctance on the part of anyone to accept a job assignment in the countryside, or anywhere away from their home region, unless it represents a step upward into cities such as Beijing and Shanghai. The ironic result of the Cultural Revolution efforts to unite city and countryside thus was a more unbridgeable gap between these two worlds in the eighties than China had ever known before. With a rigid residential permit system still in place for the forseeable future, it is now unthinkable for any young urban intellectual to take the kinds of initiative in rural and hinterland development made willingly by urban intellectuals of the Nationalist period.

There have also been other serious problems. The developmental orientation of socialist universities towards macro planning at the national level and the heavy overlay of Soviet guidelines in all areas made them even less able to undertake the task of developing a modern scholarship that has Chinese characteristics than their Nationalist predecessors. This was most notable in the social sciences which were strictly defined according to Soviet precedents and isolated in specialist institutes responsible for training the elite cadre who were to manage the system from above. At the other extreme the serious inbreeding that has resulted from universities and other higher institutes staffing themselves exclusively from their own graduates over a long period has had a debilitating effect on scholarship. These were the two poles of a system that drew universities into a vortex of change in the initial period, then subjected them to iron rules of planning that left little space for initiative except in the retention of their best graduates in subsequent years.

Primary and secondary education were less affected by the Sovietization of the 1950s, and as a consequence have been less fraught with contradictions and turmoil than higher education. At the primary level there was a steady expansion over the first three decades of socialism, levelling off in the 1980s due to demographic change. The most serious problems of the eighties include high wastage rates due to the needs of rural families for child labor under the agricultural responsibility system, and enormous gaps in the quality of provision between and among urban and rural schools in different regions. The general literacy level of the population has been raised to about 79 percent, an enormous step forward from the pre-1949 period, but there are serious problems of recidivism.

Secondary education made few substantive changes from the patterns of the Nationalist period in the fifties, remaining largely urban based and dedicated to preparing candidates for the expanded opportunities of higher education. However, in contrast to the fate of higher education in the decade from 1966 to 1976, the secondary level expanded at an incredible pace, with formal enrollments in all types of school rising from around fourteen million in 1966 to seventy-seven million in 1976. There can be no doubt that academic quality suffered, with teachers for these hugely increased numbers recruited on the basis of political attitudes rather than educational qualifications, and curricula oriented towards grassroots development and revolutionary consciousness. Nevertheless this dramatic popularization of secondary education has contributed to raising the overall education level of the population and it has become a permanent feature of secondary education at the lower level. The great pressure put on entrance to higher education by these enrollments was met by a substantial vocationalization trend in the 1980s, which has cooled the majority out of the competition and prepared them for technical, industrial, and agricultural work.

Considerable credit must be given to the patterns of the socialist West, which have been fundamental to many of the achievements described here. However, they have also produced severe contradictions in the Chinese context, most notable during the Cultural Revolution decade. With a new openness to the outside world encouraged by Deng Xiaoping after 1978, interaction with the capitalist West has been resumed and once again it is higher education that has been most affected. Two distinct forces lie behind the new contradictions that erupted in the Spring of 1989, culminating in the violent military repression of protesting students.

On the one hand rapid moves towards commodity socialism led to a commercialization of higher education curricula as students selected fields they thought would enable them to sell their talents on graduation and faculty struggled to develop training and research projects that could gain funding from enterprises or organs of government with economic responsibility. These changes led to a dramatic loosening of the controls of central planning and the beginnings of some professional mobility for intellectual workers. However, they also interfered with the ability of the government to ensure a rational geographic and sectoral distribution of professional personnel.

The other important force unleashed by these changes was a political one. In order to allow them to respond effectively to economic changes, universities had been given greater autonomy over curricula in the early eighties than ever before since 1949. The broadening of curricular specializations and the diversification and expansion of the social sciences that resulted were influenced not only by economic considerations but also by a range of philosophical influences coming in through academic exchange with the capitalist West.[18] These were dealt with in a critical way and for the first time since the fifties some independent scholarly work became possible. It culminated in lively intellectual debates over the nature of academic freedom and the need for political structure reform in 1986, and subsequently a burgeoning student movement demanding democratic reform.[19]

The Chinese leadership encouraged the economic contribution universities were able to make as a result of these changes, but was ill-prepared for the demands for political and social liberalization that came with them. The powerful and eloquent criticisms of government put forward by the student democracy movement seem to have aroused the anxiety of the conservative Soviet-oriented faction within the government to such a degree that violent military repression was resorted to. Subsequent to this, a rolling back of the pace of both economic and political reform has been accompanied by a repudiation of some curricular reforms in the social sciences and drastic enrollment cuts.

On one level the struggle has been between "hardliners" determined to maintain the rigid political and economic controls characteristic of one form of Western modernity (the socialist variety) and "reformers" who opened the door to wide-ranging experiments with another form of Western modernity (the capitalist variety). In spite of temporary successes, won by military force, the hardliners are now having to face the fact that the socialist West is rapidly abandoning the very kinds of control they are trying to reassert.

However, deeper than this tug-of-war between two forms of Westernization, each part of a distinct historical legacy, there seems to be a more serious malaise in China—the need for a vision of Chinese modernity that can give people an authentic reference point in their struggles for a better future. There is a hollow ring to the ideological campaigns now being launched by the leadership to meet this need. However, a new generation of scholars, writers, and artists are probing the fundamental changes in consciousness arising from the rapid economic changes of both countryside and city over the past decade of reforms. Their work may reveal characteristics of an emergent Chinese modernity.

But artists and scholars do not work in a political vacuum, they need a certain freedom of thought and expression for their work. The ruthless nature of the political surveillance tactics that are part of the legacy of Western socialism could operate in the present period as a kind of "random cultural force" parallel to that of Manchu autocracy, impeding the fulfillment of this task. At the other pole, the lure of Western capitalist patterns towards what are somehow too facile solutions to China's political and economic problems is also a hazard, only too evident in the posturing of the heroes of Tiananmen in France and the United States.

It remains to be seen if China's intellectuals will be able to chart their way through these hazardous seas and produce an authentic modern literature that can provide a reference point for the future.[20] The challenges facing university faculty in creating a modern Chinese social scholarship are even greater.

COMPARATIVE EDUCATION AND CHINESE MODERNITY

In this concluding section I would like to reflect back on frameworks used in comparative education from the perspective of the Chinese experience of education and modernization. I have argued that neither Western capitalist nor Western socialist patterns have been satisfactory for China so far and that a deeply felt need for China's modernity to create its own forms has found expression in each stage of development. What kind of framework might make possible some comparison of China's experience with that of other nations and at the same time take into account its unique cultural dynamics?

My limited research experience has led me to reflect on three frameworks that have had some currency among comparative educationists: the "problem approach" developed by Brian Holmes, Galtung's "world order modelling" and Wallerstein's "world systems" viewpoint. The first two I discuss briefly, summarizing some thoughts that come from earlier research within these frameworks. Then I turn to Wallerstein and the relevance of his view of the modern world system to understanding China's recent historical experience with education and modernization.

The problem approach sees educational problems as arising from asynchronous social change and leans towards a view that cultural and educational beliefs tend to lag behind economic, technological, and even political change. Holmes puts much emphasis on Myrdal's distinction between higher and lower valuations, and sees educational problems as often related to the conflict between deeply held yet unarticulated beliefs and the rhetoric that finds its way into legislation and national statements about the aims of education. His demonstration of how ideal types can be used to analyze these value complexes and so clarify difficulties that arise in implementing educational reform is extremely helpful for approaching the cultural dimension of comparative education research.[21] It makes possible the identification of contrasts and similarities across societies and a way of analyzing cultural and educational transfer.

In the case of China, I found this framework useful for looking at the development of modern higher education from 1911 to the present, and the ways in which culturally distinct Western patterns—those of the United States, Europe and the Soviet Union—related at different periods to the policies put in place by Chinese leaders. It was possible to show how certain foreign influences contributed to Chinese development goals, while others exacerbated a cultural lag already evident within the Chinese context.[22] However, the considerations left me unsatisfied with this framework. First, the view of social change underlying it is basically a functionalist one, assuming linearity in the historical process and conforming to the main lines of modernization theory. Secondly, its firm location within Popperian critical dualism and the views about scientific objectivity and the value neutral character of scholarship that arise from this leave the comparative researcher more as a technician,[23] trying to understand what is preventing change from "working" within the functionalist paradigm, than as a scholar responsible to contribute as much to the normative as to the technical dimensions of the change process.

What drew me to the group of scholars who have organized themselves around the "World Order Models Project" was their vision of a scholarship that both analyzes empirical trends of change in the global community and uses scholarly tools to build models of a preferred future.[24] Galtung's well-known structural theory of imperialism is a useful framework for analyzing the actualities of educational interaction between powerful and powerless nations, and it includes the patterns of domination that have been as strong within the imperialism of Western socialism as of Western capitalism. It further suggests ways in which the typically vertical interactions characteristic of imperialism can be modified towards greater horizontality, as part of movement towards a preferred future.[25]

This framework proved both helpful and challenging to me in analyzing cultural and educational transfer to China from various OECD countries in the eighties. It was possible to construct a value-explicit framework consisting of two opposite ideal types, a preferred and a least desirable picture of China's future. The different contributions being made by various Western patterns were assessed in relation to this vision of China's potential development.[26] It was quite a delicate task to relate these external influences to an internal contradiction central to China's change process, but there was some satisfaction in formulating a kind of evaluation that went beyond technical issues to normative ones.

However, there are problems with the analogical relation Galtung seems to assume between cultural, economic, and political patterns of domination. Many aspects of cultural interaction operate very differently from economic or even political relations. A critical study of the evolution of knowledge structures within both Western capitalist and Western socialist processes of modernization may be essential to understanding patterns of educational domination. Both Gurvitch and Habermas[27] have helpful insights on this but much work is needed to apply them to a modification of the world order models framework that would be useful for comparative education research.[28]

Let me turn now to Wallerstein and world system theory as a framework for comparative education research. From the perspective of China, it is in many ways closest to the view of China's historical development that has become orthodoxy since 1949. However, I will argue that it does not help as much as one would hope in the explication of some of the cultural and educational aspects of this process which have been discussed earlier in the chapter. I will take as my text Wallerstein's small and eloquent volume of essays *The Politics of the World Economy*, especially the last section which he calls "The Civilizational Project."[29] Here he states clearly his view of world historical development from reciprocal mini-systems through redistributive world empires to the capitalist world economy which emerged in the sixteenth century and came to dominate the globe in subsequent centuries. He sees civilizations as basically the cultural accouterments of empire and ultimately of the capitalist world order. From this perspective, the conjunction of Chinese and European civilizations in the sixteenth century and their divergent development thereafter, is fully explainable in terms of the emergence of the capitalist world economy.[30]

Within this interpretation the notion of a peculiarly Chinese approach to modernity would be seen as a mere slogan for nationalistic and anti-systemic purposes, revealing the contradiction faced by leaders who wish to capture the benefits of participation in the capitalist world system while still asserting political independence. This is certainly one way of explaining the behavior of Nationalist leaders of the thirties and Communist reformers of the eighties. But I am not convinced that cultural dynamics can be set aside quite so neatly.

There is another question central to China's experience of education and modernization which is not easily answered within this framework. Why did the Soviet socialist patterns introduced in the 1950s and seeming to have so much promise for socialist construction produce an even more violent counter-reaction in the Cultural Revolution than any set of Western capitalist patterns had ever done? Why was it that comradeship and cooperation between two great socialist nations with a common mission to build political and cultural resistance to capitalist domination ended in such a fiasco? I'm not sure how Wallerstein would answer this question, except perhaps to say that both China and the Soviet Union were inescapably a part of the capitalist world system and so the emancipatory possibilities of interaction under global socialism could not be realized at this point in history. My own sense is that there were also cultural dynamics at work that disrupted what appeared to have been a partnership with both political and economic benefits to both sides.

In a compelling analysis of the intellectual patterns that justified and made appear normal the expansion of the capitalist world economy, Wallerstein shows how the very definition and scope of the social sciences in Western universities arose from the perspectives of nineteenth century capitalist thought.[31] He does not, however, draw attention to the fact that Soviet socialism also produced its own categorization of social knowledge, one that was exported as a way of ensuring intellectual solidarity in the socialist bloc. The history of modern Chinese higher education could be sketched out from the perspective of the domination of one or the other sets of knowledge categories over Chinese thought in the vital area of the social sciences.

The 1980s witnessed a kind of hybrid of socialist and capitalist categories and it is no surprise that the present battle between hardliners and reformers in the leadership is being fought out in terms of control over the definition of social knowledge and the recruitment and utilization of students in various fields of the social sciences. What is disturbing is the fact that Soviet socialist categories have been as constraining as those of Western capitalism for China, and have made it extremely difficult for Chinese social scholarship to produce its own authentic and emancipatory literature.

Chinese modernity thus awaits forms of thought and analysis that are cognizant of without being subservient to those of either Western socialism or Western capitalism. Likewise, it seems to me, comparative educationists can make use of functionalist, Marxist, or other frameworks for modernization in a critical and exploratory way, as they seek an understanding of the particular pathways to modernity taken by one or several societies. However, the most exciting discoveries they make may be exemplars of educational patterns and forms of modernity that escape the logic of either Western orthodoxy and open up new prospects and possibilities for cultural diversity.

TAMAS KOZMA

Chapter 6

The Neo-Conservative Paradigm: Recent Changes in Eastern Europe

---

The common notion about the changes in Eastern Europe is that those events are leading to a market economy and parliamentary democracy.[1] *The transition from totalitarianism to democracy, however, goes hand in hand with the revival of conservatism.* In this chapter, I shall argue that Eastern Europe is currently experiencing a shift of political paradigms from a traditional version of socialism to an updated version of conservatism.

Before elaborating this argument I will clarify some of the concepts used in this chapter.

CONCEPTS

Conservatism and neo-conservatism. Instead of using it as a value judgement, I will use "conservatism" as a descriptive term. It will refer to a set of interrelated ideas, values, and commitments; sometimes uncertainly defined, and with changing functions. Political conservatism varies significantly in its function and its rhetoric in different societies and historical situations. Yet, it can be recognized with considerable certainty by its patriotic-nationalistic commitment, elitism, and traditional-religious values.

The interrelated ideas, values and commitments appear as a political paradigm in which the elites express their interests and explain their actions. The term "neo-conservatism" will be used as the present version of conservatism. It is related to economic ideas like free enterprise, market economy, and the restricted role of the state.

Eastern Europe. Under this term I will deal with or refer to the following countries: Poland, Czechoslovakia, Hungary, Yugoslavia, Roumania, Bulgaria, Albania (the Balkan countries), Estonia, Latvia, and Lithuania (the Baltic states). I sometimes refer to individual Yugoslavian republics or parts of Czechoslovakia and Roumania that belonged to other countries in the same region before World War II.

Although supported by political geography,[2] this definition of Eastern Europe is different from the one commonly used by other comparativists, and is in need of further explanation.[3] All of the Soviet Union is not in Eastern Europe; much of it is clearly in Asia. The USSR consists of various states, nations, and republics which have diverse historical traditions and political cultures.[4] The Baltic countries, however, share historical traditions and a political culture with other countries from Eastern Europe, especially with Poland.[5] The difference between them and the Ukraine and Byelorussia is the simple fact that the latter were never independent nations and have been central to the Russian state for centuries.

I have omitted the German Democratic Republic from my analysis. Although its economic and political system has developed under Soviet influence during the last thirty years, its institutions and traditions have different roots.

The debates reviewed in this paper assume an initial knowledge of the history and the education of Eastern Europe,[6] since I cannot hope to provide such a summary here.[7] I will begin with a short overview of the region's history and then turn to the situation in the 1980s and 1990s.

Liberals and Populists. There are various explanations for the unexpected and rapid collapse of the former regimes in Eastern Europe.[8] In the present study I will consider these changes as struggles for redistributing the economic and political powers among the middle class (the intellectuals).

It is critical to understand the middle classes of the East European societies.[9] They are not private entrepreneurs or small property holders, but state employees. They adopted the culture and the mentality of the state employee; since bureaucrats are the state employees with the longest tradition, the state bureaucrat became the role model of the middle class in Eastern Europe. They received their political legitimation from the Communist Party; and in this way the party could monopolize positions of political, economic, and cultural leadership. The professional legitimacy of the middle class came from the educational system, which, therefore, played an unusually important role in the formation of the middle class. This is the reason for referring to the middle-class peoples of Eastern Europe as "the intellectuals."

In countries where the Communist Party shared power with various groups of intellectuals the transition from a one-party system to democracy has been more or less peaceful (Hungary,[10] Bulgaria). In other countries with a strong party power monopoly the transition may even cause armed uprisings or military coups (Poland,[11] Czechoslovakia, Roumania[12]).

Of course the intellectuals were not alone in their struggle for power. They received heavy grassroots support from street demonstrators and those involved in armed insurrection. The intellectuals formulated the demands for which demonstrators agitated.

The term "liberals" refers to urban intellectuals. They used to be called the "dissidents," like the movement of the "Romania Libers" in Roumania or the Free Democrats in Hungary.[13] As the history and the leading figures of the New School of Social Sciences show, the dissidents started by criticizing "existing socialism" in the name of authentic Marxism through their rediscovery of the young Marx. In Eastern Europe today, they promote the neo-liberal initiatives in the economy, the idea of the constitutional state in politics, and the protection of human rights in civil society. As an opposition, they are well prepared advocates of the transition to a market economy and parliamentary democracy; and as members of the governments they might become outstanding advisors. As a political force, they are decisive and have good mass communication skills. As parties, however, they have only weak support, and mostly from urban, educated voters.

"Populists," like the Democratic Forum in Hungary, the Sajudis in Lithuania, the Vatra Romaneasca in Roumania, represent groups of the middle class, mostly from agricultural backgrounds, with strong ties to the countryside. They, therefore, appeal easily to religious sentiments and to nationalism as their political ideology. Nationalism, the ideology of national freedom and sovereignty, even though tainted by the fascist regimes of the 1930s and 1940s, remains strong.[14] Appealing to the peoples' original heritages, stressing the nation's own values and restoring traditional institutions like the church or the school—such political rhetoric from time to time provides the populists with mass support even if they do not have to elaborate political agendas.

Education As a Political Arena. For more than four decades, political parties in the usual sense of the word did not exist in Eastern Europe. Instead, other institutions functioned as places for negotiations, confrontations, and compromises among opposite forces. Education served as one of these semi-political arenas.

Since the new political forces (the opposition) have not clarified their educational agendas, it is sometimes hard to differentiate among them.[15] They are critical of the former regimes but their alternatives are confused. Sometimes it seems as if they do not know what they are doing. Yet, it is clear that issues like the importance of national culture, ideological housecleaning, the education of national minorities,[16] the reestablishing of traditional schools, and the influence of the church in education come from the populists. Other proposals like privitization and citizens' rights within the educational systems as well as the concern about vocational education and the new stress on foreign language teaching other than Russian are characteristic of the liberals.

In this paper I present a brief overview of some of the burning educational issues as they are reflected in the political efforts of the new forces. I shall focus on three debates, namely, nationalization of the curricula; revival of traditional educational institutions; and privatization in the educational system.

THE NATIONALIZATION OF THE CURRICULA

The most burning educational debate is about an "ideological housecleaning."[17] It has become urgent for all political movements to distance themselves from an orthodox ideology that has been taught in public schools and higher education. The ongoing changes have led to a precipitous revision of textbooks and pedagogical doctrines.

Prior to recent developments the content of ideological teaching varied in the different school systems of the Eastern European nations. Without question, the Polish system was the most liberal; there, even Christian values had been extensively taught. Hungary also adopted a kind of liberalism after 1956, and with it, the teaching of the Bible, as part of the world literature program of its secondary schools, as well as the study of the Christian church history (which was incorporated into the world history curriculum). Other systems provided much tougher indoctrination. Marxist-Leninist ideology was taught as independent subject matter in the Czechoslovakian and the Albanian curricula.[18] The Yugoslavian syllabi, which varied from republic to republic, were and still are, less liberal than expected; while the Roumanian regime developed its own version of national Marxism as its official ideology.

The extent and explicitness of the indoctrination depended upon the positions of the ruling parties. Indoctrination went on in smoother and in more sophisticated ways in countries where the political leadership felt its position to be safe, as in Hungary, Poland, Bulgaria, or in Croatia- and Slovenia-Yugoslavia. In those countries and regions, the Communist parties had gained a certain respect from the intellectuals, especially from teachers. Indoctrination was dogmatic, however, in countries such as Czechoslovakia after 1968, where party leadership could not establish solid grass-roots support or could gain credence only by portraying dangerous challenges from outside, such as the collapse of the Yugoslavian federation, a Soviet invasion of Poland, or loss of territories from the Roumanians.

These examples show also that ideological teaching had an additional function. It was necessary in order to maintain the (limited) national sovereignty of the ruling parties in the region. In the Brezhnev era, for example, the maintenance of ideological teaching could be offered as proof of loyalty to the preservation of Soviet hegemony in the region. At the same time, by emphasizing the "equality of the parties and the importance of 'national characteristics'," the ideological instruction provided the national parties with a vocabulary for conceptualizing their resistance against outside—even Soviet—influences.[19] Roumania, for example, maintained its unified territories in ideological terms, and Yugoslavian leaders always stressed the historical necessity of its federation in ideological expressions. The Polish leadership for almost a decade opposed Soviet intervention partly by displaying ideological loyalty. Marxism was the political terminology by which the Communist parties of the Baltic states expressed their independence from the Soviet party.

The abolition of the ideology from the central syllabi is one of the main requirements of the new political forces. It is so important that they combine it with the abolition of the party monopoly from their constitutions as happened, for example, in Czechoslovakia in November 1989.

As has become apparent the abolition of the state ideology revitalizes alternative values. Religion represents one of the options, and, in fact there are some who would require it as part of the school curriculum. Religion had lost its political and social influence for a long time in Europe.[20] Yet there are considerable religious revivals throughout the region, and partly among the youth.[21] Opposition forces rightly expect a growing religious influence in state education.[22]

Nationalism is another alternative. Nationalism has had a long (although checkered) history in the region since the creation of the first nation states in Europe. Nationalist values have contributed to the ideological indoctrination of youth in Roumania,[23] Poland, and in some Yugoslavian republics.[24] Hence the emphatic and enthusiastic move to revise history textbooks, the heavy demand for the use of the mother tongue as the medium of instruction, the inclusion of national literature in the curricula, the new interest in geography, environmental problems,[25] and the frequent reference to traditional symbols.

One reflection of these demands is the movement to give higher priority to "national subjects" in the central syllabi. Analyses of the central syllabi show the past dominance of science as opposed to the social sciences, civics, and humanities. Forty-seven to 61 percent of the content of the syllabi of the general schools in Hungary, or Poland, was covered by scientific subjects.[26] The new political forces, mainly the populists urge an increase in the proportion of "national studies" which would automatically mean the reduction of science.

The present textbooks of history and related fields are under siege. In the Baltic countries, the major concern is the Molotov-Ribbentrop Pact of 1939 that gave legality to the Soviet invasion of Estonia, Lithuania, and Latvia,[27] and the Polish revolts and the Warsaw uprising during World War II.[28] The Czechs and the Hungarians demand authentic interpretations of their liberation movements and the Soviet invasions of their countries.[29] The role of Tito and the present power balance is challenged everywhere in Yugoslavia.[30] It seems that history studies would turn back to the 1940s. Lithuanians have tried to use history textbooks published before 1941; in Hungary new private publishers advertise historical maps of the country; in Roumania the new political and intellectual leadership has revived issues of the old Kingdom and Great Roumania (containing Moldavia and Bessarabia) in the mass media.

The dilemma, however, is not so much the interpretation of the past as the interpretation of the present and even more so, the future. The new political forces have agreed to reject the former doctrine of "internationalism" because it involved Russification and Soviet influence. But they can hardly agree upon future steps. The liberals propose economic recovery and a political reorientation towards Europe with the hope that—in the long run—economic expansion and a free market will eliminate current national borders within a more comprehensive European framework. Populists, however, insist upon independence and sovereignty which, in turn, assumes ultimate commitment to one's own nation and homeland. Populist movements all over the region seem to be influential enough to penetrate the present subject matter debates and to initiate a kind of nineteenth-century emphasis on national studies within the foreseeable future.

The urgent necessity for textbook and curriculum revision reveals an ideological vacuum. The new, generally middle-of-the-road or conservative governments do not want to accept or suggest any official ideologies to fulfill the role of the recent state ideology.[31] They are keen to avoid any notions of ideological monopoly. In this ideological vacuum, though, the civil societies become visible[32] with their mixed, sometimes even confused values, notions, and emotions. They preserved, for decades, their private interpretations of their lives and societies. These private interpretations of national traditions create the basis of the emerging political conservatism.

THE REVIVAL OF TRADITIONAL INSTITUTIONS

Behind the debates about curriculum and textbook reforms, another issue is emerging: the reform of the schools. The golden days of the system reforms—initiated by the previous Communist governments—are over. The growing demand today is to reestablish those institutions that were closed down during the Communist takeover at the end of the 1940s. The most prestigious among them were the grammar schools (Gymnasia, Lycee), some of them owned by the churches. In current debates the "general schools," those comprehensive and compulsory basic schools meant to unify elementary education with the middle schools, are being challenged by the new political forces.

The general schools were established in the first wave of the all-embracing school reforms at nearly the same time (1944-47) all over Eastern Europe. The reforms streamlined the first three (four or five) grades of the grammar schools, unified their curricula, declared them obligatory, and administratively connected them to the elementary schools. In this way, the Eastern European countries adopted a basic education system of eight years—seven years only in Roumania[33] and Bulgaria, and nine years in Czechoslovakia. The general schools were declared to be democratic schools which would bring to an end the cultural privileges of the grammar schools.

In the early 1960s, the State parties adopted the school reforms initiated by Krushchev and his educational ideologists at the Soviet Pedagogical Academy. They began to introduce an alternative system of public education called the ten-year general polytechnical secondary school. It was introduced to the Soviet Union during the 1960s, but the Baltic states maintained their former systems of eleven-year public education.[34] The same system also was introduced (or planned) for countries with shorter traditions of grammar schools, like Roumania or Bulgaria.[35]

Though the fraternal parties were strongly advised to do so, two of them (the Czechoslovak and the Hungarian) did not adopt the ten-year system.[36] Somewhat later (1973-77) others, namely Poland, Roumania, Bulgaria, and Yugoslavia decided to adopt it.[37] The first and second grades of the secondary schools were separated from the remaining third and fourth grades and became independent, as in Yugoslavia and Roumania, or were connected to the eight-grade general schools.

In Czechoslovakia a high proportion of those who completed the general school also entered secondary education.[38] The appropriate figures were also close to the optimal in Poland or Hungary where 85% to 89% of a given age group completed the general school within eight years, and 93% to 96% within ten years.[39] Secondary enrollments in those countries were above 90%. Eight years of compulsory basic education had contributed to the formation of a new generation demanding extended schooling. A ten-year compulsory and comprehensive system seemed to meet their demands.[40] It also promised to postpone the selection year from the age of fourteen to sixteen.[41]

In the course of time however, the ten-year systems proved to be impossible to operate. After eight years of comprehensive studies the entire population of the given age group was expected to attend the same type of schools for the additional two years. But many parents did not want to send their children to classrooms "poisoned" by unmotivated and undisciplined classmates. (It was a common argument which received special publicity in Poland as well as in

Voivodina-Yugoslavia.) The governments simply declared the "new struc-ture," and they made it even mandatory. In doing so, however, they did not expand the school networks and did not hire the necessary numbers of teachers. In the name of establishing a new system, the administration ruined the existing secondary schools. So some of those restructuring actions were stopped and/or declared to be "experiments" at the turn of the 1970s and 1980s.[42]

The new political groups have become highly cautious about comprehen-siveness. The liberals argue against it in the name of the individual right to establish or attend quality schools even if they prove to be socially selective. The populists, on the other hand, emphasize that the grammar schools were always part of the educational traditions of the country and the families that had been undermined by the communists. Some intellectuals are in favor of them because they promise more rigorous academic training and a better preparation for university studies. These days only a few argue for comprehensive schools.

Reestablishing those prestigious institutions of the pre-World War II period is a clear sign of the growing strength of educational elitist ideas. Those schools were strongly selective, applied high academic standards, focused on academic as opposed to practical preparation, and stressed quality and excellence. Their revival means more than the nostalgia for the old days. They intend to serve as a model for the public education. According to this model, public schools should be achievement oriented, focus on academic preparation, and protect quality. The demand for academic selection and the search for educational excellence form part of the ideological agenda of neo-conservatism.

PRIVATIZATION IN THE EDUCATIONAL SYSTEM

The third issue under debate is the control of the school system. Different political forces, of course, have different reasons to raise the question. But for the moment, all of them agree to abolish the forty-year old state monopoly in education.

Education is one of the major human rights issue for the liberals, and the ultimate protection for exercising this right is private ownership of schools. For the populists, privatization is the necessary condition for reestablishing quality institutions owned by the churches or the local communities. For the financial experts, most of them adopting neo-liberal economics, there is an additional argument for privatization: budgetary constraints and financial necessities.

In the name of constructing socialism, the former leaders of the region tried to develop their welfare states.[43] On the one hand, they accomplished an almost total state employment of their populations. The employment rates of the active population were as high as 88-96%; Bulgaria had the highest and Hun-gary the lowest rates (data from the 1980s).

The state heavily subsidized "social services" like health care, education, transportation, housing, child-care, food supply.[44] But it paid incredible prices. Their economic policies—heavy industry, state ownership, self-reliance—did not match their social targets, including total equality and prosperity; therefore they could operate their welfare policies only at a low standard, exploiting agriculture and nature, depending on cheap Soviet energy and raw materials, and running up huge Western debts.[45] Thus, with some exceptions in Hungary and Bulgaria, the new political forces have inherited from their predecessors economic disaster, a destroyed environment, and agricultural poverty. State coffers are empty and few are free of foreign debt. (Hungary has the highest per capita rate of foreign loans and Roumania the lowest.)

One of the unintended effects of these socialist welfare policies has been the impoverishment of the schools and the teaching force. The salaries of those working in the service area are especially low. Teachers have the poorest salaries among all diploma holders throughout the region. The new governments will have to discover new resources to finance their educational systems.

One option that seems to emerge from these debates is privatization. World Bank specialists formulated and discussed this proposal recently in considerable detail (1987-88). They visited Poland and Hungary to negotiate additional loans for education and vocational training as part of their economic modernization programs.

Yet a question remains. Who will pay for the total cost of education? There are only a few calculations of the per capita costs of education in these countries.[46] According to those calculations, schools, even the most elementary types, are too expensive to be financed by individuals and without state support. Privatization, by itself, cannot save the schools and the teachers from their present poverty. So educational privatization is more a political than an economic issue on the agenda of the new political forces.

It may provide, says the opposition, better chances for individuals, families, and private organizations to influence the education system. The liberals want to save the individual's right to private teaching and learning; a right which has never been practiced without limitations imposed by the state. Populists in Hungary and in Poland tend to associate educational privatization with their community school experiments.[47] Those experiments would hand over control of the schools to local societies. Who will change the content of the education and who will modernize the system? Influenced by their decentralization and democratization rhetoric, neither the liberals nor the populists can answer these questions.

The debates on privatization leave several questions open. The most important of them is the essential contradiction between the compelling interest of the state and the opposing interests of the civil society.[48] If education is obligatory—that is, legally required—it has to be centrally financed. In this case, however, the state budget cannot be spared huge public educational expenses. Mandatory education also means that the state raises demands—even if only very broad ones—concerning the aims and goals of education. In other words, even the private schools cannot escape a certain degree of state control. These contradictions in educational privatization underscore that it is not so much an expert-oriented as an ideology-oriented proposal. And as such, it is a logical outcome of political neo-conservatism.

CONCLUSION

I started this study proposing that the East European transition from total-itarianism to democracy goes hand in hand with the revival of conservatism. I pointed out this revival involved a shift in political paradigms, and presented three burning educational issues—the nationalization of the curricula, revital-ization of traditional schools, and privatization—as examples of the neo-con-servative wave.

Yet a question remains. Which of the political forces is responsible for the shift in political paradigms from traditional socialism to neo-conservatism? On the basis of my brief analyses of the three major educational issues, I pro-pose the following answer. The change in political paradigms is a general out-come of the struggle among existing forces. *Neo-conservatism is a cooperative product of the former leadership as well as the populists and the liberals.*

The former leadership contributed to neo-conservatism by corrupting socialistic *ideas.*[49] After decades of socialist ideals and political practices none of the possible forces dare to use socialism as a rhetoric to influence the popu-lation and to win elections. Even ideas like social equality, state welfare system, or internationalism seem to have disappeared from political vocabularies.[50] These ideas were particularly absent in the debate over comprehensive educa-tion versus traditional schools.

Populist forces use patriotism and nationalism extensively. References to the tragic moments of the most recent past activate even the politically neutral populations. Religious messages further motivate the older generations, while elitist ideas appear to be especially influential among the intellectuals. These ideas—which represent the core of neo-conservatism—guarantee the largest political support. Attempts to nationalize the curricula are a clear example of this neo-conservative ground swell.

The liberals complete the new political paradigm by stressing liberalism in the economy as well as in politics. One of the rallying points is educational pri-vatization as a solution for budget tensions and as a protection of the individ-ual's rights against state monopoly. Although the liberals may receive only limited support at home, they contribute to the new image of the "East-bloc" countries. An image that is desperately needed for outside support for their economic recovery.

As a cooperative product, neo-conservatism, in turn, defines the room for political maneuvering of all political forces. As far as education is concerned, undue emphasis on individual rights may hurt the compelling interests of the newly born states. Neo-conservative emphasis on traditional institutions and national values, on the other hand, may have the unintended consequence of contributing to separation from rather than integration, with Europe and the rest of the world. In this way the shift to the neo-conservative paradigm may impede the transition from totalitarianism into democracy and may result in political and educational stagnation.

Part Three

Theoretical Frameworks

Chapter 7

Conceptualizing Education and the Drive for Social Equality

It was after the Second World War, and particularly during the great epoch of formal decolonization, from the mid-1960s to the early 1960s, that much of the rich industrialized world "discovered" the fact that a large portion of the world's population lived in abject poverty. A combination of moral sensibility and cold war imperative led many to define this new discovery as a problem, to which they should and could devote attention. In attempting to understand this problem, and to prescribe solutions for it, it was hardly surprising that western policy-makers and social scientists drew upon the experience of their own societies, as they then understood it.

Although there were fierce scholarly debates during this epoch regarding the precise nature of national "development," a fairly general consensus developed that it entailed at least three main components: (1) the generation of more wealth within a nation (economic development); (2) the more equitable distribution of such wealth, or at least more equitable distribution of opportunity for access to that wealth (social development); and (3) the organization of political decision-making structures which would be close approximations of those prevalent in the West (political development).[1] This essay focuses upon the second of these, social development, as one of the engines which has driven the massive expansion of educational facilities during the past thirty years.

Although the occasional skeptical voice was raised,[2] the general understanding during the 1950s and much of the 1960s in the West was that formal education was a major producer of upward social and economic mobility among the poor, and consequently that expansion of access to such education would naturally, and rather automatically, produce greater social and economic equality in poor societies. The prevailing belief was well captured in an essay by Don Adams.[3]

> To most American social scientists in the early 1960s, development meant a more equitable spread of wealth and a more open social structure where the main constraint to an individual's upward mobility was lack of talent. The educational system promoted opportunity for the pool—it was the great leveller of society. Within the schools, universalistic and achievement-oriented teachers made rewards essentially on the basis of talent, and once the talented were anointed with a diploma, they were guaranteed success and respect in the greater society. Thus, the obvious policy for both poor and rich nations was to expand enrollments and provide a larger period of compulsory education in order to maximize the school's influence.

Massive enrollment increases certainly resulted from the application of this view to educational policy. Between 1960 and 1975 the number of children in school in developing countries increased by 122 percent; the proportion of age-eligible children in primary schooling increased from 57 to 75 percent during the same fifteen year period, with corresponding increases at the secondary level (14% to 26%) and post-secondary level (1.5% to 4.4%). However, because population was also growing rapidly, relative to the rate of expansion of school provision, the absolute number of primary-age children out of school in developing nations increased in the same period from 109.2 million to 120.5 million.[4]

Moreover, substantial inequalities in the distribution of schooling within most developing societies appeared to be persisting, and in some cases increasing in gravity. In many societies urban children appeared to benefit more from the increased school provision than rural children. In others particular ethnic or tribal groups benefited more than others. Boys frequently received more of the newly available schooling than did girls. In many societies newly opened school places, particularly at the relatively expensive secondary and university levels, were occupied predominantly, or almost exclusively, by children of the already well-to-do. The data were especially systematic, coming primarily from unconnected case studies of different countries at different points in time, and was often interpreted differently by different scholars. Nonetheless, the newly available evidence led to a significant modification—for many observers a complete rejection—of that earlier optimistic view which had guided the actions not only of Western policy-makers and advisers, but of influential individuals in the Third World, who were themselves predominantly the product of Western education, either in their own countries or in the universities of Europe and North America.

Claims about the power of formal schooling to equalize the life chances of children who are born into very different social and economic circumstances became much more cautious. Indeed, it became increasingly popular to argue that education can have no significant equalizing or mobility-generating effect in a society which is characterized generally by a high degree of structured social inequality. It was claimed that even if the children of the poor achieve a relatively high level of education, which is itself unlikely, this will not ordinarily produce in the labor market, or in their adult lives generally, the same benefits as those received by the children of the rich because (1) the labor market (and perhaps more importantly the sociopolitical system) can be manipulated by the well-to-do to maintain their advantages for their offspring; and/or (2) as educational systems have expanded more rapidly than the modern sectors of the economy, there is increasing "educated unemployment," a phenomenon which has more effect upon the children of the poor than the rich, and/or (3) as the educational system expands rapidly the educational currency becomes devalued, so the child of the poor parent is forever pursuing a receding target (i.e., jobs that a few years ago required only a primary school certificate may now require a secondary diploma or more).

Many scholars, arguing from a Marxist, neo-Marxist, or dependency theory stance, claimed that formal education could *necessarily* do little more than reproduce structural inequalities in the existing social system; that this was its basic sociopolitical and economic function, and that this was inevitably part of the normal development of capitalist nations and of developing countries linked to such nations through dependent economic, political and social connections.[5] This view gained considerable popularity among some sectors of the scholarly community and among some policy-makers in developing nations and international aid agencies. However, it never became the predominant view. By the mid-1980s some of the academic proponents of this view began to significantly modify their earlier position, arguing that formal schooling could function *both* to reproduce existing structural inequalities and to produce structural change.[6]

Developing nations continued to invest major portions of their resources in educational expansion, and international donor agencies typically increased their investments in education, assuming (at least in many cases) that there would be over the long-term an improvement in social equality as a result. The major effect of the *revisionist* argument of the 1970s was to modify the naive optimism of the previous decade and to reduce the level of expectation regarding the equalizing effect of increases in educational provision.

It also became clear that some of the basic theoretical constructs which we have used to attempt to understand social equality within the experience of the industrialized nations of the West are not automatically applicable to the diverse and changing cultures and societies of the developing world. Particularly important is what we mean by the "social and economic circumstances" which children bring with them to the school.

All extant societies have some form of internal social differentiation, with some members being valued or rewarded more than others. However, the degree of such differentiation and its significance for the way individuals lead their lives varies dramatically across societies. Moreover, there are many different bases or criteria for such differentiation. Among the most common are occupation, race, ethnicity, regional origin, lineage, sex, income, political power, and religion. Both across and within societies there is considerable variation in which one of these, or which set of them, is most powerful as a determinant of how different people live their lives. Those of us who are creatures of the historical experience and intellectual traditions of the industrial nations of the West, whether we embrace some form of structural-functional or Marxist social theory, tend to collapse a common set of these—particularly occupation, income, and political power—into the notion of social class or social status. It is not at all clear that these theoretical constructs are generally applicable to all, or even most, less developed societies, either as accurate descriptors or as meaningful categories of social thought and behavior among individuals in those societies. In many such societies the occupation or income of a child's parent may be much less salient as a constraint upon his or her life chances than the parents' ethnic or tribal group, or their lineage, or the geographical region of origin.

Finally, we have learned over the past two decades that the concept of equality of education is much more complex and multifaceted than had been assumed. Particularly in the United States, the notion of educational equality which grew with the development of a system of tax-supported public schooling focused on *opportunity*. The general assumption was that the job of the state was to ensure that all children (with the exception in some areas of such consciously excluded groups as Blacks or Indians) had access to schools which were free of direct cost, with generally similar facilities and curricula, at least through the age of compulsory attendance. It was assumed that it was the responsibility of the child to use the opportunity thus provided. If children did not do well in school, through lack of intelligence, diligence, motivation, and so forth, the responsibility was theirs or their family's, not the state's. As it became increasingly apparent over the past several decades that large numbers of children were unable effectively to use the educational opportunity provided because of their social origins, the concept of educational equality has been gradually extended to include some notion of equal educational *results*, with the task of public policy being extended to ensure that all children, whatever their social origins, have an equal ability to benefit from the educational experience provided, in terms of what they learn and how they use their learning in later life, particularly in the labor market.[7]

It has also been found to be useful to make a distinction between *equality* and *equity*. As Bronfenbrenner has suggested, equity refers to social justice or fairness. It involves a subjective ethical or moral judgement. Equality deals with the actual patterns in which something, say income or education, is distributed among members of a particular group.[8] One can statistically assess the equality of an income distribution by measuring deviations from some hypothetically completely equal situation. But individual judgements regarding the equity or fairness of any given observed degree of inequality can and do differ; equity involves value judgements. Since societies differ in their reigning value systems, a given degree of observed educational inequality may be regarded as quite fair, or equitable, in one society and very inequitable in another. Differing interpretations of rates of female participation in education is a striking case in point.

The past three decades, then, have been characterized by increasing conceptual confusion. This conceptual confusion has been to a considerable degree the result of the circulation of a bewildering quantity of comparative information regarding the utilization of education by, and the effect of education upon the destinies of, different social groups in widely differing societies, especially developing nations. Untangling some of that data, and deriving meaning from it, with respect to equality as a rationale for educational expansion, is the task of this chapter. In the following pages I will present a "model" of educational equality which summarizes much of what we now understand by that concept and use that model to organize and summarize what much of the now available comparative data tells us about education's role in equalizing the life chances of children in different societies.

A "MODEL" OF EDUCATIONAL INEQUALITY

When considering problems of educational inequality in recent years we have come increasingly to view schooling as a long-term process in which children may be sorted at many different points and in several different ways. Recognizing that schooling operates as a selective social screening mechanism, enhancing the status of some and ratifying the status of others, we address the questions: At what points in the process, to what degree, and how are children of which social groups screened out or kept in? From this point of view, several facets of equality can be usefully distinguished.

1. *Equality of access*—the probabilities of children from different social groupings getting into the school system.
2. *Equality of survival*—the probabilities of children from various social groupings staying in the school system to some defined level, usually the end of a complete cycle (primary, secondary, higher).

3. *Equality of output*—the probabilities that children from various social groupings will learn the same things to the same level at a defined point in the
   school system.
4. *Equality of outcome*—the probabilities that children from various social
   groupings will live relatively similar lives subsequent to and as a result of
   schooling (have equal incomes, have jobs of roughly the same status, have
   equal access to positions of political power, etc.).

The first three of these types of equality refer to the workings of the school
system itself. Equality of outcome refers to the junction between the school
system and adult life—especially the labor market. With reference to the first
three, each represents a mechanism by which children are sorted and screened
by the school, and all three occur at each level or cycle of the system (i.e., a
child may or may not enter primary schooling, may or may not survive to the
end of the primary cycle, may or may not learn as much as other students do
by the end of primary; having completed primary, a child may or may not
enter secondary schooling, may or may not survive to the end of secondary,
and so on). Thus, in a three level system (e.g., primary, secondary, higher)
there are at least nine "sortings" of children; in a four level system (e.g., primary, junior secondary, senior secondary, higher) there are at least twelve
sortings. It should be noted that this classification of types of equality is itself
a simplification. For example in systems which have different types of schools
at the same level (e.g., university-preparatory and nonpreparatory secondary
schools, or universities and two-year colleges at the third level) the *access*
question is not simply whether a student enters the cycle, but the *type* of institution to which the student is given access. We should also bear in mind that
the same factors will not necessarily affect the destiny of children at all of the
sorting points. Since children confronting a later sorting point are themselves
the "survivors" of earlier sortings, we can assume that factors which are critical at the earliest points may lose their significance at later points (having
already had their effect), with new factors coming into play as the lengthy
process moves along.[9]

WHAT DO WE KNOW?

Our task here is to try to make some sense of the welter of comparative
data regarding educational equality which has been developed primarily during
the past three decades. With respect to some aspects of the model just presented the evidence is sufficient to permit a coherent summary; with respect to
other aspects the evidence is very spotty and inconsistent.

Equality of Access

For the vast majority of children in developing nations this is a problem at the primary level. A major objective of educational policy at the start of the 1960s was to provide school places sufficient to permit every child to have access to at least a few years of primary schooling. By the mid-1980s considerable progress had been made. Between 1960 and 1975 the proportion of six- to eleven-year old children in developing nations who spent at least a few years in primary school rose from 57 % to 75%, and by 1985 the primary enrollment ratio had reached 90% for middle-income nations and 76% among even the forty poorest nations of the world.[10] However, in many nations, particularly many of the largest and poorest nations, total population was growing even faster than the rate of educational expansion (which indeed decreased generally starting in the late 1970s, owing to a world-wide economic crisis). Even the most optimistic available enrollment forecasts suggest that by the end of this century no developing region as a whole will have attained universal primary schooling, although some individual countries, particularly in Latin America, may have come close to providing at least a few years of primary schooling for all of their children. But even optimistic forecasts indicate that by the year 2000 there will still be over one hundred million children in the developing world with no exposure at all to formal schooling.[11]

In those many societies which are not now able, and are unlikely for many years to be able to provide school places for all potential entrants, the salient equality question is whether the probability of entering school for any given child is independent of his or her social or economic circumstances. For such societies, wherein education is necessarily a "scarce good" which not all can acquire, the equality model becomes one of random access, with the paradigm case being a fair lottery. Even in rich societies, of course, this is the model which obtains at some point beyond the limit of compulsory schooling. Not even the wealthiest nations have yet contemplated seriously the universal provision of post-secondary formal education.

The available comparative data indicate clearly that the ideal random access situation is rarely even approximated in developing nations, although the bases for discrimination vary from society to society. In many societies rural children are much less likely to enter school than children of the towns and cities. Even in the cities, poor children are less likely than well-to-do children to enter school. In a number of societies girls are much less likely than boys to enter school. Frequently, certain tribal, religious, or ethnic groups are either consciously excluded from school, or simply ignored. If several of these bases for differential access to primary schooling overlap (e.g., if geographic differentiation overlaps with racial, tribal, ethnic, or religious differentiation) the political consequences can be explosive.

A common assumption is that the problem of equality of access to primary schooling is almost entirely a question of inadequate *supply* of schools; that an effective demand for formal schooling exists almost everywhere, and that if the resources and political will can be found to provide an adequate number of primary schools all children will attend. The obstacles on the supply side are indeed formidable.[12]

> Efforts to expand and equalize education opportunities face many constraints. The most obvious and frequent one is lack of resources—not only financial, but also physical and human. Next, geographic, and demographic conditions—vast distance, low-density population, harsh environment, and poor communications—make the construction of schools, the supply of books and equipment, and the provision of qualified teachers a difficult and costly task. Another group of constraints arises out of the cultural and sociopolitical characteristics of a country. Enrollment, for example, may not be expanded for fear of threatening vested interests, and education of the female population may be restricted by cultural factors. Finally, many countries lack the analytic and managerial capacity to perceive and implement alternative, more efficient methods of expanding and equalizing education opportunities.

In the ten years since that statement was written, the situation has worsened due to the fiscal crisis in most developing nations. If one were to meet the often-cited goal of universal access to basic education by the year 2000 (as set, for example, by the World Conference on Education for All, held in Thailand in 1990[13]), resources would have to be found, from shrinking national and international agency budgets, to create within the next decade almost as many school places as were created in the twenty years between 1965 and 1985.[14]

However, there are obstacles on the *demand* side as well. In most middle-income nations, and in some favored regions of low-income nations, there are more than enough school places, in the appropriate locations, for all age-eligible children. In such circumstances, when children do not attend school, and they often do not, it is because their parents will not send them. Parents may regard the education provided there as inappropriate (e.g., on religious or cultural grounds), or of little use, or not worth the opportunity cost of the child's labor.[15] This is a particularly serious obstacle to the enrollment of girls in many nations.

Equality of Survival

Among middle-income developing nations, between 20 percent and 30 percent of an entering grade one cohort will not complete the primary cycle. In low-income nations, the completion proportions are even lower—just over 50 percent—and have actually been declining over the past ten years.[16] In some very poor nations, the primary completion ratios are *far below* 50 percent.[17] These high rates of nonsurvival are a result of the combined effect of high repetition rates (Schiefelbein has estimated that repetition rates at the first grade level in Latin America are over 50 percent,[18] and in some societies in other regions almost all children spend at least two years in grade one[19]), and high proportions of children dropping out of school—frequently after having repeated an early grade one or more times. In most developing nations the survival rates at the secondary or post-secondary levels, for the very small proportions of the population who reach those levels, are also very low.

It is generally true that in any given level of the educational system poor children are less likely to survive educationally than are well-to-do children; that children born in rural areas are less likely to survive educationally than urban children; that repetition and dropout rates are higher among girls than boys. However, the evidence regarding the relationship between any particular aspect of a child's personal or family circumstances and the probability of achieving a given level of education is so scanty and contradictory that general conclusions cannot be easily drawn. The patterns vary dramatically from country to country, in ways which are not easily accounted for. The variations in the influence of gender on survival potential are particularly striking. For example, in a single geo-cultural area, the Arab Middle East, female enrollment as a proportion of total last year primary enrollment varies from 10.6% in the Yemen Arab Republic to 47.1% in Jordan.[20] Moreover, female enrollment ratios (compared with those among males) for the post-primary age group (twelve to seventeen) vary from lows of 1.7% (vs. 14.9% males) in the Yemen Arab Republic and 5.8% (vs. 22.3% males) in Chad to highs of 79.3% (vs. 91.0% males) in Bahrain and 82.9% (vs. 83.1% males) in Chile.[21] Schiefelbein and Farrell have suggested that the best explanation of the Chilean pattern may lie in historical factors which are unique to that society.[22] An explanation for the unusually high female enrollment in a society such as Bahrain is not available.

It is important to bear in mind that survival rates, for entire populations or for subgroups thereof, can only be understood correctly with respect to educational policy by referring as well to access figures. For example, in both Tunisia and Tanzania, approximately 77% of children entering grade one will reach the end of primary schooling. However, in Tunisia almost all eligible children enter grade one, while in Tanzania just over half do so. In contrast, Senegal has about the same grade one access rate as does Tanzania, but 86% of its entrants complete primary schooling.[23] In spite of their similarity on either equality of access of equality of survival, the interaction between the two types of inequality produce three very different educational situations by the end of primary schooling.

It is especially important to note the interaction between access and survival for particular subgroups of a population. For example, if a particular group is heavily discriminated against in terms of access to schooling, those few of its members who do get into schooling, being the "winners" in a very rigorous initial screening process, may have a very high subsequent survival potential within the school.

It is the combined effect of access and survival patterns which determines the distribution of years of schooling attained within a society. Some fascinating cross-national evidence regarding equality of years of schooling attained has been produced by Snodgrass. Using Unesco data he calculated Gini indexes of inequality[24] in the distribution of educational attainment for a large number of nations, ranging from the least to the most developed at a number of different points in time, and related these to several other development indicators. Two interrelated findings are particularly noteworthy with respect to the theoretical debate discussed above. (1) There is a strong relationship between national wealth and mean years of schooling attained in a nation (r = .726 between mean years of schooling and the log of GNP per capita). Not surprisingly, richer societies can provide more education for their citizens than can poorer nations. (2) There is a very strong negative relationship between the Gini index of inequality and mean years of schooling. That is, among societies where the average educational attainment is very low, the distribution of years of schooling attained is very unequal. As societies become able, on average, to provide more schooling to their population, the degree of inequality in the distribution of educational attainment falls off systematically. This relationship holds both between nations, and within individual nations over time. Even among those few developing societies which have relatively low inequality indexes (N = 19) most "would probably no longer be classified as developing countries today."[25] They are relatively wealthy. In sum, as one is able to provide more total education to a population, the equality of educational provision in the society increases.

It is also the case, however, that there are a few very poor societies which had quite low inequality indexes: Republic of Korea, 1953; the Philippines, 1956; Sri Lanka, 1969; Thailand, 1960; and Cuba, 1953.[26] Careful examination of these cases may provide some clues as to how or under what conditions one can provide relatively equal access to or survival through schooling when a society is not wealthy enough to improve the situation by increasing the overall availability of schooling.

Equality of Output

A system's output is whatever the system produces directly—in the case of an educational system, learning. Children with the same number of years of schooling (thus with equal access and equal survival) may have learned quite different things, or the same subjects to quite different levels. There is a great deal of cross-national evidence which indicates that differences in levels of achievement are systematically associated with differing social origins of children in a particular society. Generally, among those who have reached a given level of a nation's school system, children who are poor, or rural, or female, learn less. However, here too the differences among developing nations in the effect of these social characteristics on learning are impressive. The available evidence clearly indicates that the influence of gender on learning levels varies substantially across cultures. In some nations, boys out-perform girls on achievement tests in almost all subject areas.[27] On the other hand, a detailed eight-year longitudinal study in Chile could detect no significant sex-linked differences in achievement scores associated with the schooling process.[28]

During the past two decades there have been a large number of "educational production function" studies carried out in developing nations which permit one to examine the effect of social origin, relative to other variables, on school achievement. A very systematic pattern has emerged: the less developed a society, the less the effect of social status on learning and the greater the effect of school-related variables.[29] Different explanations for this pattern, one of the most systematic relationships ever discovered in the comparative study of education, have been advanced. Foster has suggested the following:[30]

> In broadest terms, as less developed nations 'modernize' the pattern of 'objective' differentiation of populations becomes more complex with the growth of a monetized economy and a greater division of labour. Not only this, possession of a 'modern type' occupation becomes an increasingly important factor in determining the generalized social status of an individual. In other words social strata defined in *objective* terms of occupations and income begin to emerge. Initially, however, this pattern of objective differentiation may not be accompanied by an equivalent degree of cultural differentiation as represented by increasing divergence of values, attitudes and life-styles among various subgroups. In time, however, this may occur and we move, in effect, toward a pattern of stratification that more closely resembles that obtaining in developed societies.

For example, the child-rearing patterns, attitudes toward schooling, aspirations, and other family traits which may affect a child's school success, of a newly rich African may differ little from those of families not yet participating in the cash economy, or participating at a much more marginal level, at least during the early part of the social change process. What we may be observing, then, is the educational effect of the process of "class formation" (in the Western sense) as poor societies become more like Western societies. Of course it is also the case that in societies in which standard Western indexes of social status are not, or not yet, relevant to a child's education destiny, other traditional stratification patterns may be very important, for example tribe, caste, lineage.

A different, but related, explanation is that there is much greater variation in the availability of school resources in developing nations than developed nations. For example, in rich nations almost all students have complete sets of textbooks, and the differences in the formal educational levels of teachers are relatively small, while there are great variations on such indicators within developing nations. In a poor nation, even modest increments in the provision of textbooks can thus have a major effect upon student learning, while in rich nations, where students are already abundantly supplied with books, increases in learning would require difficult and costly improvements in the *quality* of the books—assuming one knew what aspects of book quality influence student learning. In a poor nation where many primary teachers have low levels of formal schooling and little if any pedagogical training, a very modest change in pre-service or in-service training could significantly improve teacher performance and hence student learning, while in a rich nation, where almost all teachers have university degrees, high level pedagogical training, and many opportunities for in-service education, even small improvements in teacher performance are difficult to achieve and hard to identify.

Farrell has combined both of the explanations noted above into an argument that while in rich nations, which are close to the limits of perfectibility of the technology of schooling as we know it, "even modest additional gains in achievement require very difficult and costly educational effort," in developing nations, ". . . even the very modest improvements in school quality which a poor nation can realistically contemplate have the potential for providing important increases in student learning," particularly among the poorest students.[31]

The possibility of improving equality of output in developing nations within the very modest resources available to them is particularly important because the evidence indicates that levels of learning among students in developing nations are systematically lower than among students in rich nations. The cross-national comparisons of student achievement levels which have been carried out, principally under the auspices of the International Association for the Evaluation of Educational Achievement (IEA), have consistently demonstrated that the achievement test scores of children from low- and middle-income nations are lower than those of children of comparable age or grade level in industrialized nations. The differences are large in some subject areas and small in others, but they are consistent. Moreover, these studies compare young people at the secondary level, or in some cases senior primary. In most developing nations, as we have seen above, children who are neither socio-economically advantaged nor academically gifted do not typically survive to this level of schooling. Thus, the differences in learning output could be expected to be even greater at the early primary level, which is as far as most youngsters in developing nations progress in their formal schooling.[32]

There is also recently published evidence that the fiscal crisis in most developing nations, combined with expanding enrollments, is dramatically decreasing the instructional resources available per student, which is in turn increasing the "learning gap" between students in rich and poor nations.[33] This has led many observers, including such powerful agencies as the World Bank, to conclude that in many poor regions, such as Africa, further progress in improving equality of access and survival may have to be sacrificed in order to restore at least minimal levels of learning output from the educational system.[34] In sum, the argument is that neither individuals nor the society benefit from increasingly equal access to and survival through a schooling system in which students learn less and less as total available resources decrease.

Equality of Outcome

Relatively equal distributions of access to, survival through, or learning within the formal schooling system is considered socially beneficial by many only if it "pays off" for the recipients in relatively equal access to life chances (particularly jobs) as adults. To what extent does education have an intervening effect on intergenerational status transmission? To what extent and under what conditions can it produce upward social mobility rather than simply ratify or reproduce existing patterns of structural inequality? A great deal of comparative data and interpretations of theory have been produced in the past three decades with reference to this issue, and the results are empirically systematic but theoretically confusing. In 1975, Lin and Yauger reported data from Haiti, from Costa Rican communities at three levels of development, from Britain and from the United States, and concluded that "the direct influence of educational attainment on occupational status is curvilinearly (concave) related to degree of industrialization."[35] Schiefelbein and Farrell noted that data from Uganda at three points in time and from four Brazilian communities fitted the same pattern.[36] More recent results from Chile reinforce the general conclusions.[37]

In the very poorest societies, where almost everyone is engaged in subsistence agriculture, except for a few (typically young) occupants of newly created civil service posts, and some commercial entrepreneurs, education can have very little effect on occupational mobility because there are very few occupational destinations available into which one could be mobile (which partially explains the lack of effective demand for education among such populations, as noted above). As the local economy grows and becomes more differentiated, creating a variety of new job openings, and in the absence of a traditional dominant class which can exploit all of the new opportunities, formal education becomes a predominant influence on the level of job acquired, and significant numbers of even very poor children use education to obtain access to positions in the "modern" economy. (In many developing societies the growth of the educational system has surpassed the growth of the economy, producing a problem of "educated unemployment." Even in such societies children often continue in school as long as possible because the potential payoff is high if, or when, they can obtain any job at all.) As societies become very developed their economies are so complex and rapidly changing, and the possible avenues to economic success are so varied, that the independent effect of formal education begins to diminish.[38]

Evidence from advanced socialist societies suggests that there, too, this general pattern obtains.[39] Some economists have recently argued that in very advanced post-industrial economies the phenomenon of the "declining middle," the elimination of well-paying industrial jobs in favor of lower paying service sector jobs, is reducing even further the mobility-generating effect of formal schooling.[40] Pushing this argument a step further, Farrell and Schiefelbein have claimed that *all* of the major studies which have provided data regarding the effect of education on intergenerational status transmission, and which form the empirical foundation for the theoretical arguments on this question, may be flawed and uninterpretable because of a failure to take into account long-term structural changes in the economy.[41] Beyond this, a new generation of "naturalistic" studies of the ways in which youth from structurally disadvantaged backgrounds react to and use formal schooling is further confounding our understanding, from all traditional theoretical frames, of the ways in which young people are affected by and use schooling to ratify or improve their inherited life chances.[42] However, in spite of this growing empirical and theoretical confusion it is still clear that even in those societies where education has the weakest effect on intergenerational status transmission there is still *some* relationship; nowhere does the provision of formal education have *no* mobility-generating consequences.

The data noted above refer to the relationship between *years of schooling attained* and type of occupation acquired. Recently produced data from Chile indicate that educational quality variables (e.g., textbook availability, class size) also have a greater effect on the occupational destiny of secondary school leavers and graduates than does family social status.[43]

CONCLUSION

We can return to the original theme, in light of the currently available data as just summarized. While experience of the past thirty years has indicated that the highly optimistic view prevalent in the early 1960s that almost any type of increased investment in education would rather automatically reduce social inequality does not hold, the currently available data also does not support the more extreme position from the "cynical 1970s,"[44] that increased provision of schooling will either have no effect upon, or actually aggravate, existing social inequalities. At the end of the 1970s, Snodgrass argued for a "guardedly optimistic view." "As GNP per head and mean years of schooling rise, there is a broad tendency for all forms of inequality to decrease . . . there is a long term trend toward more equal distribution of schooling and probably also of earnings."[45]

Ten years later, the most appropriate stance might be called "guardedly pessimistic." In a sense, one could say that over the past thirty years we have *learned how* to use increased investments in education to improve, at least to a degree, equality on all four of the dimensions discussed above, if the available resources are used wisely by national authorities and international agencies. But, as we have seen, the poorest nations of the world have been particularly hard hit by the world-wide financial and debt crisis of the past decade, which shows no immediate sign of abating. As a result, educational expenditures, which were already very low in such nations, have been *decreasing*, in both total and per-capita terms, rather than increasing. Among the thirty-nine nations classified by the World Bank as low income, which by the year 2000 will have approximately 60 percent of the primary-school-age children in the world,[46] public recurrent expenditures per primary student declined by 11.8 percent between 1975 and 1985, and dropped from 11.0 to 8.1 percent of GNP per capita.[47] As a consequence, for almost two-thirds of the world's children, educational access equality is stagnating and survival and output equality are deteriorating. At the same time, rich and middle-income nations, where just over one-third of the world's children live, continue to increase their educational expenditures and generally to improve educational equality within their own borders. On a world basis the principal problem now is how to at least maintain the gains achieved over the past thirty years.

The probability of accomplishing even that minimum goal, or of going beyond it, is imponderable at this time. I am writing this early in 1990, in the midst of a massive and apparently fundamental change in world conditions; almost day-by-day one sees wholly unexpected changes in Eastern Europe and the USSR, and in the relationships among major political and economic power blocs. Ultimately, this could result in a collapse of the world economy, or it could free up large amounts of resources now used for armaments to address the problem just noted, or it could divert already scarce international aid resources from the poorest nations to Eastern Europe, or it could produce wholly unimaginable consequences. Each possible outcome would have significantly different effects upon educational expansion and social equality.

However that turns out, it may be appropriate to close this essay on a "guardedly optimistic" note. "Problems of inequality in the distribution of essential goods, such as education is in most modern societies, may well be an inevitable aspect of the human condition—at least no currently existing society seems to have completely eliminated them. . . . However, some kinds of problems are preferable to others."[48] What we have been observing over the past thirty years, as a consequence of the massive increases in educational provision, is a change in the critical locus of the inequality problem within many school systems. At the initial stages of development of an educational system the critical "sorting point" is entrance to primary education. As increasingly large proportions of children are able to enter primary schooling, the critical problem becomes survival—who completes and who drops out. As one approaches effective universal primary education—most children enter and most complete—attention shifts to equality of output at the end of primary schooling and equality of access to secondary. And so on. "Earlier stage" problems are not necessarily completely eliminated, but the most critical screening point for most children moves upward through the system.

From this point of view one may see investments in educational expansion, where they can occur, not in the expectation that the educational equality problem will disappear but in the hope that it will take on a more socially tolerable form and locus. As Schiefelbein and Farrell concluded in their study of social selectivity in Chilean schools: ". . . the most salient problems of educational inequality in Chile in the early 1970s—equality of output at the primary level and equality of access and survival at the secondary level—were problems to which many poorer nations were aspiring."[49]

PETER EASTON
STEVEN KLEES

Chapter 8

Conceptualizing the Role of Education in the Economy*

INTRODUCTION

Throughout the post-World War II era, and particularly since the sixties, thinking about educational policy and practice has been heavily influenced, if not dominated, by ideas about education's role in the economy. Issues of economic growth, better job opportunities, international competitiveness, education-labor market mismatch, or even fairness in the allocation of jobs, income, and other social rewards all depend critically on how one conceives of relationships between education and the economy. Moreover, if one takes a broad view of what is meant by the term "economy," including in it all organizations that produce goods and services, from the family to the government, then how we think about education and the economy critically influences discussion of major social issues that surround democracy, the environment, the community, and the family, to name just a few.

It is our contention that, despite useful ideas, we have at present no adequate way of conceptualizing the role of education in the economy, none sufficient to deal with the myriad issues suggested above. Worse yet, the view of education-economy linkages that has dominated the discussion of such issues has turned out to be a dead end. It has offered little useful guidance to policy, channeling discussion toward providing bad answers to bad questions.

For the last thirty years in the Western world, in much of the South, and even, to some extent, in the East, the dominant view of the role of education in

123

the economy has come from a few particular, and rather narrow, interpretations of human capital theory and its underlying framework, neoclassical economics. In this paper we will examine the views of education that come out of these interpretations and explain why we find them to be dead ends or worse yet, ideological biases masked as technical knowledge.

We also include a brief examination of the perspectives on education and the economy developed by other schools of economic thought, both historically and currently, plus a concluding assessment of some of the changes in direction required to "reconceptualize" the role of education in the economy. The critical question is, "What are the alternatives?" and, in conclusion, we explore some initial thoughts about this topic. The field of economics, of course, is not the only place to look for alternative ways to connect education and the economy, and it may not be the best one. In the future we need to pay much more attention to a number of other fields from anthropology to literature to religion, or "even" to education, for illumination on actual *and* desirable education-economy interrelationships.

In what follows, we begin with a brief historical look at the evolution of economic thought, both to give a sense of its range and diversity in the relatively recent past, and to better understand the current dominance of neoclassical theory in the West. Section three focuses on neoclassicism and its embodiment in the economics of education—namely, human capital theory. In section four we turn to a brief assessment of institutional and radical political economy approaches to education and the economy as alternative frameworks for conceptualizing their relationship. We conclude in section five with some thoughts about directions to take in reconceptualizing the education-labor market linkage.

ECONOMIC PERSPECTIVES ON EDUCATION: AN HISTORICAL OVERVIEW

Though the rapid development of work on the economics of education in the 1960s has been rather extravagantly termed the "human investment revolution in economic thought,"[1] in fact economists since Adam Smith have concerned themselves with education and recognized its investment value. Moreover, economic views of manpower, training, and education issues have varied considerably over the years in tenor and approach. In the eighteenth and nineteenth centuries, this interest was more implicit than explicit—Thurow lists a number of reasons why economists of the period studiously avoided adopting the notion of "human capital"[2]—but questions regarding labor and its training were never very far from the surface. Problems in accounting for the human factor in production were one of the principal factors in the break-up of classical economics, just as they were later to prove the Achilles' heel of neoclassicism. An understanding of the history of economic thought helps greatly to illuminate the stated and unstated differences in economic views of education but is more than can be attempted at any length here.[3] A few notes will nonetheless help to provide a critical backdrop for our discussion of the role of education in the economy.

The discipline of "political economy," as it was originally termed, took shape in the Western world in the late eighteenth and early nineteenth centuries as Europe was emerging from an era of nation-building and State mercantilism and glimpsing the beginnings of the industrial revolution, Commercial wealth had grown considerably since the European conquests in Africa, Asia, and the Americas, and business interests—particularly in England—were chafing under State regulation of commerce and sensing new potentials for expansion and development in the operation of free capital markets. The Classical economists (most prominently Smith, Bentham, Malthus, Ricardo and J. S. Mill) all focused their attention on explaining societal processes of production and distribution and on identifying the factors that contributed to assuring "the wealth of nations." The free operation of markets and the uninhibited movement of capital were principal among those they identified.

As codified by the last in the line, John Stuart Mill, the Classical view of the economy had, however, a number of shortcomings. For one thing, it was entirely static: though concerned at the outset with growth, the theory included no principle to explain advances in technology, industrial development or the evolution of the economic system over time. Furthermore, classical economics remained unable to resolve the quandary of "distributive shares" that had so divided its principal architects: that is, to explain how and why the economy determined the proportion of the profits of production to be attributed to each of the factors involved—labor, capital and land. Yet these were precisely the questions that the history of Western Europe in the nineteenth century was throwing into sharper and sharper relief.

The attempt to deal with such questions—and with the social reality underlying them—split the economics field into opposing schools of thought in the late nineteenth century. At least two tendencies and four main approaches can be identified. On the one hand were those, principally Marxists and proponents of the German Historical school, who maintained the classical focus on production and on the macro-institutional structure of the economy but sought to better describe the historical evolution of economic life and so to devise a dynamic model. On the other hand lay the marginalists and the Austrian economists, who shifted the focus to the micro-level of consumption and exchange and sought to understand the nature of markets and the conditions of their optimal operation. Marginalists devoted themselves to the development of mathematically precise models of market equilibrium;[4] whereas Austrians focused instead on human behavior in markets and the dynamics of entrepreneurial activity. These theoretical trends were at the same time intimately tied to real world events. To a considerable if varying degree, Marxists and German historicists were reacting to perceived excesses of capitalism, and marginalists and Austrians to perceived threats of socialism.[5]

The American Economic Association (AEA), founded in 1886 by disciples of the German Historical School who became known in the United States as "institutionalists," initially reflected much of this tension and debate.[6] Its first president, Richard Ely, oriented the association and the economic profession toward active involvement in the solution of social problems.[7] This sort of partisan commitment, however, was increasingly perceived as threatening by a discipline with scientific pretensions and growing professional ambitions. A new basis for unity on the right was forged at the end of the century by the English economist Alfred Marshall, who blended the mathematical approaches of the marginalists and the cost and production concerns of the classicists into a distinctive method of economic analysis thereafter termed the "neoclassical synthesis." Within a few years of the publication of Marshall's *Principles of Economics* in 1892, disciples of his work, or "neoclassical economists," had taken control of the American Economic Association and occupied key positions in academic and policymaking circles. Neoclassicism has been the dominant economic theory in the United States since that time.

The ascendancy of neoclassicism has not been without its problems, however. The microeconomic "perfect competition" model underlying neoclassical theory offered little help in explaining the negative consequences of capitalism that were increasingly evident or in understanding the macroeconomic shocks—recessions, boom and bust phenomena—that the United States experienced in the early twentieth century. The neoclassical school essentially split into a number of factions over the question of how best to address such issues of "market failure"—in short, how to deal with recognition that truly competitive conditions did not exist in the real world and that capitalist markets were not producing general social welfare. Those on the liberal side favored government intervention to restore competitive conditions or redress socioeconomic inequities, an approach that gave birth to the whole tradition of welfare economics and Keynesian countercyclical fiscal policy. Those on the conservative side—who in effect espoused many of the theses of Austrian economics—condemned government intervention and favored fuller reversion to laissez-faire policies.

It is significant to note that the most recalcitrant domain—both in the capitalist economy and in the discipline of economics—remained labor. The question of how to treat the human factor in production continued to prove as ticklish theoretically as it did for business and industrial practice. In both classical and neoclassical economics, workers were considered standard and uniform inputs to the production process; only their numbers entered into the mathematical formulations of the neoclassicists. However, these assumptions plus the "marginal productivity" theory of wages[8] did not yield a very good explanation of why levels of remuneration in the real world should differ as markedly as they did and no explanation whatsoever of the phenomena of strikes, labor unions, closed and open shops, and so on.

The practical consequence of these theoretical shortcomings of neoclassicism was that institutional economists, with their descriptive, sociological and meliorative bent, moved into the forefront of debate and policy-making about labor and human resources in the United States around World War I, a situation which persisted for most of the first half of the twentieth century. Students of Mitchell and Commons and economists like John Dunlop and J. M. Clark filled positions of importance in American academic and government circles and focused attention on industrial relations, labor unions, wage differences, and a host of structural phenomena in the labor market, with the result that this branch of economics became further and further divorced from the neoclassical mainstream of the discipline.

This anomaly in a sea of increasingly abstract economic thought was effectively brought into the neoclassical fold with the advent of human capital theory, whose advocates believed they had finally solved the analytical problem of treating labor like any other commodity determined by supply and demand. Economists had long admitted, but never formally recognized, that one person's work was not identical to another's, and that "labor" was therefore not an entirely homogeneous factor of production that could be measured in simple hourly units. The idea of varying quantities of "capital" embodied in human beings gave a name to these differences, yielded theories about why they exist, and led to new explanations of a variety of social phenomena in areas as diverse as economic growth, health, migration, education, and training.

In the next section, we look more closely at the current status of human capital theory and of the neoclassical paradigm that underlies it. Here it is important simply to stress two points often overlooked but of major importance to any effort to rethink the role of education in the economy. First, there is in fact a full spectrum of economic perspectives on questions of labor, human resource development, and education. Second, this variety of views did not arise overnight, but is the fruit of a rich history of economic thought—a "history," moreover, of which we are a part and which continues to unfold in sometimes unexpected ways. In the United States and Canada, the relative influence of different schools of thought has changed several times over the last century; and the current state of economics in, for example, Brazil or France is not the same as it is in the North America.

THE CURRENT ORTHODOXY:
NEOCLASSICAL ECONOMICS AND HUMAN CAPITAL THEORY

Since the 1960s, neoclassical economics has furnished the dominant paradigm for the economic analysis of education as well as the dominant template for the application of economics to issues of educational research, policy, and planning. In this section, we wish to review briefly the status of the current economic orthodoxy and its embodiment in the field of education: human capital theory.

The development of the notion of human capital in the early sixties provided the medium for applying the neoclassical model to the domain of education and human resource development. It also furnished a lens through which activities that lead to human capital formation could be seen as productive investments, at both individual and societal levels. Human capital theory thus gave neoclassical economists a rationale for involving government in educational investments and some tools for measuring their yield. It is this investment connection between education and the labor market that has dominated thinking about the role of education and the economy over the last thirty years. The dominance is at times so strong that education seems to have become no more than a conceptual appendage to the labor market and is automatically blamed for the recurrently perceived "mismatch" between the two.

The ascendancy of the economic rationale was somewhat moderated in the sixties and seventies by the attention given to issues of fairness and equity. Because of the assumed connection between education, jobs, and earnings, education and training programs were considered potentially effective means for improving the circumstances of the poor. For a while, in the 1970s, there was even a remarkable level of agreement among neoclassical economists that providing more resources to educational programs was an efficient and equitable use of public monies.

The consensus was thin, however, and the model on which it was based proved to have fundamental weaknesses. When you import neoclassical theory into the labor and education field, it should be no surprise to discover that you have also imported most of the paradigm's shortcomings and dissensions. In the following pages, we highlight some of the critical debates within the dominant paradigm over the application of economics to education, and the underlying weaknesses of neoclassical theory that this debate reveals.

Debates Over Orthodoxy

The consensus in the seventies that education could be both an efficient and an equitable social investment was undercut by the longstanding liberal vs. conservative split among neoclassical economists, and it dissolved completely in the eighties as an even more conservative view became predominant. The liberal/conservative disagreement grew sharpest over the role of the government in the economy. The key to understanding the debate lies in understanding how neoclassical economics views the public sector as a whole.

Neoclassical economics provides a very precise theoretical rationale for public sector action: government intervention is justified in cases of "market failure," that is, where the private market proves inefficient, and in instances where desirable social goals—like greater social equity and growth, or lower unemployment and inflation—cannot be achieved by reliance on the private sector. Unfortunately, this theoretical precision becomes quite fuzzy in practice. For example, to the extent that education has effects beyond the individual—on the family, neighbors, community, or nation (effects that neoclassical economists call "externalities")—neoclassical logic indicates that leaving the educational system completely to the private sector would be inefficient. One example often given of externalities associated with education is its ability to contribute to a better functioning democracy by educating thoughtful, active, and responsible citizens. To the extent that this is correct, a neoclassical economist should by rights consider the contribution of education to the functioning of democratic institutions to be just as much a part of education's "social efficiency" as its contribution to the production of goods and services. The only difference is that neoclassical economists believe they can measure the latter, while the former seems impossible to capture quantitatively, at least in the monetary terms that would allow it to be included in rate of return calculations.[9]

Consideration of the wider—though economically relevant—effects of education, or of any social intervention, obviously raises important general questions about the neoclassical analysis of the role of the public sector in the economy. To what extent are such externalities critical to the evaluation of government activities in all forms or education, and in other sectors as well? What does their presence mean the government should do? A similar aura of ambiguity surrounds neoclassicism's analysis of other instances of market failure, and there is an equivalent amount of debate over the desirability of—and means for—attaining other social goals.

This ambiguity has led to considerable divergence in the way liberal and conservative neoclassical economists interpret and operationalize their framework. Liberals tend to see myriad instances of market failure in the real world and a wide range of structural inequities which combine to justify a very strong, active, and interventionist role for government. Conservatives, on the other hand, find many fewer clear-cut cases of market failure, and many fewer instances where government intervention would help to correct such market imperfections. Moreover, they are strengthened in the conviction that less government is better by an equally strong belief that social inequities arise principally from individual differences rather than from environmental and structural causes.

Conservatives and liberals also have tended to differ on *how* the government should intervene in those cases where both camps agree it may need to. At the macroeconomic level, there has been a longstanding debate over fiscal vs. monetary policy, with the liberals favoring government spending policies and the conservatives more indirect banking system controls. At a more microeconomic level, the disagreement has often focused on how specific public sector activities could best achieve efficiency and other goals. In the seventies there were debates between those advocating more centrally controlled, technically-determined strategies to guide government social service provision and those who saw the need for more decentralized, and sometimes participative strategies.[10]

In the domain of education, rivalry and disagreement between the two camps has manifested itself in a variety of ways. Until this past decade, both liberal and conservative neoclassical economists recognized the need for considerable government involvement in education because problems of "market failure" made major private sector provision inefficient in this domain. Moreover, both recognized that government needed to play a role in ensuring the equitable distribution of educational opportunities, since these were seen to underlie a fairer distribution of economic opportunities. Yet differences over the extent of market failure and of equity justifications for government intervention led to very divergent conclusions. Liberals generally affirmed the need for public primary and secondary schooling, as well as a strong government role at the university level. Conservatives believed that the government should be less intrusive in education. In a now classic essay on "The Role of Government in Education," noted economist Milton Friedman argued for voucher schemes for secondary schooling and greatly reduced expenditure of public monies on higher education.[11]

While the conservatives did have some influence, a more or less liberal-dominated economics consensus prevailed throughout the seventies, justifying the expansion and improvement of public education, both in the western and developing worlds, as an appropriate and beneficial societal investment. In the eighties, the coming to power of Ronald Reagan and Margaret Thatcher in the United States and United Kingdom signaled a broad societal shift in both public and professional ideologies (see the Miriam David chapter in this text). In economics, this shift was led by a very conservative faction, the so-called "public choice" school, heirs in part of the Austrian economists. While conservative economists had recognized that market failure justified some, albeit limited, government intervention, the "neoconservatives" generally argued that experience showed "government failure" to be a more severe problem than market failure. That is, even if the market may not always be efficient, government interference inevitably results in worse outcomes than those it is designed to remedy. The conclusion of this strain of argument is that to improve "public choices"—that is, to increase the quantity and quality of options available to the citizenry—government should abandon much of what it does, returning many of these activities to the private sector.[12]

In recent years, public education has been hard hit by a combination of conservative and neoconservative thinking. There has been a strong movement in rich and poor countries alike to reduce the amount of government tax revenues devoted to education and to increase the share of education supplied or managed by the private sector. The World Bank now routinely recommends that Third World countries improve their educational systems through charging "user fees" and increasing privatization,[13] whereas in the seventies, similar problems of educational effectiveness and equity would have led to a call for governmental expansion and improvement of education and an increase in taxes to pay for it. If anything, this current orthodoxy strengthens the narrowest neoclassical view of the connection between education and the economy. Since, in the neoconservative view, education is principally a means for job preparation, and greater social equity is not seen as a major issue, the rationale for government involvement in education is greatly weakened.

Reflections on the Underlying Neoclassical Model

Elsewhere we have critiqued in more detail this currently dominant vision of the role of education in the economy.[14] In theory, conservative neoclassicists do recognize that education plays a variety of roles, and that some of these may be more important to social efficiency than its labor market function; and they admit that this situation could justify greater government effort and spending on behalf of education than is now the case. Yet on ideological grounds, the neoconservatives have changed the major educational policy recommendation put forward by economists from one of government investment to one of general divestment.

Criticism of neoconservative human resource economics does not necessarily imply that the liberal variant is much less problematic, however. There have been repeated attacks on human capital orthodoxy since its inception.[15] Some of the most telling critiques focus on issues and arguments like the following: earnings are a very inadequate measure of the social benefits of education; the framework ignores the very real institutional structures through which unequal power operates; it offers no satisfactory mechanism for understanding and dealing with problems of equity; and it cannot explain such phenomena as persistent discrimination along sex, race, and class lines.[16]

The weaknesses of human capital theory are symptomatic of those of the neoclassical paradigm as a whole. The linchpin assumption that wages are in fact a decent measure of productivity comes directly from the neoclassical model of the economy. Like most of the underlying tenets of neoclassicism, it is true in an ideal world of perfect competition and perfect information where personal preference functions are entirely independent, all factors of production are fully monetized, the payment to each is an accurate expression of its marginal productivity, and all the social consequences or externalities of production are accurately valued on the market. The problem is that such conditions simply do not exist, and the reasons why they do not exist are in fact quite significant: not all factors of production are monetized or monetizable, personal preference schedules are in fact interdependent, myriad externalities and social consequences do not get priced, and the topography of our economy appears fundamentally shaped by institutional realities into a welter of discrete if overlapping markets . . . to name just a few.

In the real world, therefore, wages and other prices bear scant resemblance to the signals of efficiency that neoclassical economists claim they theoretically represent. In fact, within neoclassical economics itself, the "theory of second best" says that one single "imperfection" in an otherwise perfectly competitive economy (for example, just one monopoly) sets off such reverberations and distortions that market prices for goods and services cease to give any indication of social efficiency. Under these conditions, the idea of efficiency itself becomes nonoperational, and cost-benefit calculations lose their claim to social significance.[17]

This quandary is deepened by the impossibility of separating efficiency and equity concerns in the real world. Economists cling to this theoretical distinction because it allows them to play the role of neutral "scientists" in advocating policies that they deem efficient. In practice, the groups that bear the social costs of a program are rarely the same ones that reap the majority of its benefits, and thus the real question is always "efficient for whom?" Elsewhere we have elaborated this critique in more detail.[18] Overall, our point is that the guiding concept of neoclassicism—"social or Pareto efficiency"[19]—breaks down completely once we leave the fantasy world of perfect competition and that it does not offer even partial guidance for resource allocation in the real world.

Another critical problem for neoclassical economists—as well as for researchers from other perspectives and disciplines—is the failure of empirical methods to yield the type of reliable information about causal relations that is essential to cost-effectiveness and cost-benefit calculations. It makes little sense to perform rate of return computations or to compare costs and outcomes unless you can determine the actual effects of an educational program and distinguish them from chance correlations and unrelated events. As argued elsewhere in greater detail, we believe, quite to the contrary of prevailing social science views, that the use of regression analysis methodologies (e.g., path analysis, probit, logit, LISREL, discriminant analysis, etc.) has proven to be a dead end and provides no valid information about causal impacts.[20]

Our rationale is based on theoretical and empirical grounds.[21] On the theoretical side, one can never fulfill the requirements of full and complete model specification, and the effort in the literature using regression simply leads to endless fishing expeditions through alternate specifications and no replication across studies. On the empirical side, the result is interminable debate among social scientists about the impact of any variable on any phenomenon of interest—typified, for example, by the squabbles between human capital theorists who consistently find in their regressions that structural and institutional variables have no effect on individual earnings differences, and their economist and sociologist critics who find on the contrary that they always do.

If causal linkages are impossible to determine by such quantitative means, it does not mean that data are irrelevant, but it does imply that we should adopt a much less positivistic approach to social "science" than economists (among others) have been taking. Perhaps we can not hope to answer questions about, for example, the relative impact on educational outcomes of spending additional funds on teacher training as opposed to textbooks. Perhaps, more generally, we can only rely on cross-tabulation and qualitative data as information, instead of pseudo-scientific techniques that purport to separate the effects of multiple causes. And perhaps this all implies that we must focus much more on the processes for debating our different interpretations of this evidence than on the never-ending search for some mythical scientific truth.[22]

Overall, in its theoretical and technical dimensions, the neoclassical paradigm thus seems to be in a very sorry state. It is saddled on the theoretical side with a very rigid, yet ambiguous conceptual framework that requires a strong injection of faith and ideology in order to yield policy implications and that can be applied in very different and sometimes diametrically opposed ways. On the technical side, it deploys a set of refined mathematical methods that do not work without highly unrealistic assumptions and considerable fudging. These all seem like signs of a degenerative paradigm. Why, then, is the model not supplanted? The most frequent answer from neoclassicists who admit the paradigm's weaknesses is that there are no decent alternatives; and it is to this question that we wish to address ourselves in the following section.

CURRENT STATUS OF
ALTERNATIVE CONCEPTUAL FRAMEWORKS

Defenders of the current orthodoxy in the economics of education often claim that critics have no alternative to offer, or at least nothing as fully elaborated as neoclassical theory and technique. In this section, we wish to examine briefly the current status of the institutionalist and radical political economist schools of thought and their analysis of the role of education in the economy.

Institutionalist Approaches

Whether marginal or dominant, the institutionalist movement never really disappears from the scene. Since its proponents attach a great deal of importance to the actual phenomena of social change and economic development, for them to recede from policy prominence simply means to get involved in practical issues of human resource planning and research. Examples of institutionalist economists pursuing this path might include Sar Levitan, Georgetown professor and author of numerous studies of training; or Eli Ginzberg, venerable human resource economist who over a fifty year period, from the Depression through the human capital heyday, continued to work and publish on questions of skills formation and the education-labor market linkage, whatever the current conceptual vogue.[23]

Institutionalist economics in general has, however, experienced something of a resurgence over the last thirty years, demonstrated by the founding of the Association for Evolutionary Economics and the creation of the *Journal of Economic Issues* in the 1960s, both currently going strong. In more specific reference to education and its role in the economy, institutionalists have been principally responsible for the development of theories and studies of labor market segmentation and internal labor markets—born once again from careful attention to the actual contours of the economy—which highlight the barriers to free labor mobility or to the simple productivity determination of wages.[24] At the same time, the institutionalist impulse was a predominant influence in development of the screening critique of human capital theory.[25] Though most of the mainstream response to screening consisted of efforts to sidetrack the debate into limited technical issues amenable to neoclassical treatment, the systematic articulation of alternate explanations for the education-earnings correlation had no small effect on the field.[26] Furthermore, many of the most trenchant sociological analyses of the relation of education to job markets are in effect institutionalist critiques of human capital theory.[27]

Radical Economics Perspectives

Radical political economics (or, equivalently, neomarxist economics)—and analyses of education—also experienced a considerable renaissance starting in the 1960s. The *Review of Radical Political Economy*, established in 1964, and the *Monthly Review*, which preceded it by ten years, are two prominent publications among the numerous journals that view the economy from a radical perspective.[28] Neomarxists have stressed the ways in which educational institutions reproduce existing relations of production and so the degree to which the structure of educational institutions mirrors or corresponds to the fundamental economic structure of society. During the past decade, radical political economists refined their analysis of societal superstructure—including the education system and, more broadly, the State as a whole—to bring to light the class conflicts *within* these institutions and the respect in which all such social agencies are in fact "contested terrain".[29] While there are relatively few radical economists in the United States writing about education, those few have been both prolific and influential; moreover, many researchers from other disciplines operate from, and have made substantial contributions to, a political economy understanding of education.[30] Worldwide there are many more economists working in this alternate arena.[31]

Though there is not space here to go into a detailed examination of institutionalist or neomarxist analyses of education, it is at least evident that these alternative schools of thought are alive and well. The dominant paradigm provides a methodology for the evaluation of education as an investment, and neoclassicists often fault their critics for not proposing improvements on this methodology or new ways of measuring the investment value of education. However, the critics in effect frame the entire question differently. Institutionalists view education as an historically-determined response to an institutionalized and socially-created demand; they tend to investigate the ways in which organized patterns of social behavior shape supply and demand in the labor market, and how they determine the demand for education and the uses to which it is put. Radicals view education as an apparatus for the replication of social relations of production and cultural patterns of hegemony, as well as a source for the contradictions that can produce progressive social change. They examine how these roles are manifested and developed, what determines the direction the educational system will take, and how the patterns of behavior and social status acquired in school fit with, or sometimes contradict, prevailing power relations in society.

Institutionalists and radicals concur in critiquing and debunking as "myth" the neoclassical notion that the market is a naturally occurring and naturally optimizing phenomenon. As institutionalist economist William Dugger recently phrased this general point:

> The market does not just happen. It is . . . a set of instituted social relations, a
> set of rules determining what things can be exchanged . . . how they can be
> exchanged, who can exchange them, [and] who will benefit from the
> exchange . . . . In short, the market is not a result of Adam Smith's natural system of liberty. It is a result of the exercise of power.

"In a market economy," Dugger continues, "the market becomes a powerful enabling myth: The market (not the owner) made management close the plant."[32]

It is clear to us that there is considerable conceptual vitality outside of the neoclassical camp. Yet, despite this vitality and the major deficiencies of the neoclassical model that we have highlighted, there has been relatively little use of alternative frameworks and even little debate. A number of social scientists have argued persuasively that cross-paradigmatic, even adversarial, analysis of policy questions offers the strongest basis for social decision-making.[33] In fact, however, this sort of debate rarely takes place—and is almost totally unknown in the field of economics—because the paradigms in question are not just competing theories, they are also social and political institutions. It is to this "political economy" of educational policy and planning, and to the causes and consequences of paradigm dominance, that we wish now to turn.

The Political Economy of Educational Policy-Making

If the dominant paradigm is as defective as we have portrayed it to be, and if valid alternatives do in fact exist, then why aren't these alternatives more in evidence—or, to put it in the vernacular, if you're so smart, why ain't you rich?

Elements of the answer that we would propose to this question have already appeared in the foregoing pages. As many have argued, a paradigm is not just a conceptual framework. It has a technical and sociopolitical reality as well—that is, it is at the same time a body of technique and a supporting structure of political roles and social entitlements. Such an interpretation gives a clearer meaning to the notion of paradigm "dominance" and a more critical sense of what some of the causes and consequences of that dominance may be. Most particularly, given the capitalist organization of much of the Western world, it is not surprising that the reigning version of economics is one so intricately linked to the support of capitalism.

As a consequence, proponents of the dominant paradigm virtually monopolize access to funds for research and to field contexts for the development and application of methodology. Robert Kuttner has identified the same problem in the field of economics as a whole:

> The economic orthodoxy is reinforced by ideology, by the sociology of the profession, by the politics of who gets published or promoted and whose research gets funded. In the economics profession the free marketplace of ideas is one more market that doesn't work like the model.[34]

In the arena of international educational planning, this phenomenon is clearly demonstrated by the large share of research funds regulated and dispensed by the World Bank and its affiliates. No evil intent or conspiracy to obstruct trade is required here; rather a conscious effort would be—and is—required to avoid such ideological monopoly of resources for research, planning, and policy analysis.

As one further consequence of this dominance, the neoclassical paradigm appears—at least in the eyes of its proponents—to have a virtual monopoly on applicable techniques and its competitors are seen to offer little but carping criticism. At the same time, the position of power that the neoclassical paradigm enjoys seems to incline it toward myopia and even anti-empiricism, in the sense of a lack of interest in "deviant observations" and refractory data. Neoclassical economists are notoriously disinclined to collect first-hand data or to admit the worth of anything qualitative or ethnographic, though their own basic framework is fundamentally microanalytic. Along with this myopia goes a general neglect of field work in favor of mathematical modeling. An analysis of over four hundred articles in the *American Economics Review* from March 1977 to December 1981 revealed only one piece of actual empirical research: a study of utility maximization in pigeons.[35]

In short, the relations of alternate paradigms in economics are far from perfectly competitive. Resources are distributed in such a way that there is a considerable degree of monopoly in the marketplace of research and ideas, considerable "monopsony" in the labor market for academic and policy positions; and the whole field is undergirded by relations of power that have much to do with the general political economy of our epoch. Given what we have learned from Kuhn, and, especially, Feyerabend, about the dynamics of intellectual history and the anatomy of "scientific revolutions," the dominance of a social paradigm, irrespective of its merits, should come as no surprise.[36] What can be done under such circumstances to reconceptualize the role of education in the economy? We now turn to this question in the last section of the paper.

CONCLUSIONS: RECONCEPTUALIZING THE ECONOMY-EDUCATION LINKAGE

How one conceives of relationships between education and the economy is critical to practice. What we have argued here is that, despite the existence of sensible alternatives, there has been a three decade long monopolization of debate and resources by one narrow, and, for the most part, bankrupt perspective. It is not that neoclassical economists have nothing to offer: their notion of tradeoffs and opportunity costs, and their emphasis on the need to consider the costs and benefits to all affected parties, are sensible and important. However, the baggage with which they surround such notions and collect them into one overall, integrated, and measurable idea of societal efficiency remains pure nonsense.

Clearly, this criticism has implications far beyond the education sector. Under capitalism, the "efficiency" of market solutions or of selected government actions has been an ideological bulwark and a criterion used to justify policy. If the notion is empty, current practice distorts social decision-making processes by incorrectly evaluating some alternatives and ignoring others. More broadly, we believe that this situation is part of an increasing self-delusion in our understanding of society and social policy. A technicist, rationalistic view has increasingly dominated policy debate in rich countries and poor, in capitalist countries and socialist, embodied in notions of scientific management in the early part of the nineteenth century and in cost-benefit analysis today. Yet the search for technical answers has been a rigged game: ideology chooses the dominant framework and a supposedly scientific methodology allows us to find almost any answer we choose, all done in such a way that few believe they are cheating.

In our view, there are no clear alternative perspectives that offer the same universal applicability as that (falsely) promised by neoclassical economists. Radical political economy, the most fully developed alternative, provides considerable insight in its analysis of correspondences and contradictions in the relations of education to the broader economy and within the educational system itself, but even in the eyes of its proponents, it furnishes little basis for agreement about educational practice and policy reform, especially in capitalist societies. To a neoclassical economist these radical and institutional approaches are vague and subjective. However, the only reason for the endless profusion of precise neoclassical recommendations is the erroneous belief that neoclassical economists have a technical, efficiency criterion enabling them to choose among alternatives in a manner that optimizes social outcomes. If there is in fact no overriding technical criterion to guide social choice, as implied by a conflict view of the world, then a belief in democratic values necessarily leads one to envisage a messy, participative, negotiation-oriented and collective process of defining, analyzing, and selecting among alternative policy options.

Clearly, therefore, we are confronted with a task of *re*-conceptualizing the role of education in the economy and their reciprocal relationship. At first blush, the task looks daunting and the outlook none too hopeful, given the entrenched nature of neoclassicism outlined in the foregoing section. As Amy has commented concerning the problem of supplanting or modifying the larger philosophical currents of which neoclassicism is a part, "Positivism survives because it limits, in a way that is politically convenient, the kinds of questions that analysis can investigate."[37] From where can genuine renewal be expected to come?

One thing to note is how helpful it can be to look at the question in *comparative and historical perspective*. Economic analysis of social practice is not approached the same way in France or Brazil, in the Soviet Union or India as it is in the anglophone West. Of particular interest are the political economic perspectives being developed in different portions of the world in opposition to the prescriptions of institutions like the World Bank and the International Monetary Fund. Neoclassical economists have paid scant attention to comparative economic thought. In fact, the more dogmatic positivists among them would maintain that there is only one true standard of scientific economics, and such comparisons are therefore by nature irrelevant. But as it becomes evident how highly dependent the operationalization of economic theory is upon the assumptions made—and thus, upon the ideology and general world view informing them—it likewise becomes more and more important to look at alternate specifications of the education-economy linkage. Greater emphasis on the comparative perspective, greater attention to the "naturally occurring" variation in this domain—that is, the divergent models developed and applied by economists from various societies in radically different material and social circumstances—can provide an essential source of new understanding.

Similarly, the historical point of view helps to restore some balance to the picture and to renew confidence that paradigmatic shifts are inevitable sooner or later. It is clear in an historical framework that the evolution of economic thought has been and will continue to be characterized by competing perspectives, and that neoclassicism represents an unstable compromise of a few of these tendencies at one particular period in time. The questions posed by institutionalists and radical economists have not gone away and may again move back toward the top of the social and intellectual agenda. Since neoclassicism is increasingly beleaguered within and without—and for a host of other reasons—the last decade of the millennium may be a time for some profound and widespread changes in economic perspectives. In any case, there are some reasons to be hopeful and to continue working on the nuts and bolts of alternative frameworks.

Elsewhere we have sketched out some initial ideas that we believe suggest directions for the task of reconceptualization.[38] They include the need to challenge neoclassical positions, particularly in their increasingly doctrinaire policy applications; to abandon completely the totem of "efficiency"; to forswear regression analysis and undertake alternate forms of economic research; and to focus research, policy, and planning on debate, not on some mythical technical search for "truth" and "optimality." It is also worthwhile taking a page from the institutionalists by continuing to work on practical educational issues at the local level (city, county, region), because no good concept of education will be developed in isolation from practice. As the environmentalists say (and the peace movement before them), "Think globally, act locally."

A central issue on the conceptual agenda concerns *reviving and rethinking the demand side in the education-labor market linkage,* and so getting beyond the supply-side fixation that has characterized human capital thought to date. We have accepted too long and too passively the notion that the mismatch between education and the labor market is an indictment of schooling to be remedied solely by educational reform or improved educational "efficiency". Certainly, part of the function of education is to make us better workers. But this idea has been embedded in a lot of quasi-religious nonsense about the sanctity of "the market" determining what employment should be, coupled with a belief that if we make education better, jobs will automatically become better.

This latter view is basically an incarnation of what economists call Say's Law, after the early nineteenth century French merchant and man of letters who first proposed the nostrum: supply creates its own demand. Economists have long since rejected Say's Law as an adequate description of market dynamics, and the market for labor is no exception. Yet most human capital thought betrays at its root this same oversimplification. Human capital proponents implicitly assume that the relationship between education and earnings is a causal one—a rate of return to education is based on little else—and that educated workers will automatically get jobs which match (and reveal) their potential productivity. In fact, while the supply of educated labor will surely influence the type of technologies that producers of goods and services use, and, therefore, the amount and nature of jobs created, the demand for labor depends on a host of other interrelated factors that are determined in far from perfectly competitive local, national, and global economies. To believe that by increasing the supply of educated and skilled workers, one automatically insures their employment and the productive utilization of their skills is purely wishful thinking. Worse, it is profoundly irresponsible thinking, since proponents of these views simply abandon to the market the onus of creating a world of plentiful, good jobs.

Such supply-side educational strategies are also fundamentally unworkable. How children survive and succeed through our school systems will depend largely on what they and their families see ahead for themselves, in work and in life. At present, in the United States as in many other countries, the bulk of students and their parents quite accurately perceive a lack of interesting, challenging, and remunerative employment opportunities. Nor, contrary to popular mythology, do jobs seem to be getting better, either in their nature or in their pay. Even in wealthy industrialized nations like the United States, the deskilling and automation of work seems to be increasing.[39] Under such circumstances, there are no strong incentives to study, to learn, or to think, and all the well-intentioned reforms to teach better basic or higher order skills will, at best, have very limited success.

Our point is that we have to work on *both* the supply and demand sides of the educational equation. Leaving the creation of jobs to the competitive marketplace, as much of neoclassical economic ideology argues, is not a solution, but the source of the problem. It has been the nonsensical idea of efficiency that has left the nature of work outside the public policy arena, as a derivative question for the market to determine based on available production technologies and our relative preferences for toothpaste, shoes, health care, and so forth. There is no reason to continue such neglect of one of the most basic features of our social environment.

It is not enough to seek educational policies that can yield better educated people. For such policies to work, we *must* also be thoughtful about social and economic policies that can yield better quality work opportunities.[40] We can no more leave the latter task to economists than we can leave the formation of sensible nuclear power policies to engineers and physicists. Those concerned with making educational policy must also concern themselves with policies that ensure that better education is utilized and rewarded.

Our argument implies a need to reverse the tables on the sort of mindset implicit in the title of this paper itself and of many similar reflections on the economics of education: "Conceptualizing the Role of Education in the Economy." Attention needs to be given as well to the *role of the economy in education*—that is, to the learning consequences of different patterns of social and economic organization, at the micro- as well as at the macro-level. Practicing educators have long been aware that how much and how well people learn, how much they change and grow, is highly dependent on the possibilities for application of new skills in their environment and the potential for mastering new functions and resources with the knowledge acquired. There lies at this juncture a whole field for critical research and experimentation in what might be termed—with tongue only half in cheek—"macro-instructional design," where education (both learning on the job and in school) is the dependent variable and patterns of social and economic organization constitute the independent ones.[41] What are the implications of alternate choices about social organization for the way in which people learn and grow and the way in which schools function?

In the long run, of course, it is no more adequate to say that demand creates its own supply than it is to maintain the reverse. Demand for educated manpower and labor supply arise and interact in complex and institutionally-mediated ways which can only be understood in cross-disciplinary perspective. Social, cultural, and political factors play a critical role in shaping these forces and their interaction in the labor market. The task of reconceptualizing the relationship of education and the economy is thus necessarily an interdisciplinary one.

It is therefore also a task that can only be accomplished if a host of people who have not been considered economists—or have not considered themselves that way—enter into the fray and help put the economics of education on new tracks. This means learning some unaccustomed language and opening debates to some unaccustomed participants. But the game is certainly worth the candle, as the French say. The economics of education is too important to be left to the economists.

MARTIN CARNOY

Chapter 9

Education and the State:
From Adam Smith to Perestroika

Almost all analyses of educational problems have implicit in them a theory of the state, but few tell us what this theory is. In a wide range of economic and sociological studies of education, even where the state's linkages to politics are crucial to the analysis, researchers rarely justify their underlying view of the state's role in the economy, social relations, and relations in the classroom. The varied assumptions about the state that pervade analyses of many of the hotter topics in education today—such as inequality of educational access, differential student achievement, private and public school effectiveness, teacher education, curriculum theory, and administrative decentralization—remain hidden in the background of the education debate.

This ambiguity is anything but helpful in resolving educational problems and needs to be elucidated. Understanding the state's role is part and parcel of conceptualizing schools; assuming it away as an issue creates serious difficulties in interpreting educational policy analysis. Do the conclusions result mainly from unstated political preferences (e.g., "the best government is the least government"; "the market is inherently inequitable")? Or do the results depend on the more usual implicit assumptions about how the state relates to society (e.g., "the state is independent from the economic and social structure"; "the capitalist state is a class state")?

An illustration of the first question is found in comparisons of private and public education that consistently underestimate the costs of private schooling.[1] An illustration of the second question is policy analyses of educational interventions. Most of these analyses implicitly assume that the public schools (and the state) are trying to increase all pupils' achievement but fail to do so because they are hopelessly inefficient and overly bureaucratic. The state is neutral, separate from market and other power relations outside the state, and impervious to efficiency-maximizing market forces. Effective interventions are not undertaken mainly because of these inefficiencies. Yet, an alternative theory of the state would provide a completely different interpretation. If the state—bureaucratic as it may be—systematically favors some groups over others, "effective" interventions may be ignored not because schools are inefficient but because they are *efficiently* (even if unconsciously) carrying out a particular gender, class, and race ideology as expressed through school structures and educational processes.

In this essay, I attempt to clarify these issues by (1) discussing various state theories that implicitly underlie various educational analyses, and (2) arguing (through example rather than proof) that conceptions of the state shape how we understand and interpret the educational system and its problems. Let us now turn to these various theories.

EDUCATION AND THE "PERIPHERAL" STATE

The theory of the Liberal state that emerged as a revolutionary ideology in seventeenth-century Europe stressed individual over divine rights and in that sense legitimized new bases of power, new relationships among human beings, and the human soul itself. Today it dominates neoclassical economics as applied to education and training (human capital) and conservative policy approaches to educational issues. Much of that theory was shaped by the writings of Hobbes, Locke, and Rousseau.[2] But Adam Smith, more than anyone, defined present-day Liberal thinking about the state and subordinated it to economics.[3] Smith, in Albert Hirschman's words, "established [ed] a powerful *economic* justification for the untrammeled pursuit of individual self-interest, whereas in the earlier literature . . . the stress was on the *political* effects of this pursuit."[4]

The role of the state in this conception is at best peripheral to society's principal dynamic—the "invisible hand" of the free market—a dynamic that not only should not be interfered with, but would require rather extreme human "folly" to set back significantly from its "perfection" in providing for collective material gain and therefore social betterment. "In this view . . . politics is the 'folly of men' while economic progress, like Candide's garden, can be cultivated with success provided such folly does not exceed some fairly ample and flexible limits."[5]

The proper role of the state, then, is to provide a legal framework in which the market can best maximize "benefits to mankind." At the moment in history when Smith, Rousseau, and before them Hobbes and Locke, were writing, the principal objective in this regard was for the state to use the legal process to create a market economy out of the landlord-dominated semi-feudal and mercantilist status quo. The state he railed against was the "interventionist," mercantilist state; what he called for was a body of laws and state action that would allow the free market more freedom. Of course, this involved a paradox: the state had to interfere in order to clear out the existing mercantilist framework. This interference not only meant new laws and their enforcement, but the educational function of creating a new morality.[6]

Today's Liberal theory preserves this underlying philosophy of the individual as the central force that drives both the economy and the state. The linkages between the economy and the state and the family and the state are weak, the weaker the better according to Liberal theory. The free market economy—a finely tuned, self-correcting, unbeatable, all-knowing money machine—is, in turn, the central arena shaping society's dynamic. Association with this dynamic is voluntary—made through free individual choice. Similarly, individuals voluntarily give up certain rights to the state, but control the shape and action of the state through collective political action with those who share their views.

Education in the Peripheral State. If the market is perfect, why is schooling not provided and taken as a privately produced and traded good? Many Liberals do indeed argue that were the schools themselves operated as private institutions, they would be much more efficient and respond better to public needs. But they also agree that education has a peculiar feature that causes less than optimal amounts of private capital to move into that form of investment. Because of antislavery laws, humans cannot put themselves up for collateral to secure educational loans. If public monies were not available for schooling, far less education would be taken by individuals than socially desirable. Thus, the only Liberal rationale for public education, at least for public educational financing, lies in a slight market anomaly. Yet, even in this context, state intervention is seen in terms of its relation to market forces.

One of the most important social analyses of education—human capital theory—is couched in these terms. Human capital theory is a powerful economic tool, and certainly goes far in explaining many aspects of individual behavior in a labor market where education is an important allocator of jobs and income. But it also assumes a Liberal theory of the state—hence views the state as limited to providing education in response (or failing to respond) to price changes for educated labor. In such a model, individual investors and their families, responding to market forces influencing the wages of more or less highly schooled labor, are the driving force behind the demand for education. The "good" state does no more than provide the education called for by such market forces, so state educational performance is assessed solely in terms of its meeting changing market conditions.

The Liberal theory of the state underlies many other traditional positions on educational issues. For example, should the state move to eliminate persisting income differences between United States blacks and whites through compensatory education and affirmative action? In Liberal theory, such interference in the market is not only inadvisable, it is doomed to failure. Charles Murray,[7] for example, argues that government welfare programs made blacks worse off by creating an addictive dependency on public handouts. Smith and Welch[8] contend that blacks did take increasing amounts of education anyway between 1940 and 1980 (with or without compensatory education programs), and that it was this response to market forces, not affirmative action, that successfully increased their incomes relative to whites. The message in both cases is that the market will result in the most efficient and fairest solution to social problems, and that education can contribute to that solution *but only in the market context.* It is a message that can only emanate from a theory where the markets are inherently equitable (although not equal) and (ultimately) make things best, and where the state, even with good intentions, will only make things worse.

It is also a message based on a view of state power as relatively independent of market economic power. State decisions are shaped by individuals as political actors, whereas the market functions on the basis of individuals behaving as economic actors. Adam Smith and his contemporaries were well aware of the inherent schizophrenia in such a model, but Smith for one resolved it by placing responsibility for market morality in the individual rather than the state.[9] He and Locke also assumed a classless society that conveniently avoided any inherent inequalities in economic interests and capabilities. But Rousseau was less sanguine about these "solutions" to potential market inequalities and their implications for social conflict. He saw the state as necessary to police the unscrupulous use of unequal economic power, and although Rousseau fell out of favor in the laissez-faire world of the mid-nineteenth century, it was he who, in some distant sense, inspired Karl Marx and others to develop a new interpretation of capitalism that formed the most important historical alternative to Liberal thinking.

THE INSTRUMENTAL STATE

Marxist conceptions of the state can be derived from a number of sources,[10] with a variety of possible interpretations. This feature of Marxist thought has led to a considerable debate, ranging from the more orthodox Leninist view to those who view Marx's "autonomous state" of the *Eighteenth Brumaire* (of Louis Napoleon) as the basis for analyzing the actual situation.[11] Despite these differences, however, all Marxist writers, in one form or another, do derive their state theories from some Marxist fundamentals:

1. Marx viewed the material conditions of a society as the basis of its social structure and human consciousness. The form of the state, therefore, emerges from the relations of production, not from the general development of the human mind or from the collective of people's wills.
2. Marx argued that the state does not represent the common good, but is the political expression of the class structure inherent in production. Once Marx came to his formulation of capitalist society as a class society, dominated by the bourgeoisie, it necessarily followed that the state is the political expression of that dominance. Indeed, the state is an essential means of class domination in capitalist society. It is not above class struggles, but deeply engaged in them. Given its insertion in the capitalist mode of production, it cannot be anything else.
3. By the late 1840s, under Engels' influence, Marx came to the conclusion that the state in bourgeois society is the repressive arm of the bourgeoisie. The rise of the state as a repressive force to keep class antagonisms in check not only describes the class nature of the state, but also its repressive function that in capitalism serves the dominant class, the bourgeoisie.

Although the degree to which the state in capitalist society is an agent of the dominant bourgeoisie is not altogether clear in Marx's work, it was this repressive, "instrumentalist" version that became the foundation of revolutionary Communism and hence most closely identified with Marxist-Leninism. Thus, the famous line in the *Communist Manifesto* "[T]he bourgeoisie has at last, since the establishment of Modern Industry and of the world market, conquered for itself, in the modern representative State, exclusive political sway. The executive of the modern State is but a committee for managing the common affairs of the whole bourgeoisie."[12]

The Instrumental State and Education. There is not much to say about formal education in this view of the state. Marx (and Smith), living in an age when formal public education was minimally important in economic life, gave us little analysis of schooling's role. The principal function of the state was coercion, not persuasion. Capitalist ideology was important for Marx, but it was spread and enforced in the workplace through unequal power relations and in social life through the dominance of bourgeois life styles and values. Even after the Bolshevik Revolution, Lenin saw public revolutionary education as little different from the classic capitalist education that preceded it except that it would now be distributed widely to the working class. Access—not curriculum—was the main issue for Lenin.[13]

The most important influence of this line of Marxist thought on educational analysis resides in the idea that the state providing the education is not neutral, but a class state. In contemporary works on education, such as Bowles and Gintis' *Schooling in Capitalist America*[14] or my own *Education as Cultural Imperialism*[15] this was the dominant theme. As a class state, it is at least as interested in using its institutions for reproducing the class structure as it is for their ostensible purpose of helping children reach the maximum of their learning potential. It invests public funds in schooling in a way that caters to the needs of the dominant capitalist/business—in this model, the dominant class, not citizens acting as equally powerful individuals, shape state policy on education.

But it was the work of another revolutionary, Antonio Gramsci, working in the industrial country context of post-World War I Italy, who was more impressed by the ideological function of the bourgeois state, that provided much more of a link between its "educational" functions and bourgeois dominance over the working classes.[16] Gramsci, like Marx and Lenin, believed that the capitalist state was an instrument of the dominant capitalist class. But he also argued that the bourgeoisie, in part consolidating its power through the state, reproduced the unequal social relations of production by developing its ideological "hegemony," or dominance over the way people in a society think about their relations to others and to the state. The bourgeois state was not just coercive, it was persuasive, and it persuaded by inculcating all citizens with bourgeois values and a profound belief in the efficiency and effectiveness of bourgeois institutions.

According to Gramsci, the only way to overthrow this hegemony is to develop a "counterhegemony"—an alternative set of values and a belief in the ability of the working class to develop its own set of institutions and to rule effectively. He argued that the mechanism for developing "counterhegemony" is a revolutionary political party in which everyone can become "intellectuals" through understanding the class nature of bourgeois society.

But this formulation still makes public education marginal to the revolutionary project. Gramsci considered state education an expression of bourgeois hegemony. What contemporary writers have done, however, is to take Gramsci's concepts of hegemony and counterhegemony and—now that schooling is a much more important institution than it was in the 1920s—applied it to public education's functions themselves. This interpretation/application of Gramsci's work goes far beyond what Gramsci understood as the role of schooling or even the development of counterhegemony. He never argued that state institutions (other than political parties) would be likely arenas of ideological contestation. Yet, these new writings are a fair extension of Gramsci's revolutionary intentions of "laying siege" to the bourgeois hegemonic state with counterhegemony rather than confronting the state with armed force.

Michael Apple, Henry Giroux, Jean Anyon, and Geoff Whitty,[17] to name just a few, show how the public schools' "hidden curriculum," or the unofficial message delivered in classrooms (intentionally or unintentionally) by teachers and administrators, is part and parcel of dominant class hegemony—a hegemony that is organized to reproduce inequality much more than it is to develop learning.

These writers argue, moreover, that the public school is a potential site of struggle over values and norms—a site where, through discourse, counter-hegemony is developed and therefore learning rather than reproduction can take place. In this sense, they make the schools sites of political action where, as in Gramsci's revolutionary political party, consciousness of social relations produces working class intellectuals.[18]

THE "AUTONOMOUS" STATE

The discussion in recent years among those who hold this view of the state has dealt mainly with the extent to which the state's institutions are autonomous from the business class and what greater autonomy implies for using the state itself as an arena from which to contest and redefine their shape. The debate among Marxists has focused on the absence of a clear conception of the democratic state in either Marx or Lenin. Some Marxists and many non-Marxists, drawing on Weber's institutional theories of bureaucracy, have developed theories of state autonomy that focus on the bureaucracy as an independent actor with its own dynamic, limitations, and powers of negotiation with civil society.

The Contested State. The most extensive analysis of the state within the framework of the Marxist debate was developed by Nicos Poulantzas in the late 1960s and in the 1970s. Poulantzas makes his central focus social classes and politics rather than Marxist theory as a whole. Yet, if we accept the Gramscian proposition that superstructure has a prominent place in understanding social structure and change, Poulantzas' studies of the state encompass most of the crucial elements in a theory of society—he argues ultimately that the state not only shapes and defines class conflict but is itself shaped by that conflict.

Thus, there is a different relation between social classes and the state, depending on the *stage* of capitalist development. Changes in the capitalist relations of production shaped political institutions: the "structure" of the capitalist state is not a structure at all, but rather apparatuses shaped by class struggle and by corresponding changes in capitalist production. In his last book,[19] the relative autonomy of the state is made dialectic: there is the possibility of class struggle within the state apparatuses because of the very contradictions inherent in "autonomy." The state becomes much more than the site of unifying capitalist-class fractions and the individualization and isolation of the working class. It is a site of class conflict where political power is contested; the state is shaped by struggles in production and *within* the state.

Education in the Contested State. If the state is an arena of conflict, if contradictions are part and parcel of reproduction, and if public education is essential to reproduction, then education itself has inherent in it the same contradictions that emerge from the larger political process. Henry Levin and I have developed an analysis of American education based on a model where schooling in democratic capitalist societies is characterized by two contradictory goals reflecting the broader goals of democratic states: one is to reproduce the forces and relations of production; the second is to inculcate youth with democratic norms— a belief in equality, social mobility, participative citizenship, citizen rights, responsive government, and so forth. These goals are inherently contradictory because capitalist production is neither equal nor participative and the capitalist state, rooted in these unequal relations of production has difficulty delivering on the democratic ideals it teaches in school and in other public institutions. Yet, the citizenry's willingness to accept these institutions is largely based on the very promises the state cannot deliver.[20]

Levin and I argue that much of the way the educational system works can be explained by its inherent contradictions. For one, the state is an active participant in shaping educational policy, for it is only in this way that it can control the mix between reproductive and democratic goals. But because the state cannot limit itself to educate for reproduction, it often appears that it is responding to consumer demand for more education. We argue that the degree to which the state does respond to business' reproductive mandate versus consumers' democratic mandate depends on the force of social movements in influencing state behavior. In periods of intense social activity, social spending and educational access increase sharply. In periods of social passivity, the class state reemerges to bring education back into line with the business class' perceived reproductive goals.

The necessary presence of state activism in education that goes far beyond providing the level of resources to meet optimum social investment in human capital provides a clear contrast between this and the Liberal model of education. Those who call for the privatization of educational delivery must assume that the state's educational function could be limited to financing. In the contested state model, state involvement (including the judicial system) in the management of the educational process is a crucial activity both for the dominant groups (to try to control reproduction) and the citizenry at large (to try to gain increased access and improved performance). It is the state that necessarily arbitrates this contested process. Even though business and parents attack the educational bureaucracy, without the state apparatus in education, neither the dominant not subordinate groups in society can achieve their goals. The spread of private education, in a contested state model, would require costly state monitoring agencies that would begin to look like the state itself.

The difference between the peripheral and contested state theory's view of the state role in the educational process also pervades models of educational production. Assuming that the state is peripheral leads to a modeling of educational delivery as a private firm maximizing educational achievement. The contested or institutional (see below) theories lead to a model where educational delivery is necessarily public and therefore has features very different from private firms, including teachers with professional independence and school administrations that organize schooling around political more than achievement objectives.[21]

The Carnoy-Levin model is different from the modern Gramscian interpretation, where the school is a potential "site of struggle" between hegemonic and counterhegemonic activities. That view regards the school as a public firm characterized by a special set of social relations and in which the principal output is hegemonic ideology. The state represents business class interests in the schools, attempting to reproduce the social relations of production by imposing that class's values, norms and views of how social output is and should be distributed. In the contested state theory, business class intentions are contested in the arena of the state as a whole, and the contested state brings to the schools the product of mass-base social movements' previous victories. These include the possibility of using the educational system for social mobility and the relative autonomy of school bureaucracies and teachers' unions. Many of the important struggles about schooling, such as increased access and teacher treatment of colored minority children, are fought outside the school in broader conflicts about civil rights, the role of minorities in the labor market and the larger society, and the distribution of educational funding. Most of the gains in black children's test scores in the last fifteen years, for example, have occurred in the South, probably because of drastic improvement in black teachers' pay and education and increased funding for predominantly black schools.[22] These improvements were the result of social struggles that extended far beyond the schools themselves.

The Institutional State. The state autonomy debate has other roots, namely in Max Weber's writings on bureaucracy. Weber and many contemporary sociologists and political scientists reject the Marxist axiom of the class state. Rather, they assume that the state is autonomous because the public bureaucracy takes on a life of its own—the state attempts to shape policy as much in its own conception of social and economic progress as in the name of one or another interest group. There are many versions of this "institutional" state in the contemporary literature. Foucault[23] sees it as organizing society in some form of bureaucratic "order" that overshadows classical economic markets and shapes the private economic institutions that operate within them (the corporation, for example). Evans, Rueschemeyer and Skocpol[24] argue that the really interesting problems regarding the state reside in understanding how the state bureaucracy develops and implements policies that then influence behavior in civil society.

The common theme of these different interpretations is that the state is a highly autonomous actor in shaping social and economic behavior and that this autonomy is not rooted in the social relations of production. In that sense, the state bureaucracy has real power of its own—to the extent that it has the resources and the decision-making legitimacy, it can develop society in *its image*, not the image of an economic class. Elites may emerge in such a model, but these are just as likely to be power elites with their base in the state as economic elites with their base in capital. In different historical periods, the state bureaucracy may ally itself with capital or with labor or with the popular classes to achieve its social goals. This does not mean that the state can formulate policy independently of those actors; it still must answer to them for its legitimacy. But it does mean that the legitimate state is an innovator and source of change.

The Evans-Rueschemeyer-Skocpol research argues that the modern capitalist state is not only autonomous from the dominant business class, but develops its own policy agenda based on the internal dynamics of the state bureaucracy: "Unless such independent goal formulation occurs, there is little need to talk about states as important actors. Pursuing matters further, one may explore the 'capacities' of states to implement official goals, especially over the actual or potential opposition of powerful social groups or in the face of recalcitrant socioeconomic circumstances."[25] The view rejects state bureaucracies as necessarily serving or not serving the reproduction of a particular configuration (structure) of social relations. "Strategic elites" in the state can seize and revamp state power, can take action independent of dominant social classes (even destroying them), and reshape the configuration of class "from above", using the state's repressive ideological apparatuses.

This is a state that Liberals agree exists but should not. They can agree that it exists because it is not a state shaped by class relations in production. A *limited* state autonomous from the economy is consistent with Liberal theory: the extension of the state against the common good is also a possibility, even though it is precisely what is not needed. It interferes with free market resource allocation, and separates political action from individual sovereignty.

But how, then, can the bureaucracy gain legitimacy for its interferences if they are inherently against the public interest? To begin with, state interventions may not be against the public interest. According to Foucault, the modern state is a historical phenomenon that has its roots in a need for order in a world passing from feudal traditions to the uncertainties and seeming chaos of markets and rapid change. The state was the one institution that could organize the new society in an orderly way. Skocpol and others have focused on individuals' desire for state intervention in order to shield them from excesses and fluctuations in the market economy and provide financial security.[26] During the Great Depression, the state became the planner in industrial economies the world over, and it was broadly supported in these interventions. The issue in this theory is not *whether* the state should intervene, but only the *degree* of state intervention and the role of the bureaucracy in various aspects of social and economic life.

The contested and institutional state theories differ in one other important way from both the Liberal and Marxist instrumentalist theories: they shift the focus of social analysis from the economic to the political. In the contested state, this shift is only in the "last instance"[27] since the economic class structure is still the ultimate source of contradictions in the political arena. Even so, politics becomes crucial to the dynamics of change.

Education and the Institutional State. With the state much more central to the shape of the social dynamic, the institution of public education is likely to be the product of bureaucratically originated policies catering to bureaucratic conceptions of the public good. Such policies are not necessarily based in any class' interests or even in contested class interests, although the bureaucracy has to consider conflicts outside the state and education when making policy decisions. But as it is more likely to be aware of and respond to conflicts within the bureaucracy (organizational conflicts), educational models based on this theory stress organizational objectives and responses to them.[28] The expansion of schooling, its institutional forms, and the similarity of those forms worldwide has also been analyzed from the standpoint of the spread of the modern state and its bureaucratic dynamic.[29]

State autonomy and bureaucratically-driven educational policy does not, however, mean the absence of class-structured education. In their classic study of French education, Bourdieu and Passeron adopted the Foucault version of the institutionalist state and argued that the state *develops* the social class structure through the widely accepted "meritocracy" of the educational system. Children of the elite, whether it be a state-based bureaucratic elite or a bourgeoisie, come to schools with "cultural capital," a home background with rich (and proper) language usage and socially "correct" behavior patterns, that positions them to do better than others in terms of schools' meritocratic norms. These norms are themselves the basis for elite status, so confer on elite children such status in their own generation.[30] Why do nonelites accept a meritocracy that is biased against them? Bourdieu and Passeron argue that the larger legitimacy of the democratic state gained in matters other than education, especially in representing national interests against other states, plays an important role. Since this otherwise legitimate state confers on teachers (the school's bureaucracy) the "expertise" to decide who is meritorious or not, parents and children tend to accept school decisions about elite status.

The Bourdieu-Passeron model is less applicable in the United States only because schools as institutions and teachers as experts have been increasingly delegitimized as part of the Liberal assault on the state. This has shifted debate from the class nature of American schools to their ability to correct racial and class inequalities—all in terms of the capacity of state power to affect any social change. The belief in the state as social engineer reached its height in the Kennedy-Johnson administrations of the early 1960s. With programs such as Head Start attempting to correct for early disadvantage on the one hand and the affirmative action recruitment of minorities into universities to overcome past discrimination on the other, it was hoped that increased education would help bring minorities into the mainstream of America's middle class.

It is that belief and its alleged failure to effect change in the 1970s that draws Liberals in the Reagan-Bush era to expound on the limitations of state policies to alter the "natural course" of market forces. Whatever the economic arguments used to justify or criticize affirmative action and compensatory education, the real argument is about the state. And, interestingly, there is little disagreement between Liberal thinkers and the institutionalists on what the capitalist state *is*. Both analyses assume that the state is interventionist and that politics matters a great deal. Yet, what the state *should be* is another matter. Should it be an innovator and allocator, possessing a wisdom and a broader vision unattainable by narrower-interest private enterprise and organized labor? Or should it be peripheral to the market, limiting itself to those infrastructural responsibilities that the market will not, for various reasons, assume?

The educational policy discussion has always been set in this larger philosophical framework. The major attack has been on affirmative action as an inefficient policy costing billions in lost productivity.[31] But public schooling itself has long been a target of Liberal critics,[32] and more recently as part of concerns about U.S. education in a more competitive world economy, studies showing higher student achievement in private schools have resurrected calls for vouchers and greater choice.[33]

THE STATE IN TRANSITION

Capitalist societies are marked by a major paradox: the source of their dynamic is in the economy, but social change takes place in the arena of the state. It is through democratic political processes that capitalism is shaped and transformed. This is why Liberal philosophy—once revolutionary in providing the intellectual justification for transforming the absolutist state—is now inherently so conservative. By restricting the state's legitimacy as an arbiter of the common good, Liberals limit the very arena where present social relations can be recast. No matter how conservative the democratic capitalist state is at any moment in history, political power relations are contestable and changeable. This is the nature of democratic politics. But social relations in a market protected by the prerogatives of private property ownership are inherently undemocratic and inherently less changeable. Changes do take place in the economic sphere, and some of these changes are substantial—witness the technological and organizational innovations in the twentieth century. But power relations have only changed in the economy when the state intervened, and some of these changes have been substantial as well—Sweden and Austria are good examples of capitalist societies that have reshaped capital-labor relations through state action.

The reshaping of such relations was felt especially rapidly in the educational system, where expansion took place at all levels (particularly in Sweden) as the state bureaucracy focused on providing the working class with new opportunities for social mobility. Even in today's Europe, where some countries with conservative governments, such as Britain and West Germany, have constrained the expansion and democratization of higher education, Sweden and other Socialist governments, such as Spain, France, Denmark, Norway, and Finland have promoted freer access to university and graduate education.[34] The Scandinavian countries and France are also at the forefront of investing in high-quality child care (early education).

This paradox of change coming through the capitalist state means that transitions from traditional capitalism to other social organizations occur when the state, not the economy, is transformed. Social transition can be defined, in effect, as the shift of social dynamic from the economy to the state. Marx, Lenin, and Gramsci all understood this at some level, yet paid little attention to its main implication: rather than the state "withering away" in Lenin's famous phrase,[35] all three writers thought it would become the primary institution of the new society. The structures of decision-making in the political arena would determine the shape of the new society, in the same fashion as capitalist organizations of production determined the shape of capitalist society. Just as generals preparing for war always fight the previous war, twentieth-century Marxists prepared their revolutionary utopia on the basis of the system they were overthrowing. They ignored the obvious: once the revolution greatly diminishes the political power of the capitalist and large landholding classes, the economy is a sphere of activity subordinated to politics. They also came to ignore the corollary of that axiom: An undemocratic state would necessarily define production and all other spheres of life in inherently undemocratic ways.

The dominance of the state in the transition to what are known as socialist societies is therefore the logical outgrowth of the nature of the transition itself. But is the hyper-bureaucratization of socialist society also a necessary outcome of this shift of dynamic to the state, as Liberals claim? This is a more difficult question to answer.[36] Some argue that in practice there is no example of democratic socialism; therefore, democracy is a form that must be associated with capitalism. But others point to Sweden as a possible version of "market socialism" where the economy is a highly regulated capitalism and the state is politically dominated by organized labor and is highly democratic. Indeed, capitalism in Sweden has been reshaped by decades of state intervention.[37]

Besides its democratic state, or perhaps because of it, the Swedish economy, regulated as it is, has been able to generate a standard of living for the average Swede that is one of the highest in the world and to continue to compete favorably in the world market in increasingly sophisticated manufactured goods and services. This contrasts with the typical Eastern European socialist state or the Soviet Union, which—burdened by huge military spending and unable to diffuse technology to commercial, consumer-oriented, flexible production—ran out of economic steam in the late 1960s. Once the economic capability of these authoritarian states became questionable, their own rationale for that form of the state disappeared. The will to produce for the collective goals of the state also withered away.

Education and the Transition State. Despite its generally authoritarian form, the state "in transition to socialism" has everywhere invested heavily in education, health care, and other forms of human capital. Samoff and I conclude that this is partly because of highly unequal access to such investment in the "conditioned" capitalist societies that preceded the transition and partly because of the Marxist emphasis on labor rather than capital as the source of economic value. Education and other human services represent one important way that state bureaucracies can deliver popular public goods to the population at large—goods that are immediately accessible to every family and that put the government very much in the public eye. In these "socialist" societies, the traditional reluctance of propertied classes to spend on public services is, of course, nonexistent, so spending on education and health also has much lower negative political impact. The main political cost is in terms of short- and long-run economic growth. But this cost, too, appears lower because of the belief in labor as the primary source of economic value. All these factors shift resources more to human resources (mainly from consumption goods production) than in capitalist societies.

However, when the state is authoritarian and bureaucratic, schools and other human service institutions are organized in that undemocratic image. Little, if any, discourse takes place in classrooms, and discipline and order are just as much, if not more, stressed than in capitalist schools. There is greater emphasis on "socialist values": the organic relationship between mental and manual labor, group work, and achieving for collective goals rather than individual aggrandizement. But the collective goals are rarely themselves discussed or set by the participant students. There is also more emphasis on schooling for particular occupations. This is in the European tradition, but it is carried to an extreme in a planned economy because of a fundamental faith in being able to match specific knowledge to specific tasks. Unfortunately, any change in technology and the specific knowledge—even high-end engineering and science—learned in Soviet and Eastern European universities becomes obsolete.

The Redemocratized State. It is not surprising that political activity, when it occurs in authoritarian states, springs up mostly outside state institutions—in clandestine worker organizations and in the church—and in the one state institution that seems universally unshieldable from counterhegemonic political activity—the university. And it is not surprising that such activity is specifically antistate bureaucracy and pro-democracy.

But defining the economic structures that should emerge from this democracy is somewhat more problematic. Consider the situation: The state in Eastern Europe has been the source of the social dynamic and all energy has focused on the state for at least two generations. The state has been authoritarian but it has also been a mass state, where power is at least legally vested in the population as a whole and where the working class has been the "ruling class." And the working class and peasants believe they have real political power, a belief brought to reality by the overthrow of the Communist bureaucracy that had held the state hostage against them and by the absence of any authentic bourgeoisie to contest that power. In addition, the fruits of capitalism have become known to these workers and peasants and so have its drawbacks— much more unequal wealth and income distribution, unemployment, economic insecurity, individual competition, and so forth. And finally, the mass of people in Eastern Europe are relatively well schooled, literate, and all allowed to vote and hold political office.

How different this is from the original capitalist revolutions in the eighteenth and nineteenth centuries. Will the overthrown socialist states become capitalist states under these conditions? Will the high level of social services, including massive spending on education, social security, and guaranteed employment, be subordinated to the interests of a new capitalist class emerging largely from the former Communist director-bureaucrats of state enterprises?

Przeworski and Wallerstein[38] have written of the worker-capitalist compromise in social democracy, and it is this compromise that is at stake in Central and Eastern Europe. One important variable for workers in giving up political and economic power to a new bourgeoisie is how real and imminent the fruits of capitalism are. Greater economic insecurity and social inequality is more acceptable if the economic payoff to market structures is early and large. The promise of Deutschemarks and Western goods flooding into East Germany was the key factor in elections that brought on economic union with the West. But the East German economy collapsed in the backwash of the unification decision. In Hungary, Czechoslovakia, and Poland, the potential gains of free market capitalism are as desired, far more distant, and the measures perhaps somewhat less dramatic both in implementation and impact.

Yet, even should these countries (and the Soviet Union) transform their economies into a market system, as they will, the state and the economy will continue to be arenas of sharp political conflict. The state will also be even more interventionist than in Western Europe because of its historical role and because of popular movements' strength in defining it.

Education and Redemocratization. Education is crucial in this transformation. Since Communist regimes invested heavily in schools and universities, the issue is not the number of places in schools, but what is learned there, especially in physical and social sciences and engineering. The past focus on specific skills for specific jobs does not produce the kind of science and engineering needed for developing and applying rapidly changing technologies in the information age, and will have to be changed. There will also have to be a restructuring of the research and development system, with more research and development moving into firms and greater interaction between firms, universities, and research institutes. To make such reforms requires a highly interventionist state, and their success would strengthen the legitimacy of the interventionist role.

But the reforms are only one part of education's fundamental role in a changing Eastern Europe and in defining the state's role as part of those changes. It is likely that the educational system will also serve as a special arena of conflict. At one level, it will be highly politicized as students continue to question both the Communist past and the contested future. At another, different visions of Eastern Europe's future will be contested in curriculum and faculty hiring reforms. The conflict could be the source of new knowledge and ideas—as it has until now—or it could hamper their production and dissemination. But it is clear that the state has a vested interest in taking an active role in shaping the universities and cannot help being shaped by them.

SOME CONCLUDING REMARKS

Education is an integral element of the state's relation to civil society, so how the state relates to civil society is fundamental to interpreting educational structures and processes. The most important differences in such interpretations arise from two opposed state theories, one which argues that the state is independent of civil society and "interferes" in the workings of social welfare-maximizing free market, and the second which assumes that the state's behavior *reflects* and *reinforces* power relations that *derive* from those free market economic relations. Another set of differences in interpreting the educational system comes from differences in valuing independent state interference in free market activities. A theory that defines the state as almost always increasing inefficiency in an otherwise efficient system narrowly constrains the possibilities for excellence in public sector activities, including schools. Institutionalist views of the autonomous state, however, are more sanguine about the need for the state to use education, among other public instruments, to correct significant inequalities that result from an unfettered free market. For the institutionalists, the state is (potentially) the good cop. It represents democratically expressed interests to equalize opportunities and outcomes. Efficiency, for the institutionalists, is a broader concept than in the free market definition, and is partly the domain of public intervention.

Depending on the underlying theory of the state, then, education can perform well (a) only when it smoothes the operations of the market (the peripheral state); (b) only when the state is no longer an expression of unequal class, race, and gender relations inherent in the market (the class state); or (c) only when it is both smoothing market relations and correcting its worse excesses (the institutionalist state).

And, conversely, when political/economic systems change as in Eastern Europe, the role education plays depends on the role that the state takes in the new social relations under formation. Again, there are many possibilities for education, but understanding the state is the only way to sort them out.

Part Four

Contemporary Reform Movements and Emergent Issues

NOEL F. McGINN

Chapter 10

Reforming Educational Governance: Centralization/Decentralization

Decentralization of the governance or control of education is today often recommended as a solution for low levels of participation by communities, teachers, and parents in decision making. Increased local participation, it is argued, will help resolve problems of insufficient finance and management inefficiency.[1] What are we to make of these proposals? Do they reflect a genuine shift in power toward those who believe in popular democracy? Would decentralization improve education in an equitable fashion?

This chapter argues that there is no simple correspondence between degree of popular participation in State power and the form of governance or control of that State's education system, for at least three reasons. First, State power generally is held by coalitions of groups; these have different views on which form of governance will best serve their interests or goals. Control of education is one of the factors that these groups will exchange in bargaining for positions within the State. Second, education is a complex enterprise and the governance that at one level best serves a group's goals may not be as effective at another level. Third, beliefs about which form of governance is most effective are derived from interpretations of particular and changing experience and situations.

These points are illustrated by an historical review of reforms in governance in Europe, the United States and Latin America. This review shows how both the intent as well as the meaning of reforms in governance has changed over time, with shifts in sponsorship between those seeking greater social equality through education and those opposed to democratization.

We should, therefore, examine the motives as evidence of those who propose changes in the form of governance of an education system. Proposals for decentralization, or centralization, have no intrinsic merit, but they can be evaluated in terms of which groups in society are most likely to benefit from their imposition. The chapter suggests several factors to be taken into consideration by those who wish to both improve efficiency of educational institutions, and enhance social justice.

TYPES OF GOVERNANCE REFORMS

The more common decentralization reform has been a *deconcentration* of government authority accomplished by moving officials from central toward more local offices.[2] The Board of Education of (the city of) New York in the late 1960s created a series of mini-boards of education dotted across the city.[3] The federal ministry of education in Mexico began in 1978 to open branch offices in the states.[4]

A second type of decentralization reform involves the *delegation* of authority for the control and governance aspects of education to another organization, generally at a lower level in the hierarchy of size. For example, some major public universities are autonomous; although funding comes from the national or state government, allocation of funds and decisions about students, staff, curriculum, and physical facilities are the responsibility of the university.[5]

In a third kind of decentralization, sometimes called *devolution*, the more central authority turns over all responsibility, including that of funding, to a more local organization. For example, Nigeria's 1979 Constitution turned responsibility for basic education over to the states (which in turn delegated responsibilities to local education authorities). *Privatization*, in which public institutions are handed over to individuals or corporations, is one form of devolution.

Centralization of education has been accomplished by consolidation of smaller units, imposition of regulations by higher-level agencies, and creation of higher level boards and planning agencies. The long-term trend in the United States has been toward consolidation of school districts. The national government of Colombia increased its control over state education agencies by offering additional funds in return for conformity to higher qualifications for teachers.[6] Budget increases for universities also have been tied to development of plans subject to approval by central government agencies,[7] and some governments have moved to eliminate university autonomy.[8]

SOCIAL FORCES PRODUCE COMPLEX FORMS OF GOVERNANCE

At any given moment in history it is possible to find several forms of control existing side by side. In Brazil, for example, some states have both state and municipal systems of primary education. Public secondary education is largely but not exclusively the responsibility of the state government. There are both federal and state universities, many of which are autonomous, but some of which are controlled by state ministries of education. An autonomous federal agency is responsible for skill training for workers. In Kenya and Indonesia, on the other hand, primary education is run by the national government, and local communities have autonomy to set up secondary schools. In many countries private schools and universities receive subsidies from either state or national governments, and follow government regulations with respect to curriculum and teachers.

The simultaneous coexistence of diverse forms of governance results from a complex political process in which improvement of education is not always the major goal. As a consequence, there is no reliable relationship between form of governance, the efficiency or effectiveness of the education system, and equity. The long-term worldwide trend toward increased overall centralization of national education systems[9] has not, therefore, been accompanied by reliable changes in efficiency or equity.

In the examples that follow, we can see how centralization, and decentralization, of education have been intended to accomplish contradictory purposes. We will also see an increasing sophistication in forms of educational governance.

European Examples. Prior to the emergence of nation-states[10] most education in Europe was under the control of either the Church, municipalities, or individuals. None of these welcomed external participation in governance of their schools, but some religious communities governed themselves democratically (e.g., election of abbots) and admitted all who applied to their institutions. As early as 1600 all the cities of France had lay public schools supported by local taxes. Their egalitarianism appalled Henry IV's advisor Richelieu, who feared the spread of democratic values:

> it is the ease of access to this bewildering number of colleges that has enabled the meanest artisans to send their children to these schools, where they are taught free of charge—and that is what has ruined everything.[11]

Under State sponsorship the Church began to take over management of municipal schools, until by the middle of the eighteenth century almost all were run by religious communities. The Church developed the first professionally trained teachers, who developed a graded curriculum, standardized examinations, and systems of financial accounting, which enhanced centralized control.

The French Revolution saw centralized education as a means to achieve goals of equality, and the mobilization of the French people against the forces of reaction. Napoleon in turn saw in the centralized system a means to extend the power of the State into an expanded France. All public schools were put under control of the national government. Teachers were made national employees and trained in national institutes. They taught a single curriculum and were supervised by national inspectors. The royalists who replaced Napoleon kept central control but reduced coverage. The democrats who pushed out the royalists further extended centralization in order to increase coverage. Each group saw in centralized bureaucratic control a means to insure the realization of their goals for education.

Although the British national system of education took power from private teachers (and the working class), in comparison with the system of France it was highly decentralized.[12] As late as 1985 local education authorities in Great Britain had virtual autonomy with respect to hiring and salaries of teachers, in-service training, construction and closing of schools and examinations between primary and secondary levels. There was no national curriculum, nor regulations with respect to conditions of work for teachers.[13]

Recent reforms in governance have made the two systems more alike. Arguing for the benefits of increased efficiency through decentralization and privatization, the Thatcher Government in 1988 passed legislation to centralize control of curriculum and examinations. At the same time it took control of teachers and school administration away from local education authorities in municipalities and counties, and gave it to governing boards of individual schools. These boards are now empowered to privatize their schools, that is, to substitute private for public funding. In France, decentralization reforms since the Crisis of 1968 have moved in the direction of greater curriculum autonomy for the twenty-six geographic regions, and encouragement of local community participation in administration. At the same time, the national ministry is using results of national examinations to signal regions as to what should be emphasized in their curriculum.[14]

The net effect of these reforms is, in both cases, to *increase* central government control over critical aspects of education, while relieving central government of other responsibilities. This is possible because the traditional contradiction between centralization and decentralization no longer applies. Recent developments in management technologies allow central governments to control the *products* of educational institutions (through examinations and certification mechanisms) without having to control *inputs* (e.g., number and salaries of teachers, books in libraries, etc.).[15]

The United States Case. The first communities in New England established locally-controlled (but not private) schools. With Independence state governments were made responsible for education but most delegated control, and finance, to local communities. As late as 1850 half the school finance in the

United States was private.[16] Before the turn of the century, however, public education had grown until it had nearly a monopoly on schooling. Prior to 1900 the tradition of control of schools by locally-elected lay school boards was maintained. There were at that time approximately 160,000 school districts in the United States, each with an elected school board. In cities boards were large, with more than twenty members each. Most cities had neighborhood school boards that enjoyed considerable influence over the central city board.[17]

Trends toward centralization were noticed as early as 1897.[18] By 1913 the average size of urban boards had been reduced to ten members, and neighborhood boards had been abolished. Prior to 1900 board members were elected on a ward or precinct basis, and represented their local community; by 1913 most members were elected at large. Zeigler et al. attribute this shift in power to the concern of "liberals" that working class control of school boards had led to political corruption and low quality of education. Arguing that education should be made "nonpolitical" reformers devised means to insure that political groups with working class support had less chance to place their representatives on school boards. Boards were made smaller and small school districts were consolidated to make larger ones. By 1930 there were only 130,000 independent school districts, covering many more students and teachers. School board elections were made nonpartisan and scheduled to not coincide with state and federal elections. Participation in elections declined sharply.

In some cases these reforms were justified by reference to "efficiency" but "others were quite open in their assertion that only 'successful' people should serve on school boards."[19] School boards had previously drawn members from all the community; now almost all members were from the business or professional class.

Education professionals contributed to this shift from local to more centralized control. Schools of Education developed programs of educational administration, arguing that "schools, like businesses, should be run by experts."[20] Both parental involvement in decision-making, and that of classroom teachers, were reduced to a minimum.

Beginning in the late 1950s and early 1960s, liberal and progressive groups attempted to use education as a means to correct serious inequities in American society, and to restore some measure of democratic participation in decision making about education. The major mechanism to achieve the first goal was the federal government. Federal courts were willing to overturn long-standing patterns of discrimination by state and local governments against minority populations. Congress and the Executive branch financed and implemented programs that provided resources to groups of children systematically deprived of educational opportunity for generations. Even though the total expenditure on education by the federal government was a small fraction of that of state and local governments, the effect was to reorient school districts toward compliance with federal guidelines.

The reformers were less successful in terms of restoring some measure of control to local citizens. Efforts at decentralization created new layers of bureaucracy between central administrators and parents and generally failed to increase actual parental control over either the content or the process of education.[21] Consolidation of school districts continued; in 1988 there were approximately fourteen thousand.[22]

The election of Ronald Reagan as President in 1980 signaled a major shift in the balance of forces in U.S. society, and led to further changes in governance of education (see David's chapter in this text). The conservatives favored minimal reduced federal government involvement in education, and federal support of education diminished. But at the same time conservatives were successful in limiting the revenue-raising capacity of local governments and school boards. The net effect has been to increase state control over local schools but at least one state has moved to restore neighborhood school boards.[23]

At the same time, explanations for the poor performance of the national economy have been sought in the poor performance of American school children on international examinations. The President and the National Governors Association have called for national goals and standards for education, and the President of the American Federation of Teachers has recommended a national curriculum.

Examples in Latin America. Education in Spanish Latin America was modified in the nineteenth century to conform to the Napoleonic model. In some countries reformers opposed groups sympathetic to the Catholic Church, and imposed control over private (Church-run) education as well. In other countries public and Church-run systems operated side by side. In both cases teachers, local communities, and parents had little or no say over the process and content of education.

Indigenous groups resisted the imposition of national public education systems from the beginning; most were unsuccessful.[24] The first successful challenge to State control of higher education was in Argentina in 1928, when progressive groups opposed to conservative Catholic dominance in the national government sought autonomy for the university. In Mexico during the same period conservative Catholics protected their control of the national university by successfully resisting a Socialist government's attempts to manage the university through the Ministry of Education.[25]

Both conservative and progressive groups in Latin America adopted national planning beginning in the 1950s, but some groups simultaneously encouraged a modest decentralization. The emerging Christian Democratic parties, whose constituency was a modern middle class and peasants, promoted a "communitarian" ideology which included regionalization of education.[26] National planning was successful in massification of public education, but also demonstrated the limitations of central control. By the late 1970s many countries were urging regionalization as a means of reducing bureaucratic inefficiency and improving the match between programs and regional economic needs.[27]

In Peru seizure of power by a progressive faction within the military in 1968 was followed by an attempt to delegate control over education to local community members. A national plan for reform built on previous experiences with decentralization established a hierarchy of regional and local offices to provide training and support services to clusters of local schools. Teachers, parents, and local authorities were to participate in management of the school clusters, mobilizing local resources, and interpreting national curricula to fit local requirements. The promise of participation did not attract much support from parents, and teachers actively opposed what they defined as the government's attempt to shift attention away from demands for higher pay.[28]

In Mexico a modernizing urban elite sought to weaken control over the education system by a traditional bureaucracy linked to the national teachers' union. Among the methods chosen was a delegation of authority for disbursement of funds for basic education to officials operating at the state level. This reduced the union's control over appointments and "sweetheart" contracts, and led to ascendancy of "breakaway" groups within the union who pushed for democratic election of leaders and teacher participation in decision-making about education. For awhile the modernizing elites at least tolerated the democratic opposition within the teachers' union, but when these groups demanded more local control over education, and began to make alliances with local communities, the modernizers rebuilt their coalition with the conservative union. Decentralization did increase participation in decision making for education at the level of state elites, but made no difference at the level of communities.[29]

The most celebrated experiment in decentralization of control over education has taken place in Chile, where a right-wing military government attempted to privatize the education system. Beginning in the late 1970s the government delegated administration of primary and secondary education to municipal governments, and provided each municipality with annual funding based on the number of students enrolled. Legislation with respect to teacher qualifications and salaries was rescinded; municipalities now set qualifications and salaries. The municipalities were allowed, if they desired, to sell their schools to private owners. Individual citizens or groups were also allowed to start schools, and to receive government subsidies, if they would follow the national curriculum and submit to inspection.

Only one municipality chose to completely privatize its system. Private spending on education rose from about 15 percent to 25 percent of the national total, most of that in the aided schools that received government subsidies.

There has been no significant change in the proportion of the age group enrolled, nor in the internal efficiency of schools, nor in available measures of achievement. Enrollments in universities, which now charge sizeable fees, have declined. Parental participation in education has increased, at least in private aided schools, which often are run by collectives of parents. Participation of parents and teachers in decision making in public schools has declined, and the once powerful teachers' union now has little or no say in national dialogue on education policy. The distribution of spending on education has shifted noticeably. The previous Christian Democratic and Socialist governments distributed funds for schooling to compensate for income differences between regions. Under the military's municipalization scheme, all regions received the same amounts. In Chile, "decentralization" increased participation by some middle class parents, but decreased others' share of resources.[30]

In a review of the history of efforts at decentralization in Chile, Nuñez insists on the importance of distinguishing between:

1. a democratic State,
2. the unity and coherence of an education system, and
3. centralization of governance of education.[31]

A democratic State seeks to maximize participation in decision making, while at the same time attending to an equitable distribution of access to resources. There is a dialectical tension between participation and the coherence and unity of an education system. Participation can lead to increased diversity and reduced coherence. Centralization does not necessarily produce coherence, however, and it is also possible for a centralized state to encourage diversity in its constituent regions.

Although progressive educators in Chile (beginning in the 1940s) were concerned with local control over schools, and favored school-based management and school-based curriculum, they were also concerned for social equity, and the integration of Chilean society to overcome profound class differences. The educators chose to promote integration of the education system, seeking to break down the barrier between primary and secondary school, and to build integrated administrative structures and processes, and larger public schools in which gender and class mixing would promote social coherence.

It was these progressive educators who pushed Chile to lead Latin America in extending access to education to all children. Centralization to achieve integration was carried out in the name of increased democratization, by people who preferred a decentralized system of governance. Under the military, decentralization has maintained central control over the content and process of education, but has allowed those with resources to distance themselves from those without.

HOW CAN PROPOSALS FOR REFORM BE EVALUATED?

It is possible to increase local control over some aspects of education by centralizing other aspects. What label is applied to a given reform will, therefore, depend on who is asked. Whether or not a given policy of centralization/decentralization will be implemented depends in part on the political commitment and resources of the group behind the program, but it also depends on the extent to which there is an opposition with resources and commitment. The struggle between those who propose and those who resist centralization/decentralization programs affects not only whether the program will be implemented at all, but also the ways in which the implemented program will affect the system.

For these reasons, technical analysis is seldom sufficient to predict the outcome of a given program of centralization/decentralization. The point here is not that the theories of governance are wrong, but that because they cannot predict the new balance of forces that will emerge in a given political struggle, their accuracy in prediction of outcomes of a particular reform is limited to the short-term. Consider the following.

Some elements of curriculum—for example, national history and language—perhaps can best be determined nationally, while other elements might be chosen regionally or locally. If students are expected to remain in the areas in which they are educated, a localized curriculum may be seen as reasonable. But if most students live or work outside their local community, then localization of curriculum may be seen as a disservice and resisted.[32]

From the perspective of good pedagogy, it can be argued that teachers should be allowed to select and develop methods of instruction to fit the children and subject matter they are teaching. But when teachers have low levels of both academic training and skills in pedagogy, both teacher and student learning can be increased by centralization of instructional methods.[33] Encouragement of local resource mobilization—through voluntary or imposed fees, for example—can compensate for inadequate allocations made by central governments and increase access to schooling, but may also reduce the overall quality of education provided.[34] Increased authority for administrators can increase initiatives in local solutions for local problems, can improve school-community relationships and increase donation of labor and materials to schools, and can increase teacher and student morale and attendance and reduce failure rates.[35] But this can also draw resources away from some schools, favoring those which already have more than their share.

Participation in decision making about education depends not so much on the location of that decision making, but on the existence of mechanisms to facilitate participation by all relevant groups. Considerable public discussion about and participation in decision making for education policy can even take place in a highly centralized education system, if the political system is essentially democratic.[36]

The vitality of mechanisms for democratic participation is reduced by two forms of decentralization—professionalization and privatization. Professionalization refers to management of schools by specialists in educational administration, and should not be confused with other forms of teacher participation. "School-based management" and other proposals for "restructuring education" can include teachers and parents (or local community) as partners with specific responsibilities in management of the school. In Great Britain, for example, the Taylor Report of 1977 called for "A New Partnership" between teachers and parents in which the former would handle technical aspects of teaching, and the latter would monitor their performance.[37] Parental supervision is not always welcome, however, especially when teachers define themselves as the legitimate agents of change,[38] or when any professional group sets itself up as "expert" and argues for a strictly "technical" solution to problems.

Privatization acts to limit democratic participation in several ways. First, it reduces the effectiveness of existing political organizations developed over time as mechanisms to express popular will. Second, unless there is a strong central effort to equalize resources, privatization favors those who already have a disproportionate share of resources, and worsens inequities in participation. Third, privatization encourages diversity not only in solutions to immediate problems (which is good) but also in fundamental political values. This leads to a weakening of commitment to any form of shared or collective action. Without the possibility for collective action democratic participation is a hollow phrase.

Proposals for reform of governance should be evaluated not in terms of labels such as centralization or decentralization but rather in terms of their likely impact on the means by which people can participate in decision making, and in terms of their impact on commitment to that participation.

JANDHYALA B. G. TILAK

Chapter 11

Public and Private Sectors
in Education in India

INTRODUCTION

In the contemporary context of increasing demand from various competing sectors on diminishing public resources, soft sectors like education become vulnerable to severe budget cuts all over the world and especially in the developing countries. Accordingly, the need for diversification of the sources of educational finances is widely felt. Among the alternative sources of funding education, "privatization of education" is being given increasingly serious attention. While privatization takes various forms, at least two forms are noteworthy. They are: (1) an increase in the contribution of the private sources in the form of the introduction/increase in user charges or fees, and (2) an increase in the role of the private corporate sector in education, in the form of an increase in the number of private educational institutions. Arguments favoring privatization are implicitly based on assumptions that (a) expenditure of households on education is rather trivial; (b) opportunity costs of education in developing countries, characterized by massive unemployment, are also not significant; (c) the ability of households to pay for education is not efficiently tapped and, as a result, (d) households can be asked to pay substantial amounts as fees for education. It is also viewed that without fees, it is impossible to achieve even minimum educational goals. These implicit assumptions also find partial support in the existence of excess demand for education (over and above the supply of public education), and the growth of demand for private education by small but socially and economically powerful strata in the society, who pay

173

huge amounts in the form of fees and "other" contributions. Those who advocate privatization often overlook the costs the society has to pay in the long-run in the form of increasing socioeconomic inequities that result from the creation of dual structures of education.

The present chapter proposes to analyze some of these aspects with the help of available evidence from India. Specifically the chapter examines household expenditure on education and the role of the private corporate sector in education. These two forms of privatization have been in existence in India for a long time. They originated not necessarily in response to the past or recent economic problems like the world recession and external debt. But they assume significance in the present context of economic austerity all over the world. They are examined here in the same context. I will begin by discussing the need for "mixed" (public *and* private) support for education. Subsequent sections are respectively devoted to a detailed discussion on household expenditure and the role of private enterprise in education. I shall show that families invest considerable amounts of resources in education, and that the private corporate sector's contribution is significant neither in terms of finances, nor in terms of improving socioeconomic equity in India. All this leads me to be skeptical of the widely suggested proposal of privatization of education. The chapter ends with a short summary of the analysis and the main arguments.

THE NEXUS BETWEEN PUBLIC AND PRIVATE GOODS

Education can be considered both a private and a public (social) good. The social benefits of education are not simply equal to the sum of private benefits. Nonprivate benefits of education are substantial. It is necessary to recognize the distinction between individual and public domains in education.[1] The decision-makers in the two sectors are different, may have different objectives and constraints, and have different time horizons in making decisions. State planners, for example, consider externality and neighborhood effects of education, and equity in making decisions about public investment in education, while these aspects may not be important for families while deciding to invest in education of their children. That education and life-time earnings are positively related may be of concern for individuals. On the other hand, state planners may be interested in efforts that far exceed one life-time. Hence individual household and government investments do not necessarily always match and this results in either over or under optimum social investment in education. Familiar to us all are the differences between private demand and the manpower needs of the economy, or differences between the private and social rates of return to education. Further, household decisions to invest in education depend upon microeconomic factors such as improvement in households' socioeconomic conditions, while decisions regarding government investment are influenced by macro-level factors, such as national economic growth, income distribution, and equity.

Families as well as governments invest sizeable amounts in education. Both government and family investments in education are of significance not only because of their magnitudes, but also because of the nature and characteristics associated with those investments. Although public investments can provide the educational facilities, corresponding individual investments are equally important for human capital formation, as without individual investments one cannot realize the benefits of public investment in education. While this has been recognized, the complementarity between family and government investments is relatively little examined. Education is an important area where the interaction between government and households is particularly significant. Government may be thought of as deciding upon an "optimum" or a desired level of national investment in education, and accordingly invest such amounts, taking into account household investments as to make the total social investments equal the desired levels. On the other hand, individual households seek to effectively take advantage of public investments in education and limit their contribution to cover benefits they perceive in their own personal, rather than societal, interests. Government and household expenditures are so interrelated and interdependent that, the absence of either is likely to result in under allocation of total societal resources for education. They do not necessarily substitute for each other. On the other hand, family expenditures may complement government expenditure and vice versa. As human capital formed through the process of education depends on investments made in the two complementary parts, and decided in the two domains, the two have to balance each other. This has been argued by many. "Unless the two kinds of investments match there can be only empty, or over crowded, classrooms and under or oversubscribed training programs."[2] Hence many rightly feel the need to achieve a balance between public and private financing of education.[3]

Public financing of education, in general, is required essentially due to the positive social effects of education. Education being a public good,[4] its social benefits exceed private benefits significantly. In fact, externalities of education are believed to outweigh the direct benefits. Accordingly, government's role in education is important for the following reasons:[5]

1. Neighborhood or externality effects of education are quite significant. Social benefits are far greater than those perceived by individuals. Accordingly, private markets fail to provide optimum education relative to its social merits, and government involvement becomes critical.
2. To ensure equality of opportunity in education, state funding of education becomes necessary. State responsibility for minors has long been estab-

lished. Children cannot make decisions on their own regarding their future education, and not all parents have the ability to make wise decisions about investing in their children's schooling. If a bright child of an illiterate parent does not get enough education, the loss of future welfare for the whole society may be large.

3. The quest for common values in the society, and the role public education can play in inculcating common values among the children, necessitate active involvement of the government in the provision of education. In most democracies, the role of education in making democracy work is believed to be quite significant, providing better citizenry, reducing crime, and inculcating democratic values among the people.

4. Education is subject to technical economies of scale and it is more efficient for the government than private individuals to provide it.

5. Effects of education on economic growth, reduction in poverty, improvement in income distribution, and improvement in the physical quality of life provide a strong case for public investment in education.[6]

Given all this, some rightly feel that education publicly provided and funded, accessible to all, is the *sine qua non* of the public good.[7]

At the same time, education cannot be considered a pure public good like defense, or clean air, where all people in the society receive equal benefits. Neither is it a pure private good like food, the benefits of which are exclusive to those who consume. Education is a semi- or quasi-public good, where both social and private benefits are important. Since it is a quasi-public good, 100 percent public financing of education can be seen as economically unjustified. Since private individuals also benefit, it is reasonable they share a proportion of the costs. As the private rate of return to education is higher than the social rate of return, one expects individual families to invest in education higher amounts than governments.

However, where should public financing of education end and where should family financing begin? No theory of the optimum mix of public and private financing of education has to date been generated. Earlier research analyzing alternative mixes of public and private finances for education has only pleaded for more experimentation with different combinations of public and private financing.[8] The actual mix of public subsidies and private finances for education in a society reflects the economic policies of the government, the traditions and social policies in the society. A few general principles that might guide policies seeking to optimize the mix between public and private expenditures in education are as follows:

1. Since social benefits of education exist along with individual benefits, the government should fund education. If social benefits exceed private benefits,

the government's share of funding should be relatively larger than an individual's or family's share. Where social benefits exceed private benefits in such a way that private benefits become relatively less significant, total public subsidization of education may be required. An excellent example is elementary education.

2. Since education is a social good, it should not be rationed on the basis of ability to pay by the consumers.[9] Government subsidization hence becomes necessary.

3. The "Robin Hood principle" suggests that public financing of education should result in a transfer of resources from the rich to the poor, and not the other way.[10]

There is little empirical evidence on government and family finances for education and on their effects on educational development in developing economies to warrant unquestioning adoption of the principles enunciated above.[11]

The rest of the paper analyzes empirically the growth of government and private investments in education in India.

HOUSEHOLD AND GOVERNMENT
INVESTMENTS IN EDUCATION

Private, including household expenditures on education, have not received serious research attention. Research tends to consider government's expenditure on education as the total social investment in education. This is the case with most statistics on expenditure on education, including national and international statistical handbooks/yearbooks. Further, opportunity costs rarely figure in national income accounts. Hence, most analyses do not present comprehensive estimates of true social investment in education.

In India, the National Sample Survey Organization collects data on household expenditure on various consumption activities, including education. However, few details on the nature, scope, and definition are available regarding these data. Table 11.1 presents long-term trends in the growth of such household expenditure along with government expenditure on education in India during 1960-61 and 1984-85, a period for which both sets of data are readily available. Family and government expenditure on education increased remarkably between 1960-61 and 1984-85 in current prices. Household expenditure grew fourteen-fold while government expenditure thirty-two-fold. The increases have not kept pace either with inflation or with population growth. In constant prices household expenditure increased by only two and a half times, and the government expenditure six times, and the real increase per capita is still less in either case.

TABLE 11.1
Government and Household Expenditure on Education
(Rs in 10 millions)

	Government Expenditure			Household Expenditure		
	Total (at 1970-71 prices)	% of Total Expenditure	% of GNP	Total (at 1970-71 prices)	% of Total Expenditure	% of GNP
1960-61	452	9.4	1.7	520	2.3	1.9
1965-66	634	9.1	2.0	697	2.6	2.2
1970-71	928	10.8	2.3	983	3.0	2.5
1975-76	1163	9.7	2.5	882	2.4	1.9
1980-81	1725	11.1	3.1	1058	2.4	1.9
1984-85	2673	10.5	4.0	1308	2.5	1.9

Notes. Expenditure in current prices is converted into constant prices with the help of national income deflators (base: 1970-71).

Source. Tilak, "Family and Government Investments in Education," *International Journal of Educational Development* 11, no. 2 (1991), pp. 94, 96.

More interestingly, household expenditures were higher than government expenditures until 1973-74. After 1973-74 household expenditures have been lower than government expenditures, and the gap between the two has widened slowly. During the 1970s, the real expenditure on education declined both on the part of households and government, but the decline is more significant and longer lasting in the case of households. India's economic problems in the mid-1970s, particularly high rates of inflation, affected household budgets more severely than government budgets, as far as education is concerned.

How much should families spend on education? There is no clear theory to determine this.[12] Generally, economists agree that it should be based on parental ability to pay. The proportion of budgets spent on education indicates the relative importance assigned to education. The relative priority allocated to education in the household and government budgets is computed here as a percent of total final consumption expenditure in the case of households, and as a percent of total government expenditure.

In households, education's share has been around only 2.5 percent (with an all-time high of 3.1 percent in 1971-72). In the government sector around 10 percent is devoted to education. On the whole, both in cases of household and government budgets, education's share suffered during the mid-1970s, and recovered somewhat gradually during the first half of the 1980s.

The relative priority accorded to education in the national economy by both households and the government can be denoted by the percent of gross national product (GNP). Analysis of data on the share of education in GNP indicates that the government expenditure has been slowly but steadily increasing from 1.7 percent of the GNP in 1960-61 to 4 percent in 1984-85. The household expenditure on education as percent of the GNP increased to 2.5 percent by the beginning of the 1970s, and then declined to less than 2 percent, where it remained stable during the 1980s. Like the trends in total expenditure on education, household expenditure as percent of GNP was either higher or about equal to government expenditure until 1973-74. Since then government expenditure has been higher than household expenditure.[13]

Besides direct monetary expenditure, students forgo substantial earnings due to their participation in education. These foregone earnings, also called opportunity costs of education, are quite sizeable in India and are quantitatively comparable with the direct public investment in education. For example, according to one estimate, [14] the opportunity costs in 1979-80 constituted 4.2 percent of GNP, while the public investment formed 3.9 percent of GNP.[15] Thus, total household investment—household expenditure plus opportunity costs—in education is indeed very high. These figures are particularly high when examined in the context of relatively low levels of living and the high incidence of poverty in India,[16] and also when compared with even high income countries. For example, the percentage share of education in total household expenditure was 0.3 in France, 0.5 in Australia, 1.6 in Greece, 1.9 in the United States, and 2.3 in the United Kingdom and Spain.[17] As a proportion of GNP also, household expenditure on education in India is very high, compared to less than 0.5 percent in several Organization for Economic Cooperation and Development (OECD) countries.[18] All this suggests that the scope for enhancing the contribution of the households to education in the form of raising school fees in India is not as great as generally has been believed.

However, given that students in higher education do not belong to a homogeneous socioeconomic group (in fact, the distribution of students is found to be skewed in favor of higher income groups), there exists some scope for a discriminatory fee system, which requires high income groups to pay higher levels of fees and lower income groups either no or lower levels of fees. This policy would not only generate additional resources (which may not necessarily be significantly large), but it also has the potential to make the system less regressive.[19]

PRIVATE SECTOR IN EDUCATION

In a mixed economy where the private corporate sector has contributed significantly to industrial and agricultural development, the role of private enterprise in education needs a detailed analysis.[20] This is particularly the case during the periods when the growth of public resources for education has been minimal, but when the requirements of education for both quantitative and qualitative development have been growing very fast. In this context, two aspects are important: the role of the private sector in financing education, and the role of the private sector in administering, planning, and managing education. The role of the private sector in education is totally different from that of the private sector in the economy in general. Private education or private schools necessarily mean a privately managed system, and not necessarily a privately funded system of education. Even with respect to management and decision-making, private schools still can be "controlled" by public authorities. The controls may extend to the use of funds, fee levels, staffing patterns, and salary scales.

There are at least four forms of educational systems in India: (a) publicly managed and funded (e.g., government primary schools), (b) publicly managed, but publicly and (relatively less) privately funded (e.g., government secondary schools and colleges/universities), (c) privately managed but largely publicly funded (e.g., aided schools and colleges), and (d) privately managed and funded (e.g., unaided schools and colleges). Most government schools in India belong to category (a), and to a lesser extent to category (b). Most private schools and colleges in India, as in many countries belong to category (c): they are privately managed, but receive as much as 95 percent or even higher proportion of their expenses from the state exchequer. Schools in category (d) are very few in number. More than 40 percent of the secondary schools, and three-fourths of the colleges are privately managed, but publicly funded institutions. A few missionary institutions that were opened with philanthropic motives also receive substantial government aid, and are also subject to state controls. Except for a few such institutions and a few autonomous colleges, most private institutions, which have been founded in the recent past, are operated as commercial enterprises. They had to survive for a few years before they could qualify for government financial aid. Both during initial and later periods, they might make profits by under paying teachers and other staff, charging various types of non-tuition fees, and through other questionable practices.[21] Thus expansion of the private sector through public funding may not be socially and economically justified.[22] It only leads to the enrichment of the private sector at public expense, as the so called private "non-profit" institutions become "profit making" institutions with the help of state aid and undesirable practices.

While a vast majority of the private schools and colleges in India are funded by the public exchequer and hence are called "aided private institutions," there are a few private schools (category *d* above), called "public schools," that do not receive any state subsidy and are least regulated by public authorities; but they constitute an infinitesimally small proportion of the total number of schools in the country.[23] In 1986 private unaided primary schools constituted 2.5 percent of the total number of primary schools in the country,

8.4 percent of middle schools, 12.7 percent of secondary schools, and 6 percent of higher secondary schools (table 11.2). It may be noted that the share of the private unaided sector increased noticeable in the recent past (between 1978 when the earlier *survey*[24] was conducted, and 1986).

TABLE 11.2
Government and Private Schools in India, 1986-87

School	Government*	Private		Total
		Aided	Unaided	
Primary	89.0	8.4	2.5	100 (529)
Middle	73.8	17.9	8.4	100 (139)
Secondary	43.5	43.9	12.7	100 (52)
Higher Secondary	41.7	52.4	6.0	100 (16)

Note. *Includes schools run by local governments. Figures in ( ) are number of schools in thousands.

Source. Fifth All-India Educational Survey: Selected Educational Statistics. New Delhi: National Council of Educational Research and Training, 1989, pp. 24-25.

The share of the private finances in total educational finances in India is very limited. Ignoring the unaided private institutions for a moment, the contribution of the private sector to educational finances in the form of gifts, donations, endowments and so forth, was a petty 3 percent of the total educational finances. This was around 12 percent at the time of inception of planning in the country, that is, in 1950-51 (table 11.3).

It is not possible to state exactly how much of the financial support for pri-

TABLE 11.3
Government and Private Finances for Education (%)

	1950-51	1960-61	1970-71	1980-81
Government Sector				
Central and State	57.1	68.0	75.6	80.0
Local Governments*	10.9	6.5	5.7	8.6
Private Sector				
Fees	20.4	11.2	12.8	8.8
Endowments,				
Donations, etc.	11.6	8.3	5.9	2.6
Total	*100.0*	*100.0*	*100.0*	*100.0*
	(114.0)	(344.4)	(1118.3)	(3546.9)

Note. *Includes *Zilla Parishads, Municipalities, Panchayats,* etc. Figures in ( ) are Rs. in 10 millions.

Source. Education in India, New Delhi: Ministry of Education, Government of India (various years); and *Statistical Abstract of India 1986,* New Delhi: Central Statistical Organization, 1988.

vate institutions in India comes from the private corporate sector, as no country-wide data on private unaided schools are available. Given that such institutions are very few in number, their share in the total educational finances cannot be significant. The scanty evidence available indicates that private institutions have grown largely in response to prospects of making "quick profits,"[25] and/or for political power, and that they are detrimental to all but few.[26] "Motives of profit, influence, and political power conspired," as Rudolph and Rudolph observed in a recent study, "to accelerate foundings as local politicians created colleges to secure the reliable political machine a loyal staff and students could provide."[27]

The private institutions, more particularly the unaided ones, practice exclusiveness through charging high tuition fee, and alarmingly large "capitation fees" or "donations." The tuition fees in the private institutions are so high that few lower and middle class households can afford even to apply for admission in these schools. For example, in Bombay, compared to tuition-free education in government schools, private schools (excepting a few private schools that have been established as charities) charged during the 1970s tuition fee ranging from Rs.4-5 a month to upwards of Rs.200 a month.[28] In Delhi, nowadays, a typical private school charges Rs.200-400 per month as tuition fees alone. In addition, it charges annual fees, about Rs.100 per month towards transportation, and miscellaneous fees like art and music classes, computer instruction, clay material, and so on. These figures need to be compared with the prevailing wage structures. A majority of the unskilled and semi-skilled labor force hardly earns a four-digit figure as monthly wages. Many "public" schools quite deliberately exclude lower socioeconomic strata, taking economic status of parent as a criterion.[29]

In higher education, the growth of private engineering and medical colleges has been a recent phenomenon. As a market response to the unmet private demand of the upper classes for higher education, there has been a proliferation of such colleges. Private unaided engineering and medical colleges are allowed by the governments in Karnataka, Tamil Nadu, and Maharashtra, and recently in Gujarat and Andhra Pradesh. There are presently about one hundred sixty-one private engineering colleges in the country which charge either capitation fees or considerably higher tuition fees than the colleges run by the government.[30] These colleges receive little public support, but charge "hefty" donations and capitation fees from the students. Engineering colleges in Maharashtra in 1989, for example, charge donations anywhere between Rs.50,000 and Rs.90,000. These are in addition to tuition and other normal fees (which may be over Rs.8,000 per annum), compared to Rs.500 in government colleges.[31] Private colleges for general education, such as the "parallel colleges" in Kerala, have also been operating on more or less the same lines. The tuition fees in these colleges are two to three times higher than in government colleges.[32]

Over the course of time, ostensible merit-ordered criterion for admissions into the private institutions have been replaced by ability to pay criterion; and the high fees, not to speak of capitation fees, effectively bar students from middle class, even upper middle class families, not to mention the lower income families. Kothari expressed these concerns in a study on Maharashtra, when he noted that "the objective of equal opportunities for education would be jeopardized in a big way. The overall effect would be to convert education into a force for reinforcing the existing stratification of the society."[33]

That there are strong disequalizing forces inherent in the private educational system is well noted by some protagonists of privatization themselves. A World Bank study rightly fears that private schools might "turn out to be socially and economically divisive in the future."[34] In case of India, it has already been found that there are disequalizing forces inherent in private education and that the government school system has not been adequate to counteract them. As a result, the whole educational system has become a disequalizer accentuating income inequalities.[35] No evidence is available to show that the external efficiency, as measured by say rate of return to education, of these private schools and colleges is higher than that of education in the government schools. Earnings associated with private schooling are not significantly higher than the earnings associated with government schooling, but private costs of education in private schools are quite high. As a result, the rate of return to private education could be quite less when compared to that of education in state run schools.[36]

To sum up, the conflict between the vested interests of the ruling elite on the one hand and social realities, specifically the government's lack of political will to fund the provision of good quality education to all on the other, led to the emergence of a dual system of education, a tiny sector providing expensive quality education for the privileged few through the private schools known paradoxically as "public" schools, and private colleges and cheap education of poor quality for the masses in the public sector. The private schools and colleges, aided as well as unaided, in India are found to neither fulfill the efficiency criterion or the equity principle, nor contribute significantly to educational finances in the country. Yet they grow in number, particularly in cosmopolitan urban areas to satisfy the needs of, according to a report of the Ministry of Education,[37] "gullible parents." Furthermore, some state governments support their expansion, so long as they serve their vested interests. With the emergence and growth of such private schools, "the system of interlocking interests of capital, educated elites, bureaucrats and politicians is thus mutually supportive and complete."[38]

Given all this, it seems right to argue that the benefits of education in private schools accrue largely to the elites, as the private sector attracts mainly the elites. These schools provide expensive and presumably "quality" education.

On the other hand, the benefits of education in public schools in general go to the masses, as the public schools are compelled generally to choose quantity in the quantity-quality trade-off, and accordingly, provide inexpensive and poor quality education.

SUMMARY AND CONCLUSIONS

Inadequacy of financial resources is widely considered to be one of the critical reasons for the desperate state of affairs in education in developing countries. It is generally believed that family investments in education are trivial, and governments finance nearly the whole of educational investments in developing countries. As the public investment in education dwindled during the late 1970s and 1980s, as compared to the earlier halcyon days of the economics of education, household investment has become a focus of attention. This new emphasis implicitly assumes that family and government investments substitute for each other. But in actual practice, families and governments may complement each other in their respective efforts to improve educational investments, as long as the total investment in education is below the optimum level.[39]

In the context of growing budget squeezes on education, it is also increasingly believed that in a mixed economy like India the private corporate sector may play an important role in easing the financial crisis in education in the form of an increase in the number of private schools and colleges, and in the form of donations and endowments to education.

Empirical evidence on these aspects in developing countries is limited. This chapter is a modest attempt in filling such gaps. It is found here that family expenditures on education are sizeable. They form nearly one-third to a half of total (government plus family) expenditures on education in India. If opportunity costs are also included, family investments in education are about double the government investment in education.

Little reliable information is available on the price elasticity of demand for education in the developing countries. It is yet to be seen whether increases in fees would reduce enrollments and improve quality, as argued by some in another context.[40] Without also exploring other forms of mobilizing additional resources, it may not be right to argue, that without an increase in fees it is impossible to fulfill even basic needs in education.[41]

All this suggests that the scope for enhancing the family contributions to education in India, in general, is not as high as generally thought. At the same time, carefully planned reforms in fees in higher education, such as introduction of differentiated fees, may generate a few additional resources for education, and more importantly may make higher education more equitable.

The experience of India also shows that the contribution of the private corporate educational sector to educational finances is extremely limited; and the role of the private sector in the overall educational development, including administration, management and financing aspects of education, is indeed not conducive to the development of the welfare state. Instead, it may be socially divisive and financially ineffective. That privatization of education can be a major barrier to equity is not yet empirically challenged. The available evidence shows that the over all contribution of private institutions to educational development in India is indeed negative.

Thus privatization, including an increase in the number of private schools and colleges and a general increase in user charges, may not only not solve the financial crisis in education, but also might create new serious problems both in terms of equity and efficiency. Governments in countries like India that aim at equity in social and economic sectors will have to continue to bear increasingly more responsibility for education and continue their search for more efficient and equitable measures of generating additional resources for education.

HAROLD J. NOAH
MAX A. ECKSTEIN

Chapter 12

Comparing National Systems of Secondary School Leaving Examinations

A vast literature deals with examinations in particular countries, spanning the entire range of examination-related topics: psychometrics, mechanics of examinations, standards of achievement, the effects of examinations on the rest of the education system, various kinds of biases (social, cultural, and gender) in examinations, and (to a lesser extent) the effects of examinations on social status, employment opportunities, individual life chances, and the like. Reports about secondary school examinations in other nations appear from time to time in the popular press, although usually in the context of news, typically describing outbreaks of student protest over examination practices or policies. By contrast, relatively little systematic cross-national comparative work has been done, and the comparative study of examinations seems to have been a largely neglected aspect of comparative education.

However, comparative study of examination systems finds its strongest justification when nations seek ways to bring about educational change, especially when the concern focuses on raising the level of school achievement. Whether justified or not, there is a tendency to believe that certain foreign models (e.g., the Soviet Union in the 1960s , Japan in the 1990s) merit close attention, and possibly even emulation. Foreign examination systems may be viewed as doing a better job of stimulating student achievement, defining the curriculum for teachers, providing taxpayers and administrators with indicators of school quality, and preparing school graduates for subsequent education and work.

While examinations exert a powerful influence on schooling arrangements, social and educational developments in turn affect examinations. The advent of mass education, especially at the secondary level, has profoundly altered the nature and purpose of secondary school completion examinations. From being almost exclusively directed at regulating credentials for entry into higher education, examinations have become increasingly multipurpose, certifying completion of the upper secondary level of schooling, and controlling access to a variety of further education and training opportunities far beyond the traditional institutions of higher education. If only because they now touch the lives of so many more young people, secondary school completion examinations fully merit our close attention.

There are other, more general justifications for concern with these examinations in contemporary society. As economic and social life becomes more formalized and bureaucratized, schools are drawn to fit their procedures to the surrounding society. Certificates of completion of a course of study become valuable pieces of property, and examinations are a way to ensure that such certificates reflect degrees of learning, rather than simply attendance. What each nation considers to be the most desirable opportunities after the end of secondary school are necessarily limited relative to the demand for them. Thus, examinations are accepted as a politically and ethically defensible way of deciding which high school graduates to reward, and which to deny.

From time to time, nations have tried to abandon examinations at the end of secondary school, but have then been moved to backtrack. China offers a contemporary example. During the Cultural Revolution (1966-76), China broke with its well-established tradition of reliance on examinations to control admission to higher education and further training. Certification of political activism and "correctness" of social origin took their place. But when Mao's widow and her colleagues fell from power in 1976, one of the first changes made by the new regime was to return to using examination results for allocating university places. The Soviet Union also tried to do away with such examinations in the 1920s, but under Stalin they were reintroduced and they are now a well-entrenched feature of Soviet education.

Indeed, with the notable exception of the United States and Sweden, it is difficult to name a modernized or modernizing nation that does not rely on secondary school completion examinations in one form or another to certify completion of secondary education, to allocate opportunities for further education/training, or to regulate hiring.

Alongside these manifest functions of examinations are some equally significant additional functions. Examination results can be used to evaluate (with greater or lesser validity) the "quality" of a teacher or a school. They can be used to establish preferential treatment in the allocation of money for salaries, buildings, materials, equipment, and the like. Examinations can serve to motivate teachers and students, stimulating teaching and learning efforts by specifying in detail the system's expectations of students' learning. In consequence, examination requirements can lead to undue concentration on the material to be examined, to the exclusion of other elements in the school curriculum. Indeed, examined subjects can drive unexamined subjects out of the school timetable entirely. Above all, examinations can serve as a way of legitimizing knowledge, signaling the acceptance of a new school subject. For these reasons, examinations are expected to serve as influential means of implementing new school practices and educational reform programs.

Examination systems in particular countries demonstrate different ways of fulfilling these functions. They illustrate how changing social circumstances create pressures to change examinations, both directly and indirectly via changes in educational arrangements. In addition, they provide illustrations of the different patterns of intended and unintended effects examinations have on school systems. Eight national systems (Japan, France, the Federal Republic of Germany, the Soviet Union, England and Wales, Sweden, China, and the United States) have been selected for discussion, because each illustrates at least one important feature of the relationships among examinations, schooling, and society.

Japan. Japanese society and schooling place extraordinary emphasis on scholastic success, as measured by examinations. Educational practice appears to give wholehearted support to the thesis that education is primarily about examination success. In ninth grade, at the end of lower secondary school, a fiercely competitive set of examinations regulates admission to upper secondary schools of high prestige. Although nearly all lower secondary graduates go on to upper secondary school, admission to the "right" school is extremely important in determining future academic opportunities and eventual employment, for the hierarchy of upper secondary schools is well defined and widely recognized. In twelfth grade, at the end of upper secondary school, comes the second stage of the selection process, the university entrance examinations. Performance in the examinations is once again absolutely critical to a young person's subsequent chances for education and, as a consequence, employment. "More than any other single event, the university entrance examinations influence the orientation and life of most Japanese high school students, even for the many who do not go on to postsecondary education."[1]

About three-quarters of university students attend private universities. Some of these are quite prestigious, but most of them enjoy a lower reputation than the national (public) universities attended by the remainder. (There is a small local public university sector, with about 3 percent of total enrollment.) To gain admission to a public university in Japan, it is normally necessary to take two examinations. The Joint First Stage Achievement Test (JFSAT) is a nationwide, centrally administered, governmental, public examination. The results of the JFSAT are used to steer students to apply to a university likely to accept him/her. The JFSAT is followed by an examination set by the university to which the high school student has applied. These examinations are very highly competitive. In a typical year there are about four candidates for each public university place, so the university entrance examination results serve as a way of rationalizing allocation of high school graduates to a sharply defined hierarchy of higher education institutions, ranked explicitly in quality and reputation.[2]

One of the side effects of the intense competition generated by the examination system has been the development of the minor industry of *juku*, private cram schools, to improve a candidate's chances. Another side effect has been the emergence of a large group of overage candidates *(ronin)*, who have failed to gain entrance to the university of their choice the first or second time of trying, and are studying at specialized juku, termed *yobiko*, to retake the entrance examinations.

Serious concern has been expressed about the intensity of student competition, and about testing that stresses recall of isolated fragments of information, while neglecting comprehension. The term "examination hell" has been applied to the last couple of years of high school leading up to the JFSAT. On the other hand, there is strong support in Japan for the present system that, it is claimed, rewards those who are prepared to work hard and serves the interests of the Japanese nation. A movement to reform the school curriculum and to reduce the examination load on students was instigated in the mid-1980s by no less than the Prime Minister, but came to nothing.[3]

France. French invented the device of a certificate gained through national, noncompetitive examination and designed to be both the necessary and sufficient condition for entry into higher education. Since then, forms of the *baccalauréat* in a multitude of variations have been adopted in scores of countries. For this reason alone, France has a strong claim for inclusion in a cross-national survey of secondary school completion examinations. In addition, the significant changes that have been made in the baccalauréat since the 1960s, together with the implications of those changes for schooling and employment, heighten the significance of France in the realm of examinations.

The French educational system is probably even more centralized than Japan's. Control by the national Ministry of Education insures that for each school subject, the baccalauréat examination is uniform in timing, content, and structure across the entire nation, as well as in France's remaining overseas dependencies.[4] However, what used to be a single baccalauréat examination and credential has over time diversified into more than thirty lines, all built on a strong base of academic study in the humanities, mathematics, and the natural sciences, and providing a moderate degree of specialization, especially in the final year of secondary education. The diversification of the baccalauréat has been a powerful instrument for widening the curriculum of French secondary schools, and for undermining the privileged position of the academic *lycées*, which formerly enjoyed a monopoly in preparation for the baccalauréat.

In contrast to the Japanese practice, passing the baccalauréat examination confers legal entitlement to university entrance anywhere in France (some restrictions apply in some popular faculties, such as medicine, dentistry, and engineering). In 1986 overcrowding, especially in the University of Paris, and decline in physical and academic conditions of study and standards of work led to government proposals for greater differentiation of standards within and across the universities, and for granting some autonomy in admission decisions to individual institutions of higher education. However, the draft legislation intended to introduce such changes provoked such widespread student protest and political opposition, in the form of mass demonstration on the streets and outside the National Assembly, that the responsible minister was forced to resign and the government withdraw its legislative proposals entirely. These events called seriously into question the government's ability to institute changes in both higher and secondary education.

To some extent the proposed legislation would have merely given formal recognition to changes that have been growing over past decades. The baccalauréat has become less and less an automatic passport to the higher education of one's choice. Instead, there has developed what has been termed a *université à deux vitesses* (a two-speed university). Admission to the ordinary university (the slower track) is still open to all baccalauréat holders. But admission to the fast track institutions is restricted. Approximately 10 percent of the students in French higher education attend the specialized *grandes écoles*, access to which is determined by highly competitive examinations (the *concours*), run separately by some individual grandes écoles, and in groups by others. To prepare for the concours, students are admitted to the preparatory classes attached to lycées, on the basis of their baccalauréat results and their record of school work. Preparation normally lasts for two years. There are several science specialties, leading to a common concours for such grandes écoles as Mines et Ponts and Saint-Cyr, a special examination for entrance into the Veterinary schools, a special literary examination for other groups of grandes écoles, and so on. Successful candidates for entry into one of the most prestigious of the grandes écoles, the *Ecole Nationale d'Administration*, are offered cadet appointments in government service, together with salary while studying, and in return must sign on for ten years service in a specific government appointment on graduation.

While admission to a university in France has become much more open during the past twenty years (the proportion of the age-group in university-type education has quadrupled since 1955, from about 5.5 percent to well above 20 percent), the grandes écoles remain very restricted. Compared to the universities, they enjoy immensely superior facilities and staffing ratios. Graduation from them opens the door to the highest levels of responsibility and reward in government, the professions, and business in France. In addition to the concours for the grandes écoles, there are other highly competitive examinations to regulate access to particular fields of study in the universities (e.g., medicine, pharmacy, and dentistry). For these segments of higher education, in particular, the make-or-break features of the French examination system closely parallel those of Japan.

*Federal Republic of Germany.** The FRG offers a major variant on the basic French model, which has relied so heavily on standardization and control from Paris to maintain academic standards. Instead, the Federal Republic has secured a relatively high and uniform degree of academic quality at the end-point of secondary education, while according a large measure of regional and local control of the examinations.

The credential at the end of upper secondary school (the *Hochschulreife*), or "certificate of readiness for higher education," is commonly known as the *Abitur*, literally "exit credential." Like the French baccalauréat, the Abitur has national currency. It, too, is at once a necessary and sufficient qualification for admission to higher education. However, unlike French practice, the examinations are locally set and administered (by the examination board of the secondary school), though arrangements are subject to criteria established by the provincial Ministry of Education.

There are two types of Hochschulreife/Abitur, "general" and "specialized," plus other certificates that are awarded to those who have completed other secondary school courses that are shorter than the full course at the *Gymnasium*, or academic high school. The general Abitur certificate is acquired through study and examination in the Gymnasium, following thirteen years of education. In the late 1980s, just over 20 percent of the age group was enrolled in the Gymnasium, preparing for the Abitur. A further 10 percent were in other secondary schools, preparing for a vocational/technical form of the examination. As most students who prepare for the examinations pass them, the last few years have seen about 30 percent of the age group receiving their Abitur certificate. The certificate serves both as evidence of completion of academic secondary school, and as an entitlement of entrance to higher education. The specialized certificate is awarded after examination in a more limited number of subjects, and entitles the holder to entry into higher education in the related speciality (e.g., agriculture, engineering, technology, or computing). The specialized Abitur can be converted into a general certificate by sitting a supplementary examination in a second foreign language.

In the past, a holder of the Abitur was entitled to admission to study in virtually any faculty, under any professor. However, the numbers of those achieving the Abitur increased to quite unprecedented and unexpected levels, from a mere 57,000 in 1960 to almost 300,000 by 1986, (of whom some 66,000 received the specialized certificate which did not even exist in 1960).[5] In consequence, a progressive erosion of this entitlement has occurred in the last fifteen years. Many institutions and faculties now impose limitations on entry (the so-called *numerus clausus*) into some oversubscribed fields, such as medicine and dentistry. As part of these changes, a measure of performance during the course of secondary school is added to examination results, to arrive at the applicant's total score. In addition, the percentages achieved in the Abitur examination, rather than the simple fact of passing, have become important for obtaining entrance to the popular faculties and institutions.

Changes have taken place in the structure of German education that could scarcely have been foreseen in the 1960s. The Gymnasium has become differentiated, and is no longer restricted to the single model based on classical languages. Enrollments in these academic high schools, and in the scarcely less academic *Realschulen*, have burgeoned. Between 1965 and the late 1970s and early 1980s, the number enrolled in the Gymnasium jumped from 860,000 to about 2,000,000; in the Realschulen from 600,000 to 1,350,000. During the 1980s the absolute numbers have fallen off, as the size of the age-group has declined, but the proportion of the age-group attending either Gymnasium or *Realschule* has kept increasing. This, in turn, has had implications for the Abitur, which is no longer considered exclusively as a ticket to higher education. Instead, a growing fraction of Abitur holders (now reaching about 10 percent) are choosing to enter the "dual system" of apprenticeship training. For Germany, this is an astonishing development, showing that the function of even the most firmly entrenched examination credential can change in the face of severe social pressures, in this instance rising unemployment among those with solely academic education.[6]

*Union of Soviet Socialist Republics.*** The Soviet Union combines features of the German, French, and Japanese approaches to high school completion examinations. A substantial degree of local administration of the examination provides the parallel with the FRG; as in France, there is a strong framework of central directives; and, as in Japan, applicants for higher education admission must compete in a second-stage entrance examination specially arranged by individual institutions. Thus, the high school completion certificate in the Soviet Union is a necessary, but not a sufficient condition for admission. Indeed, relatively few applicants will be accepted into full-time higher education; most will have to be content with part-time or correspondence study.[7]

Each of the fifteen Union republics exercises formal control over its schools, although in practice there is considerable uniformity of educational structure, content, and procedures across the entire USSR. A de facto national curriculum with a strongly academic bias has been established, with only minor variations to take care of republic and local differences (mainly of language). Moreover, the curriculum offers very few elective subjects and, within subjects, very little discretion over the material to be studied. However, despite this high level of uniformity, there is no central school examination authority, and no secondary school completion examination at the level of either the Union or the republics.

As in the Federal Republic of Germany, each school examines its own students for graduation, even continuing the older German tradition of oral examinations. The candidate appears before a small board of examiners, and chooses from among a number of face-down question cards. A little time is then allowed for the candidate to prepare an appropriate answer which he/she is then invited to present orally. Supplementary questions may then be posed by the examiners.[8]

Secondary school completion is certified by the award of the "certificate of maturity" *(attestat zrelosti)*, based upon satisfactory completion of courses during the previous two (now three) years of senior secondary school and satisfactory performance at the oral examinations. The quality of the attestat is an important datum for admission to higher education, but is not the only factor considered: letters of recommendation as to character, community service, and political reliability are also taken into account. But most important of all are the applicant's results in each university's or higher technical institute's entrance examination.[9]

In general, the Soviet authorities have made only cautious changes in their secondary school structure and curricula, and in the regulations governing admission to higher education and other education/training opportunities. An exception was provided by Khrushchev, who enthusiastically supported the introduction of labor training in the secondary academic schools, and set a work experience requirement for admission into higher education. These innovations were quickly abandoned on his downfall, although the labor training requirement is now being reintroduced, characteristically quite cautiously under the Gorbachev regime. Underlining the slow pace of change in the Soviet educational system, the regulations and procedures for high school graduation, especially the emphasis on the cumulative grade record in the courses taken in high school, have remained unchanged, as has the necessity to sit for a particular higher education institution's entrance examinations. The Soviet system thus provides an example of exceptional stability of examination structures, content, and credentials, in a society that has also been constricted by a powerful ideology and a strong state apparatus.

The Soviet Union has carried over into a socialist society many of the goals and methods of earlier nonsocialist European systems of academic secondary education, with the important exception that it has sought to make access to complete secondary education universal across the entire nation. As a consequence, the numbers receiving the *attestat zrelosti* have far outstripped the capacity of Soviet higher education to accommodate them. Competition for admission has elevated the significance of the university examinations, and this has reinforced the already strong academic emphasis in the Soviet school curriculum. It has also led to the creation of a large network of postsecondary, non-higher education institutions, to accommodate those who could not gain a coveted place in higher education.

Over and above these questions of educational structure and articulation is the much larger question of the dynamics of a society in which the state and the Party have for decades sought to maintain tight control on public information, attitudes, and action, while the population at large has been endowed with ever increasing amounts of secondary education and the credentials that go with it. Gorbachev's slogan, *glasnost*, and the ferment of opinion and political activity in the Soviet Union and Eastern Europe is some evidence that the tradition of state and Party monopoly on information cannot for ever withstand the critiques of a better educated and more credentialled citizenry.

England and Wales. England presents a set of secondary school completion examinations and higher education admission procedures quite unlike those of other Western European countries. In England and Wales, the college or even the academic department chooses the students it wants, on the basis of criteria it sets for itself. If this is familiar to the American observer, it is quite different from Western European practice, where it is the student who chooses the university to attend and the faculty in which to study.

The customary examinations taken in England and Wales toward the end of secondary schooling provide a credential that is neither legally necessary nor formally sufficient for entrance into higher education. Until recently, in practice, a candidate with the "correct" choice of subjects and a good set of scores could expect to find a college place. This is no longer so, since the Thatcher government took the quite unprecedented step (for Britain) of setting an upper limit to the number of places that can be offered. The imposition of an across-the-board numerus clausus has transformed what was a largely noncompetitive set of examinations into an implicitly competitive one.

Consistent with the British tradition of decentralized education, about a dozen regional authorities have provided the examinations normally taken by students toward the end of secondary schooling. Beginning in 1950 and until 1988, the major examination was the General Certificate of Education (GCE). The GCE Ordinary Level examinations were normally taken at age fifteen or sixteen, in four to eight subjects, and were intended to certify completion of a standard, academic, five-year general secondary education. The GCE Advanced

Level examinations were taken after an additional two years of specialized study, either in the humanities, the natural sciences, or the social sciences and business related subjects.[10] Because college education in England and Wales is typically highly specialized (a student goes to college to read English Literature, or German, or History, etc.), there has been great pressure to offer a combination of A-Level subjects that is closely related to the desired course of study at college. Most candidates offer not more than three Advanced Level subjects, and the results have been very important, though not decisive, in determining university admission.

In the early 1970s an additional examination, the Certificate of Secondary Education, was introduced. It was designed for students leaving comprehensive secondary schools at age sixteen, and was much less dominated by university entrance interests than the GCE. The CSE was developed as part of the mounting effort to reduce inequalities of esteem among different types of secondary schooling and categories of students. The new examination introduced two innovations: local authorities and teachers' groups could develop question papers based on their own syllabi, and marks for course work were included in the final examination grade. However, since 1978, a reformed national system has been promoted under the title, General Certificate of Secondary Education. It is designed to integrate the older, predominantly academic university entrance examination (GCE) with the more general purpose examination (CSE). While the GCSE will be administered through regional boards, and will continue to be strongly influenced by university interests and the teaching profession, it was the central government's Department of Education and Science that took the initiative in instituting the new arrangements. The examination may include locally (school) determined components, but the Department of Education and Science has moved to reduce sharply the number of examining authorities, and to take more power to determine the structure of the examinations, and the levels of grading. The intent is to have a single major examining system for all students. Candidates will be awarded passes at different levels, and papers in different subjects can be taken over a period of years, with a student accumulating a series of passes at different levels in different subjects. Thus, the newly instituted GCSE examination is to cover the widest possible student population, and be intended to serve all three common functions of secondary school examinations: as a diploma of completion; as a device to assist employers in hiring decisions; and as a guide to institutions of postsecondary education in their admission decisions.[11] The first administration of the new examination took place in 1988, to many complaints that not enough time had been provided to prepare the new curricula and that grading standards had not been established fairly. These early problems seem to have diminished.

The examination system that has developed to satisfy the university entrance requirements has led secondary school students into exceptionally early and intense subject-specialization. The British are quite divided about this feature of their upper secondary schooling. The persistence of GCE A-Level examinations, despite reform efforts, suggests that a majority still judges the high level of specialization in Sixth Form (grades twelve and thirteen) to be a most positive feature, leaving only a minority to deplore the fact that English youngsters can (and typically do) abandon the sciences and mathematics, or the humanities, or the social sciences by age sixteen, to concentrate on their Sixth Form studies. England and Wales thus provide an example of an examination system that has made little or no effort at the upper secondary level to insure some equivalent of the French *culture générale*, or the German, *allgemeine Bildung*, let alone the Soviet polytechnical ideal.

Sweden. A preoccupation with fairness and equity in access to higher education led to a gradual change in Swedish government policy with regard to secondary school examinations. In considerable contrast to the FRG and France, Sweden today relies on a nationally provided, but locally administered, system of regular assessment of individual student achievement. Sweden has abandoned the *studentexamen*, once equivalent to the Abitur and the baccalauréat. In the 1950s, as part of its larger goal of secondary school reform, the Swedish government began to introduce exceptions to the traditional practice of university selection by examination results alone. By 1972 the new system was in place. Since that time, no school leaving examinations has been required, only certification that a given program of study has been satisfactorily completed. However, locally administered assessment of achievement on the basis of tests sent out from the Swedish National Board of Education is mandatory in the final years of secondary school. The system is not without its problems. Minimizing variation in grading standards from one high school to another requires a good deal of interschool consultation, and there is a complicated system for weighting some school subjects more than others in computing a final grade point average.[12]

Sweden has gone further than the other nations we have considered in being willing to tailor curricula to suit individual choices, and to relate them to employment. It now possesses a highly differentiated upper (post-compulsory) secondary school system, from grade ten on. Many of the twenty-seven tracks defined as alternative programs of study at the upper secondary school level are avowedly vocational. All, in theory, are of equal status and, with regular testing, lead to equal rights to enter higher education and further training. In practice, a hierarchy of prestige and opportunity continues to exist.[13] However, Sweden's decision to abolish the final examination and replace it with in-school assessments has noticeably attenuated the importance of simply achieving success in leaving examinations in determining future study opportunities.[14]

The People's Republic of China. China is the birthplace of the first and most influential of all examination systems, by means of which individuals were selected for high officer and public responsibility. Instituted in 909 A.D., the Imperial Examination System was retained through successive regimes until the overthrow of the Qing Dynasty in 1909.[15] Advancement to postsecondary education continued to depend upon examinations in subsequent decades, but the very idea of this unique, highly centralized, nationwide procedure was rejected after the Cultural Revolution, which in fact closed down the universities entirely between 1966 and 1971. While admission tests continued to exist, acceptance into higher education was determined largely by class background, work experience, and recommendations concerning political reliability. Academic examinations were rejected both as a symbol of traditional oppression and a powerful means of maintaining social differentiation.[16]

However, in its recent moves to improve educational efficiency and quality, the Chinese government has reintroduced examinations as a means of rationalizing the distribution of scarce resources. Examinations at the end of the nine-year compulsory period of schooling now determine entrance to the various forms of upper secondary education: general academic schools, 'key' schools (designated for selected, superior students and receiving superior resources), and vocational/technical schools. A subsequent examination at the end of upper secondary school determines university entrance. Standards of passing are very much influenced by availability of places, and quotas are related to overall plans for institutional and economic development.[17]

Control of the systems for testing and admission to various types/levels of schooling differs. The central government's Ministry of Labor and Personnel prepares a nationwide entrance examination for the skilled worker schools (though authorities in the major cities of Beijing, Shanghai, and Tientsin prepare their own). The national State Education Commission prepares an examination for prospective students of technical schools and the universities. However, this is administered by the provincial Higher Education Bureaus which in turn assign candidates to schools based on their scores and specialties, and the places available. Entrance examinations for the various forms of upper secondary schooling are prepared by the provincial education bureaus and administered on a city-wide basis.

Examinations were reinstated in China to help deal with the nation's labor market and educational deficiencies, especially the low overall quality of the teacher cadre, severe shortages of high level personnel in many sectors of society, and constraints on opportunities for advanced education. Deficiencies of personnel and facilities have led to great pressures on selection devices, and the problematics of selection are further complicated by ideological considerations, which place emphasis on political correctness. Nevertheless, examinations are regarded as essential tools of technological, commercial, and educational modernization. Their reinstatement marks an important victory for those who place efficiency and academic quality above the rhetoric of egalitarianism.

United States. The United States has no official, national system of examinations at the point of graduation from high school. Regulation of the requirements for graduation is largely in the hands of the education authorities of the fifty states, and difference among the states in their minimum requirements can be quite substantial. Only a few states (notably New York and California) provide statewide achievement tests to validate the award of a high school graduation certificate. Moreover, as many states control their local school districts quite loosely, there are important variations in standards and requirements within states, as well as among them. For most young people, the high school diploma is awarded after satisfactory completion of a required number of courses, distributed in accordance with state regulations, and with no public examination necessary to validate the grades awarded during high school.

What the United States lacks in terms of official national examinations is in part balanced by the development of a system of tests that are essentially privately organized, developed, and administered, and are designed to assess achievement in school subjects toward the end of secondary school, as well as aptitude for college-level studies. Two organizations dominate in providing these tests, the Educational Testing Service (which provides the Scholastic Aptitude Test (SAT), "regular" Achievement Tests and "Advanced Placement" Tests in individual school subjects), and the American College Testing Program (which provides the American College Test, or ACT). Most, though not all, colleges and universities ask applicants to supplement the record of their high school work with the results of a test of scholastic aptitude, administered by one or other of these private testing agencies.

In conformity with so much of the within-school examining and testing in the United States, these aptitude and achievement tests are predominantly multiple-choice and machine-scorable. (The Advanced Placement Tests are a notable exception, but less than 5 percent of all high school graduates take these tests.) This contrasts with the more traditional format for the examinations: a German, French or Soviet student will spend most of the examination time writing out lengthy prose answers, or detailing each step of a mathematical proof or computation. These requirements send a strong signal to teachers and students that the ability to provide answers framed in a connected, literate manner is very important.

Criticism of the U.S. practice of multiple-choice testing has not been lacking.[18] The tests have come under increasing criticism for their alleged undesirable effects on what and how teachers teach, on student learning, thinking, and their ability to write acceptable prose, and for the message they convey to students about the nature of academic skills and knowledge. The criticisms appear to be having some effect. The American College Test now advertises itself as more than an aptitude test: and the Educational Testing Service is reported to be working on an extensive revamping of the SAT. This will entail two major changes: moving the SAT away from its claim that it is primarily a test of "aptitude" for college level work, toward being a more explicitly achievement test; and introducing more items requiring extended prose responses, in place of the checking-off of alternative answer boxes that the present format permits and indeed requires.

The contrast with the more formally organized and nationally regulated systems described above is striking, especially the reliance on nonofficial, private agencies to provide nationwide reference points for college admissions officers. The U.S. approach both reflects and reinforces its bias toward a highly decentralized school system.[19] For this reason, although many reports on reform of secondary schools have recommended the strengthening of examinations, in the hope that this will raise the achievement levels of high school graduates, state action to impose examination requirements along the lines of Western European countries is nowhere in sight.[20]

Conclusion. Viewed in cross-national perspective, secondary school completion examinations share a largely common set of functions, but they differ substantially in their modes of control, clientele, and implications. Examinations can be set by national or regional, governmental or nongovernmental authorities, involving participation by quite different sets of interest groups. They may be uniform across the country, or vary by region, and even by school or higher education institution. The examination system can be concerned largely or exclusively with promotion to more advanced academic study, but it can be used also for regulating entry into various opportunities for work in business and industry.

The credential gained may be both necessary and sufficient in order to proceed to further education (as in France and Germany). It may be a necessary, but not sufficient, condition (as in Japan, China, and the Soviet Union). It may be neither legally necessary, nor sufficient (as in England). It may be conventionally necessary, but sufficient only for entry into some higher education institutions (especially the state colleges and universities), but not for others (as in the United States, where the high school diploma can be acquired in most school districts without formal final examination). Finally, a nation may abolish entirely the formal final examination for the secondary school completion credential, and award it on the basis of satisfactory performance on tests and course work done during the last few years of school (as in Sweden).

Rising enrollments at upper secondary school levels have had a powerful effect on examinations. In the space of thirty years or so, the percentage of the relevant age group completing upper secondary education has more than doubled in virtually all the countries we have studied. As the number of candidates for the end-of-school examinations has increased, pressures to diversify the examination have become difficult to resist. In France, the baccalauréat used to offer little choice of subjects and levels of difficulty; the examination now has a long menu of alternatives; to a somewhat lesser extent, Germany has followed the same route. The Soviet Union continues to hold out against such diversification, though political changes may lead to substantial differentiation in what until now has been a remarkably undifferentiated system of examinations.

Another aspect of the changes overtaking examinations is change in the way achievement is assessed. In the PRC multiple-choice questions are increasingly being used, while in the United States alternatives too such convenient, yet suspect, techniques are under serious consideration. Most importantly, reliance on the one-shot, one-style examination is coming more and more into question, whether for validating graduation from high school, or for determining university entrance. The quality and range of schoolwork are heavily weighted as part of the final score in Germany, and also in England in some subjects. In Europe, in particular, attention is being given to replacing examination results with profiles of achievement. These would combine records of achievement and activities in school and out-of-school, based on tests, examinations, self-reports, and portfolios of work.

It is also important to note that examinations may prove to be obstacles in the way of changes in education in one country, while being used as levers of change in another. Thus, although the JFSAT appears to remain a very strong impediment to relaxing the pressures placed on Japanese schoolchildren, in England the government has placed great store on the power of a new set of examinations to shift curriculum emphases toward a national pattern and to raise levels of academic achievement in general.

Last, pressures to change national examination systems come not only from within the school system, but from outside. Prospective employers, government paymasters, parents, and the public at large express their views about what the schools should "produce" in order to serve better the civic and economic needs of the nation. In addition, important questions of equity, fairness, and relevance of examinations are perennial topics of debate (and even litigation), helping to shape changes in examination systems. While there is little evidence that the nations under study are moving towards congruence in their examination practices, it is clear that in many instances they are moving away sharply from past forms and practices.

Chapter 13

A Cross-National Study of Teachers

This chapter is presented as one example of a study in comparative education based upon certain deliberately chosen principles.[1] No claim is made for the exclusive superiority of these principles, which must nevertheless be identified at the outset. Even a cursory examination of work undertaken under the generous banner of comparative education will reveal the width of choices of style and method available to the student and the writer. Some authors elect to write one-country studies and abstain from considerations of a comparative order.[2] Others more adventurously seek for supranational rules or underlying general principles: what interests them is always the generalizable rather than the specific.[3] Others, with equal legitimacy, exploit the insights furnished by comparative education in order to identify precisely that which is specific to a culture, and to show how that specificity in educational practice is related to the politics, history, and context of that same society.[4]

This study belongs to this last tradition and addresses one tightly focused theme. Two questions are posed: How are teachers perceived, in terms of their status and role? How are those perceptions changing, and for what reasons? The enquiry is limited to two societies, the United States on the one hand and England (with Wales) on the other, on the grounds that close and specific comparison will elicit not so much general rules as a sharper sense of what determines such perceptions in the two countries.[5] In that sense, the study chooses to be contrastive rather than comparative. It is, in other words, cross-national rather than supranational. Other important studies of teachers have instead chosen to search for the general rules and to embody them in overarching principles.[6] But this enquiry, to which a third country will be added at a later date, lies in the tradition of comparative education as an exercise in the interpretation of culture, as that term is understood by Clifford Geertz:

> The concept of culture I espouse . . . is essentially a semiotic one. Believing with Max Weber that man is an animal suspended in webs of significance he himself has spun, I take culture to be those webs, and the analysis of it to be therefore not an experimental science in search of a law but an interpretive one in search of meaning.[7]

It is especially appropriate to address this particular question in the 1990s. In both countries, albeit in revealingly different ways, such themes as the quality, preparation, motivation and role of the teacher are at the heart of the so-called reform movements and relate directly to questions bearing upon the relationship of schooling to social purpose, political authority and economic survival. An added importance is therefore given to the public perceptions of teachers. A common, and not wholly discredited, method of locating perceptions of the role and status of the teacher in any given society is to apply the test of "professionalism." Is teaching, within the country in question, acknowledged as a professional activity? What does that word mean within that society? Are some groups of teachers viewed as members of a professional class, and others not? Do the categories of the minor profession and semi-profession illuminate these and similar questions? How do the criteria of professionalism refer to the structures and procedures of education and training, and in particular to the mainstream of higher education? Does the answer to the key question, and to those derived from it, change over time and if so then in what ways and at what speed? These are not trivial questions, and addressing them as preliminaries to a more subtle series may be useful. Their usefulness is nevertheless limited, and becoming more so. The growing diversification and specialization of high status activities within developed societies is eroding the traditional concept of professionalism. Nothing very precise or impressive is represented by the public insistence that airline pilots should be professionals (rather than enthusiastic amateurs) or by the corporate insistence of advertising agents that they should be regarded as professionals (rather than unlicensed charlatans). Relatively few of the traditional criteria apply in such cases as these. Accompanying this loosening of traditional definitions of professionalism (erudition, autonomy, public service) is an enlarging and probably healthy disenchantment with the tendency of professional groups within society to employ the techniques of mystification in order to claim power, wealth, or freedom from public accountability.[8]

Some serviceable generalizations can, however, be derived even from a cursory application of the criteria of professionalism to teachers in both the United States and the United Kingdom. It is certainly not difficult to parade the reasons which would generate, in both countries, a negative response to the question: Is teaching a profession?

In both countries the reasons for the negative response are intuitive but, given that the issue is one of public perceptions, not for that reason any less powerful. In the United States there are over two million teachers, and only about half a million doctors: the number of doctors in the United States is comparable with the number of teachers in the United Kingdom, whereas the population is some five times greater. In the past, professions have defined themselves in terms of membership in an elite minority; that claim is tenable for teachers in no developed society. Equally widespread is the general sense that—however varied and numerous the qualifications and exceptions—members of a profession are expected to receive fees rather than salaries or, even more obviously, wages.

The symbol and reality of the fee is important in that it identifies and honors the relationship between the parties to a contract. Members of a profession relate to a client rather than to a customer or an undifferentiated mass of persons entitled to some publicly provided service, and their overriding duty is to protect and promote the best interests of that client. But who, for most teachers in most schools, is that client? There is a wonderful confusion of competitors, both in the United States and in the United Kingdom: the parent or parents, the community, the School Board, the local Education Authority, the national government, or even in reified form society itself or the economy. Any identification of the student himself or herself as the client is uncomfortable, since it seems to impose upon the teacher a professional duty to promote the interests of that student, if necessary at the expense of others competing for attention or resources.[9]

These factors—the size of the relevant work force, the fee-relationship, the tight link of that relationship to client status—are unlikely to be fundamentally modified in either the United States or the United Kingdom.[10] The bid by teachers for recognition as professionals is rooted in powerful aspirations to improve their status and to dignify the tasks which they perform. The consideration of other relevant factors—rules for admission to the ranks of teachers, formal licensing, the control of standards—leads to a similar conclusion. These are matters over which control has not been, and in no conceivable future will be, handed over to teachers.

There is, then, a dispiriting sameness in the answers proffered on either side of the Atlantic to well-rehearsed questions about whether or not teaching is or could be a profession. The similarity of the answers emphasizes the characteristics common to perceptions of teaching in the United States and the United Kingdom and from it may be derived a transnational rule: teaching cannot be perceived in those countries as a profession insofar as it incorporates a large and unwieldy occupational group, is not client-based, enjoys little corporate autonomy, and so on. There are, however, some important characteristics—much less frequently discussed—which elicit differences of perception in the two nations. Five of them are identified below. An analysis of these characteristics dissolves the crude homogeneity of public perceptions, and also demonstrates that significant contemporary changes can be observed when the two societies are compared. The differences between the two countries taken together with the movement within each of them provides an exemplary natural laboratory within which to test more subtle hypotheses.

The five characteristics are labelled as Nationality, Stratification, Syndicalism, Autonomy, and Unity.

NATIONALITY

The questions at issue here turn upon the extent to which the teaching force in a society (for the moment, the United States and the United Kingdom is perceived as being national in character, rather than regional or local. The secondary, but important, question relates to the speed at which and the direction in which such a perception is currently being modified (the dynamic element in this analysis). On a number of counts the United States earns a low rating with regard to this first characteristic of Nationality. It is, for example, a source of some legitimate pride to the fifty states that each of them controls standards of admission to licensed teacher status, and to the sixteen hundred local school boards that each of them is the employer of teachers and prescribes their conditions of service. Superannuation and other benefits are rarely transferable from one district to another, even within one state.[11]

The contrast with the United Kingdom is striking. Since the end of the First World War, salary scales and conditions of service have been settled nationally.[12] The Secretary of State for Education and Science determines the conditions under which status as a qualified teacher may be given or withdrawn and controls the mechanisms for giving effect to such policies. Teachers move freely, within the general limitations of job opportunities, from one employer to another.

So much is obvious. In each case, however, there is at present an important shift of perception: and in each case that shift is "upward" on the Nationality characteristic. Within the United States, the states have become more active in setting the rules within which the school districts must operate: the setting of minima for teachers" salaries is an obvious example. More recently and at a national (albeit not a federal) level an authoritative report from the Carnegie Corporation has stressed the importance of establishing national standards validated by a national examination for certification: an emphasis which is specifically linked to the systematic pursuit of professional status.[13] A National Board for Professional Teaching Standards has now been established.

At the same time within the United Kingdom a high score on the characteristic here being discussed is being driven even higher by well coordinated efforts by the Government in London. After painfully long and unsuccessful negotiations the Secretary of State intervened decisively to introduce nation-wide conditions of service for teachers. The Government had already published the criteria to be satisfied by programs—of teacher education and created body to ensure that those criteria are duly respected.[14] By the Education Reform Act of 1988 the same Government has introduced a national curriculum defining the limits within which teachers must teach and a national program for the testing of students to ensure that the required standards are achieved by those teachers.[15]

The virtues or vices of such policies are not here under discussion. Their only relevance is to illuminate the differences in perceptions of teachers between the two countries and more particularly the ways in which such perceptions are being changed. The conclusion at this point is that with regard to Nationality the United States has a low score and the United Kingdom a high one, but that in both countries there is a marked movement upwards on this particular scale.

STRATIFICATION

An interestingly different conclusion emerges from a review of the second characteristic, which relates to the importance for teachers of formal and informal hierarchies. For this characteristic the United States score is again low. There is little differentiation of a formal kind among teachers within a school: the principal is regarded not as superior teacher but as an administrator, salary scales are not designed to reflect or reward differences of responsibility within a largely bureaucratized work force, the only way upwards for a teacher is outwards from teaching itself into other branches of the so-called education professions.[16]

In the United Kingdom, on the other hand and especially in secondary schools, a high degree of stratification has developed and is faithfully mirrored in salary scales and related payments. School principals, whatever they may be called, see themselves and are generally styled as "Head Teachers" and would generally resent being classified as administrators. Departments within a school are strong and their heads formally designated and given considerable responsibility for the management of other teachers.[17]

In each country, however, the readings for this second characteristic (Stratification) can be shown to be changing. In the United States there has been a wide but by no means universal movement towards such concepts and practices as merit pay and the career ladder (certainly a significant metaphor in this context). Two influential reports published in the mid-1980s stressed the desirability of making firm and indeed hierarchical distinctions among teachers, based upon differing levels of responsibility, expertise and qualifications.[18] Here the movement is therefore up this particular scale.

In the United Kingdom a good deal of smoke still lies over the battlefield.

The whole issue of Stratification and its relationship to salaries is contentious, with some protagonists asserting the need for greater differentiation and others praising the virtues of a relatively uniform structure with a "main professional grade" of salaries for teachers. Whatever the outcome of these lively and continuing debates, it is at least clear that there will be movement on this particular scale, and that its direction and pace will be closely related to the rhetoric of professionalism and to the realities of political and trade union power. One powerful cross-current may indeed push the system away from nationally agreed salary scales with all that they imply—thereby driving down the United Kingdom reading on the Nationality characteristic. Indeed, movements of emphasis within several of the characteristics will prove to be closely linked.

SYNDICALISM

There is often, within groups enjoying or aspiring to professional status and rewards, a profound conflict between the use of trade union tactics to achieve immediate goals and the rejection of such methods and styles as inappropriate to the dignity of a respected group within society. The more threatening to life or welfare such action is and the more vulnerable (the sick or the young) those who must suffer from it, the more inappropriate such action becomes. Such tensions raise important questions about the analysis of the behavior of organized groups of teachers.[19]

Readings for this characteristic assessed for the early 1960s would have been low in both the United States and the United Kingdom. In the United States strikes by teachers were in many places formally outlawed and collective bargaining unheard of, while the National Education Association, in particular, behaved in a gentlemanly or ladylike manner and covered a wide range of potentially divergent interests, including those of the administrators or managers within the school system.[20] There was a strong parallelism in the United Kingdom, where the polite consensus of the 1950s had not yet been broken by the bitter salary disputes that arose a few years later.[21] Strikes were, for most teachers as for the public at large, rejected as unsuitable behavior for a group claiming professional status. There had indeed been heroic action of this kind in the past, but it was important only in the folk-memory of teachers and not as a guide to policy in the modern world.

A simple description of these circumstances evokes a sense of the rapidity of change since the early 1960s: in both countries the movement has been up the scale for this third characteristic. Collective bargaining has become in the United States the commonplace procedure and is now technically illegal in only two of the states, whereas strikes of greater or lesser severity are taken for granted among the predictable hazards of life.[22] The world of teaching was permanently changed by the events in New York in the 1960s. In the United

Kingdom the contrasts over time are even more salient, if only because of the high score in that country under characteristic one. Action by teachers' unions is usually nationwide and for that reason highly visible and certain to generate public attention and concern. The precedents for trade union type activity were set in the later 1960s, and conflict between teachers, their employers and the Government in London achieved new levels of recrimination in the period between 1985 and 1987.

AUTONOMY

Trade union type activity of the kind which is now common among teachers in the United States and the United Kingdom is generally perceived as conflicting with the traditional claim of a professional group to be trusted always to set first the interests of the client or patient and to eschew actions calculated to damage those interests. Some would, of course, argue that all such claims are in fact rhetorical (and often employed to consolidate the power or monetary advantage of the organized group), and that trade union tactics may in any case be necessary as a short-term means to achieve the long-term goals represented by professional status.

However that may be, a quarter of a century ago—and the links with characteristic three are as obvious as they are important—the United Kingdom readings for the Autonomy characteristic were dramatically different from those in the United States. In Britain the score was high, even if it turns out on examination to be higher in perceptions than in reality. The centrally orthodox view then was that teachers, like other professionals in this respect, knew best and should be entrusted with educational decisions—on the choice of curriculum, text books, teaching methods, internal school organization, methods of discipline.[23] This prevailing orthodoxy was about to acquire a novel form with the foundation in 1963 of the Schools Council, a body which for most of its uneasy life canonized the notion that teachers should be in charge of the curriculum, as doctors saw themselves as being in charge of medicine.[24] This development did, however, represent a subtle shift from the belief that teachers (individually) should have that control towards the doctrine that the teachers (collectively) should be so empowered. This mutation was caused, in my view, by the corresponding rise in the United Kingdom score for characteristic three and contributed in its turn to the rise in the score for characteristic one.

At the same period, the United States score for Autonomy as a characteristic of teachers and of perceptions of them was very low. The schools belonged not to the teachers (an excusable exaggeration of the United Kingdom perception) but to the community—a perception tidily linked to the low score on characteristic one. Teachers were therefore accountable to that community through administrators acting as managers. Nor is it clear that this perception has been fundamentally modified. The model is unashamedly industrial with an emphasis, going back at least to the beginning of this century, upon efficiency and control and the limited delegation of carefully specified tasks. This important and historic characteristic has been particularly well analyzed in the literature.[25]

So much for the (static) perceptions of the early 1960s. For the United Kingdom, the shift in these perceptions (the dynamic in this analysis) has been dramatic and unambiguous. Consider only some of the indices of that change. The Schools Council, the epitome of syndicalism-autonomy, has been abolished as part of an effort to establish a national curriculum, defined for and not by teachers.[26] Two successive and very different Governments have made clear their discontent with the performance of the educational system and in particular with the unacceptably wide range of diversity within it. The machinery for negotiating teachers' salaries has broken down under considerable strain, and the Secretary of State for Education and Science has felt himself obliged to use his powers to prescribe a settlement and to associate with it novel arrangements for the appraisal of teachers—a clear sign of the application of the classical US view of teachers as functionaries within a system, or even in some exaggerated forms as workers within a factory. It is not a coincidence that this sharp fall in the United Kingdom score for characteristic four is associated with equally clear rises for three and for one.

Comparably clear conclusions do not emerge from a study of the United States case, where the reactions are more confused and contradictory. On the one hand, it can be argued from much of the evidence that the score is falling even lower. Many of the policy initiatives within the so-called educational reform movement of recent years emphasize the desirability of exercising even greater control over teachers, subjecting them to tests of basic competency, motivating them by the inducements of merit pay, requiring them to work longer hours, specifying their duties in greater detail, measuring their performance by recording and evaluating the test results of their students, and so on. This is probably the prevailing tendency, and obviously suggests a declining score for the characteristic being discussed in this section.[27]

Running contrary to this prevailing tendency is evidence of disenchantment with the top-down model clearly implied by that tendency. It may be better to describe this countervailing evidence as one theme in the literature of educational reform, rather than to search for a set of observable changes in the operation of the system itself. The 1986 reports of the Carnegie task force and of the Holmes Group at least gestured towards the hope that teachers (or, more precisely, the genuine professionals among them) will be allowed a great deal more autonomy within a reconstructed framework of teaching as a high-level activity. In such proposals, and particularly in the Carnegie version, there is a marked stress upon accountability for the attainment of agreed goals as a necessary restraint upon such autonomy.

Arthur E. Wise provided in 1979 a lucid critique of the limitations of educational policies which reinforced models of educational efficiency by incorporating a belief that if schools and teachers were more firmly controlled they would produce better results.[28] More recently Linda McNeil, in an empirical study of great importance exploring the contradictions within the educational reform movement, has succeeded in demonstrating the lowering effects upon teacher attitudes which ensue when collegial styles of decision-making and of action are abruptly supplanted by the prevailing orthodoxies of control.[29] Her work suggests that, in such circumstances, to specify is in effect to limit. Lying behind both these works are the scholarly and imaginative explorations of teachers and teaching by Dan Lortie and Philip Jackson.[30] Arguments for greater freedom and flexibility for teachers might also be supported by attempts to redefine good management techniques. Some recent studies suggest that, even within the world of business itself, older versions of how to improve performance and manage large systems are themselves coming under attack.[31] At some point the powerful emphasis within the US upon the importance of controlling from above and outside the daily life of schools will collide with a growing conviction, at least among teachers and those who write about them, that if teachers are to perform effectively as professionals in some kind of new order they need to be freed from much of that control.

UNITY

The discussion of this last characteristic of perceptions of teachers, analyzed cross-nationally, will focus upon the extent to which teachers are perceived as belonging to a single and relatively homogeneous group within either of the countries, without regard to the type of school in which those teachers work or to the ages or abilities of those whom they teach. By these criteria and until recently the score for the United Kingdom would be low. The structures of teacher education reflected this, with the Training Colleges (to be renamed as Colleges of Education in the 1960s) producing the teachers for the elementary schools while the universities provided those for the academic secondary schools, whether public or private.[32] This symmetry was, of course, disrupted first by the introduction after the 1944 Education Act of universal secondary schooling and, perhaps even more fundamentally, over the past two decades by the secondary comprehensive school. These developments have softened the distinction between the schoolmaster or mistress who was a graduate and may or may not have received any special training before teaching older and more academic pupils, and the elementary school teacher who attended a college for teachers for two years, taught younger pupils and had no degree.

Although the lines of such a distinction are still quite clear in some other

European countries, they have effectively disappeared in the United Kingdom. It is, nevertheless, still a widely shared prejudice that teachers in secondary school teach subjects while those in primary schools teach children. Such a perception is much less prevalent in the United States. There have for example never been two separate unions or associations for teachers in the two categories of school. Junior high and middle schools occupy an important position at the heart of the system. The American rejection of the selective academic school makes it improbable that a clear line will ever be drawn between two distinct categories of teacher. The score for the United States under this characteristic is therefore high and it is not obvious that there is at present any noticeable movement. In the United Kingdom, on the other hand, the score is low with a tendency to rise over time as a result of the reorganization of secondary schooling, itself reflecting powerful social movements.

CONCLUSIONS

The main purpose of this chapter has been to clarify intranational concepts and perceptions by cross-national analysis. Concentration upon one theme—teachers—enables their place in the national system to be examined across five dimensions. Such an examination clarifies what is distinctive to teaching (and therefore to schooling, education and social patterns) in the two societies under review. It also sharpens awareness of the intentions and effects of the changes now visible within the two systems: again, by contrast rather than comparison. Some at least of these threads may now be drawn together.

The order in which the five characteristics were discussed was, inevitably, arbitrary and therefore concealed some important structural connections. These may now be clarified. In the case of the United Kingdom, a national system of education introduced by successive legislative acts led naturally to the identification of teachers as a national resource to be managed. The Government in London was not (and still is not) their employer but it is the regulator of standards and the main source of resources for teacher training and for schooling itself. But until the 1960s at least that Government did not as a general rule directly concern itself either with the nature of teaching or with the content of the school curriculum. It, like the literate public at large, was content to accept the historical distinction—common throughout Europe—between a popular and elementary education for the masses and a classically academic education for those who could afford to purchase it or who won it in a selective examination. Small wonder, then, that elementary and secondary school teachers were throughout this earlier period perceived as belonging to two culturally distinct groups, differently educated and trained and addressing unrelated sets of professional concerns. Because explicit public expectations of schooling were ill-defined, and against the background of a laissez faire liberal tradition hostile to the formal public prescription of curriculum, teachers were indeed conceded a high degree of autonomy. Neither central nor local government enjoyed a publicly acknowledged right to define what should be taught and how. Such minimal decisions as were necessary on such matters could be arrived at by consensus and the unions, or "associations" as they were more politely described, played an important part in that process. They were co-opted into the establishment and generally eschewed adversarial positions. Entirely consistent with such a set of values and assumptions was the collegial style of much school management. Wide authority was delegated to the Head Teacher who, within a stratified system of teacher organization, was indeed the first and best among the teachers and not an administrative careerist agent of an external authority placed in the school in order to control the teachers. In this way were (to vary the order of presentation in the text of this chapter) the perceptions of Nationality, Uniformity, Autonomy, Syndicalism and Stratification integrated within the British system.

I write "were" because much did indeed change over the period between 1965 and 1990. The extent of such change can again be measured by reference to shifts within the five characteristics, and this dynamic element in the analysis has been at several points important. Even before the Conservative victory in the election of 1979 the static quality of the older system was already under open attack, although it was not until the 1980s that the fundamental nature of the educational and social revolution became clear. Government showed determination to take a firm grip upon national education by regulating rather than centralizing it. A national curriculum, anathema to the Conservatives of previous generations, and national systems of pupil-testing would control the schools, albeit by submitting them to market forces rather than to formal local control. On the contrary, the power of democratically elected local authorities was to be systematically weakened. Teachers had to be trained in order to deliver the national curriculum and, in the traditionally comfortable sense, their autonomy was weakened. Relations with Government, especially central government, were strained as conditions of service and wage settlements were imposed, and unions became aggressive. The growth of comprehensive schools, and the repeated challenges to the relevance and utility of a pure academic curriculum, eroded the distinction between primary/elementary on the one hand and secondary on the other—as did the emphasis upon continuity across all stages of the national curriculum. In such ways were the rising scores for the characteristics of Nationality, Syndicalism and Unity systemically linked with a corresponding decline for Autonomy.

What of the United States, in terms of the network of perceptions of the five characteristics? One of the most powerful American educational traditions relates to the common school. In marked contrast to developments in the United Kingdom and elsewhere, the high school developed as an outgrowth of the elementary school. The colonial example of the Latin School did not become the national model for the secondary school; in the United Kingdom the medieval precedent of the grammar school and the nineteenth century ideal of the independent boarding school did become such a model.

Nationally, therefore, the high school came to be regarded (and correctly so) as the property in every sense of the local community and of its school board, rather than as a colony planted by the university. A community which owned such a school would of course require of those who staffed it that they should reflect the character and ambitions of the community, and teachers would be hired in order to work towards those ends. Their autonomy would be limited, they would be perceived as a local rather than as a national resource, they would not be expected or even allowed to unionize, they would not be encouraged to form quasi-professional hierarchies among teachers within the school, they would not be divided in the public mind into one group (elementary) which extended the functions of the family and another (secondary) which imported the purposes of an external academic community. With the growth of big city systems and a parallel emphasis upon the importance of efficiency narrowly defined, such powerful ideas were given a new but entirely predictable force. The role of the principal and that of the superintendent (a profoundly significant term) was distanced from that of the teacher, teachers themselves were bureaucratized, measurement and testing became the appropriate methods of evaluation and control.

Within the American System therefore, in its own classical form, a high score attributed to Unity is ineluctably connected with relatively low readings on all four other characteristics: popular systems of education, locally controlled, are unlikely to favor the growth of strong national systems, or of powerful and respected unions (which in any case often depend on strong central government for their own authority), or of professional styles of autonomy for teachers, or of stratified responsibilities among those teachers. Of course, the American system is no more static than is the British even if the latter, for good or ill, can be given a stronger coordinated impulse. Current reform efforts in the United States do however at least aspire towards securing a greater autonomy or empowerment for teachers, as well as a clearer nationwide identity for them and a more elaborate grading of responsibilities in their ranks. It is unhelpful to speak of educational reform as though it were some kind of disembodied international movement. But a cross-national perspective, focusing as in these pages upon the distinctive and the integrated relationships among apparently discrete characteristics, may be illuminating. It at least suggests that, in the American case, the tightly linked perceptions with which this chapter has been concerned will be shifted with difficulty, if at all. For that reason alone, it may prove as hard to modify perceptions of the teacher in the United States as it is already proving to promote the growth of decentralization in France.

Chapter 14

Education Reform in Britain and the United States

Education reform was the leitmotiv of education policy in both Britain and the United States in the 1980s. With the benefit of a decade's hindsight, there is a remarkable similarity in the ways in which educational policy issues were addressed in both countries. The language used, too, was also very similar, with the notion of education reform as a commitment to excellence and academic standards uppermost in the debates. Both Britain and the United States had witnessed the ascendance of right-wing administrations by the beginning of the 1980s, coming to power on the basis of their commitment to solve each nation's current economic problems. Schools, indeed, were scapegoated for the perceived economic ills and education became a major focus of the debates. In this paper I shall compare and contrast the ways in which the Thatcher and Reagan administrations introduced education reforms and ponder the likely impact of these changes in education policy in the 1990s.

ORIGINS OF THE EDUCATIONAL RIGHT

The origins of the movement to the right in both Britain and the United States are to be found in the politics and policies of the 1960s and 1970s. It has been argued by many political and social commentators that there was a political consensus in advanced capitalist societies on the need for some measures of social and educational provision and support to industry to sustain economic growth after the Second World War. Mishra has claimed that in both Britain

215

and the United States a "bipartisan political consensus" prevailed consistent with a liberal or social democratic political ideology.[1] There were political disagreements between the major political parties about the means of ensuring a healthy mixed economy but Left and Right alike agreed that state intervention was necessary to ensure the smooth running of the economy.

This political consensus reached its apotheosis in the 1960s first in the United States, followed later in Great Britain. In the United States, the policy achievements associated with this were named by President Johnson as the Great Society legislation and the War on Poverty. Education policy was key, with a commitment to the principle of equality of educational opportunity through the expansion of early childhood education, compensatory education, and financial equity programs in schools and higher education. Indeed, in announcing this panoply of legislation, Johnson stated: "The answer for all our national problems comes to a single word. That word is 'education'."[2] Johnson and his administration focused on using education to reduce differences between individuals on the basis of their family and socioeconomic circumstances, to achieve economic opportunity and "get poverty out of the people."

In Britain in the 1960s, there was a similar commitment to the role of the welfare state as a means of stimulating economic growth. Indeed, many of the policies to expand educational and, socioeconomic opportunities were borrowed directly from the United States—in particular, dealing with social and economic disadvantage through compensatory education, early childhood education policies to direct resources to disadvantaged areas, and comprehensive secondary education.[3]

The extension of educational and economic opportunities aimed at reducing differences in socioeconomic background came under criticism from right-wing political groups in the late 1960s and early 1970s. Conservative dissent had always existed in the 1960s. Its rallying cry was "excellence in education" and it upheld standards, placing them in opposition to equality of opportunity.

In Britain, right-wing academics and political commentators voiced these concerns in a series of pamphlets, they called "the Black Papers" (which gave a hint of possible British officialdom given that statutory publications are called White or Green papers). Five different pamphlets were published between 1969 and 1977, all dedicated to the same themes of "more means worse" and "the egalitarian threat."[4] In the 1975 pamphlet, a ten point set of "Black Paper Basics" was produced which included these four points:

> If the non-competitive ethos of progressive education is allowed to dominate our schools, we shall produce a generation unable to maintain our standards of living when opposed by fierce rivalry from overseas competitors.

It is the quality of teachers which matters, rather than their numbers or their equipment. We have sacrificed quality for numbers, and the result has been a lowering of standards. We need high-quality, higher-paid teachers in the classroom, not as counselors or administrators.

Schools are for schooling, not social engineering.

You can have equality or equality of opportunity; you cannot have both. Equality will mean the holding back (or the new deprivation) of the brighter children.[5]

These criticisms remained marginal right-wing political concerns in the 1970s. They had relatively little influence on the development of British social and educational policies, despite the fact that between 1970 and 1974 there was a Conservative government in power, with Mr. Heath the prime minister and Mrs. Thatcher his Secretary of State for Education. However, the government remained committed to equality of educational opportunity as a means of maintaining economic growth. Mrs. Thatcher was the author of a government White Paper in late 1972 entitled "Education: A Framework for Expansion" which proposed, inter alia, nursery education for a majority of preschool children. A clear program was developed which set 1980 as the target date for providing nursery education for three and four year old children. It also emphasized social mixing to achieve equal opportunities.

The international oil crisis of 1974 put an end to many of these plans. The Heath government fell as a result of serious economic mismanagement. It was replaced by a Labour government which came to power with a slender majority. Although the Labor Party remained committed to the expansion of equal opportunities through education, programs to advance such goals became more difficult to achieve given recurring economic crises. In 1976, Mr. Callaghan replaced Harold Wilson as Labour's prime minister and immediately focused on education policy. By the mid-1970s, right-wing pressure groups had grown in strength and number, and were beginning to influence the parameters of the political debate. Three years later, Stuart Hall, an academic, claimed in a paper entitled "The Great Moving Right Show" that "the Tories had gained territory without taking power."[6]

"The great debate on education" was launched by Callaghan in 1977 specifically to consider how to restructure the educational process so that it tied education and training more clearly to the needs of industry and economy.[7] Expanding educational opportunities was no longer seen as consonant with economic growth. The Labor government focused on ensuring that parents played a role in this process of restructuring, arguing that there was a clear parallel between parental and state needs. Callaghan prefaced his introduction to the debate with the comments: "What a wise parent would wish for their children, so the *state* must wish for its children."[8]

The "Great Debate on Education" was narrowly drawn. The Labor government's commitment to equal opportunities was ignored. "The question of racism was not confronted," nor was that of sexism.[9] The outcome of the debate was an official government Green paper, which was a prelude to legislation. "Gone were the references to any egalitarian ambitions for schooling,"[10] and the Green paper focused on how children should be prepared for work through schools and other forms of training in further education or "on the job." The paper also proposed a common core curriculum for all schools to consist of three basic subjects, to be taught, throughout schooling, to all children, namely English, Math, and Science with Technology. These proposals were not implemented. However, they did provide the starting point for subsequent right-wing debates about education.

By the end of the 1970s British educational policy was no longer officially debated in terms of its ability to aid in the process of, and achieve, equal opportunities. This occurred despite the creation of two quasi-nongovernmental bodies charged with monitoring those processes for minority ethnic groups and on the grounds of sex. These two bodies were the Commission for Racial Equality (CRE) created in 1976 and the Equal Opportunities Commission (EOC) created in 1975. They covered equal educational opportunities, requiring special quasi-judicial processes in both cases.[11] Yet the two Commissions never influenced the educational debate, except to the extent that a special governmental inquiry was set up to investigate the education of West Indian children in the late 1970s. The scene was set for a rightward move as education was increasingly blamed for the economic ills of the nation. The increasingly influential right-wing arguments were that children were not educated with the skills and habits necessary for the "world of work" and that the education system was too distant from the needs of the economy.

A similar process had occurred in the United States over the same time period. When President Nixon came to power in 1968, it had been assumed that this signalled a move to the right. However, during Nixon's period of office social programs, including education, continued to expand. As in Britain, there were plans to extend early childhood education through the Comprehensive Child Development Act. However, Nixon vetoed this plan, seeing it as committing the vast moral authority of the nation to socialism. He favoured instead a Family Assistance Plan aimed at giving a basic minimum income to families. Although his measure was never fully implemented, it was seen as "Nixon's Good Deed."[12]

Under President Carter, spending on social programs still continued to rise and plans to expand both education and training continued apace. The Comprehensive Employment and Training Act of 1976, for example, opened up a range of new training initiatives. The Education of All Handicapped Children Act of 1975, attempted to ensure equal opportunity to handicapped children.[13] A number of measures were enacted to reduce inequalities in educational opportunities for racial minorities and women.

In the 1970s, the American right-wing was becoming vocal. The right was critical of increased social spending and its impact on the state budgets. It also opposed educational expenditures designed to achieve some measure of educational equity. The right furthermore, from moral and religious stand points, questioned the content of schooling in terms of the kinds of subjects taught and books use. While these criticisms were expressed both by individuals and by groups on the right, there was no one single set of right-wing educational programs. Religious groups, such as the Moral Majority, had one set of educational agendas, while neo-Conservatives who focused less on the content of educational programs and more on limited social spending had different concerns. Still other groups emphasized declining academic standards and perceived growing 'mediocrity'.[14]

THE RIGHT EDUCATION IN THE 1980s

By the end of the 1970s, the New Right and/or neo-Conservatives were in the ascendance in both the United States and Britain. They blamed state social and educational policies for causing their country's serious economic decline. Thatcher (in May 1979) and Reagan (in November 1980) obtained political office through a critique of social democratic policies, particularly those relating to education. Both pursued similar themes in articulating their agendas for educational and social reform despite differences in contexts. By the end of the 1980s, both administrations had come to similar points in the transformation of their nation's respective education systems. They abandoned a commitment to equal opportunities and instead emphasized consumer choice and academic standards. I shall first examine the process of change in each country separately.

The Educational Right in Britain

In Britain, Mrs. Thatcher came to power in May 1979 with a new rightwing platform. Her aim was to reverse Britain's economic decline with new monetarist economic policies and reduced social intervention. Educational policies which aimed at equal opportunities were seen as part of the problem. However, the first Thatcher administration did not focus its energies on education reform directly, rather it dealt with education by stealth.[15] Thatcher focused on reducing spending on education through various local fiscal controls and the reform of local government expenditure.

Three major pieces of educational legislation, all fairly limited in their scope, were enacted. The first, passed in 1979, reversed the central government requirement that local education authorities (LEAs) reorganize their secondary schools on comprehensive lines. By 1979, however, most LEAs had reorganized their secondary schools and were loath to undo what had been a costly and difficult process of educational change. The 1979 Education Act did reintroduce some selective education in a few areas.

The 1980 Education Act, which was the second piece of education legislation, borrowed extensively from the Labor government's policies and proposals.[16] The major aim of the legislation was to make schools more open and accountable to the public, particularly parents. The legislation required schools and LEAs to make public both their "planned admission levels" or entry numbers and their educational strategies and results annually. Parents were given more rights both to complain about procedures on an individual basis through a national ombudsman and to be involved, through parental representation, on school governing bodies. Parental governors came to be one of four types of governor in the first level of school management. However, the role of school governing bodies remained quite limited, and were not a strong influence in the process of education decision-making.

The 1980 Education Act, like its successor in 1981, did not dwell on curricular issues; rather it was concerned with educational rights and relationships. The 1981 Act required all LEAs first to produce a statement of need for the parents of each child with special educational needs and second to attempt to integrate all such "handicapped" children into mainstream educational provision. Here it was essentially concerned with the dual issues of parental rights and limited educational expenditures.

Two other measures implemented during this first Thatcher administration signalled the shape of things to come.[17] The first was concerned with the redirection of educational expenditure across different types of schools, and the second, the control of these expenditures in higher education. In 1981, the government announced a modest diversion of public expenditure from state schools to individual children of academic ability who passed a selective test to an independent private secondary school. If the child's parents were of low income, the state would pay the school's fees. This reintroduced a form of selective academic education. In the past, a small number of schools participated in a similar scheme. This Assisted Places Scheme widened the range and number of private independent schools which were eligible to participate. It also provided an additional indirect subsidy to the private schools, apart from their charitable tax status. Since 1981, the scheme has grown and blossomed.[18]

In higher education, as in state schools policy, the central government's initial policy was to provide fiscal and other measures of central control over institutional spending. The government required individual higher education institutions to reduce or curb spending within clear national financial limits.

Economies in funding were achieved largely by means of rigorous selective criteria, in terms of both disciplines or subjects and students. The conditions of change were, therefore, largely negative.[19]

The second plank of the Conservative program, launched after Mrs. Thatcher's reelection in May 1983, was the definite attempt to transform the welfare state by putting in place the idea of a market for social and education provision, with consumer choice its chief selling point.[20] Thatcher aimed at enabling consumers to demand higher educational or academic standards. Such ideas were presaged in the Conservative manifesto for the election where the then Secretary of State for Education Sir Keith Joseph argued for "the pursuit of excellence." The focus was on developing quality rather than equality in schools through schemes which attempted to differentiate between teachers and between pupils. For instance, proposals for merit pay for teachers were mooted and new forms of assessment, through pupil profiles and records of achievement, were initiated. These, and changes in the system of examination to a composite examination at age sixteen were intended not only to placate parents as consumers but also industrialists and employers, as were the introduction of new technical and vocational courses and qualifications.

Although attempts were made to transform school curricula, these were not easily implemented because of the financial stringencies applied to schools at the same time. Thus teachers were continuously involved in action over their pay and conditions for a two year period. During this time, the government also tried, through legislation, to set limits to school curricular debates and to alter the decision-making processes.

The 1986 Education Act signalled the beginnings of the new, more coherent approach to school reform. It set limits to the kinds of subjects taught in schools, such as political and peace studies, aspects of multi-culturalism and sex education. Attempts were made to distinguish between education and indoctrination on lines similar to those set out by a new group of right-wing pamphleteers.[21] Parents were given rights to withdraw their children if they did not approve the school's approach to sex education which was not taught according to the traditional family centered approach. Parents were also afforded a more significant role in the running of schools, through revision to the system of governing bodies. The 1986 Act gave parents a majority vote and required the publication of annual reports from schools and the holding of a school annual general meeting on business lines.

In 1988 the Thatcherite project in education came to full fruition in the form of one comprehensive piece of legislation called the Education Reform Act (ERA). The Act was unique in the history of British educational legislation both in the sense that it covered both schools and higher education and that it allowed for education institutions to be removed from state financial control with impunity.[22]

The ERA gave school governing bodies the power to ballot parents to decide whether or not they wanted to remove their school from the local education authority (LEA) system and become directly financed by a grant from central government. (The "grant," in the long run, however, would be recovered from the LEA, on the same criteria as the LEAs' other schools.) LEA financial management of all higher education formerly under LEA control ended and these institutions became financially independent, bidding for resources from the central government. Key to the legislation was the financial autonomy of each educational institution. Schools that chose not to opt out of LEA control also had to assume more financial responsibility. A new system of local management of schools was introduced whereby school budgets were set by the LEA but controlled by the school's governing body. Each LEA was itself to be more controlled by external forces, through parallel moves to alter the funding of local government through the poll tax. A new set of education institutions called City Technology Colleges, financed by business in partnership with government and aimed at enhancing technical and vocational skills, were introduced.[23] At the time of writing, this scheme has not yet attracted the funds from industry predicted for it, and the majority of funding has come from a single patron of the arts. Educational institutions were afforded the freedom to raise funds and control their expenditures within clear financial parameters, the aim being to ensure that consumer demand would determine the schools' styles of spending.

A second key feature of the Education Reform Act was the designation of specific "standards" for schools and the development of a national curriculum. The Act specified assessment tasks or targets as well as forms of age-related testing. Since the Second World War, there had been no agreed set of subjects to be taught to school children, except those enjoined by external examinations. The Education Reform Act has required ten compulsory subjects, including the three core disciplines of Math, English, and Science, and seven foundation subjects, namely a modern foreign language (not required in primary schools), technology, history, geography, art, music, and physical education. Precisely what would be covered was to be determined by a National Curriculum Council, working groups in the key subject areas, a School Examination and Assessment Council, and specific task groups on assessment and testing.

The aim was for schools to spend about 80 percent of their time on state-mandated subjects, with almost half of all school time devoted to the three core subjects. Schools also would be required to continue teaching religious education. Attainment targets were to developed for seven, eleven, fourteen and sixteen year olds and a system of nationally prescribed assessment tests were to be established.

The subjects specified in the National Curriculum represented a very traditional view of education. This could be imputed even by the concept of "national," with standards related to a traditional academic curriculum.

The traditional approach was further elaborated through specification of the kinds of modern languages considered appropriate, namely French, German, Spanish, and Italian. European and non-European languages spoken by Britain's minority ethnic groups are noticeably absent. Bilingual education was encouraged only for Welsh speakers. In a 1985 Government sponsored inquiry into multi-cultural education, eventually published after lengthy controversy, bilingual education and the teaching of and in the languages of Asian minorities were rejected as "linguistically impoverishing."[24] The intention of the government, in the National Curriculum, was to inculcate a specifically British set of standards, related to an academic curriculum, judged relevant to more able children. No concessions were made to children from family circumstances where such quintessentially British experiences had been unknown before the experience of schooling. Rather, all children were expected to adapt to a specifically British form of education, valuing only traditional English subjects and knowledge, rather than appreciating the diversity and richness of the varied cultures of British citizens. The 'British' approach was further implied by explicit legislation to ensure that religious education, and daily religious assembly, including the daily act of worship, were specifically Christian, which was seen as the main religion of the country.

By the end of the 1980s, the education system of England and Wales had been reformed so that it bore only slight resemblance to that created after the Second World War. The Thatcherite reforms had set in place educational institutions competing with each other for both finances and students. They required that the subjects taught in all schools be the same and conform to national curriculum with its nationalistic emphasis. In all other respects, schools are likely to develop differently dependent upon their clientele, their abilities and susceptibilities. Indeed, some LEAs have already begun to develop magnet schools, focusing on particular subjects within the required National Curriculum in order to build up particular competences, such as skills in science and technology. Within the schools, too, the variations in the levels achieved in relation to the age specific attainment targets is likely to vary, dependent upon children's prior backgrounds and knowledge. Selection on the basis of merit has been encouraged, support for disabilities and educational disadvantages discouraged. As a result, there is already clear evidence of diversity in the supply and morale of qualified teachers to provide this kind of selective education. In some places, there are simply no qualified teachers and uncertified people are now being positively encouraged to become involved in the classroom. The transformations in all levels of education have taken their toll on teacher supply.

Education Reform in the United States

In the United States, the same themes of education reform were pursued as in Britain. Indeed, it could be argued that Britain followed rather than led the

United States. Historically speaking, however, some of the US reforms occurred at a later stage. Indeed, the complexities of the American political system, interwoven with the legal system, meant that national educational reforms were initially harder to achieve. Federal involvement in education had been part of the liberal programs of the 1960s and the Federal Department of Health, Education, and Welfare had been given power to provide fiscal equity in educational provision among the individual states and between school districts. One of Reagan's first aims was to reduce such a federal role and to abolish the federal department of education. These goals were not easily achieved and the federal role has continued. It has shifted to fanning public disquiet about the future of the nation's schools, especially the secondary schools and their curricula.[25]

The Reagan administration, like Thatcher's government, supplemented massive cuts in public expenditure and used those cuts to try to reorient the school system. "These cuts were particularly difficult, since many programs mandated by the federal government had to be maintained regardless of federal funding."[26] Federal legislation also continued to require many recent developments as in Britain, such as "the mainstreaming of handicapped students," by integrating them into regular classrooms with other students.

Reagan's Education Secretary appointed a National Commission made up of America's corporate as well as educational elite to inquire into the question of "Excellence in Education." Its report, published in 1983, was followed by a spate of other reports from different agencies, a few research-based studies and wide public debate and discussion. Altogether about a dozen major reports were produced all with different approaches but essentially arguing for changes in schools and, given the notion that "the nation [was] at risk," a back to basics approach.[27] As Altbach noted:

> There is unison on the need to improve standards, stress science and ensure that students are 'computer literate'. In general, there is a concern for the role of education in equipping America for participation in a cut-throat global economic war.[28]

In addition, there were recommendations, as in Britain, for foreign-language instruction, relating the school curriculum to the perceived needs of industry, and the improvement of the quality of teachers through merit pay. Such was the range of recommendations from these diverse but primarily business sources that it too was named a "great education debate." But as Kelly has noted the main theme was to shift responsibility from government, at any level (federal, state, or local), to parents, business, and the local community.[29]

In other words, the role of government and the courts in ensuring some measure of social justice and quality of educational opportunity for minorities, women and handicapped people had been reduced and reoriented. The reports themselves produced a spate of responses. One conservative writer argued, in support of the report's recommendations, that the fifty state legislatures should take an easier path to reform, unleashing the resources and power of citizens, teachers, and principals, to rebuild a diverse and locally rooted set of public schools. This would be the only means to provide quality education to children, through the American "glorious experiment in self-governance."[30]

Indeed, these 'conservative' arguments about a reduced federal role—despite the counter-arguments also raised by the right, for a curriculum to reflect the needs of modern industry and technology to improve America's competitive edge—won out by the mid-1980s. Margaret Goertz, summarizing the education politics of the 1980s, has argued that during the Reagan years, the federal government influenced education policy with moral suasion rather than federal aid, emphasized demonstration over intervention; and decentralized the administration of federal programs. The abandonment of education by the federal government created a *leadership* as well as a financial vacuum so that the 1980s reform was dominated by business leaders and elected public officials.[31] She went on to note that "the absence of a broad consensus about the purpose of education led to a *patchwork* of state education programs to meet the demands of different and competing interests."[32] She also noted that it was "unique" in the politics of state education that education interest groups played a "relatively unimportant role . . . in the formulation of new state policies."

In any event, President Reagan and his Secretary of Education, Terrance Bell, began, in the second administration, in 1985, to argue "strongly in favor of business support of education to compensate for federal spending cuts particularly in the areas of vocational and adult education."[33] Ray and Mickelson went on to add that by 1987, more than three hundred business-initiated studies about the quality and content of education had been completed.[33] The process was one of government reducing its role to be replaced by business leaders.

The process of educational reform in the United States was somewhat different from that in Britain. Given the evidence and ideas underpinning the voluminous national reports in the early to mid-1980s, the approach was one of continuing to reduce the federal role, rather than to use central government, as in Britain, to command that reduction. It therefore is not surprising that little federal (as opposed to a plethora of state) legislation, contrary to Britain, was attendant upon the spate of recommendations.

Indeed, the approach of the moral right in the United States in the early 1980s may have been an object lesson for the neo-conservatives and the corporate and business elites.[35] There were two relatively unsuccessful attempts to reorient aspects of the school curriculum through the Family Protection Act in the early 1980s. This Act was described by the *Congressional Quarterly* as a "tidy wish list for the New Right."[36] It attempted to control the content of school textbooks in terms of their portrayal of sex roles and the nature of sex education provided. The moral right also attempted to introduce school prayer and religious education into hitherto secular schools. These issues were dealt with only cursorily by the federal government. The Family Protection Act also provided for tuition tax credits for private schools (which was subsequently taken up in a number of states). Nevertheless, the legislation did not provide the new framework initially hoped for it. The dominant approach in the United States became that of fiscal restraint and moral persuasion rather than federal legal edict. This process has been followed through by President Bush. His first budget included new initiatives in education costing some $450 million, of which the majority of the funds were earmarked for awards to excellent schools, alternative systems of certification for educational personnel, educational tax credits for low income families, the Drug Free Schools and Communities Act, the Youth Entering Service program, and magnet schools (with a special admonition that funds not be used to foster desegregation). The new programs emphasized institutional and individual competition to de-emphasize the monopoly of the public schools, for example, magnet schools, excellent schools, tax credits, alternative certification routes. Bush, in other words, has continued the educational stance of the Reagan administration structurally, substantively, and affectively.[37]

By the end of the 1980s, decentralization, devolution to the states, and the reduction in the federal role appeared to have been relatively well achieved.

PROSPECTS FOR THE 1990s: A NEW ERA?

In both Britain and the United States, by the end of the 1980s, the process of educational reform seems to have been accomplished, although by very different means. In Britain, the central government has played a key role in attempts to diversify and decentralize the school system, to such an extent that there no longer appears to be anything that could be graced with the term "system." In the United States, decentralization to states and school districts and to schools themselves has occurred through drastic reductions in the federal government's role in education. Moreover, in the United States, the recommendations for a national school curriculum have not been implemented by federal legislation—rather individual schools (private or public, parent, or religious) have been encouraged to foster their own initiatives and developments. This is in marked contrast to Britain where the main emphasis has been on the detailed specification of a national curriculum not only for state schools, but also for private, independent schools. The national curriculum may in the 1990s end up by being the specification of minima rather than what was initially intended as the raising of academic standards and stemming "weaknesses in the education system." This may be because of the effects of other government legislation on local government finance and economic and demographic trends. The educational reforms of the 1980s are likely to widen social inequalities.

In the United States, the term "risk" was used for precisely these problems. Clark and Astuto point out that from the National Commission on Excellence in Education on, the right have misdirected the attention of the American people. The researchers claim that the "risk factor" is the poor children in American education who lag behind in school achievement. They provide evidence that such children only have a 50 percent chance of finishing high school. If they do not, they are likely also to be unemployed.[38] The risks of poverty, especially for minority children, have increased at alarming rates in the United States in the 1980s and, given the lack of federal intervention, continue to rise. The Commission on Minority Participation in Education and American Life noted that by the year 2000, 16 percent (21.8 million persons) of the United States labor force would be non-white and *one-third* of all school age children will be minorities. Yet policy analysts and politicians alike have not attended to the potential consequences of these demographic shifts.

Although there are differences in the proportion of minority children in the schools, similar changes are occurring in Britain. Simultaneously, female participation in further and higher education in the 1990s has risen dramatically in the face of growing demand for female participation in the labor force. There are as yet no plans to cope with these likely shifts in the school population and the gender balance in the labor force. The new National Curriculum will not produce equal opportunities, particularly for women or minorities, given the ways in which it was debated and introduced.[39]

Educational policy which aims to increase rather than decrease inequalities in educational and socioeconomic opportunities, and which ignores the consequences of governmental inaction, will only serve to exacerbate rather than contain these risks and compound the "weaknesses" that conservative politicians hoped to address. As Roxanne Bradshaw stated:

> Reduced education spending and the subsequent demise of educational opportunity cannot possibly produce good results. We must understand that research and education are the engines of our society. And without them we will go nowhere. We will only restrain progress, we will restrain prosperity and we will jeopardize our security.[40]

Given current policy trends and demographic developments there will be a recreation of social diversity and a perpetuation of sexual difference in the 1990s: for women, for blacks and other minorities, for the poor and working class. Education policy as currently specified by the right in Britain and the United States will contribute to these trends, unless there is concerted political action to stem the process. Such right-wing education policy will indeed produce a new era, which will be far from committed to equal rights and opportunities. The 1990s will be predicated on individual competition, consumerism, and educational inequalities. The era will witness, at the very least, a bifurcation of society in terms of class, race and gender.

In the United States, however, there are beginnings of a new movement to reverse these trends in favor of the traditional American dream. Many aim for schools to "become truly public spaces and truly democratic institutions" reversing the trends in the 1980s towards private institutions and individual benefit.[41]

There has not, as yet, been a similar glimmering of a new movement to reverse the trends established by the educational legislation Thatcher enacted in Britain. There have been a number of powerful intellectual critiques, which eliminate the trends and mourn their development.[42] Together, they show how the Conservative dream of individuality, competitiveness, and consumerism will create a patchwork of educational institutions in Britain. Chances for a good education will depend on parental socioeconomic circumstances, area of residence, ability to make demands upon individual schools, as well as intellectual ability and the power to be educated. By the mid-1990s, if the Conservative education policies are successfully implemented, there will no longer be a public network of educational institutions teaching to a common academic set of standards, but variety and diversity. These arguments have not yet been voiced so powerfully in Britain and yet they are beginning to be asserted against the previous Conservative dream of individuality, competitiveness, and consumerism.

It is never easy to predict the political consequences of government policy. It may well be that changes in demographic trends and socioeconomic circumstances will prevent the full achievement of Conservative education policy. The new era may well be vitiated. It may be replaced by a concern for equality of opportunity, especially for women and minority ethnic groups. Yet, given the account of the development of Conservative education policy, in both countries, this seems unlikely.

HENRY M. LEVIN

Chapter 15

Effective Schools in Comparative Focus

INTRODUCTION

The terminology of "effective schools" has become very common in education in both the developing and industrialized world. It connotes both the existence of a knowledge base on what makes a school effective and how to implant that knowledge in existing schools to increase their effectiveness. The purpose of this chapter is to survey that knowledge base in the context of the quest for improving school quality and participation and seeking a more efficient use of school resources.

Both industrialized and industrializing countries face a host of common problems in providing sufficient education of high quality. Although the problems may be more severe in the industrializing countries, they are not unique to those countries. Typically, these general challenges break down into matters of participation, costs, and quality. For example, almost all countries in the industrializing world "guarantee" that children of primary age, usually between the ages of about seven through twelve, will be provided with a public education. In the poorest of the developing societies, this goal has not been met and seems to be farther and farther from reach as high birth rates exceed the fiscal and organizational capacity to increase school spaces. Although a high proportion of students begin primary school, relatively few complete it.

In the development decade of the sixties with its great optimism about economic growth, family planning, and educational planning, universal primary education seemed to be around the corner. Instead, much attention during that decade was devoted to the expansion of secondary and tertiary schooling and the directions that those levels of schooling should take. But, in the nineties it is clear that much of Sub-Saharan Africa and parts of Latin America and Asia have not and will not come close to meeting universal primary participation for the foreseeable future. In fact, some of these countries are farther from this goal today than they were a decade ago.

The costs of a modest school program for all primary-age children vastly exceeds the resources that are available in the poorest countries. Even school participation data do not tell the entire story. Expenditures per student are declining, and double and triple shifts of a few hours are becoming the norm in some regions. School years have been shortened, and teachers' salaries have declined so much that fully qualified teachers are often a luxury and teacher turnover and attendance are problematic. Even with low salaries, almost all of the school budgets are spent on personnel, so there is little left for school textbooks and other instructional materials. These situations contribute to a schooling experience of low quality and its attendant problems of low achievement and high rates of grade repetition and dropping out.[1]

Although these extreme conditions are not typical in the industrialized societies, they are characteristic of the education of immigrants and other marginalized populations. For example, in countries like the United States the most rapidly growing enrollments are composed of students in at-risk situations: the poor, racial minorities, immigrants, and those from broken families.[2] These students tend to complete primary school and some secondary school, but they drop out before high school completion. Of course, even minimal high school participation would be a level of educational attainment not even dreamed of in the rural areas of many industrializing countries, but it does not qualify students for most employment in the United States. Further, at-risk students have levels of educational achievement as reflected by test scores that are considerably below the average for other students at similar educational levels.

What do these situations in the industrializing countries and among at-risk populations in the industrialized countries have in common? The first is that they both address children from marginalized and impoverished populations, those who are at the margins of both economic and political power. The children of families of wealth and power are not caught in this situation. Second, the schools do not provide the educational and social mobility that is associated with the popular image of education as a liberating force. School quality is poor and educational expectations are low; resulting in educational achievement that is also low. Finally, the available resources that their societies are able (in the poorer industrializing countries) or willing (in the richer industrialized countries) to apply to education are inadequate to make meaningful changes.

Traditional educational policy in both types of societies has sought out potential improvements at the margins of the educational system rather than its core. Such alterations have generally been piecemeal, leaving intact the infrastructure of institutions that are failing to serve the needs of their students. Typical of such policies have been those of improving teacher training and retraining, more and better instructional materials, reductions in class size, and the use of educational technologies such as television and computers. While the intent behind such efforts is well-meaning, the record of success is meager for such incremental changes.

Beginning in the seventies, educational reformers began to argue that schools did not work for these populations because they were simply not designed to meet their needs. That is, the very nature of existing schools must necessarily serve to undereducate, miseducate, and fail students from marginalized populations.[3] The underfunding of these schools was at least as much a symptom of the problem as it was a cause. And, simply providing more resources was not likely to make the substantial change in the character of education that was needed to succeed. Some critics argued that unless the operation of schools was shifted from a "monopolistic" state to a competitive marketplace, it would not be possible to substantially improve matters.[4] Others argued that within the public school system, we could create effective schools. In general, the term effective schools was used to refer to schools that had the same characteristics as ones which had been shown to be successful in research.

This comparative review of effective schools will be devoted primarily to elementary or primary schools. The reason for this limitation is that primary education is considered to be a basic necessity around the world, while secondary education is often considered a luxury. Moreover, if students do not succeed at completing primary school, they will not have access to secondary schools. Finally, most of the studies of effective schools address primary schools rather than secondary ones.

In the next sections I will present examples of effective schools movements as they are found in both industrialized and developing countries. I will differentiate particularly between movements that have arisen from statistical research that has identified a checklist of characteristics of effective schools from those based upon a more holistic approach which grows out of a strong educational philosophy of what is considered to be effective. In the final section, I will summarize some common features of effective school strategies that seem to be promising.

EFFECTIVE SCHOOLS IN THE
UNITED STATES AND UNITED KINGDOM

The notion of creating a different kind of school that would be more effective with children from marginalized or poverty backgrounds can be found in many places. However, the coining of the effective school movement is usually associated with the work of Edmonds and Brookover and Lezotte.[5] These authors raised the question of why there are some—albeit only a few—schools that seem to get good educational results for at-risk or marginalized students. They hypothesized that if they could identify those schools, they could ascertain how they differed from the more typical school educating at-risk children. They could then create school reforms based on effective school practices so that ineffective schools could be transformed into effective ones.

Using test scores as the criteria, they carried out a statistical analysis for schools that were supposed to be serving student populations that were similar in race and socioeconomic status of students. Based upon this analysis they identified statistical outliers that were performing much better and much worse than average. In turn, they studied the two groups of schools to find out how they differed. Although the different researchers came out with slightly different lists of characteristics—and earlier lists were augmented by later authors, the most commonly cited list is that compiled by Edmonds.[6] Edmonds identified the following characteristics of effective schools:

1. strong leadership of the principal;
2. emphasis on mastery of basic skills;
3. a clean and orderly school environment;
4. high teacher expectations of student performance; and
5. frequent assessments of student progress.

Edmonds and his colleagues began to disseminate these results widely at educational conferences, and they were accepted as the basis for educational reform by large numbers of school authorities. The unusually receptive response to the results by educational practitioners seems to be related, in part, to the argument that they were based upon sophisticated statistical inquiry and, in part, to their appeal to common sense. In any event, U.S. schools sought out training in effective school practices. The success of this proliferation is evidenced by the fact that the General Accounting Office of the United States published a report in 1988 that found that 41 percent of the nation's school districts claimed to follow effective schools principles, and another 17 percent reported that they were planning to do so.[7]

What is unique about the effective schools strategy is its emphasis on transformation of the entire school, rather than on a specific aspect of curriculum or instructional strategies, or school organization. More typically school improvement has focused on the adoption of a large number of piece-meal changes which are often unconnected. Thus, a new reading series might be adopted; class size might be reduced; computers might be brought into the classroom; teachers might be retrained in providing mathematics instruction, and so on. But, the effective schools approach argued that research proves that effective schools for at-risk students are different in systematic ways from ineffective ones; and that the core characteristics of effective schools could be imparted to ineffective ones to increase their effectiveness through school-wide transformation rather than piecemeal reform.

As compelling as the effective schools movement has been to educators, researchers found much to criticize in the underlying methodology. The critics analyzed test performance of students and found inconsistent results from grade-to-grade and from year-to-year in terms of which schools were statistical outliers. That is, if the analysis were done in a particular grade and a particular year, a school might be shown to be statistically effective; for another grade or for another year, the same methodology would show the school to be ineffective. Further, the characteristics of effective schools were charged as being excessively vague, particularly when one was trying to replicate them in other schools.[8]

A search for evidence of schools that had improved student achievement by following the recommendations of effective schools research was unable to locate any documented cases based upon acceptable evaluation methods.[9] This absence is rather remarkable when one considers that over half of U.S. school districts had adopted or planned to adopt the approach. However, a recent statistical analysis of schools in one metropolitan area of the United States found that "effective schools" characteristics were modestly associated with higher student achievement.[10] The effective schools variable used in this study incorporated such dimensions as teacher involvement in decisions and parental involvement in schools. Although these particular factors are widely viewed as important to school success, they were not incorporated initially into the effective schools movement. In fact, that movement placed much greater weight on a strong leader who is held accountable for results than the diffusion of that power and accountability through sharing of decisions with other school staff.

United Kingdom Studies

During the same period, a group of British researchers undertook studies of both elementary and secondary schools. The secondary school study was the first to be published.[11] The elementary school study was published almost a decade later.[12] Both studies followed students over time; studied their teachers, classrooms, and schools through direct observation; surveyed teachers, parents, and students; and evaluated the connections between school and home influences and student test scores. They concluded that there are a range of school practices that can elevate the performance of students, regardless of socioeconomic background.

At the secondary level Rutter and his colleagues concluded that effective schools have the following characteristics: (1) group management in the classroom; (2) high expectations and standards; (3) positive teacher models; (4) feedback on performance; (5) consistency of school values; and (6) pupil acceptance of school norms.[13] The elementary school study found the following to be features of effective schools: (1) purposeful leadership of the staff by the headteacher; (2) involvement of the deputy head; (3) involvement of teachers; (4) consistency amongst teachers; (5) structured sessions; (6) intellectually challenging teaching; (7) a work-centered environment; (8) limited focus within sessions; (9) maximum communication between teachers and pupils; (10) record keeping; (11) parental involvement; and (12) positive climate.

Both of the United Kingdom studies asserted that schools with similar student intakes showed very different educational results and that these school characteristics explained the vast differences in effectiveness. However, these studies were not associated with the same type of explosive school effectiveness movement that was witnessed in the United States where there was a concerted attempt to transform schools into those with effective schools characteristics. Accordingly, there are no evaluations of United Kingdom effective schools—schools designed to embody these characteristics on the basis of the research—that I am aware of.

CHECKLISTS OR PHILOSOPHIES

Both the effective schools movements in the United Kingdom and United States were based upon research studies of schools in which statistical models and other techniques were used to ascertain the characteristics of effective schools. These characteristics were used, in turn, as guidelines for transforming ineffective schools into effective ones. The particular characteristics that are viewed as integral to effective schools are ones that are identified through research comparing effective with ineffective schools. But, the question that must be raised is whether effective schools can be replicated by trying to duplicate a relatively short checklist of characteristics.

An alternative perspective is that such characteristics are merely manifestations of a larger underlying philosophy and mode of operation. That is, effective schools are different from ineffective ones not only in these characteristics, but also in the myriad details of their practices which are rooted in an overriding philosophy. Effective school approaches that are based upon particular philosophical perspectives can not be replicated without wholesale changes in the overall ethos, orientation, and operations of schools. This is a more holistic perspective which can not be summarized by a checklist of characteristics. The following three examples represent effective school movements based upon distinct philosophies of what makes for effectiveness.

Yale Child Study Center

One of the earliest of these philosophical approaches to school effectiveness for at-risk students is the one developed by James Comer and his associates at the Yale Child Study Center School Development Program.[14] The Comer team has worked with schools in the city of New Haven, Connecticut since 1968, and in other cities in more recent years. Much of the available information is on the transformation of the King School (a school covering grades kindergarten through fourth). Student enrollments in the King School are predominantly black and from low income families. At fourth grade the students were almost two years behind national norms on standardized tests in 1969.

Comer used a process model in which administrators, parents, teachers, and support staff collaborated to address the problems of the school. A mental health service team was used to provide support to the school in carrying out a comprehensive plan for improving school social climate, academic performance, and staff development. The mental health team consisted of a psychiatrist, social workers, and psychologists. They were especially equipped to relate parental, family, and community needs and practices to school practices in a way which would enhance the academic and social performance of students. Planning was done collaboratively and included the establishment of new instructional programs and curriculum. Parents and teachers had important roles in governing the school and contributing to school decisions, and the overall approach was one of problem-solving rather than finding fault.

The Yale approach assumed:

> . . . that the vast majority of children can acquire the psychological, social, and academic competencies needed to function adequately in and after school when the school environment is adequate. The hypothesis is that as the organization and management system of a school successfully provides all participants in the education process—school staff, parents and students—with adequate educational and interactional skills and support, the academic achievement and social performance of students will improve and provide residual academic, social, and psychological benefits to students.[15]

This collaborative approach, using a mental health team for staff support, showed strong results over time, ones that have been sustained after the intervention team left the school. In 1986 fourth grade students in the King School scored about a year above grade level in the Iowa Test of Basic Skills with a socioeconomic composition similar to that in 1969 when students scored almost two years below grade level.[16] Student attendance went from one of the poorest in the New Haven to one of the best, and staff attendance was among the highest and staff turnover among the lowest in the city.

A follow-up study of graduates of the King School found that among seventh graders who had attended kindergarten to fourth grade at the School, former King students were performing better than a group of otherwise similar "control" students who had attended other schools.[17] For example, former King students showed total language scores at a 7.7 grade level in comparison with control students with a 5.3 grade level. Differences were also pronounced in mathematics and other skill areas.

Accelerated Schools

The accelerated schools movement is also a holistic attempt to transform both the governance and content of schooling to bring at-risk students into the educational mainstream by the end of elementary school.[18] This movement had its origins in a study of schools serving disadvantaged or at-risk students in the United States in the early eighties. That research found that at-risk students started behind other students and got farther behind the educational mainstream the longer that they were in school. And this problem did not appear to stem from a lack of teacher dedication, a charge that had often been made. Paradoxically, it occurred because compensatory programs for the disadvantaged are designed to slow down the instruction of such students, assuming that they are less capable than others. Such students are placed into less demanding instructional settings—either by being pulled-out of their regular classrooms or by adapting the regular classroom to their "needs"—to provide remedial or compensatory educational services. While this approach appears to be both rational and compassionate, it has exactly the opposite consequences.

First, it reduces learning expectations on the parts of both the children and the educators assigned to teach them, and it stigmatizes both groups with a label of inferiority. Second, it slows down the learning process so that at-risk students get farther and farther behind the mainstream, the longer that they are in school. Third, the approach to remediation is to provide repetitive practice of low-level basic exercises through endless drill and practice. This educational experience is empty and joyless because it fails to incorporate a rich curriculum, student involvement and discourse, interesting applications of concepts, active problem solving, and learning activities that build on the strengths of the students and their backgrounds. Finally, this remedial approach does not draw sufficiently upon parental and community resources, nor does it provide for the participation of school-based educators to influence the programs that they must implement.

The study concluded that an effective approach to educating the disadvantaged must be characterized by high expectations, deadlines by which such children will be performing at grade level range, stimulating instructional programs, planning by the educational staff who will offer the program, and the use of all available resources including the parents of the students. The approach should incorporate a comprehensive set of strategies that mutually reinforce each other in creating an organizational push towards raising the achievement of students to grade level.

The Accelerated School is premised on a philosophy that views at-risk students as gifted and talented students who can excel if they are placed in accelerated and enriched educational environments. The schools have a unity of purpose around their focus on acceleration, and both the staff and parents at the school site have responsibility for both decisions and for the consequences of those decisions. School programs are chosen directly by school staff to build on student strengths and to be rich in challenging applications and problem-solving situations. Heavy emphasis is also placed on creating a positive emotional climate for all students.

Since 1987 some forty pilot accelerated elementary schools have been established, most of them in the 1989-90 school year. It is expected to take six years to fully transform a school into an accelerated entity, but early evaluations have shown dramatic results for student achievement, parent participation, and school climate. Although the program takes about six years to fully transform a school from its traditional practices to accelerated ones, the improvements are dramatic even in the first years. For example, in its third year (1989-90) the Daniel Webster School in San Francisco had the largest increase in standardized tests of language and the second largest increase in mathematics among the seventy-two elementary schools in that city. Accelerated schools in Texas, Missouri, and Illinois had the largest improvements in student achievement in their school districts.

Accelerated schools have also reported sizeable increases in parental participation (e.g., 95 percent of parents attending parent conferences with teachers, up from 30 percent some three years before), reductions in grade repetitions, and improvements in attendance. These results are found in schools in which the vast majority of students are at-risk and in which there have been only nominal increases in expenditures—averaging about 1 percent to 2 percent of the budget to support the program.

Coalition of Essential Schools

One other major, philosophically-based movement of effective schools in the United States involves secondary schools, the Coalition of Essential Schools.[19] This movement arose out of a study by Theodore Sizer exploring secondary schools. That study was based upon a large number of case studies of both public and private secondary schools and concluded that much is wrong with secondary education in the United States. Such schools were considered too large to provide a caring and interpersonal environment; too departmentalized and with too many electives to provide an essential common core of integrated learning; and too contrived and controlled to permit active learning by "students as workers."

Although the Coalition of Essential Schools that emerged from this study does not focus on disadvantaged or at-risk youngsters and is devoted to secondary schools, some of its conclusions overlap with those of the other effective schools movements. For example, it is premised on a philosophy of a common academic focus for all students with active teacher and student involvement and a minimum of bureaucratic impediments. In 1989 there were about seventy schools affiliated with this movement, all dedicated to a statement of principles rather than to a checklist of school characteristics based upon statistical research.

EFFECTIVE SCHOOLS IN INDUSTRIALIZING COUNTRIES

Effective schools approaches in the industrializing countries are primarily based upon a philosophical perspective rather than checklists. These strategies are almost never based upon statistical studies of successful versus unsuccessful schools. Rather, they are premised on central themes about what is required to meet the educational needs of their countries or regions within countries. Approaches in the developing societies also have a much greater preoccupation with both resource adequacy and with how to get more from existing resources and to uncover additional resources. In particular, there is a concern with how to create effective schools that are consistent with providing primary school participation for the entire eligible population. The following programs provide concrete examples of this quest.

Impact

Impact stands for Instruction Managed by Parents, Community, and Teachers.[20] It was designed to provide mass primary education that was of relatively high quality and that could be delivered effectively and economically. Although initiated in the Philippines and Indonesia in 1974, similar projects were established in Malaysia, Jamaica, Liberia, and Bangladesh. At the heart of Impact were three major themes: (1) the use of pedagogical strategies that would permit increased student-teacher ratios without sacrifices in quality or with rises in quality; (2) increased involvement of parents and communities in the provision of resources and in instruction; and (3) and the use of teachers with poorer formal qualifications.

It was believed that these three steps could reduce the cost of schooling in order to expand participation. The ability to maintain or improve school quality under these changes was based upon the production of high quality instructional modules consisting of materials and self-instructional units that were supported by instructional radio. Classroom activities were designed to be individual and self-paced with a diminution of the standard age and grade-level divisions. In this respect, it was believed that higher quality materials, curriculum, and educational technology would allow for teachers with lower qualifications while educational quality might even be increased. In this way, the savings from teacher salaries could fund the other improvements.

Each of the six countries had a different experience with its Impact projects, but none succeeded in fulfilling the ambitious plans that had been formulated at the outset. For example, each country's program was designed to have a major impact on introducing the innovations into mainstream schooling, but not a single country succeeded in this transformation. In all cases it appears that resistance to change from traditional educators and the educational bureaucracy was far more powerful than was anticipated. Perhaps the major triumph was in the addition of schools in isolated and sparsely populated rural areas where schooling was of lower quality or nonexistent. In the Philippines and Liberia, the program seems to have had the greatest overall success in demonstrating relatively high achievement, cost-savings potentials, and innovation. Even in these countries, the adoption and implementation were met with great resistance and the movements were limited. In many respects, Impact represents the most important example of a multi-country attempt to establish effective schools within a context of very limited resources. It has important lessons for those who would attempt to establish and implement a national system of effective schools.

Integrated Centers of Public Education

Integrated Centers of Public Education (CIEPs) represent a movement of schools established in the state of Rio de Janeiro and other parts of Brazil in the early eighties to serve economically disadvantaged students at the primary level.[21] The CIEPs were viewed as an alternative to a public school system in which only about one in two Brazilian youngsters even made the transition from the first to the second grade. The CIEPs differed from the conventional public schools in a number of ways.

First, the program encompassed a full day, some ten hours divided equally between instruction and extra-curricular activities. This full day program was designed to be of assistance to working parents as well as providing exposure of students to such subjects as art, music, physical education, dance, and topics. Second, the curriculum of the school was structured around an integrated curriculum in which central topics were used to teach all of the standard subjects in an interrelated and interconnected way. A central focus of the curriculum was the incorporation of the culture, folklore, and traditions of the local community into learning experiences which would integrate all of the school subjects.

Third, the pedagogy emphasized higher order thinking with active learning experiences and extensive dialogue and discussion. Student opinions were given respect by teachers as a way of engaging pupils and building self-esteem. The pedagogical approach also placed a heavy stress on developing close relations with parents and community through parent participation in the school and school participation in community activities.

Teachers were provided with training in a literacy method that was an adaptation for children of the method that Paolo Freire had developed for adults. Teachers worked together in the CIEPs to strengthen and apply the underlying philosophy as a community in contrast to the more individualistic patterns found in traditional schools. This collegial approach extended to the development of lessons and the exchange of ideas on school program. There was a great deal of agreement and solidarity about school goals among school staff.

In the mid-eighties the CIEPs movement suffered a setback because its political supporters were defeated in the elections, changing the educational focus of the government. Thus the development of the CIEP program and its expansion were seriously undermined. However, a political shift in 1988 brought the CIEPs sponsors back into power, with sixty such schools functioning by 1989. Some one-third of these schools were following the original plan. However, the tumultuous political changes have meant that the schools have been characterized by fits and spurts and have not been evaluated for their effectiveness. Such an evaluation is expected to begin shortly.

The New School

Probably the most ambitious undertaking to transform primary schools in rural areas into more effective schools is The New School (La Escuela Nueva) sponsored by the Ministry of Education in Colombia.[22] This program was organized in 1975 as a response to serious and persistent problems that characterized rural schools in Colombia including high dropout rates and repetition rates in the first two years of primary school; low educational attainments; and poor educational quality. The rural schools lacked educational materials, parent and community involvement, a relevant curriculum for rural areas, and inappropriate teaching methods. Even in 1985, only 45 percent of rural first graders made the transition to second grade.

The New School was established in 1975 as an attempt to integrate curricular, community, administrative, financial, and training strategies in an effort to expand primary education to all students and to improve the quality of that education. Its central philosophy is to establish rural schools based upon a system of active instruction, a strong relation between the school and community, and a flexible promotion criterion that could reflect the lifestyles of rural children who are called on to help their parents in agricultural activities.

The program is a highly integrated one based upon four major components of curriculum, training, administration, and community connections. According to the program's founders, the curriculum was designed to promote:

> ... active and reflective learning, the ability to think, analyze, investigate, create, apply knowledge and improve children's self-esteem. It incorporates a flexible promotion system and seeks the development of cooperation, solidarity, civic participation, and democratic attitudes.

These goals are implemented through study guides or self-instructional materials which promote active learning, discussion, group decision making, and the development of applications within the community setting. A core national curriculum is combined with possibilities for regional and local adaptions during teacher training. Each school has learning activity centers in the four curriculum areas (mathematics, natural science, social studies, and language) which contain objects and other manipulatives that can be observed and manipulated to reinforce learning. Local materials and applications are also brought into the learning centers to reinforce local culture and experiences.

Each school has a student government made of committees that are linked to community and school projects. These teach decision skills, responsibility, solidarity, and cooperation and link the school with the family and community. A library of about one hundred volumes including literature and reference materials is provided in each school. The library is organized and maintained by the children and represents a resource for active learning.

The New School is characterized by an extensive teacher training program with follow-up at school sites to assist teachers to apply what they have learned in the training. To a large degree the training exemplifies the activities that teachers will apply in their classrooms. Regional administrators are also provided with training. Initial training is followed by workshops on the use of the study guides and organization of the school library, and reinforced by monthly meetings involving teacher discussion and exchange of ideas. Demonstration schools representing model programs provide opportunities for visits by teachers so that they can see the ideas in practice.

The community component is based upon involving parents and other community members in school activities. Community members are engaged in assisting the school in its activities, and teachers are expected to get to know the community and to use it as a learning resource. An effort is made to see how the school can benefit the community and meet its needs. Cultural elements from the community are incorporated into the curriculum and school activities.

Administrators are trained to carry out the functions of the school and to visit the local school sites with follow-up activities and support. This process of reinforcement is carried out primarily through monthly workshops.

The New School was initiated in 1975 with a pilot program that encompassed about five hundred schools. The program was expanded to some three thousand schools between 1979 and 1986 with both national support and funding from international organizations. During these stages the program was continuously deepened and improved as evaluations provided a basis for new directions. In the latter period, the Interamerican Development Bank and the World Bank provided considerable support.

In 1985 the Colombian government adopted the New School as the strategy for providing universal primary education in rural areas. By 1989, some eight thousand schools had been established with a target of twenty-seven thousand schools by 1992. Evaluations have shown that children in the New School have higher self-esteem and superior test score results in academic subjects than students in traditional rural schools. The estimated incremental costs for the program are estimated at about $82 for each teacher per year of training: $150 for the library; and $15 for the study guides for the four subjects. Since trained teachers can teach for many years, the library has a considerable life, and the study guides last for about four years, the annual incremental cost per student is very modest.

While no formal analysis has been done, the reduction in repetition and dropout rates suggests that the cost per educated student is probably lower under the New School strategy. It appears that the New School represents the most successful example of the application of an effective schools model to expanding primary school participation and quality. Even so, the path has not always been smooth. The implementation and expansion of this type of movement requires constant monitoring, problem solving, and adaptation. The transformation of teacher attitudes and skills to create effectively functioning New Schools is particularly challenging in many rural settings.

Thailand

A number of other examples of effective school applications are worth reviewing. In an important paper, Nicholas Bennett has analyzed examples of such strategies in Thailand, Nepal, and Ghana.[23] Here I will review briefly the Thai project. This project focused on education in the most impoverished areas of Thailand with the highest rates of illiteracy. An integrated strategy was developed to combine adult literacy training with the reform of primary education. Adult literacy training was provided through Freire-like techniques building on learning meaningful words and text and engaging in discussion on content with simple looseleaf materials that were adapted to the regions of the country. Extraordinary literacy gains were made.

Simultaneously, the primary school shifted from a traditional emphasis on teaching abstract "subjects" to the exposure of the child to his or her own world beginning with the child and extending over time to his/her family, school, community, district, and by the end of the fourth grade, the Nation. This focus was intertwined with the study of language, mathematics, hygiene, nutrition, and other subjects that were pertinent. Test scores in Thai and mathematics improved significantly.

Emphasis shifted from textbooks to teacher's guides, supplementary readers, and kits for practical work. A massive training program was established for teachers and administrators to support the new pedagogy and school organization. Although the reform took many years, it was successful in providing a basic education to a majority of rural Thai children. Bennett points out that its success stemmed from an integration of efforts to change both formal and nonformal education (such as adult literacy) in tandem; to push for uniformity and structure as an overall strategy with adequate room for flexibility and differentiation to meet local needs; and to build on local differences in language, culture, religion, and perceived needs of the people.

COMMON FEATURES

It is important to note that virtually all of the versions of and strategies for effective schools that were reviewed here were developed independently to address particular challenges and situations. Accordingly, one would hardly expect them to have identical features. Yet, my interpretation suggests that most share a set of common features. These may provide a basis for considering generic approaches to developing schools that will be more effective within resource stringencies. In this final section I will set out eight dimensions that seem to be common to what I consider to be the most successful of the effective school strategies. These dimensions might be viewed provocatively as a basis for considering the development of effective schools' strategies in other contexts. These conclusions represent a personal interpretation rather than the results of a "scientific" investigation.

Central Philosophy. The most effective schools are characterized by a central philosophy that provides a guiding spirit to the design and implementation of results. The reforms seem to be inspired by a serious and persistent set of educational concerns towards which a profound transformation of schools seems to be the only solution. The philosophy of each effective schools movement is cohesive, overarching, and holistic rather than being a collection of piecemeal and incremental changes. This philosophy is embodied in a movement which has a spiritual and reformist appeal as opposed to the more traditional techno-cratic and mechanical approach to school improvement. This means that an effective schools movement must go beyond a mere checklist to an organic approach that encompasses these features in a natural way rather than mere "add-ons" to existing schools.

Overall Strategy. The overall strategy is to use the central philosophy to design an ideal school and school program. This ideal is used as a basis for a compre-hensively conceived curriculum, training program, materials, administration support, and uniform approach to school change at a macro-level. At the same time, local flexibility, adaptations, and variations are encouraged to meet local needs within the overall program boundaries.

Community Involvement. Community involvement is central to the ideal of the effective school in two ways. First, the community is expected to contribute local resources to the school through the provision of in-kind contributions and voluntary participation in school activities.[24] In addition, families have particular responsibilities to support and reinforce the education of their chil-dren. Second, the school is expected to contribute resources to the community by addressing community needs in its programs and getting students to work on community problems and projects. The community is expected to be an asset to the school and vice versa.

Empowerment. A principal emphasis is placed on empowering teachers, stu-dents, parents, and the community to take responsibility for making educa-tional decisions and for the consequences of those decisions. At the heart of the educational philosophy is the view that a meaningful education requires active participation among all who are involved in the process rather than following a script or formula set out by higher levels. Schools are expected to choreograph their own activities within the framework of the larger effective schools pro-gram.

Active Learning. The emphasis on student learning is to shift from a more tra-ditional, passive approach in which all knowledge is imparted from teachers and textbooks to an active approach in which the student is responsible for learning. Effective schools' approaches emphasize self-instruction, the use of manipulatives and objects around which activities are built, problem solving, and meaningful applications. Active learning also means the application of learning activities to the local context.

Focus. Effective schools tend to delineate the scope of their programs, often focusing on accomplishing well a narrow set of objectives rather than address-ing ineffectively a much larger set of goals. The Coalition for Effective Schools stresses that "less is more." This view is also found in accelerated schools where acceleration often means to cover fewer topics and activities in depth rather than more topics in rapid profusion. The New School is clear about its four curriculum areas. Each of the programs seems to emphasize a clear and manageable focus rather than a proliferation of goals.

Teacher Expectations. Either explicitly or implicitly, each of the approaches is premised on high teacher expectations. The view is that students can succeed if the right conditions and support are provided to ensure their success. This view is embodied in the central philosophies of the programs as well as in the training and curriculum.

Funding and Resources. To a large degree the programs are premised on the view that effective school transformation can be done largely without new infusions of resources with the exception of those resulting from community involvement. While this assumption is not necessarily integral to effective schools, it emanates from the fact that substantial additional resources are not likely to be available. Accordingly, any additional resources must come from the community or from more efficient use of existing resources.[25] For example, Impact was premised on raising student to teacher ratios by increasing self-instruction, low-cost educational technologies, and community participation. A major source of additional resources can be found through the reduction of the high rates of retention. Clearly, if students do not have to repeat grades, those resources can be used to expand enrollments and improve educational quality.

SUMMARY

This review has suggested that the evidence on effective schools' strategies is mixed. There is probably no formula for effective schools that can be reduced to a checklist derived from statistical comparisons of effective and ineffective schools. Certainly, such research—if well-executed—can provide guidelines for informing the development of an effective school strategy. But, the more promising direction is the formation of a highly integrated approach to developing effective schools that are based upon a clear educational philosophy and mission. That central focus is the basis for curriculum, instructional strategies, teacher training, instructional materials, and so on. In general, it should build on the eight principles that were derived from the cases.[26]

Part Five

Assessing the Outcomes of Reforms

Chapter 16

Policy Impact of IEA Research*

We are concerned in this essay with the effects of various International Evaluation of Educational Achievement (IEA) studies. The history of the IEA has been considered elsewhere, as has the substantive analysis of many IEA reports and documents.[1] The association has been one of the most influential research efforts in the history of educational research, and it certainly has done the best-known international research on education. It is, therefore, useful to explore the policy impact of the IEA over the years. It is particularly relevant to consider this topic as a new series of IEA studies is about to be released in a period when there is great concern about educational "standards" and "excellence" in many countries.

TWO CATEGORIES OF "CUSTOMERS": POLICYMAKERS AND PRACTITIONERS

There are two categories of "customers" for IEA research: (1) policymakers, most of them at the national level, and (2) educational practitioners at both the national and "grass-root" (i.e., school and classroom) levels. The two cannot, however, be regarded as clearly distinct from each other. What is policy-relevant research is often closely dependent on a given time and place. The same applies to practice-relevant research. Schwille and Burstein point out that instructional variables "have been growing in policy relevance not because of any enlightenment about their true nature, but because the political climate has turned increasingly critical toward teaching and has challenged educational researchers to provide some remedy."[2] What they mean is that concern about the quality of teaching has emerged in the United States in the wake of criticism of the quality of student performance. This is reflected in the fact that the U.S. researchers participating in the Second International Mathematics Study (SIMS) have paid much more attention to the mathematics curriculum and how the subject is taught than was the case in the first study sixteen years earlier, when the emphasis was on advancing fundamental knowledge about determinants of student achievements and on the standing of American students relative to those in other countries.

Policymakers are on the whole more interested in findings pertaining to the structure of the system of education: what subject areas should be studied, the relative amount of instructional time allotted to them, and, moreover, the evaluation of the system and its schools. Educational practitioners primarily pay attention to teaching-learning problems: classroom practices, instructional methods, teaching materials, and the assessment of individual student progress.

When the first IEA survey was launched, attempts were made by the IEA researchers from (then) twelve countries to accommodate the rather diversified interests of the two major consumer groups within the design of one single investigation. Thus, in reporting the First International Mathematics Study (FIMS) hypotheses and findings were presented under three major headings: (1) problems of school organization (e.g., age of entry, size of class, size of school, selectivity vs. comprehensiveness); (2) problems related to curriculum and methods of instruction (e.g., opportunity to learn, use of inquiry-centered methods); and (3) effect of social factors (e.g., home background, urban-rural environment, amount of homework).[3] In the Six-Subject Survey, the relative importance of various "input" factors for student achievement were studied by means of multivariate analyses, which focused on between-school and between-student differences more than on between-country differences. These analyses were conducted for each country separately, and therefore comprised a series of replications. The hope was that one would thereby arrive at more valid generalizations than by conducting such analyses in one single country only. But a shortcoming of all IEA research up to this point in time was that it was cross-sectional in nature. Student progress during a particular school year could not be linked to what happened to students because of the lack of baseline scores (pretest scores). Furthermore, student scores could not be linked to the particular teacher who taught the actual class but to all teachers in the sampled school.

ATTEMPTS TO BRING OUT POLICY IMPLICATIONS

After the Six-Subject Survey had been completed, IEA as an organization tried to bring out the policy implications of its research. According to the IEA statutes, one major aim is "to promote research aimed at examining educational problems common to many countries and thereby devise evaluative procedures which can provide facts which can be useful in the ultimate improvement of educational systems."[4]

In the wake of the Six-Subject Survey, as mentioned above, most countries prepared national reports in which analyses of policy problems in their own systems were conducted. Several national studies of this kind, such as the one on the effects of the new science curriculum in England or sex differences in science achievement and attitudes, were published in a 1974 special issue of the *Comparative Education Review*.[5]

The Harvard University Graduate School of Education organized a conference in 1973 to present IEA findings and discuss their implications for educational practice and policy.[6] At the 1974 IEA General Assembly meeting held at the Max Planck Institute in Berlin, I presented a paper on the policy implications of the IEA findings and a more complete review of policy ramifications at the IEA General Assembly meeting in Rome in 1977. The Italian minister of education, Franco Malfatti, commented on the effects of the IEA findings in Italy, saying that "an electric shock" had been administered by the IEA.[7]

Until the late 1970s, the IEA only conducted large-scale surveys of student achievement in specific subject areas. This, in part, drew the attention of policymakers and the general public to what has been referred to as the "Olympic Games" aspect of the research. Other aspects, such as the policy implications of variables within countries affecting between-student and between-school differences in achievement, were, as pointed out by Marklund, neglected even though they had been reported.[8] But as the IEA began to investigate other problem areas— such as classroom environment, transition from school to work, and effects of preschool education—other comparative aspects began to be considered.

The IEA findings have on several occasions become major news items, even front-page news. In 1967, when the FIMS was published, press conferences were held in Chicago and London, the latter for the international press. In the United States, the findings were commented on by the major magazines and newspapers, such as *Time* magazine and the *New York Times*. When the printed reports from the first three subject areas in the Six-Subject Survey were available, an international press conference was held in Stockholm. Fred Hechinger of the *New York Times* and Stuart Maclure of the *London Times Educational Supplement* spent a week at the IEA secretariat in order to learn more about the research.

CROSS-NATIONAL AND POLICY-RELEVANT
EDUCATIONAL STATISTICS

In April 1985, the National Center for Educational Statistics (NCES) in the U.S. Department of Education invited university researchers, policymakers and administrators to a conference on international educational statistics held in Washington, D.C. The aim was to obtain suggestions from researchers, policymakers, and others about the substance and format of future studies on international education statistics. Behind this was evidently a heightened interest in finding out what kind of indicators one should try to establish in order to make fruitful cross-national comparisons. Judith Torney-Purta, for example, pointed out the importance of identifying "comparative reference points" for policy decision making. On the whole, since the IEA researchers were the only ones who had experience in collecting empirical and more quantitative cross-national information on student achievement, they could provide the NCES with certain suggestions.

It was pointed out at the NCES conference that participation in a major study in which many schools and researchers in a country are involved is "an intervention in itself"—irrespective of the eventual outcomes of the study—in that it contributes to alerting educators and researchers to problems they have previously not been aware of. It was also suggested that governments build into the IEA surveys tests and questions that they would otherwise administer as part of their own efforts (such as the National Assessment of Educational Progress) to monitor the development of their respective systems.

At the NCES conference, "The U.S.: Lessons in the First and the Second IEA Studies," Alan Purves pointed out that the FIMS, with its demonstration of superior Japanese performance, contributed to the demise of the "new math" in the United States and raised questions about grouping practices in American schools.[9] The first science study put state-developed curriculum guides in question. The reading and literature studies revealed that secondary school students were not performing well on comprehension skills and identified an underclass of bad readers. The civic education studies showed that attitudes could be learned and taught in school but not always the ones intended or expected. The language studies demonstrated a high correlation between time on-task and language acquisition. The opening of educational opportunities to those who had previously been more or less excluded had not inhibited the achievements of more privileged learners.

When the secretary of state in the Dutch Ministry of Education, Gerard Van Leijenhorst, opened the IEA General Assembly meeting in Enschede in 1983, he commended the IEA for the use of modern survey techniques. Such research can help "to answer the question we all ask ourselves from time to time: Can the education we offer our children stand up to the test of criticism, when we compare it to what other countries offer their children?" At the same time, however, he expressed some reservations about the way in which the dissemination of results was undertaken because the IEA has not developed close relationships with relevant national or international public authorities and organizations.

THREE POLICY PERSPECTIVES

Three policy perspectives have been enriched by the empirical evidence produced by the IEA surveys of national systems of education.

Overall Social and Economic Policy

Educational policy could be studied in the context of the overall social and economic policy because of the information collected in the national case studies but also thanks to the background information collected for each student.[10] Certain overriding national objectives emphasized in several OECD countries since the late 1960s, such as equality of educational opportunity and particularly equality of results, are of a social nature. One problem in this context is the extent to which an educational system takes care of socially and culturally handicapped students.

Cross-national comparisons of student achievements and attitudes provide a unique opportunity for disentangling the relative effect of the factors that the child brings to school. These are the social influences at large and home background in particular, on the one hand, and the key factors operating in the school situation on the other hand. The soaring cost of school education have made policymakers ask themselves questions about how much schooling per se can accomplish in achieving the changes in cognitive competence and inculcation of attitudes that it is supposed to bring about and how much of the achieved competence is simply a reflection of the society in which the school operates.

School and society interact in such complicated ways within the educative process that we might well heed some doubt expressed about the adequacy of the analytic techniques that the IEA and other researchers have employed: for disentangling the relative importance of the two sets of factors. Schooling after all operates within the socioeconomic context at large.

Structure of Formal Schooling

The effects of the structure of formal schooling, particularly the structure of basic schooling, can be studied by comparing student achievement and student motivation in various types of school systems. The structural changes in the direction of greater comprehensiveness in many industrialized countries have been accompanied by a vivid debate on the relative advantages and disadvantages of the previous "parallel" system as compared with the new, more unified one. The pervasive issue in countries where, during the last few decades, one has discussed the "democratization" of secondary education has been the one of elitism or selectivity versus greater comprehensiveness. One operationalization of the principle of equality of opportunity is, To what extent should there be a dualism between a common school for everybody on the one hand and a separate school preparing for the university on the other! What age range should be covered by a unified school catering to all young people throughout their entire compulsory education?

It is interesting to note that, depending on political affiliations, research findings about the school structure in a given country have been used as arguments both for and against greater comprehensiveness. The Swedish findings were used by German Social Democrats and Liberals as a support for the *Gesamtschule* but by the Christian Democrats in the same country as a confirmation that comprehensiveness would lower academic standards.[11] The same happened in Britain in the 1960s. The minister of education in the Labor government, Anthony Crosland, took a keen interest in the Swedish studies on the social and pedagogical effects of comprehensive schooling and considered them a support for his own plans of increasing the comprehensiveness of British secondary education. But in the so-called Black Papers, issued by a group of right-wing conservatives, the same studies were considered proof of the failure of the comprehensive setup.[12]

Curricular Problems

Curricular problems pertaining to objectives, time (number of years of study, number of periods per week, appropriate age for introducing a subject), and *methods of instruction* can be studied and elucidated within a cross-national perspective. At the outset, the IEA surveys were planned and methodologically designed with the ambitious aim of assessing the relative importance of the different factors constituting school resources and instructional processes.[13] It is common sense that factors such as per-student expenditure, class size, number of periods of instruction, teacher subject-matter competence, availability of teaching aids, student-activating methods, and the like all make a difference, in that they influence how much students learn.

However, the relative effects of these factors depend very much on the *context* in which they operate. In a given national context, the variability of certain factors is usually, due to the uniformity of national policy, very limited. In country A, where the average class size is above the critical level of manageability, a reduction of a few students in the class could have a significant result on outcomes of teaching, whereas in country B, with a consistently small class size, an equal change in the average number of students would not seem to make any difference at all. When talking about the context, we ought to consider the socioeconomic structure at large, within which a given national system of education operates; its resources; and the instructional strategies employed. Increased resources and/or improved instruction in one setting with poor resources might enhance the quality of outcomes considerably, whereas the effects in an affluent system of the same additional resources could well be, at most, marginal.

FINDINGS RELEVANT TO EDUCATIONAL POLICY IN A WIDER CONTEXT

Policymakers, as well as media people, tend to be primarily preoccupied with national mean scores and comparisons among them—a kind of "cognitive Olympics." This happened in the first international mathematics and science studies published in 1967 and 1973, respectively. Soul-searching questions began to be raised in countries with low means, such as about thirteen-year-olds in the mathematics survey in Sweden and the United States. In Sweden, the low score was cited by critics of school reform in the election campaign of 1970. In the United States, members of Congress began to ask what use one had for the substantial and well-financed programs for upgrading mathematics education by federal funds.

In Sweden, the relatively low level of mathematics performance was attributed by conservatives to the change in school structure from a parallel to a comprehensive system. It readily confirmed the misgivings among critics that the abolition of the structural differentiation between academic and nonacademic students would lead to a lowering of standards. Divergent political perceptions tended to confuse the issue, as usual. In interpreting the differences between countries, very few took into account the fact that in both Sweden and the United States students in the ten to thirteen-year-old age range attended comprehensive schools, whereas in England and the Federal Republic of Germany, for example, they were divided between academic schools for a select minority and common elementary schools for the remaining majority. This meant that certain abstract topics in mathematics, such as algebra and geometry, were not introduced into the mathematics curriculum until after the age of thirteen in the former countries, whereas they were taught to an elite group in the latter countries. Thus, a considerable part—but by no means all—of the mean difference in mathematics performance between thirteen-year-olds in England and the Federal Republic of Germany on the one hand, and in the United States and Sweden on the other, was accounted for by differences in opportunity to learn certain topics in mathematics.

In the Federal Republic of Germany, an intensive debate followed the publication of the mean scores in science and reading for the various Länder.[14] The Länder had different school structures: Bavaria, for instance, had more of the traditional parallel school structure than Hesse did. Conclusions were, in many quarters, readily drawn about the "efficiency" of the two different systems. However, in the case of Germany, the sample drawn at best represented the Federal Republic in its entirety. The number of schools drawn for each *Land* was generally too small to permit inferences about relative levels of competence because the small number of schools within a *Land* was associated with big standard errors of sampling—a point that was overlooked in the German debate.

In the SIMS, the relatively low Swedish mean score among thirteen-year-olds became a major item for the newspapers and caused quite a lot of concern in the Ministry of Education. Headlines such as "Sweden at the Level of Developing Countries" and "Sweden Close to Swaziland" were found in the newspapers. The minister of school education decided to appoint a task force, chaired by the director-general of the National Board of Education, charged with taking a hard look at mathematics education. A study of the competence of teachers in the middle grades (four through six) was launched.

In Finland, new legislation on the establishment of school governance provided the students the opportunity to participate in the planning and practical organization of the schoolwork.[15] The long-range objective of these changes was to enhance the students' ability to participate in the social affairs of adult life. The launching of the IEA Civic Education Survey provided an opportunity to investigate the relation between the power structure in the (secondary) schools and the attitudes of teachers and students.[16]

FINDINGS RELEVANT TO THE
STRUCTURE OF SCHOOL SYSTEMS

C. P. Snow, in "The Two Cultures," expressed concern about the lack of communication and understanding between natural scientists and men of letters. One main reason for the gap was said to be the narrow specialization in science and classical-humanistic tracks in the upper-secondary school. Since the IEA tested the science, reading comprehension, and literature achievement of the same students in a number of countries, there was a unique opportunity to test the "two-culture" hypothesis on a multinational scale. This was done by Richard Wolf of Teachers College, Columbia University, using a special analysis.[17] Out of nine countries, only in England and New Zealand was there support for the existence of "two cultures."

In most social systems, even in those that are relatively ascriptive and show little social mobility, lip service is paid to the principle of equality of opportunity, particularly in getting access to further education after mandatory schooling. In the industrialized IEA countries, practically 100 percent of the fourteen-year-olds are in full-time schooling, which means that the enrollment by and large reflected the social composition of the entire population. By the early 1970s, at age eighteen or nineteen, the proportion of the age-group still in full-time schooling varied from 3 percent to 76 percent. The enrollment in all countries showed a much higher representation of students from the higher social strata. The imbalance in participation between strata were in some countries so striking that they could only be explained by a built-in bias in the system.

Planners and policymakers can get important leads by comparing various national systems with regard to structure, selection practices, and social bias in secondary education enrollment. The IEA data have quite a lot to offer with respect to policy issues related to the structure and selectivity of educational systems, particularly at the secondary level. The IEA surveys have, in that respect, been an evaluation of the consequences of the introduction of mass education at the secondary level. In some countries universal, or close to universal, lower secondary education had been achieved by 1970, whereas in others there was still a sorting and sifting of the students at the age of eleven in order to select those who are supposed to be academically oriented for university-preparatory schools. The crucial issues could be stated as follows: those in favor of elitist sorting at an early age maintain that broadening of access to quality secondary education would lower the standards. In other words, "more means worse." Those in favor of a more comprehensive system maintained that the opening of opportunities would infuse new blood into the traditional academic elite by taking care of talent from lower social strata.

The analyses conducted on both mathematics and science data unequivocally showed that the most able students, say, the top 5 percent to 10 percent, do as well in an egalitarian as in a more elitist system. In other words, the "best children" seem to achieve the same standards in both types of systems. In addition, the mass systems show a significantly lower degree of social bias in enrollment at the preuniversity level.[18]

In a parliamentary statement in Belgium, the prime minister raised the question of how well the able student were taken care of at the secondary level.[19] Since the tests in literature were the same for the fourteen-year-olds and the preuniversity students, their achievement could be compared. It was noted that there was a general decline of high achievers from the first to the second age level. The main explanation advanced was that many of the high achievers dropped out between the ages of fourteen and eighteen, which seemed to account for the low Belgian achievement by international standards among the preuniversity students. An interesting observation, however, was that there was no decline—on the contrary, there was an increase—in the number of high scorers in the comprehensive system, which was seen as an indication that the comprehensive system took better care of the elite than the selective one.

The National Institute of Educational Research in Tokyo, which is the

Japanese national center for the IEA surveys, published three national reports on the outcomes of the SIMS in 1984-85. The first of these reports, "Mathematics Achievement of Secondary School Student" (original in Japanese), was simply a descriptive report on student achievements in 1964 and 1980, respectively, with main emphasis on item performance. The second report focused on learning conditions. The third report dealt with methods of instruction and their effects on achievement at the lower secondary level. Japanese students at the preuniversity level tended to perform better in 1980 than they did in 1964, which was ascribed to the revision of mathematics curriculum after the FIMS. However, no improvement was found at the lower secondary level. In the framework of an overall superiority in mathematics as compared with Western Europe and America, the Japanese students performed relatively better in mechanical operations than in higher mental processes required in problem solving. This caused concern and was interpreted as an outcome of the heavy emphasis put on computational skills and the nature of entrance examinations, which do not put heavy emphasis on problem solving. This matter became the focus of commissions composed of mathematics teachers and specialists in Japan.

Finally, let us take an example that shows how IEA findings definitely resolved a national policy issue. In the late 1960s and early 1970s, there was in Sweden a spirited debate referred to by Dunlop as the "foreign language teaching controversy."[20] At issue was, on the surface, the proper method of teaching English. But, in a deeper sense, the worthwhileness of teaching foreign languages to all students in undifferentiated classes was at issue. The critics maintained that the curriculum and the concomitant methods of teaching recommended by the National Board of Education unduly favored a "direct" approach and discouraged the use of the mother tongue, orally or in print, as a medium of instruction. It was further maintained that complaints from university English departments about entrants lacking basic knowledge of grammar could be attributed to the "extremist" approach of teaching English in school, allegedly recommended by the central authorities. Finally, and this was the most serious accusation, it was maintained that the standards of English in secondary schools had been considerably lowered as a result of the allegedly prescribed methods of instruction.

Dunlop analyzed the Swedish data on the teaching of English. First, he showed that very few teachers employed the extreme direct method that the critics had described.[21] The great majority employed what Dunlop referred to as a "modified" grammar approach. Second, in all four skill areas (listening, reading, speaking, and writing), Swedish students at both the fourteen and eighteen-year-old level tended to perform at least as well, and often better, than their agemates in other countries. Thus, empirical evidence did not support the notion that the standards were lower due either to the employment of extreme methods or to the teaching of English to all students. The latter was said to hold back able students in Sweden, in comparison with countries where foreign languages are taught only to select students in academic schools or tracks.

FINDINGS RELEVANT TO
INSTRUCTIONAL RESOURCES AND CURRICULUM

The implications of IEA findings for curriculum policy and development have been dealt with in depth by specialists in the various subject areas. I shall, therefore, limit myself mainly to the role played by *time* in school learning. But, before doing so, I shall briefly deal with some pedagogical implications of the multivariate analyses conducted with the aim of identifying key school factors affecting learning.

Rosier tried by means of multivariate analyses to identify learning conditions that were most important for Australia in accounting for between-student differences.[22] He came out with four factors, all of which are related in one way or another to time: grade level, hours of studying science, hours of homework, and hours of teacher preparation of lessons.

To say that time is important in learning would state the obvious. But it is not as trivial as it might appear. Time can mean many different things, such as the age or grade level when the student begins and finishes a particular school subject, the number of years he or she takes the subject, the number of periods per week instruction is given in the subject, and the number of hours devoted to homework. John B. Carroll, who served as chairman of the International Committee on French, has developed a model of school learning in which time is the cardinal variable.[23] Most of the time, variables of the kind that I have exemplified above show, due to uniform national curricula, very little spread within a given country. But the variability between countries is the more striking. Thus the IEA foreign language studies offered a unique opportunity to elucidate the effect of time in the acquisition of skills that constitute mastery of a foreign language.

When the national mean scores in reading, listening, speaking, and writing of French were plotted against the adjusted means of the number of years that French was taken, the resulting plots were close to the regression lines, which indicated high correlations between number of years of taking French and student competence. The overwhelming portion of the between-country variance in performance in French was accounted for by the number of years of study. In the United States, where French at the high school level is taken for only two years, the level of competence achieved was dismal. The same applies to Swedish students, who take French as the so-called C-language for only two or three years. Carroll was able by his international comparisons and analyses to show very convincingly that for the majority it takes six or seven years of study to acquire satisfactory proficiency.[24]

In the 1960s, new science curricula began to be developed in Britain supported by the Nuffield Foundation. Studies of the teaching of science in England, as well as the launching of the Nuffield Program, were inspired by concerns about the substantial reduction of students taking science both at the upper-secondary and university levels. The objectives for this comprehensive Nuffield project in biology, chemistry, and physics, which consisted mainly of developing new teaching material, were stated as promoting "science for understanding," "learning through investigation," and stimulating "curiosity and enquiry." About half the number of schools in the English sample had to a varying degree adopted the Nuffield program in their teaching.

The attitudes among students, as assessed by the IEA instruments, were rather negative to physics and chemistry, whereas biology rated in the main cluster of subjects such as English, history, and geography. Significant sex differences in attitudes (and achievement scores) were found in physics and chemistry, and rather small ones in biology.

It was found that students in schools teaching the Nuffield program were much more positive to biology and moderately more positive toward chemistry than in other schools, whereas the differences in attitudes toward physics were rather small. Controlling for verbal intelligence, it was found that in all types of secondary schools those who were taught according to the Nuffield program scored higher in the Test on Understanding Science (TOUS) than those taught according to traditional programs. The evaluation of science teaching in England offers a good illustration of how national sample surveys of this kind can serve monitoring purposes in curriculum revision.

In the foreign language studies, the question at what age the first foreign language—if any—should be introduced in school has in many countries been a longstanding issue among teachers and educational planners. It has generally been believed that a certain level of intellectual development had to be reached before the student could be expected to deal successfully with the grammatical rules.

The IEA French survey covered eight countries with widely varying practices with regard to the age level when French was introduced. A finding of great significance was that students starting at later age or grade levels showed faster rates of learning than those who started early. Such a finding has far-reaching policy implications. It has been maintained that, by starting foreign language teaching in the primary grades, one could at the secondary level save time for the benefit of other subjects. Even if this is so, one should not forget that learning a foreign language could be made more challenging to a teenager than to a ten or eleven year old. At the primary level, students find all kinds of learning challenging, whereas at the secondary level, say at the age range twelve to fifteen, many find most of it a drudgery, particularly the repetition of subject matter that they began to learn earlier in primary grades. A late start of a subject could entail some extra motivation because of its novelty.

The "Paradigm" Problem

One interesting result of the IEA has been the discussion in some scholarly circles of the use of the empirical, quantitative paradigm. The bulk of the IEA's research has been cross-national sample surveys of student achievements. The criticism of this methodology has had three foci.

The IEA Has Been Accused of Favoring One Particular Methodology. The methodology is the strictly quantitative, "positivist" one, which by the middle of this century was developed in survey research in Anglo-Saxon countries and became "normal science." By its very nature, this kind of approach tends, according to adherents of the critical school, to accept and preserve the existing social order in education and not contribute to any critical examination of the establishment. The IEA, according to some critics, should have employed alternative approaches of a qualitative and participatory nature.

The Adequacy of the Survey Research Paradigm for Developing Countries Has Been Questioned. The IEA has supposedly failed to meet their particular needs and priorities. In accordance with the now popular dependency theory, it has even been maintained that the IEA exerts a kind of "methodological neo-colonialism." It increases dependency and legitimizes First World country supremacy in the research domain.

The IEA Research Is Accused of Being Not in a True Sense Cooperative and Comparative. The "developed" countries, according to critics, tell the "developing" countries what to do. The IEA has not listened to what the developing countries say their needs are. To quote from a letter to a researcher in an African country wanting to join the IEA from a representative of an agency providing research support to LDCs: "We are not entirely happy with regard to the conceptualization process, the organizational structure and the division of labor in IEA studies."

The launching of the IEA survey research twenty-five years ago has to be viewed and appraised against the background of the trends and tendencies that dominated the research milieu of its "founding fathers" in the late 1950s and early 1960s.

First, the belief in what science, in this case social science, would be able to achieve had grown to an all-time high. This belief had its roots in the Enlightenment, when people like Condorcet saw a close connection between what was true and what was right. The scientific researcher could by his or her methods reveal what was true and thereby show the direction for right actions.

A systematic collection of facts would by itself contribute to the establishment of a better and more Just society.

Second, the decade after World War II saw the breakthrough of a social science that, by means of its empirical, quantitative methods overlaid by sophisticated analytical statistics, would play a decisive role in social reconstruction and improvement. Philosophically, these expectations were supported by the neopositivist conception of valid science as spelled out by the "Vienna article" about philosophers who had gained a strong influence, particularly those in the United States.[25] Within a few decades, social scientists in some quarters were regarded as the high priests of modern society. In other quarters, they were seen as subversive revolutionaries.

Third, international and comparative aspects of social science research were inspired by rapidly expanding international communication, by trade, and by military competition between the superpowers.

One ought to have this background in mind in order to put the criticism leveled against IEA survey research into a proper perspective. The founders of the IEA, who also provided the intellectual leadership during the first years of its existence, were, of course, products of their time. What they did or did not do should not be judged by the hindsight knowledge and eventual wisdom of today. Most of these founders had their background in educational psychology, particularly psychological testing as applied in education. Psychology was expected to provide the "facts" in the fields of learning, child development, and testing that educators needed. It was expected to contribute to a school and a society guided by scientific rationality. The methods applied were those that had proved to be successful in the natural sciences. Important dimensions of human behavior were measured, and the data obtained were subjected to complex statistical analyses.

It is worth pointing out that the IEA began its work three years before Thomas Kuhn published *The Structure of Scientific Revolutions*, a book through which "paradigm" and "normal science" became buzzwords.[26] The IEA feasibility survey in twelve countries was planned and executed in 1959-61.[27] Out of this grew the FIMS, 1962-65, followed by the Six-Subject Survey, 1966-73.

Given the international character of the IEA enterprise, methodological or paradigmatic catholicism is surely in order. But the main IEA projects during its twenty-five year history have been cross-national evaluations of standards achieved by students at certain age or grade levels. The purposes of these projects determine the general orientation of the research and, by necessity, set certain rather narrow limits for the methodology employed. The approach or "paradigm" is simply geared by the objective of the particular research endeavor. If the purpose is to assess on a cross-national, comparative basis the level of competence achieved in, say, mathematics, then the quantitatively designed sample survey is the self-evident choice. Ethnographic methods, including participatory observations employed in the respective countries, would not yield very useful and reliable data from which accurate conclusions could be drawn about relative standards.

The survey approach can provide global parameters, such as mean scores and spread, for an overall assessment of a large system of education. However, such an approach cannot tell us in a more detailed way about the subtle and multifaceted infrastructure of pedagogical processes of teaching and learning going on in the classrooms. Data collected by means of mass-distributed questionnaires do not yield the same type of data as from observation schedules or ethnographic studies often conducted on a small number of teachers and students. Data collected in such a way can be systematized so as to provide quantitative information. That is what was done in the IEA Classroom Environment Study, which grew out of self-criticism about the shortcomings of survey methods.[28]

From what has been said above, it follows that the so-called paradigms, depending on the purpose of the research, would have to be complementary and not mutually exclusive. One cannot arrive at any valid and reliable information about standards achieved in, for instance, science in Chinese secondary schools simply by visiting a number of classrooms and collecting impressions. Even a highly experienced teacher would not be able to draw any accurate inferences about the quality of instruction of a region or a whole country from such visits, let alone be able to make comparisons between national systems. A few years ago, the minister of education of China visited Stockholm to learn, among other things, more about the IEA from its headquarters. In a long conversation, he spelled out to me that he wanted science competence among secondary school student in China to be evaluated according to the standards employed in the industrialized countries. Soon thereafter China joined the IEA SISS.

This request brought up not only the issue of the adequacy of the IEA methodology but an ethical issue as well. The first issue could be resolved by working with Chinese colleagues adapting questionnaires and trying out test items in Chinese schools. The latter was, indeed, more difficult. Should I have told the minister that he should forget about an IEA survey because of its allegedly inadequate, or even "neocolonialist," nature, or should I go along with his wishes! I opted for the latter alternative. I have posed this question to critics of the IEA approach. They too thought that I did the right thing.

We cannot come to grips with the problem of imbalance in methodological and other resources between the "center" and "periphery" by simply relinquishing the entire research tradition of the "center" countries and by relying more or less entirely on indigenous methods of a more qualitative or "barefoot" nature when the objective is to assess and monitor the system of education of a whole country. A colleague at one of the leading "center" universities, who had expressed concerns about what he perceived as methodological dominance of center researchers, was asked whether his criticism implied relinquishing the more complex center methods. He thought that this was "the price we had to pay" in order to achieve self-reliance on the part of Third World countries. The logical consequence appears to me to have been that he should have recommended that his university stop taking on graduate students from Third World countries, in order to avoid socializing them into the center paradigms.

We would, indeed, be in bad shape as scientists if we were to think that there were no common denominator of concepts and methods across cultures and nations. If we accept such a pessimistic view, we might just as well abandon all our attempts to conduct cooperative and comparative studies across cultures and nations. There is certainly a need for IEA self-criticism inspired by informed criticism from outside. Complementarity of methods is called for, but—in the last run—the methodology has to be geared to the objectives of the studies and the kind of problems tackled.

CONCLUSIONS

The IEA large-scale sample surveys of national systems of education have, by both international and national reports, had implications for educational policies in the participating countries under three different perspectives: (1) the overall quality and/or performance of the entire national systems of education, including the role of education in achieving certain social and economic objectives, such as greater equality of opportunity; (2) the structure of the formal system and its influence on student achievement; and (3) the influence of school resources and methods of instruction on learning.

Media, the general public, and policymakers tend to pay most attention to the national mean scores achieved by students at certain stages in respective educational systems. The mean score is perceived as an index of relative performance ("standard") of the system, which in the last run is to be accounted for by the overall educational policy. A study of the press reactions as well as parliamentary debates triggered by the outcomes of surveys indicate that the "Olympic Games" aspect of the IEA surveys is the one that attracts most attention.

The IEA findings can contribute to elucidating educational issues of high priority common to many countries. Many issues vary, however, in character and priority between countries, which calls for secondary analyses of the data sets in order to obtain information relevant to national policy. In some cases, such analyses need not have any comparative dimension. In other cases, the comparative perspective can contribute to answering questions about how efficiently national educational policies have been implemented. As pointed out by Marklund, in spite of the high priority attached in many countries to egalitarian policies in education, few IEA studies have been made on between-school and between-student variability across countries.[29] Analyses on a comparative basis that provide a fruitful perspective on national policies could contribute to providing answers to the following problems.

How big are the between-school differences, and what accounts for them? How big are the increments in competence from one level to another, for instance, in reading from the ten to the fourteen year old level? How is competence in the respective subject areas developing over time? The SIMS showed a slight improvement of competence in most countries, except one or two, from 1964 to 1980. How should these changes be accounted for? National surveys with regular intervals could serve important monitoring purposes, particularly in systems where major reforms are in the process of being implemented. Cross-national comparisons can enrich the policy perspective.

The methodology employed must be geared to the aims of the comparative research studies. National standards of achievement can best be assessed by quantitative surveys based on probability samples. The intricacies of the interactions in classroom processes can best be assessed by qualitative approaches. The IEA tried to achieve both through survey methods. The criticism leveled at the IEA has led, at least, to an insight into the complementarity of various approaches.

GAIL P. KELLY

Chapter 17

Education, Women, and Change

Since the 1960s women's educational enrollments have grown considerably at the primary, secondary and tertiary levels. More women than ever before have had an opportunity to attend and stay in school. Paradoxically, while schooling at all levels has become more accessible to women, the number of women illiterates has been growing as has the number of females left unschooled or semi-schooled.[1] This chapter focuses on changes in women's educational enrollments world-wide since the 1960s. It will show that, while female educational enrollments have dramatically increased in most countries, these increases have occurred in the absence of specific policies focused on bringing greater educational equity to women. Second, changes in enrollment which in many countries have closed the gap between male and females in education, even at the tertiary level, have had little effect on women's income or their participation in the paid labor force. More women than ever before have had access to education. Despite this the economic outcomes of education have not been the same for women as they have for men. Why this is the case is explored in this chapter.

CHANGES IN WOMEN'S EDUCATION: EXPANSION SINCE THE 1960s

Women's educational enrollments at all levels have grown spectacularly since the 1970s. The numerical rise in female enrollment in some countries has been impressive, growing threefold or more. In Ethiopia, for example, the number of females in primary school went from 349,000 in 1975 to 1,097,000 in 1987,[2] in Nigeria they rose from 2,625,061 to 6,331,658 between 1975 and 1983. The doubling of the number of females attending primary school is common throughout the Third World in the decade or so since 1975.

Primary Education. While in most of the Third World the number of females attending primary school rose markedly, in most of Eastern and Western Europe, North America, and a few Asian countries, the number of girls studying at this level declined. In Canada, for example, 1,190,489 girls were in primary school in 1975, in 1987 1,104,550 girls were enrolled. Corresponding numerical declines for the United States were 14,820,000 in 1975 versus 13,127,000 in 1986. These declines, for the most part, are a function of zero population growth in systems where, with the exception of China, universal primary education had been long achieved.

While the numerical increases in female enrollment at the primary level are dramatic, particularly in the Third World, male enrollment rose as rapidly, if not more than that of females, leaving the gap between male and female enrollments scarcely touched. For example, females were 31% of all students in Benin primary schools in 1975; after their number doubled between 1975 and 1987, they were 34% of all enrollments. In most of Africa the female share of primary school enrollment grew one percentage point in nine countries and by between two and four percentage points in sixteen countries. They stagnated or declined in another twelve countries including Burkina Faso where girls are still 37% of primary enrollments.

In Central America, South America and the Caribbean the female share of primary school enrollments have more or less stagnated at between 48% and 50% particularly in those countries which had universal primary education.

In Asia, only in Afghanistan and Nepal were female increases in the share of primary enrollments dramatic, going from 15% in 1975 to 29% in Nepal and from 15% in 1975 to 33% in Afghanistan in 1987. Elsewhere, except for Bangladesh where female enrollment rose to 44% of the total in 1987 versus 34% in 1975, female shares of primary school enrollment stagnated. In some twelve countries they remained between 47% and 49% of all enrollments from 1975 to 1987.

In the Middle East, female shares of primary enrollment climbed in most countries. For example, in Algeria they rose from 40% in 1975 to 45% in 1987.

Females' share of primary school enrollments remained stagnant, at about 49% to 50%, in Europe and North America between 1975 and 1986, despite the numerical decline of female enrollment in the time period.

The data clearly indicate that since 1975 world-wide there has been an equalization in male/female enrollments at the primary level. Table 17.1, which presents enrollment ratios for males and females at the primary, secondary, and tertiary levels, underscores this movement to equality. It also indicates that the greatest increases in female enrollment on the primary level occurred between 1960 and 1975. In that period, female enrollment ratios jumped from 72.9 world-wide to 86.7—a leap of 13.8 points. Between 1975 and 1987 the increase was slightly smaller. In Sub-Saharan Africa female enrollment ratios almost doubled between 1960 and 1975 going to 53.9 from 29.6. Their increase halved in the 1975 to 1987 period, going from 53.9 to 68.2. Similarly in Asia, the increase in the enrollment ratios of females grew from 68.5 in 1960 to 88.5 in 1975 while the increase between 1975 and 1987 was from 88.5 to 95.8 or less than half the gain of the earlier period. A similar phenomenon holds for the Middle East. In Latin America and the Caribbean also the greatest gains were between 1960 and 1975. By 1980 universal primary education was reported throughout the region. The gains in female enrollment ratios have been consistent everywhere but in Subsaharan Africa. Here, female enrollment ratios reached 70.9 in 1980 to plummet to 66.5 in 1985. By 1987 they had risen to 68.2.

Secondary Education. Women's access to secondary education has grown every bit as dramatically, if not more so, than has their access to primary schooling, but there are greater inequalities between males and females in the secondary sector. The numerical increases in female enrollment are startling. In many countries female secondary enrollments tripled between 1975 and 1987. In other countries, particularly in the Third World, the increases were substantial but less dramatic.

In North America, Japan, and much of Europe, the numbers of females in secondary schools either declined or registered small gains in the period. In these countries secondary education tends to be universal, female enrollments had been equal to those of males on the secondary level, and population growth was quite low. In these countries, while the numbers of females in secondary education declined, the female share of enrollments did not.

While the numerical increases in secondary education are dramatic, changes in the female share of secondary enrollments have been slow to increase. In most of the Third World women are a minority in secondary schools. In many countries of Africa for which data are available, female share of secondary school enrollments has remained the same between 1975 and 1987. In fourteen countries girls' share of enrollments has risen, but only by a few percentage points while in three countries females' share of secondary enrollments declined. A similar picture emerges in the Caribbean, Central America, and South America.

In Asia females' share of secondary enrollments grew, except in Japan, where women's share approached equality. In some countries, the increases

TABLE 17.1
Enrollment Ratios for Primary, Secondary and Higher Education
1960-1987

Regions	Year	Primary Education			Secondary Education			Higher Education		
		Total	Male	Female	Total	Male	Female	Total	Male	Female
World Total	1960	84.1	94.8	72.9	27.6	31.3	23.7	5.3	7.1	3.5
	1970	88.5	95.8	80.8	36.2	40.7	31.5	8.5	10.4	6.5
	1975	94.5	102.0	86.7	42.7	47.8	37.4	10.6	12.4	8.7
	1980	96.1	103.5	88.3	44.6	49.6	39.4	11.5	12.9	9.9
	1985	98.8	105.7	91.6	46.1	51.4	40.5	12.1	13.4	10.7
	1986	99.6	106.3	92.6	47.3	52.6	41.7	12.3	13.6	10.9
	1987	99.6	106.1	92.8	48.6	54.1	42.9	12.6	14.0	11.1
Sub-Saharan Africa[1]	1960	40.4	51.2	29.6	3.5	4.9	2.2	0.3	0.5	0.1
	1970	52.0	61.6	42.5	7.9	10.5	5.3	0.8	1.2	0.3
	1975	63.1	72.2	53.9	11.0	14.3	7.7	1.1	1.7	0.4
	1980	80.4	89.9	70.9	18.7	24.0	13.5	1.6	2.6	0.6
	1985	74.4	82.2	66.5	22.7	29.5	15.8	2.1	3.4	0.9
	1986	74.4	81.5	67.3	24.1	31.6	16.6	2.2	3.4	0.9
	1987	75.3	82.3	68.2	25.9	34.0	17.8	2.2	3.5	0.9
Asia[2]	1960	85.6	101.7	68.5	20.9	26.1	15.5	2.6	3.9	1.2
	1970	89.8	99.9	79.1	28.0	34.2	21.4	3.5	5.0	2.0
	1975	98.9	108.8	88.5	34.9	41.9	27.4	4.7	6.4	2.8
	1980	97.0	106.6	86.7	37.8	44.7	30.5	5.6	7.5	3.5
	1985	103.4	112.4	93.8	39.0	45.9	31.8	6.5	8.3	4.5
	1986	104.9	113.6	95.7	40.4	47.2	33.2	6.8	8.7	4.8
	1987	104.7	113.2	95.8	41.8	48.7	34.4	7.2	9.2	5.1
Arab States of Africa and Asia	1960	48.3	63.0	33.2	10.2	15.0	5.3	2.0	3.2	0.7
	1970	62.5	77.9	46.4	20.4	28.1	12.5	4.1	6.3	2.0
	1975	73.1	88.9	56.5	28.3	36.4	19.8	6.9	9.6	4.0
	1980	79.9	92.5	66.8	38.0	46.7	29.0	9.5	12.8	6.0
	1985	81.8	92.6	70.6	47.1	55.5	38.4	10.8	14.2	7.2
	1986	82.3	92.5	71.6	48.4	56.7	39.8	11.2	14.3	7.8
	1987	83.1	93.3	72.4	49.3	57.2	41.0	11.3	14.5	8.1

Region	Year									
Latin America and the Caribbean	1960	72.7	74.7	70.7	14.6	15.2	14.0	3.0	4.2	1.8
	1970	90.7	91.9	89.4	25.5	26.3	24.6	6.3	8.0	4.5
	1975	97.0	98.5	95.5	36.6	37.4	35.7	11.7	13.5	9.9
	1980	104.8	106.4	103.3	44.9	44.4	45.4	13.5	15.3	11.7
	1985	106.4	108.7	104.1	50.7	49.0	52.4	15.9	17.3	14.4
	1986	107.2	109.5	104.8	51.7	49.9	53.5	16.2	17.2	15.1
	1987	107.9	110.1	105.5	53.7	51.7	55.6	16.9	18.0	15.7
Europe (including USSR)	1960	106.7	107.7	105.8	54.5	56.2	52.7	10.3	12.9	7.6
	1970	105.1	105.6	104.5	72.7	73.8	71.6	17.3	19.4	15.0
	1975	101.9	102.0	101.9	81.6	81.9	81.3	20.3	21.8	18.8
	1980	103.0	103.3	102.8	83.6	82.4	84.9	22.1	23.0	21.1
	1985	103.1	103.6	102.7	86.4	86.3	86.6	24.3	24.6	24.1
	1986	103.3	103.7	102.8	87.8	87.8	87.7	24.5	24.6	24.4
	1987	103.0	103.5	102.6	89.4	89.3	89.5	25.2	25.6	24.7
North America	1960	105.8	107.0	104.6	87.4	87.2	87.6	28.9	36.2	21.5
	1970	103.2	103.5	102.8	93.1	92.6	93.6	45.4	52.8	37.8
	1975	99.2	99.8	98.6	99.8	101.0	98.6	53.2	57.9	48.5
	1980	99.4	99.7	99.0	89.4	88.2	90.7	54.3	52.1	56.5
	1985	99.9	99.8	98.1	98.1	98.4	97.7	60.4	56.6	64.3
	1986	100.7	101.5	99.9	99.0	98.5	99.5	62.6	58.1	67.3
	1987	101.1	101.9	100.3	101.2	100.8	101.7	63.8	60.0	67.7
Oceania	1960	109.1	110.0	108.0	54.2	55.5	52.8	9.9	14.0	5.7
	1970	111.7	113.8	109.6	70.8	72.3	69.2	14.2	18.3	9.9
	1975	108.8	111.2	106.4	76.0	76.2	75.8	20.4	24.2	16.4
	1980	110.2	111.8	108.5	74.6	73.2	76.1	22.1	24.3	19.9
	1985	108.3	109.6	106.9	79.9	78.9	81.0	24.4	25.3	23.3
	1986	108.8	110.0	107.5	80.5	79.5	81.5	25.3	25.8	24.9
	1987	109.4	110.7	108.1	81.0	80.0	81.9	26.0	26.4	25.6

1. Excludes Arab States of the Middle East
2. Excludes Arab States of Asia

Source. Derived from *UNESCO Statistical Yearbook, 1989,* Table 2.10, pp. 2-31, 2-32.

were great. For example in Pakistan, females went from 23% of all secondary enrollments in 1975 to 28% in 1987; in Nepal they climbed from 17% to 23% in the same time period while in Bangladesh they went from 11% to 33% in 1986 and in Korea they rose from 41% in 1975 to 47% in 1987. In China, Hong Kong, Malaysia, and Singapore, females' share of secondary school enrollments rose between one and two percentage points between 1975 and 1988. In the Philippines it fell by one percentage point.

In the Middle East, females' share of secondary school enrollment grew the most . In Algeria, between 1975 and 1986 the percentage rose from 34% to 41%; the same increase characterized Libya and Tunisia. In Iraq females' share of enrollment went from 29% to 37% between 1975 and 1987; in Jordan the increase was from 41% to 48% while in the United Arab Emirates females went from 38% to 50% of secondary school enrollments.

Females' share of secondary enrollment stagnated in most of Europe and North America. In these countries universal secondary education had long been attained. In some countries, like Finland, Czechoslovakia, and France, the percent of the secondary school female population exceeded that of males.

The gains in females' access to secondary education are quite real world-wide and outpace those females have made in primary schooling. Worldwide, as Table 17.1 shows in 1987, 42.9% of girls ages twelve to seventeen, went to secondary school (as opposed to 54.1% of boys) . World-wide the gap between males and females at the secondary level has been closing, but these gaps are still, as Table17.1 indicates, very great in Africa, where the enrollment rates for boys was twice as high as for girls in 1987.

The trend toward equalization solely concerns access to secondary education, but females do not receive the same kind of secondary education as do males. In most countries, secondary education is highly diversified and consists of not only academic secondary education but also teacher training and vocational education.[3] A few examples will illustrate the differences between males and females' educational routes at the secondary level. In Botswana, where females were 52% of all secondary enrollments in 1986, they were 84% of students in teacher training courses and 31% of vocational school students. Fifty-three percent of students in academic secondary schools were girls. In Tunisia, where girls were 42% of all secondary students in 1987, they were 43% of those in academic secondary education programs, 71% of enrollments in teacher training courses and 34% of vocational school students; in Zimbabwe where females were 40% of secondary students in 1988, they were 13% of vocational school students. In Cuba, where 51% of secondary school students were female in 1987, females were 52% of the students in academic courses, 77% of those enrolled in teacher training classes and 46% of vocational school students. These patterns hold through most of the Third World, regardless of the proportion female of secondary students. Women are disproportionately enrolled in general academic courses which tend to ill prepare them for the workforce that most will enter upon completing secondary school. Most women will not go on to university. Females are also disproportionately represented in secondary programs designed to prepare elementary school teachers. Overall females' secondary school enrollment patterns presage the sex segregated workforce in which women become unemployed or primary school teachers and clerks. Women are underrepresented in vocational and technical schools preparing skilled workers. The extent of that underrepresentation varies from country to country. In the 1980s there has been a tendency to increase female access to vocational schooling. In China, for example, women went from 34% to 43% of vocational school students between 1975 and 1987; in Indonesia their share grew from 29% to 36% of vocational school students. Despite this, the largest increases in female secondary school attendance between 1975 and 1987 in the Third World appear to be in teacher training, except in a number of countries which have relegated all teacher preparation to tertiary level institutions.

Female enrollment patterns in Europe and North America replicate those found in Third World countries. In Austria, for example, females were 50% of all secondary school students in 1987 and 64% of all students in teacher preparation courses and 53% of vocational school students. They were 48% of students in academic programs. In the German Democratic Republic in 1987 they were 48% of all students in 1987 and 43% of vocational school students while in Greece females were 48% of secondary students and 29% of vocational school students.

Statistics are not available as to the type of gender differentiation which exists among vocational school students. For the most part, girls, even when they gain access to vocational training, which seems to be increasingly the case, receive preparation in different kinds of skills than do boys. They tend to be shunted off to secretarial and clerical preparation, and to other programs training students for "female" occupations. Women do not enter programs that prepare students for traditionally male occupations in the skilled trades—carpentry, masonry, electronics, mechanics, and so forth. Increasing preoccupation with the articulation between secondary schooling and employment has meant greater gender segregation within the secondary sector, paralleling the sex segregation of the modern workforce. The change, in short, in secondary education has meant females everywhere have greater opportunity to study, but they do not have the opportunity to pursue the same kind of secondary education as do males.

In addition, many of the gains females have made in secondary education since 1960 were greatest before 1980. Between 1975 and 1980, female secondary school enrollments grew 3.5%; after 1980 they grew 2.3%. In Sub-Saharan Africa these rates more than halved in the two periods—the rate of growth was 15.8% between 1975 and 1980; it slowed to 4.9% between 1980 and 1987.[4] While the rates of increases in female enrollment in secondary education in the Third World slowed most in Sub-Saharan Africa, they also fell in Latin America and the Caribbean and in Asia.

Higher Education. Inequality in educational enrollments between males and females is greater in higher education than it is at the primary and secondary levels. In most countries of the world, women are in the minority. In only twenty-four countries as of 1986 did the proportion of female students equal or exceed those of men.[5] In sixteen nations, on the other hand, women constituted less than 20% of all tertiary level students and in an additional sixteen women were between 20% and 29% of all students. These inequalities in enrollment persist despite the fact that the rate of expansion of higher education has been far greater than that of either primary or secondary education and the increases in female enrollment have been greater proportionately than at other levels.

The changes in the number of women enrolled in higher education are dramatic but still the absolute number of females in higher education in many countries is low.[6] In most of Sub-Saharan Africa the number of women students in higher education grew tenfold since 1965. For example, in Ethiopia there were 152 female students in higher education as of 1965, by 1981 their number reached 4,881. In Ghana in 1965 there were 346 women pursuing higher education studies, by 1981 there were 3,326. In Asia the increases were about fivefold or more. In India 200,480 females were enrolled in the tertiary sector in 1965, by 1986 the figure had risen to 1,396,466. In the Philippines the increase was from 282,266 in 1965 to 1,070,045 in 1985. Similar increases can be charted for the countries *of* the Middle East and Latin American and the Caribbean. The number *of* women enrolled in higher education in Europe and North America grew between three and tenfold between 1965 and 1986. In Belgium, for example, female enrollments expanded from 27,523 to 118,491 in this time period while in France they went from 167,810 to 653,330. The increases in the Federal Republic of Germany were even greater. In the former Soviet bloc nations of Eastern Europe the changes in female enrollment are no where near as dramatic as they were in the rest of the world, with exception of the German Democratic Republic where the number of women students rose from 24,186 in 1965 to 236,383 in 1986. More characteristic of these countries is Bulgaria where the number of women students increased from 43,427 in 1965 to 69,498 in 1986 or Czechoslovakia where the corresponding growth was from 54,049 in 1965 to 71,664 in 1986.

Not only did the numbers of women entering higher education grow, their proportion also grew (except in a few countries like Angola, Congo-Brazzaville, Togo, Mozambique, Afghanistan, Hong Kong, and Fiji). For example, in

Ethiopia, women's share of higher education enrollment rose from 7% to 29% between 1965 and 1985; in Ghana it went from 8% to 21%; in Rwanda the corresponding increase was from 1% to 14%. Similar gains characterize Asia, Latin America and the Caribbean and the Middle East.

In Europe and North America the gains in the proportion of female students in higher education were less spectacular but nonetheless substantial, especially given the numerical stagnation, even decline of enrollment at the primary and secondary levels. In most of these countries women became 40% or more of all students in higher education. In Finland the number of women tripled, while their proportional representation in higher education remained static at 53%. In France, however, women's share went from 30% to 51% between 1965 and 1986; in Greece it rose from 32% to 48%. In the United Kingdom the percent of students who were female rose from 30% to 45%; in the United States it went from 39% to 53%.

Table 17.1, which charts enrollment ratios on the primary, secondary, and tertiary levels for males and females, indicates that world-wide female enrollment ratios in higher education still lag behind those of males, although the gap between the two has consistently narrowed since 1960. The table also shows the gaps are greatest in Sub-Saharan Africa, the Middle East, and Asia. In Sub-Saharan Africa the gap between male and female enrollment ratios never narrowed between 1960 and 1987; rather it widened considerably. This is also the case in Asia and the Middle East although on a less exaggerated scale. Only in Latin America and the Caribbean, Europe, and North America have the gaps really closed. In North America female enrollment ratios in tertiary education actually came to exceed males' by far by 1987.

While the number and in most countries the proportion of women enrolled in tertiary education have grown, so also has gender stratification in higher education. Females tend more than men to receive their higher education outside of the university—in teacher training institutions, colleges of nursing, or "distance" or correspondence courses. Fragmentary as they may be, UNESCO data indicate that as of 1986 women tend to disproportionately enroll in nonuniversity based tertiary institutions.[7] In some countries females are 85% of all enrollments in nonuniversity higher education. In a number of nations female enrollments in tertiary education outside of university settings exceed their enrollment in universities. In some countries the number of females enrolled in nonuniversity based higher education is four times greater than the number of females attending universities.

In the majority of countries, one-third to one-half of all women in higher education attend nonuniversity based tertiary institutions. This is the case in countries as diverse as Poland, Israel, Sweden, Syria, Switzerland, Gabon, Afghanistan, and the United States.

Within universities, women are usually segregated from men by field of study.[8] In most nations, 40% or more of all female students specialize in Education, the Humanities, and the Social and Behavioral Sciences. In Lesotho 83% of all women were enrolled in these fields by 1985, the corresponding figure for Nepal was 72%, Israel, 68%; the Sudan, 62%; Iran, 49%; Turkey, 48%; the Republic of Germany, 47%; Italy, 46%; Spain, 45%; the United Kingdom, 44%; and Nicaragua, 42%. The sex segregation is so great in some countries, like Argentina, that women are 92% of all education students. In Poland 80% of all education students were female as of 1985.

Women are excluded in most countries from a number of specializations. They are noticeably absent from Engineering, Mathematics, and Computer Science Programs. In 1985 only three countries—namely the former German Democratic Republic, Israel, and Turkey—did as many as 10% of all women specialize in Engineering. In most countries less than 5% of all women study Engineering. Less than 3% of all women in the vast majority of countries studied Mathematics or Computer Science by 1985. Women also tend not to be enrolled in the Natural Sciences either. In no country in 1985 did more than 10% of all women in higher education study natural sciences.

There are a number of fields in which women's share of enrollment vary considerably by nation. In 1986 women formed a disproportionately high proportion of Law students in fifteen countries, while they were a disproportionately low percent of students enrolled in that field in thirty countries. In another twenty-one countries the percent of women studying Law was equivalent to their share of enrollment in higher education as a whole. Women's enrollment in Social and Behavioral Sciences follows a similar pattern.

Sex segregation in higher education has increased, rather than decreased, as more women have entered universities. Women tend to enter fields which already have substantial numbers of women enrolled in them. Thus, Humanities and Education, which always had female students, as higher education expanded, became female ghettos in much of the world.

Expansion of female enrollments has also meant increasing sex segregation by level of study in most of the world. The greatest gains in female higher education have been on the undergraduate level. In Sweden, for example, in the mid-1980s women were 60% of all undergraduates and 30% of students pursuing post-baccalaureate degrees.[9] In Australia women received only one-third of all graduate degrees in the 1980s.[10] Only in the United States did women constitute half of Master's degree recipients; most of these were in Education.[11] In Norway of 6,632 women enrolled in the Humanities in the 1983-84 academic year, only 168 were in graduate programs.[12] Similarly patterns exist world wide, as Kathryn Moore's and Margaret Sutherland's respective works have amply pointed out.[13]

Thus, while women's gains in higher education have been substantial, they have, as in the secondary sector, been accompanied by increasing differentiation between courses of study females versus males pursue. The type of programs in which women enroll at both of these levels accounts in large part for the patterns of occupational segregation in the contemporary workforce.

THE WORKFORCE OUTCOMES OF WOMEN'S EDUCATION

Research has in the past documented a strong relationship between educational levels and workforce participation and education and income. Indeed, human capital theory draws these linkages quite strongly particularly in the case of males. The remainder of this chapter asks whether the dramatic increases in women's education at the primary, secondary, and tertiary levels have changed women's rates of participation in the paid labor force or affected their income.

Since 1960, despite the massive changes in female educational levels, world-wide women's workforce participation rates have stagnated. In 1960, 47% of women over the age of eighteen worked for a wage; in 1980 46% of women over 18 were in the paid labor force. (The decline women experienced was accompanied by an even greater decline in men's workforce participation rates. In 1960 90% of all men between eighteen and sixty years of age were in the paid labor force, by 1980 85% were in the paid labor force. This decline was in large part due to mechanization of agriculture and western forms of wholesale marketing which displaced both male and female labor in most Third World countries.)[14]

Although women's participation in the wage-earning workforce stagnated world-wide, there are differences between industrialized versus Third World countries. In twenty-eight industrialized nations, including the United States, Canada, France, United Kingdom, the USSR, and Poland, there was an increase in female participation in the paid workforce—in 1960 52% of all women were employed; this figure rose to 57% in 1980. In Third World nations, where increases in female education particularly on the primary and secondary levels were most dramatic, the rate of women's participation in the paid labor force dropped from 45% to 42%. The declines were greatest in Oceania, where women's workforce participation rates fell off six percentage points, and in Asia where they decreased five percentage points.[15] In large part this reflects the stagnation of many Third World economies where the number of potential entrants into the waged labor force has exceeded the number of jobs available. In such cases women became disproportionately unemployed relative to men, despite their rising educational levels. Such a phenomenon has been noted in India, Nigeria, Zaire, Peru, Chile, Mexico, and Bangladesh.[16]

There are differences among individual countries as to women's workforce participation rates. In general these rates are higher in the former Soviet bloc countries of Eastern Europe than they are in Western Europe and Canada. The rates in Vietnam and China, when compared to other Asian countries like India or Bangladesh, are high. Socialist governments have strongly encouraged women to enter waged labor whether they are educated or not. Changes in education in such countries may have less to do with women's workforce participation than do economic policies aimed at exploiting women's labor, particularly in China and the Soviet Union.

While the rates of female participation in the paid labor force has remained stagnant and in some countries declined, the work women do has changed in large part because of their changing educational levels. The occupational structure has been transformed in most countries, demanding higher levels of education and skills of those employed. In industrialized nations like Sweden, France, the United States, the Soviet Union, Germany, Canada, and the United Kingdom, women have increasingly moved into occupations requiring secondary and tertiary level education. Many of these occupations, which are expanding, like primary and secondary school teaching, nursing, and social work, have traditionally been "female" occupations. Increasingly, also, women have been entering low-level white collar jobs, technical employment, and work in health-related professions, all of which require secondary or higher education. Undoubtedly, without education, many women would join the ranks of the unemployed. In a number of these countries, as the statistics presented earlier on higher education indicate, women are staying in school longer to qualify for employment in the new jobs that require secondary or better education.[17] Unskilled jobs which traditionally employed women, such as domestic service and secretarial work, have ceased to expand or have even begun to decline. A number of studies of women in Third World settings have also shown that in some of these nations women stay in school longer than men because the only paid employment open to them requires at least secondary schooling.[18]

The trend in much of the industrialized world for women to obtain more education than men is attributable to the sex-segregated occupational structure and the fact that women need stronger credentials than men to enter occupations which employ an almost exclusively female workforce like teaching. Most women work in occupations that are predominantly female, so much so, that it has been estimated that in countries as diverse as Canada and the Soviet Union, three-fourths of workforce would need to change jobs so that males and females would be equally represented in all occupations.[19] Sex segregation in employment closely parallels the segregation of women into secondary school tracks and into specialized fields of study on the tertiary level.

In the Third World female employment patterns have also changed, but somewhat differently. Third World labor markets are segmented and two separate markets exist: one is traditional and involves subsistence farming and petty trade; the other is a modern industrial urban economy. In much of Africa and in parts of Asia and Latin America, women's labor force participation has been traditionally high, although women have been self-employed concentrated in the traditional economy. In the process of modernization, women's work in the traditional economy has been increasingly displaced by mechanization, by the incorporation of land holdings, and the extension of corporate retailing. Women displaced from traditional sector employment, cannot easily transfer into the modern, industrial labor force where education has increasingly become an important credential for obtaining employment and where employment opportunities have shrunk.[20] In these cases the undereducation of women, coupled with stagnant job markets, is somewhat related to women's declining rates of entry into paid labor in the Third World. Simultaneously, much of the work women have held as unskilled factory laborers in light industry in the urban workforce has disappeared in the face of greater mechanization. Thus, the relation between women's education and employment for a wage has in many Third World countries become J-shaped.[21] Poor uneducated women enter the urban workforce, filling low-skill, low-paying jobs. These women account for the vast majority of women in the labor force. Most take up jobs as domestic servants and in trade. (Domestic labor remains the largest single form of employment for women in Latin America and Southeast Asia.) Women with primary education tend to withdraw from the urban labor force unable to find appropriate employment, while women with secondary or better education have been entering the workforce in greater numbers taking up clerical, semi-professional, and professional employment. In some countries, like Turkey and Egypt, this has meant greater female participation in the professions while the overall workforce participation rates of women have declined.[22] Given these trends, the increases in female primary education have little meaning for women's entry into paid labor in labor markets in which secondary or better education has become prerequisite for employment. As was noted earlier, it is on the secondary and tertiary levels where the greatest inequalities between males and females appear.

While there have been changes in women's educational levels relative to men's and in the kind of work women do, women still earn 75% of men's wages worldwide.[23] There are some variations among countries. In Japan, for example, in 1980 working women earned 53.8% of working men's wages; in Canada women earned 58%. In the Netherlands, however, in 1982 women's average wages were 76.7% of men's.[24] In some Third World countries, where women's participation in the paid modern labor force is low and on the wane, there is less wage inequality among men and women earning a wage. In Egypt, for example, women in the modern labor force earned 93.7% of men's wages; in Venezuela in 1983, women earned 79.1% and in Sri Lanka in 1981 women's wages were 93.3% of men's in the modern workforce. In these countries only a few highly educated women enter paid labor. When the paid workforce expands to include more women, it tends to absorb women at the lowest rungs of the occupational structure in low wage positions. Ironically, wage equality tends to be more prevalent in those countries where few women are in the modern workforce.

Over time, particularly in industrialized nations where female paid workforce participation is heavy, the disparities between males' and females' wages are the greatest and have increased over time as more women enter the labor force with higher educational levels. In Japan in 1975 working women earned 55.8% of men's wages; in 1980 their wages had dropped to 53.8% of men's wages. While Dutch women earned 79% the salary of men in 1971, in 1982 they earned 76.7%. In South Korea women earned 47.2% of men's wages in 1975; in 1983 their wages fell to 46.6%.[25]

The data presented here suggest that improvement in women's education simply means increasing women's education. It does not mean women enter the paid workforce in increasing numbers, nor does it provide increase in income, as charted for men, or income equality. Rather, the trends suggest that changes in education mean only that women are better educated—it has not meant economic equality.

EDUCATIONAL CHANGE AND WOMEN'S STATUS

As the data presented in this chapter have indicated, world-wide there is a trend toward equalizing access to all levels of schooling for men and women. Throughout the world, primary schooling has become both obtainable and attainable for females. Third World countries, hit hard by the economic crises of the 1980s, have been slow to equalize secondary and tertiary education. In the 1980s growth in females' share of education at these levels has slowed and in some countries regressed. In the industrialized world equality of access is close to a reality in many countries; in a number of nations females surpass males in enrollment in academic secondary schools and in institutions of higher education.

While equality in educational access is achievable in most countries and has occurred without major specific government policies encouraging females to enter school and continue their studies, great inequalities have emerged in the kinds of education women versus men receive. In secondary education women have been allocated to general academic studies, to preparation programs for elementary teachers, and to "female" vocational training for positions as secretaries and clerks. Males, on the other hand, have been channeled into technical, vocational training which articulate more closely with the changing structure of employment. In higher education, women have come to dominate the

Arts and Humanities and teacher preparation programs; men, on the other hand, have maintained Engineering, Business Administration and Computer Science as their preserves. It is little wonder then that women's role in the workforce has eroded in the face of economies increasingly based on extensive use of computer-based technologies.

The type of education women versus men obtain explains in part the erosion of women's participation in the paid labor force and in their income relative to men. The lack of change in sex role division of labor in the family and the lack of social legislation recognizing family organization and women's role in it has also prevented women from using their education in the same way as do men and has encouraged women to enter low-wage female occupations. The connection between women's education and employment as a condition for gender equality was premised on the idea that education would enable women to work for a wage like a man, but, unlike men, would also work in the family without a wage. Indeed, the very idea that education may be an enabling condition of workforce entry and of gender equality presumes that lack of qualification is at the root of inequality between men and women. It also presumes that women's lack of status and authority stem from wage earning. Ignored are the structure of the family, and the differential impact of marriage, child bearing, and child rearing on men versus women. Education is only a means of integrating women into male-dominated social structures on males' terms. It is little wonder, then, that educated women have sought out work for a wage that could most easily be combined with wageless work in the family— teaching, nursing, and so on. Few efforts have been made to change women's role expectations in the family, the structure of occupations to accommodate family responsibilities, discrimination against women in employment or remuneration, or the vertical as well as horizontal sex segregation of the workforce. Schooling alone can only provide women with knowledge, skills, and credentials, but the extent to which these translate into equality between men and women in society depends on whether the structures that keep women subservient to men are themselves changed. This extends beyond, but includes, the workforce and most certainly involves changes in the family and women's roles in it. As long as the domestic sphere is women's primary domain, unless impoverished, women are unlikely to seek work that does not allow them to combine waged employment and their unpaid responsibilities at home. Achieving equality in access to education is quite possible; it can be and has been done. Achieving gender-based equality in the workforce and in society, however, takes more than opening schools to women.

ROBERT F. ARNOVE
HARVEY J. GRAFF

Chapter 18

National Literacy Campaigns in Historical and Comparative Perspective: Legacies, Lessons, and Issues*

This chapter examines national literacy campaigns in historical and comparative perspective. We maintain that a focus on campaigns facilitates analysis of literacy goals and outcomes in particular historical and social contexts, providing insight into the relationship between the spread of literacy and its various uses. The theme of a campaign is timely: 1990, the "International Year of Literacy", marked the commencement of a decade of internationally coordinated medium- and long-range strategies and programs to eliminate illiteracy and provide universal primary education (UPE) by the year 2000. After briefly reviewing data on the extent of illiteracy both globally and regionally, by level of economic development and for significant populations, we discuss what lessons might be derived from a review of past literacy campaigns and what tensions are likely to persist during and after even the most successful of campaigns.

EXTENT OF ILLITERACY

Although significant gains were registered in the number of adults who have become literate in the past two decades, the absolute number of illiterate individuals fifteen years of age and older has also increased. While the percentage of adult illiterates decreased between 1970 and 1990 from 33 percent to 25 percent, the absolute number increased from 760 to 882 million. UNESCO estimates that there were more than 880 million illiterate adults in 1990 and that the number will reach one billion by the year 2000. A majority of the world's illiterate adults live in only two countries—the People's Republic of China and India—but Africa is the region with the highest illiteracy rate—47 percent in 1990.

Table 18.1 indicates significant differences between rich and poor countries, and between men and women, in literacy attainment. According to Lind and Johnston, "In the 25 least developed countries (with a per capita product of less than 100 U.S. dollars per year) the illiteracy rate was more than 80% in 1970 and around 68% in 1985."[1] Ninety-eight percent of the world's illiterate are found in developing countries, although the figure of 2 percent for industrially developed countries fails to convey the existence of large pockets of illiteracy.[2]

TABLE 18.1

Number of Illiterates and Illiteracy Rates in 1985 for the Adult Population Aged 15 and Over

	Absolute number of illiterates 15 and over (in millions)	Illiteracy rates (age 15 and over)		
		Both sexes	Men	Women
World total	888.7	27.7	20.5	34.9
Developing countries	868.9	38.2	27.9	48.9
Least developed countries	120.8	67.6	56.9	78.4
'Developed' countries	19.8	2.1	1.7	2.6
Africa	161.9	54.0	43.3	64.5
Latin America	43.6	17.3	15.3	19.2
Asia	665.7	36.3	25.6	47.4
Oceania	1.6	8.9	7.6	10.2
Europe (including USSR)	13.9	2.3	1.6	3.0

Source. UNESCO Office of Statistics, *The Current Literacy Situation in the World* (UNESCO, July 1985); cited from Agneta Lind and Anton Johnston, *Adult Literacy in the Third World: A Review of Objectives and Strategies* (Stockholm: Institute of International Education, University of Stockholm, and Swedish International Development Authority, 1986), p. 13.

As UNESCO and many adult educators have pointed out, the world map of illiteracy is the map of poverty and, we would add, powerlessness. As a case in point, women who have suffered historically and universally from various forms of subordination, from both the sexual division of labor and from male control over female reproductive rights, as noted by Stromquist, have the highest illiteracy rates, with poor women being even more disadvantaged with regard to access to and participation in literacy programs.[3] UNESCO estimates that of the 882 million illiterate individuals over the age of fifteen in 1990, 553 million were females.[4]

Ethnic minorities and rural populations also register disproportionately high levels of illiteracy. Heath, in a report to the Interagency Commission for the World Conference on Education for All, observed that over 800 million illiterates are located in areas with numerous languages and complex patterns of language use.[5] Minorities are defined not only by their numbers, but principally with regard to the power of groups to influence national political, educational, and cultural policies. For example, statistics for Africa do not include persons literate in languages other than official ones (notably English, French, Portuguese, and Spanish). According to African educator Baba Haidara, "Africa south of the Sahara is perhaps the only region of the world in which the languages of instruction (and often of literacy) are not utilized by the immense majority of the population."[6]

Rural populations, historically, have not wielded the same political clout to shape educational benefits or gain access to educational resources and services. To take the case of India, the country with the largest number of illiterates: in 1981, the illiteracy rate for urban populations was 34.9 percent; and for rural populations, 67.3 percent. The highest literacy rate was found among females living in rural areas—82.4 percent.[7]

These patterns of state educational provision and literacy acquisition by different subpopulations are not unique to the contemporary period, although there also have been interesting and significant historical variations. For example, historically, literacy campaigns have not been tied to the wealth, industrialization, urbanization, or democratization of a society nor to a particular type of political regime.

NATURE OF LITERACY CAMPAIGNS

Although there is a tendency to consider large-scale efforts to provide literacy a phenomenon of the twentieth century, we contend that major and largely successful campaigns to raise levels of literacy have taken place over the past four hundred years in the West, beginning with the Protestant Reformation. Both historically and comparatively, literacy campaigns have formed part of larger transformations in societies. These transformations have attempted to integrate individuals into more comprehensive political and/or religious communities.

The efficacy of literacy and the printed word itself has been an article of faith since the sixteenth century in Europe. Then, as now, reformers and idealists, shakers and movers of societies and historical periods, have viewed literacy as a means to other ends, whether to a more moral society or a more stable political order. No less today than four hundred years ago, individuals have sought and used literacy to attain their own goals.

In the twentieth century, particularly from 1960 on, pronouncements about literacy have deemed it a process of critical consciousness-raising and human liberation. Just as frequently, such declarations refer to literacy as a means to perhaps diametrically opposing goals—to the ends of national development and to a social order that elites, both national and international, define.[8]

In the following section, we review some principal findings from an analysis of national literacy campaigns over a four hundred year period in over a dozen societies.[9] By pointing out the following lessons derived from our analysis we intend to do more than provide practical guidelines for campaigns; we endeavor to illuminate the dynamics and tensions that characterize literacy provision and acquisition.

LEGACIES AND LESSONS

Among the lessons we have culled from our examination of efforts at literacy provision are these:

— that literacy efforts need to last long enough to be effective,
— that local initiative should be mobilized in conjunction with national will,
— that there will be a significant minority who will oppose or not be reached by literacy efforts of centralized authorities,
— that eventually emphasis will have to be placed on schooling for youth (in order to head off future illiteracy), and
— that literacy must be viewed and understood in its various contexts.

CAMPAIGNS LAST YEARS

In a UNESCO-commissioned review of twentieth-century national literacy campaigns, Bhola defines a literacy campaign as a "mass approach that seeks to make all adult men and women in a nation literate within a particular time frame. Literacy is seen as a means to a comprehensive set of ends—economic, social-structural, and political." He notes that "a campaign suggests urgency and combativeness. It is in the nature of an expectation, it is something of a crusade." Sometimes largescale attainment of literacy becomes the moral equivalent of war. By contrast, a "literacy program . . . even though planned, systematic and designed by objectives may lack both urgency and passionate fervor."[10]

Although a limited time frame is considered to be a defining characteristic of a mass campaign, those national cases frequently pointed to as exemplars of twentieth-century literacy mobilizations commonly took one or more decades. Bhola's examples include the USSR (1919-39), Vietnam (1945-77), the People's Republic of China (1950s through 1980s), Burma (1960s through 1980s), Brazil (1967-80), and Tanzania (1971-81). Only the Cuban literacy campaign spanned a period of one year or less. The Nicaraguan Literacy Crusade of

1980, not studied by Bhola, lasted only five months; but immediately following the 1980 *Cruzada*, the Nicaraguan government instituted a campaign in indigenous languages for non-Spanish speaking populations of the Atlantic Coast Region, and it established, in the same vein as Cuba, a program of continuing basic *(popular)* education. Some seven years after the 1980-81 mobilizations there were renewed calls for a campaign to reach those adults who had lapsed into illiteracy because of the war situation in the country.

As literacy campaigns are usually initiated during periods of upheaval, revolutionary transformation, and civil strife, the difficulty of achieving and sustaining lofty educational goals—which frequently characterize new political regimes—is not surprising. The Soviet Union, for example, stands out as the first case of a country adopting a war-siege mentality to combat illiteracy. The December 29, 1919 Decree on Illiteracy required all illiterates eight to fifty years of age to study, empowering local Narkompros (People's Commissariats of Enlightenment) to draft citizens to teach, and making it a criminal offense to refuse to teach or study.[11] Five years after the passing of comprehensive legislation and the establishment of a national literacy agency and of "liquidation points," Minister of Education Anatoly Lunacharsky complained that "the society for the liquidation of illiteracy passes wonderful resolutions, but the concrete results of its work are despicable."[12] N. K. Krupskaya, Lenin's wife and a renowned educator, complained ten years after the passage of the 1919 literacy decree that not a single article had been implemented.[13]

Further insights are provided by Lind and Johnston in their review of objectives and strategies of adult literacy efforts in Third World countries in the post-World War II period. They found that most adult literacy programs have a low level of efficiency with often far less than 30 percent of individuals who enroll in a literacy program successfully passing a final test to certify minimal competency. As they note, "Only the very large single 'campaign to eliminate illiteracy' has been able to reach and retain a sizeable number of adult learners." They conclude: "Where strides towards eradicating illiteracy have been made, it has usually been by incorporating very large numbers of people in each stage of the total effort and 'passing' a low proportion, and not by 'passing' a large percentage of a small number enrolled."[14]

NATIONAL POLITICAL WILL IS IMPORTANT— BUT SO IS LOCAL INITIATIVE

While it may take ten years or more for a campaign to take hold, nationally orchestrated literacy programs are usually preceded by grassroots initiatives. Moreover, the fanfare heralding tremendous achievements brought about by new political regimes generally obscures local educational efforts and accomplishments upon which national policymakers build.[15]

Perhaps the most striking example of the successful attainment of high literacy levels through decentralized efforts is that of nineteenth-century America. Unlike the German, Swedish, and Scottish campaigns of the seventeenth and eighteenth centuries, there was no centrally determined policy that brought the power and resources of the nation-state to bear on the problem of literacy. Instead, the competition of religious denominations, the proliferation of religious and secular presses, the exhortation of leading secular and clerical authorities, and local civic initiative came together to promote literacy activities.[16] Most activity was organized and directed by the individual states rather than the federal government.

In the twentieth century, the most striking examples of mobilization involve national, centrally organized efforts that are waged in terms of a "war on ignorance." But these efforts also have depended heavily on local initiative and popular organizations to recruit teachers and to implement instructional activities. The People's Republic of China, with the most massive mobilization of people (over 137 million people), was, according to Bhola, "centrally instituted and nationally orchestrated, but carried out in a decentralized manner, leaving much to local choice and initiative."[17] China illustrates, in extreme form, the importance of national political will to achieving widescale literacy in a poor country.[18] Other prominent examples include Cuba, Tanzania, and Nicaragua. By contrast, advanced industrialized countries like the United States, the United Kingdom, and France represent, according to Limage, societies that have not committed the resources and efforts necessary to resolve substantial literacy problems.[19] The success of large-scale mobilizations, particularly in socialist countries, is often the function of mass organizations such as youth, worker, neighborhood, defense, and women's associations. A national campaign, by mobilizing large numbers of people and strengthening mass organizations, creates opportunities for large-scale citizenship participation in decision making. But such mobilizations and organizations may also serve as instruments for exercising cultural and political hegemony by dominant groups or state apparatuses.

As the International Council on Adult Education has noted, "If literacy programmes are imposed on people and are not related to development and or local conditions, they have little chance of improving people's lives; they should encourage participation and self-management.[20] One of the consequences of state authorities imposing literacy and educational program on local populations is resistance.

RESISTANCE

History offers countless examples of people, individually and collectively, resisting such imposition. The German literacy drives elicited this response from peasants as early as the sixteenth century. Russia offers abundant instances before and after the 1917 revolution of peasant populations setting up their own schools and employing reading materials that did not accord with the designs of state authorities. Eklof chronicles peasant attacks on State appointed teachers in the late 1920s and early 1930s. He also describes how, in later years, despite intense efforts at censorship, readers pursued their own interests, frequently of an escapist nature: "Library subscribers took out books on politics in far smaller number than their availability. Books checked out were concentrated in the areas of travel, biography, and history (primarily on World War II, military memoirs, spy documentaries, regimental histories)."[21]

Similar accounts of reading habits from Tanzania and the People's Republic of China indicate that peasants and workers may be less interested in reading about how to construct a latrine or organize a cooperative than they are in romance and adventure stories. Gillette, who participated in the evaluation of the UNESCO-sponsored eleven-country Experimental World Literacy Program (1967-73), sums up the difficulty of controlling outcomes of literacy campaigns: "Happily, literacy like education more generally cannot be reduced to behavioral conditioning. It endows people with skills that they can (although do not always) use to receive and emit messages of an almost infinite range, a range that in any event escapes the control of those who imparted literacy . . . . Literacy is potential empowerment."[22] Similarly, Noor notes that attempts to define literacy too narrowly, in terms of "functional work needs may alienate." He recommends that ". . . the content of learning materials should be culturally oriented . . . and relevant to adult perceptions."[23]

One question that is pertinent here is how are illiterate people treated by the increasingly literate population. As learning to read, possibly to write, involves the acquisition or conferral of a new status—membership in a religious community, citizenship in a nation-state—literacy often carries tremendous symbolic weight, quite apart from any power and new capabilities it may bring. The attainment of literacy per se operates as a badge, a sign of initiation into a select group and/or a larger community. The opposite side of the coin is that those who do not participate in a campaign or who continue to be illiterate may be labeled as deviant and denied full membership rights in a more comprehensive community. Historically as well as more recently, those who oppose literacy efforts may be viewed as dissident, unassimilated, counterrevolutionary, or enemies of the state.

SIGNIFICANT POPULATIONS ARE NOT REACHED

In addition to the resistance of people to control or to content that is alienating, there are other seemingly intractable problems. As noted earlier, class, ethnic, racial, geographical, and gender differences in literacy acquisition have been ubiquitous over the past four hundred years. Historically and comparatively, rural populations, the working class, ethnic and racial minorities, and women have been the last to receive literacy instruction and to gain access to advanced levels of schooling.

Women, in the past as in the contemporary period, have been the most disadvantaged group. From the time of the Protestant Reformation, when household heads were held responsible by the state for literacy instruction and for supervising reading, men typically have benefited most from education campaigns. Moreover, when reading was extended to women, men received preference in the teaching of writing. However, in early modern Sweden and the nineteenth-century United States, perceptions concerning women's special "mission" as educators in the home and as school teachers propelled their rates of literacy upward, sometimes rivaling those of men. More recently, the Cuban and Nicaraguan campaigns reveal a new potential for breaking this pattern. In both countries, a majority of the literacy workers were women. The results from other campaigns, such as Tanzania, indicate, however, that women predominate at the lower levels of literacy attainment; at the highest levels, corresponding to functional literacy, males predominate.[24]

Overall, according to Stromquist, "Except for a few countries (particularly Jamaica and Lesotho) women have lower levels of literacy than men." There is a difference of twenty-one percentage points between men and women in developing countries, and while 58 percent of adult illiterates were women in 1960, the figure had increased to 63 percent by 1985.[25] As cases in point: in Asia, while the number of illiterate men decreased from 247 to 233 million, the number of illiterate women increased from 390 to 418;[26] in Africa, of an estimated 169 million illiterates in 1990, 105 million were women.[27]

Despite the intensity and scale of efforts, and whether by intent or not, an unmistakable pattern emerges from an historical analysis of campaigns from cases as diverse as preindustrial Germany, the Soviet Union (1919-39), Tanzania (1970-83), and Nicaragua (1980-86). Regardless of date, duration, or developmental level, approximately 85 percent adult literacy is achieved.[28] It seems that an irreducible minimum remains of at least 10 percent to 20 percent. This finding places in question notions that, except for a small minority of severely handicapped and institutionalized populations, it is possible to achieve literacy rates of over 95 percent in advanced industrialized societies.

SCHOOLING BECOMES THE VEHICLE FOR ATTACKING ILLITERACY

The intractability of adults, who do not wish to learn in ways prescribed by state authorities or be converted to a different set of beliefs, is a common occurrence. An important legacy of the German Reformation campaigns is Luther's shift in attention to shaping the young, as opposed to his earlier focus on all members of the community.[29] The dilemma faced by Luther, whether to concentrate literacy efforts on the young (who may be less "corrupted" and more malleable) or on adults, is a strategic issue in almost all subsequent mass campaigns. In twentieth-century campaigns, despite initial large-scale efforts aimed at entire populations, a narrowing eventually occurs with greater emphasis placed on the formal education of the young. Thus, as Lind and Johnston observe: "The provision of 'basic education' for all children and adults has in the 1980's become a major concern in the international community, which has led to the promotion of both mass adult literacy campaigns and UPE (Universal Primary Education) for children in a reformed, more 'relevant' and 'cost-efficient' primary school."[30]

It is not surprising that literacy provision and socialization of individuals over time have merged and been institutionalized in state systems of formal education. From the earliest campaigns, the goals of literacy provision have been the propagation of a particular faith or world view through the reading of prescribed texts under the supervision of teachers of a certain moral persuasion and of an upright character. Historically, the religious orientation of school systems has given way to a more secular faith in the nation-state and/or the propagation of an ideology such as capitalism or socialism. State organized and regulated systems of schooling represent, for political elites, an efficient means of achieving these goals. While bureaucratic systems of education with their attendant centralization of decision making, standardization of routines, and uniformity of curriculum, may bring certain benefits, such systems also lead to alienation and academic failure—possible illiteracy—of substantial numbers of individuals who do not fit into such structures.

Data from Africa and Latin America are suggestive of the difficulties educational reforms face in tying gradual elimination of illiteracy primarily to provision of basic education to the young. In Latin America, school repetition rates are as high as 25 percent to 30 percent in the early grades when children are learning to read. According to Tedesco, a high percentage of students' first experience with schooling is that of failure. In many Latin American countries, less than a majority of a student cohort complete five or six years of primary schooling, with the highest dropout rates being registered by working class children, rural populations, females, and ethnic minorities. Between 1980 and 1990, as Tedesco goes on to note, the rhythm of school expansion was interrupted by the severe economic crises affecting the region, especially the high foreign debt that led to cutbacks in funding of social services.[31]

A similar pattern obtains in Sub-Saharan Africa where high levels of illiteracy combine with low levels of school penetration. Although the absolute number of school-going children increased between 1970 and 1985, the percentage of the relevant age group attending formal educational institutions dropped from 75 percent to 57 percent. According to Haidara, policymakers face the twin problems of population growth and dysfunctional systems of education that absorb a high percentage of governmental budgets.[32]

Worldwide, there are an estimated 100 million children without access to basic schooling. Moreover, one of the legacies of literacy campaigns, and a salient lesson that emerges from an historical analysis of past campaigns, is that the widespread provision of literacy usually leads to a dramatic increase in the demand for formal schooling on the part of newly literate populations, whether they be youths or adults. Post-literacy programs that are not tied to a credentialing school system are unlikely to satisfy, for long, the heightened expectations of individuals who have successfully completed literacy programs.[33]

Thus the prospect for the future is both that of increasing numbers of youth and young adults achieving literacy through schooling but also substantial numbers and percentages who either do not achieve a basic level of formal education or who will leave school illiterate or with minimal literacy skills. These patterns suggest the need for educational policy makers to continue to mount large-scale literacy efforts to reach those populations never reached by school or poorly served by formal education.

For the past two decades notions of lifelong education have formed part of the international agenda of educational reform and visions of what education systems would and should be like in the future. Tied to notions of lifelong opportunities for individuals to improve their knowledge and skills and develop a broad range of talents are changing definitions of literacy.

LITERACY MUST BE CONTEXTUALLY DEFINED AND CONTINUALLY REAPPRAISED

Literacy takes on meaning in particular historical and social formations. The status of literate persons and the multiple competencies that are required to interpret texts and communicate with others must be viewed in relation to the demands of specific settings. In industrialized societies, a variety of qualifiers are used in conjunction with the term literacy: one commonly hears references, for example, to computer and scientific literacy, and even "cultural" literacy.[34] It is generally considered that more sophisticated reading and writing skills are required in more complex technological environments, and comprehension of various print materials necessitates background knowledge of both national and international contexts. Thus, it is likely that there will continually be calls for renewed efforts to reach and impart literacy-related skills of a higher order.

On the other hand, a radical political economy critique of industrialized societies is likely to point out that a process of deskilling has been going on in the workforce of countries like the United States.[35] If the fastest growing sectors of the economy are not in high technology areas involving robotics and computerization, but in the service sector and, in particular, areas like fast food restaurants and security services, then there are unlikely to be sufficient economic incentives and rewards for individuals to develop higher order communication and computation skills.

In a similar vein, Kelly and Wallace point out in their examination of adult basic adult education program that:

> The goal . . . is not ultimately a critical and imaginative literacy but an *etiquette*, an ability to perform tasks whose value refers not to the life experiences of the student but to the institution of education. The student's willingness to perform literary tasks, to adopt good study habits, to respect authority and the rules of educational institutions, etc., are the values of employability. Employment is not the purpose of literacy but rather a certain behavior: passive obedience to authority.[36]

Viewing literacy in context also contributes to an understanding of why literacy is only potential empowerment, and why certain groups try to prevent or control the provision of literacy. Cases from rural India to inner city Los Angeles underscore how the acquisition of literacy by previously dispossessed and dependent individuals represents a threat to dominant groups. Powerful landlords, commercial groups, economic and cultural brokers will resort to violence against literacy teachers and community organizers who teach individuals and collectivities, in the words of Freire, to "read the world" by learning to read the word. Restraints and conflicts that operate in the public domain are also mirrored in the private domain as women who attempt to gain literacy skills and take on new roles in society encounter the resistance of their male counterparts.[37]

Consideration of context contributes to a greater understanding of the common assertion of literacy scholars and activists that illiteracy must be seen as a symptom rather than a cause of underdevelopment. Illiteracy must be viewed in relation to political, economic, cultural, and social factors that encourage or limit the development and expression of human talent generally and communicative competencies in particular. The imperative to study literacy in context further underscores the futility of attempting, in narrowly positivistic and functionalist terms, to reduce literacy to a specified set of skills that are universally the same.[38]

CONCLUDING REFLECTIONS AND QUESTIONS

A historical and comparative review of national literacy campaigns leads us to conclude that there are many paths to literacy, that literacy's interaction with political, economic, and social development is complex, that the quantity and the quality of literacy (and the acquisition and use of literacy) are not linearly related, that the consequences of literacy are neither direct nor simple, and that literacy is never politically neutral.

Ultimately, contextual factors—the opportunities for using literacy skills, the transformations that occur in social structures, the ideology of national leaders—determine whether or not individuals acquire, retain, and use literacy skills. Whether literacy and postliteracy campaigns use materials and methods that are truly designed to equip people to play more active roles in shaping the direction of their societies or, instead, use materials and methods aimed at inducting people into predetermined roles is a telling indication of the ideology and intent of these campaigns.

Once we assume that the necessary contextual factors obtain, we move on to other considerations. One set of questions concerns whether or not political and educational policymakers are willing to dedicate sufficient resources and time to the endeavor, while encouraging local initiative and input. Another set concerns the extent to which they will take into account the reasons for resistance to such national efforts, and find the means to reach previously ignored or discriminated against populations with materials and methods that serve the interests of these groups.

From current and past literacy campaigns, literacy planners and political leaders have learned a number of lessons about the factors that contribute to the success of a campaign or cause it to fall short of its goal. But the extent to which international and national authorities have grasped the implications of these lessons and are committed to applying them remains in question. The lack of resolve of political and educational leaders in many nations may be attributed to the fact that widespread literacy within a populace can have uncontrollable, contradictory, and conflicting consequences.[39] Reluctance on the part of policymakers is especially understandable in the light of the rhetoric and ideology of recent national campaigns which have stressed literacy for "critical consciousness," "liberation," and "empowerment."

As Cairns has observed, literacy is fundamentally a political issue involving these questions: "What sort of society do we want? Are we seriously interested in improving the skills and training of the poorly educated? Will we make this a priority, and commit funds and expertise in an age of dwindling resources?" He goes on to note that these questions lead to others which "starkly clarify the values we put on people and their ability to realize their full potential."[40]

Notes

CHAPTER 1

1. For an elaboration of these "identity" crises, see Gail P. Kelly, Philip Altbach, and Robert Arnove, "Trends in Comparative Education: A Critical Analysis," in Philip Altbach, Robert Arnove, and Gail P. Kelly (eds.) *Comparative Education* (New York: Macmillan, 1982) pp. 505-533.

2. *Ibid.* See also, Harold Noah and Max Eckstein, *Toward a Science of Comparative Education* (New York: Macmillan, 1969); Gail P. Kelly and Philip Altbach, "Comparative Education: Challenge and Response," *Comparative Education Review* 30 (February 1986): 89-107.

3. Isaac L. Kandel, *Comparative Education* (Boston: Houghton Mifflin, 1933). Nicholas Hans, *Comparative Education* (London: Routledge and Kegan Paul, 1949), was also an early influential work.

4. See Andreas Kazamias, "Woozles and Wizzles in the Methodology of Comparative Education," *Comparative Education Review*, 14 (October 1970): 255-261.

5. *Ibid.* See also Noah and Eckstein, *Toward a Science of Comparative Education*, *op. cit.*

6. George Z. F. Bereday, *Comparative Method in Education* (New York: Holt, Rinehart, and Winston, 1964).

7. Noah and Eckstein, *op. cit.*

8. See especially C. Arnold Anderson, "Methodology of Comparative Education," *International Review of Education*, 7 (no. 1, 1961): 1-23.

9. See, for example, Irvin Sobel, "The Human Capital Revolution in Economic Development: Its Current History and Status," *Comparative Education Review*, 22 (June 1978): 278-307; Philip J. Foster, "Dilemmas of Educational Development: What

We Might Learn from the Past," *Comparative Education Review*, 19 (October 1975): 375-392; A. M. Kazamias, "Comparative Pedagogy, *Comparative Education Review* 16 (October 1972): 406-411.

10. See Philip G. Altbach, "Education and Neocolonialism," *Teachers College Record*, 72 (May 1972): 543-558; Martin Carnoy, *Education as Cultural Imperialism* (New York: McKay, 1974); Philip G. Altbach and Gail P. Kelly, eds., *Education and Colonialism* (New York: Longmans, 1978).

11. See, for example, Dean C. Tibbs, "Modernization Theory and the Study of National Societies: A Critical Perspective," *Comparative Studies in Society and History* 15 (1973): 199-226; Rolland G. Paulston, *Conflicting Theories of Social and Educational Change* (Pittsburgh: University of Pittsburgh Center for International Studies, 1976).

12. Carnoy, *op. cit.*; Michael W. Apple, "Ideology, Reproduction and Educational Reform," *Comparative Education Review* 22 (October 1978): 367-387.

13. See, J. D. Cockcroft, Andre Gunder Frank, and D. L. Johnson, eds., *Dependency and Underdevelopment: Latin America's Political Economy* (Garden City, NY: Anchor Books, 1972).

14. Altbach, "Education and Neocolonialism," *op. cit.* P. G. Altbach, "Literary Colonialism: Books in the Third World," *Harvard Educational Review*, 45 (July 1975): 226-236; Carnoy, *op. cit.*; Robert F. Arnove, "Comparative Education and World Systems Analysis," in Philip G. Altbach, Robert Arnove, and Gail P. Kelly, eds., *Comparative Education* (New York: Macmillan, 1982), pp. 453-468.

15. See, A. M. Kazamias, "Comparative Pedagogy," *op. cit.*; Rolland Paulston, *op. cit.*; Lois Weis, "Educational Outcomes and School Processes: Theoretical Perspectives," in Philip G. Altbach, Robert Arnove, and Gail P. Kelly (eds.) *Comparative Education* (New York: Macmillan, 1982), pp. 485-504; Vandra Lea Masemann, "Critical Ethnography in the Study of Comparative Education," *Comparative Education Review* 26 (February 1982): 1-15.

16. Apple, *op. cit.*; Arnove, *op. cit.*; Carnoy, *op. cit.*; Rolland Paulston, *op. cit.*; Hans Weiler, "Legalization, Expertise, and Participation: Strategies of Compensatory Legitimation in Educational Policy," *Comparative Education Review*, 27 (June 1983): 259-277; John Bock, "Education and Development: A Conflict of Meaning," in Philip G. Altbach, Robert Arnove, and Gail P. Kelly, eds., *Comparative Education* (New York: Macmillan, 1982), pp. 78-104.

17. See, for example, Harold J. Noah and Max Eckstein, "Education and Dependency: The New Simplicitude," *Prospect* (1985):; Keith Watson, "Dependence in Education? Two Cases from Post-Colonial Southeast Asia," *International Journal of Educational Development*, 5 (no. 2, 1985): 83-94; Martin McLean, "Educational Dependency: A Critique," *Compare*, 13 (no. 1, 1983): 25-41.

18. Erwin H. Epstein, "Currents Left and Right: Ideology in Comparative Educa-

tion," *Comparative Education Review*, 27 (February 1983): 3-29.

19. Paulston, *op. cit.*

20. See, for example, George Psacharopoulos, "The Planning of Education: Where Do We Stand?" *Comparative Education Review*, 30 (November 1986): 560-573; Steven J. Klees, "Planning and Policy Analysis in Education: What Can Economics Tell Us?" *Comparative Education Review*, 30 (November 1986): 574-607.

21. See Gail P. Kelly, "New Directions in Research on Women's Education in the Third World: The Development of Women-Centric Approaches," in David H. Kelly and Gail P. Kelly, *Women's Education in the Third World: An Annotated Bibliography.* (New York: Garland Publishing, Inc., 1989), pp. 15-37.

22. See, for example, Hans N. Weiler, "Educational Planning and Social Change: A Critical Review of Concepts and Practices," in Philip G. Altbach, Robert Arnove, and Gail P. Kelly, eds., *Comparative Education* (New York: Macmillan, 1982), pp. 105-118.

23. Sobel, *op. cit.*; Klees, *op. cit.*

24. Psacharopoulos, *op. cit.*

25. See, for example, George Psacharopoulos, "The Perverse Effects of Public Subsidization, or How Equitable is Free Education?" *Comparative Education Review*, 21 (February 1977); 69-90; Martin Thobani, "Charging User Fees for Social Services: Education in Malawi," *Comparative Education Review*, 28 (August 1984): 402-423; Alain Mingat and Jee-Peng Tan, "Who Profits from the Public Funding of Education: A Comparison of World Regions," *Comparative Education Review*, 30 (May 1986): 260-270.

26. See World Bank, Education in Sub-Saharan Africa, "Summary of World Bank Report, 1988 (Symposium: World Bank Report on Education in Sub-Saharan Africa)." *Comparative Education Review*, 33 (February 1989): 93-104.

27. Ivan Ilich, *De-Schooling Society.*

28. See, for example, Steven J. Klees, "The Need for a Political Economy of Educational Finance: A Response to Thobani," *Comparative Education Review*, 28 (August 1984): 424-440.

29. See Mingat and Tan, *op. cit.*; Thobani, *op. cit.*; Mateen Thobani, "A Reply to Klees," *Comparative Education Review*, 28 (August 1984): 441-443.

30. Ruth Hayhoe, "A Chinese Puzzle," *Comparative Education Review*, 33 (July 1989): 153-175.

31. George Psacharopoulos, "Comparative Education: From Theory to Practice, or Are You A: \neo.* or B:*.ist?" *Comparative Education Review*, 34 (August 1990): 369-380. Quote is from p. 369.

32. Don Adams, "Commentary: Analysis Without Theory is Incomplete," *Com-*

parative Education Review, 34 (August 1990): 381-384; Rolland Paulston, "Commentary: From Paradigm Wars to Disputatious Community," *Comparative Education Review*, 34 (August 1990): 395-400.

CHAPTER 2

1. Emile Durkheim, *The Division of Labor in Society* (New York: Free Press, 1933).

2. Emile Durkheim, *Moral Education* (Glencoe, IL: Free Press, 1961).

3. Talcott Parsons, "The School Class as a Social System," *Harvard Educational Review* XXIX 4 (1957): 297-318; Robert Dreeben, *On What is Learned in School* (Reading, MA: Addison-Wesley, 1968).

4. Samuel Bowles and Herbert Gintis, *Schooling in Capitalist America* (New York: Basic Books, 1976); Michael B. Katz, *The Irony of Bureaucracy and Schools: The Illusion of Educational Change in America* (New York: Praeger, 1975); Ake Isling, *Kampen for och mot en demokratisk skola (The Struggle for and Against a Democratic School)*(Stockholm: Sober, 1980); Bengt Sandin, *Hemmet gatan fabriken eller skolan. Folkundervisning och barnuppfostran i svenska stader 1600-1850 (Home, Street, Factory or School: Popular Education and Child-Rearing in Swedish Towns 1600-1850)* (Ph.D. diss., University of Lund, Sweden; Lund: Arkiv, 1985).

5. Ingemar Fagerlind and Lawrence Saha, *Education and National Development* (Oxford: Pergamon, 1983).

6. Randall Collins, "Functional and Conflict Theories of Educational Stratification, " *American Sociological Review* 36 (1971): 1002-19, and "Some Comparative Principles of Educational Stratification," *Harvard Educational Review* 47 (1977): 1-27.

7. Margaret Archer, *Social Origins of Educational Systems* (Beverly Hills: Sage, 1979.

8. Cf. Bernard Bailyn, *Education in the Forming of American Society* (Chapel Hill: University of North Carolina Press, 1960).

9. Joel Spring, *Education and the Rise of the Corporate State* (Boston: Beacon, 1972).

10. Alex Inkeles and David Smith, *Becoming Modern: Individual Change in Six Developing Countries* (Cambridge: Harvard University Press, 1974).

11. For example, Collins sees compulsory schooling laws in the American states as a solution to multiethnic conflicts—they made "training in Anglo-Protestant culture and political values compulsory for all children up to a certain age." Randall Collins, *The Credential Society: A Historical Sociology of Education and Stratification* (New York: Academic Press, 1979).

12. On Europe, see Mary Jo Maynes, *Schooling in Western Europe: A Social History* (Albany State University of New York Press, 1985); on the United States, see John G. Richardson, "Historical Sequences and the Origins of Common Schooling in the American States," in *Handbook of Theory and Research for the Sociology of Education*, ed. John G. Richardson (Westport, CT: Greenwood Press, 1986).

13. See, respectively, I.N. Thut and D. Adams, *Educational Patterns in Contemporary Societies* (New York: McGraw-Hill, 1964); Bernard Jolibert, *L'enfance au XVII siècle* (Paris: Librairie philosophique J. Vrin, 1981); Henry Barnard, *National Education in Europe* (Hartford, CT: Frederick Perkins, 1854); Jean-Luc le Cam, "L'introduction de l'obligation scolaire dans l'Allemagne protestante du XVIe au XVIIIe siècle: Un problème d'interprétation et de mesure," in *Introduction, Development and Extension of Compulsory Education*, vol. 1 of Conference Papers for the Eighth Session of the International Standing Conference for the History of Education, ed. Giovanni Genovesi (Parma: University of Parma and Centro Italiano per la Ricerca Storico-Educativa, 1986), pp. 55-64.

14. M. Krupa, "L'Introduction de l'obligation scolaire dans la Pologne, la Prusse et l'Autriche," in Genovesi, pp. 197-203.

15. Knut Tveit, "School and Literacy: Introduction of the Elementary School in Norway in the 1730s and 1740s," in Genovesi, pp. 175-84; Jens Vibaek, *Danmarks historie, v. 10: Reform og fallit 1784-1830 (History of Denmark v. 10: Reform and Decline 1784-1830)* (Copenhagen: Politikens Forlag, 1964); Peter Flora, *State Economy and Society in Western Europe*, vol. 1 (Frankfurt: Campus Verlag, 1983); David Tyack, Thomas James, and Aaron Benavot, *Law and the Shaping of Public Education 1785-1954* (Madison: University of Wisconsin Press, 1987).

16. J. F. Braster and N. L. Dodde, "Compulsory Education in the Netherlands: A Problem in the 19th Century, a Solution in the 20th Century," in Genovesi, pp. 163-73; Donald K. Jones, *The Making of the Education System 1851-81* (London: Routledge & Kegan Paul, 1977); Paul Gerbod, "L'obligation educative en France des origines a nos jours," in Genovesi, pp. 43-54.

17. Paul Willis, *Learning to Labor* (Lexington: Heath, 1977); Arthur Stinchcombe, *Rebellion in a High School* (Chicago: Quadrangle Books, 1964).

18. Michael Olneck and D. Bills, "What Makes Sammy Run? An Empirical Assessment of the Bowles-Gintis Correspondence Theory," *American Journal of Education* 89 (1980): 27-61.

19. John Boli and Francisco 0. Ramirez, "World Culture and the Institutionalization of Mass Education," in Richardson, *Handbook of Theory and Research for the Sociology of Education*.

20. John Boli, *New Citizens for a New Society: The Institutional Origins of Mass Schooling in Sweden* (Oxford: Pergamon, 1989); Collins, *The Credential Society*.

21. John Boli, Francisco 0. Ramirez, and John W. Meyer, "Explaining the Origins

and Expansion of Mass Education," *Comparative Education Review* 29: 145-170; Francisco 0. Ramirez and John Boli, "The Political Construction of Mass Schooling: European Origins and Worldwide Institutionalization," *Sociology of Education* 60 (1987): 2-17; Boli and Ramirez, "World Culture and the Institutionalization of Mass Education."

22. John A. Hall, *Powers and Liberties: The Causes and Consequences of the Rise of the West* (London: Basil Blackwell, 1985); Michael Mann, *The Sources of Social Power Vol. 1: A History of Power from the Beginning to A.D. 1760* (Cambridge: Cambridge University Press, 1986); George M. Thomas, John W. Meyer, Francisco 0. Ramirez, and John Boli, *Institutional Structure: Constituting State, Society, and the Individual* (Beverly Hills: Sage, 1987).

23. Guy Swanson, "An Organizational Analysis of Collectivities," *American Sociological Review* 36 (1971): 607-23.

24. Max Weber, *Economy and Society*, two volumes (Berkeley: University of California Press, 1978); Jacques Ellul, *Le système technicien* (Paris: Calmann-Levy, 1977).

25. Cf. the papers in Michael Carrithers, Steven Collins, and Steven Lukes, eds., *The Category of the Person* (Cambridge: Cambridge University Press, 1985 .

26. Erving Goffman, "The Nature of Deference and Demeanor, " *American Anthropologist* 58 (June 1956): 473-502; Emile Durkheim, *Professional Ethics and Civic Morals* (New York: The Free Press, 1958). Durkheim's analysis of the individual is discussed by Anthony Giddens, "The Individual in the Writings of Emile Durkheim," *European Journal of Sociology* 12 (1971): 210-28, and Charles Marske, "Durkheim's Cult of the Individual and the Moral Reconstitution of Society," *Sociological Theory* 5 (1987): 1-14.

27. Walter Ullman, *The Individual and Society in the Middle Ages* (Baltimore: Johns Hopkins University Press, 1966); Louis Dumont, "The Modern Conception of the Individual: Notes on its Genesis and that of Concomitant Institutions," *Contributions to Indian Sociology* VIII (October 1965): 13-61 .

28. Reinhard Bendix, *Nation-Building and Citizenship* (New York: John Wiley, 1964); George M. Thomas, *Revivalism and Cultural Change: Christianity, Nation-Building and the Market in Nineteenth-Century United States* (Chicago: University of Chicago Press, 1989).

29. Philippe Aries, *Centuries of Childhood* (New York: Vintage, 1962); Jolibert, *L'enfance au XVII siècle.* For a critique of the Aries thesis that nevertheless finds "...an increased emphasis on the *abstract* (her italics) nature of childhood and parental care from the 17th century onwards," see Linda Pollock, *Forgotten Children: Parent-Child Relations from 1550 to 1900* (Cambridge: Cambridge University Press, 1983), esp. pp. 263-269.

30. Charles Tilly, "War Making and State Making as Organized Crime," in *Bringing the State Back In*, ed. Peter Evans, Dieter Rueschemeyer, and Theda Skocpol (Cam-

bridge: Cambridge University Press, 1985); Reinhard Bendix, *Kings or People: Power and the Mandate to Rule* (Berkeley: University of California Press, 1978).

31. Reinhard Bendix, *Nation-Building and Citizenship* (New York: John Wiley, 1964).

32. Yet the contradiction between the state and the individual is equally clear: the state restricts individuals, individuals resist the state. But the conflicts involved also strengthen both the individual and the state as social entities.

33. Collins, "Functional and Conflict Theories of Educational Stratification."

34. Collins, *The Credential Society*; Boli, *New Citizens for a New Society*.

35. Emile Durkheim, *Education and Sociology* (New York: Free Press, 1956); Francisco O. Ramirez and Richard Rubinson, "Creating Members: The National Incorporation of Education," in *National Development and the World System: Educational, Economic, and Political Change, 1950-1970*, eds. John W. Meyer and Michael T. Hannan (Chicago: University of Chicago Press, 1979).

36. James Bowen, *A History of Western Education, Volume 3: The Modern West, Europe and the New World* (New York: St. Martin's Press, 1981); John Sommerville, *The Rise and Fall of Childhood* (Beverly Hills: Sage, 1982).

37. See the papers in Genovesi (1986).

38. Max Weber, *The Protestant Ethic and the Spirit of Capitalism* (New York: Scribner's, 1958); Thomas, *Revivalism and Cultural Change*.

39. Robert Nisbet, *History of the Idea of Progress* (New York: Basic Books, 1980); Hans Kohn, *The Age of Nationalism* (New York: Harper & Row, 1962); Sven Goransson, *Folkrepresentation och kvrka 1809-1847 (Political Representation and the Church 1809-1847)* (Uppsala: Almqvist & Wiksell, 1959).

40. Edward Reisner, *Nationalism and Education since 1789* (New York: Macmillan, 1922); Herbert Tingsten, *Gud och fosterlandet: studier i hundra ars skolpropaganda (God and the Fatherland: Studies of a Hundred Years of School Propaganda)* (Stockholm: Norstedt, 1969).

41. Richard Rubinson, "Class Formation, Politics, and Institutions: Schooling in the USA," *American Journal of Sociology* 92 (1986): 519-548; Ira Katznelson and Margaret Weir, *Schooling for All: Class, Race, and the Decline of the Democratic Ideal* (New York: Basic Books, 1986).

42. Boli, Ramirez, and Meyer, "Explaining the Origins and Expansion of Mass Education."

43. Francisco O. Ramirez and Marc Ventresca, "Across Time and Space: An Event History Analysis of Compulsory Schooling Legislation, 1810-1985." Paper presented at the annual meetings of the American Sociological Association in Washington, D.C., 1990.

44. Benedict Anderson, *Imagined Communities: Reflections on the Origins and Spread of Nationalism.* (London: Verso edition, 1983.

45. Gabriela Ossenbach-Sauter, "Notes for a Pattern of Analysis of Compulsory Education in Latin America During the Nineteenth Century" pp. 111-120 in Genovesi (1986).

46. Yasemin Soysal and David Strang, "Construction of the First Mass Education Systems in Nineteenth Century Europe." *Sociology of Education* 62 (1989) 277-288.

47. José Luis García Garrido, "Primary Education on the Threshold of the Twenty-First Century" International Bureau of Education: *International Yearbook of Education,* vol. 38, 1986.

48. Aaron Benavot and Phyllis Riddle, "National Estimates of the Expansion of Mass Education, 1870-1940" *Sociology of Education* 61 (1989) 191-210; John Meyer, Francisco 0. Ramirez, Richard Rubinson, and John Boli-Bennett, "The World Educational Revolution, 1950-1970" *Sociology of Education* 50 (1977): 242-258.

CHAPTER 3

I am indebted to Robert Arnove, Gail P. Kelly, and Lionel Lewis for their comments on this essay and to Lalita Subramanyan for her assistance with editing. A modified version of this chapter appears in *Prospects.*

1. For a historical perspective, see Charles Haskins, *The Rise of Universities* (Ithaca, NY: Cornell University Press, 1957).

2. Philip G. Altbach, *The Knowledge Context: Comparative Perspectives on the Distribution of Knowledge* (Albany, NY: State University of New York Press, 1987).

3. For further discussion of this point, see A. B. Cobban, *The Medieval Universities: Their Development and Organization* (London: Metheun, 1975).

4. The history of British higher education expansion in India and Africa is described in Eric Ashby, *Universities: British, Indian, African* (Cambridge, MA: Harvard University Press, 1966).

5. Irene Gilbert, "The Indian Academic Profession: The Origins of a Tradition of Subordination," *Minerva* 10 (July, 1972), pp. 384-411.

6. For a broader consideration of these themes, see Lawrence Stone, ed., *The University in Society* (2 volumes), (Princeton: Princeton University Press, 1974).

7. Joseph Ben-David, *Centers of Learning: Britain, France, Germany, United States* (New York: McGraw-Hill, 1977), pp. 16-17.

8. Friedrich Lilge, *The Abuse of Learning: The Failure of the German University* (New York: Macmillan, 1948).

9. Charles E. McClelland, *State, Society and University in Germany, 1700-1914* (Cambridge, England: Cambridge University Press, 1980). See also J. Ben-David and A. Zloczower, "Universities and Academic Systems in Modern Societies," *European Journal of Sociology* 3 (no. 1,1962): 45-84.

10. In the German-originated chair system, a single full professor was appointed in each discipline. All other academic staff served under the direction of the chair holder, who held a permanent appointment to the position. Many other countries, including Japan, Russia, and most of Eastern Europe, adopted this system. In time, it was criticized as too rigid and hierarchical.

11. Laurence Veysey, *The Emergence of the American University* (Chicago: University of Chicago Press, 1965). For a somewhat different analysis, see E. T. Silva and S. A. Slaughter, *Serving Power: The Making of the Academic Social Science Expert* (Westport, CT: Greenwood, 1984).

12. In Egypt, the Al-Azhar University still offers Islamic higher education in the traditional manner. There are virtually no other universities which fundamentally diverge from the Western model. For a discussion of the contemporary Islamic university, see H. H. Bilgrami and S. A. Ashraf, *The Concept of an Islamic University* (London: Hodder and Stoughton, 1985).

13. Philip G. Altbach, "The American Academic Model in Comparative Perspective," in P. G. Altbach., ed., *The Relevance of American Higher Education to Southeast Asia* (Singapore: Regional Institute for Higher Education and Development, 1985), pp. 15-36.

14. For a case study of British higher education policy in India, see David Lelyveld, *Aligarh's First Generation: Muslim Solidarity in British India* (Princeton: Princeton University Press, 1978).

15. Michio Nagai, *Higher Education in Japan: Its Take-off and Crash* (Tokyo: University of Tokyo Press, 1971).

16. See Philip G. Altbach and V. Selvaratnam, eds., *From Dependence to Autonomy: The Development of Asian Universities* (Dordrecht, Netherlands: Kluwer, 1989) for case studies of a variety of Asian universities.

17. See Philip G. Altbach, David Kelly, and Y. Lulat, *Research on Foreign Students and International Study: Bibliography and Analysis* (New York: Praeger, 1985) for a full discussion of the issues relating to foreign study.

18. A telling example in this respect is that the number of American students going abroad is only a small proportion of foreigners coming to the United States—and the large majority of Americans who do study in other countries go to Canada and Western Europe and not to the Third World. See also Robert Arnove, "Foundations and the Transfer of Knowledge," in *Philanthropy and Cultural Imperialism*, ed. Robert Arnove (Boston: G. K. Hall, 1980), pp. 305-330.

19. For a discussion of higher education development in the NICs, see Philip G. Altbac et al., *Scientific Development and Higher Education: The Case of Newly Industrializing Countries* (New York: Praeger, 1989).

20. Martin Trow, "Problems in the Transition from Elite to Mass Higher Education, (Paper prepared for a conference on mass higher education held by the Organization for Economic Cooperation and Development, Paris, 1975).

21. For documentation concerning African higher education, see World Bank, *Education in Sub-Saharan Africa: Policies for Adjustment, Revitalization and Expansion* (Washington, D.C.: World Bank, 1988), particularly chapter 6.

22. Philip G. Altbach et al., *Scientific Development and Higher Education: The Case of Newly Industrializing Nations* (New York: Praeger, 1989).

23. Max A. Eckstein and Harold J. Noah, "Forms and Functions of Secondary School Leaving Examinations, *Comparative Education Review* 33 (August, 1989), pp. 295-316.

24. It is also the case that academic institutions serve as important "sorting" institutions in modern society, sometimes diverting students from highly competitive fields. See, for example, Steven Brint and Jerome Karabel, The *Diverted Dream: Community Colleges and the Promise of Educational Opportunity in America, 1900-1985* (New York: Oxford University Press, 1989).

25. Roger L. Geiger, *Private Sectors in Higher Education: Structure, Function and Change in Eight Countries* (Ann Arbor: University of Michigan Press, 1986). For a focus on Latin America, see Daniel C. Levy, *Higher Education and the State in Latin America* (Chicago: University of Chicago Press, 1986).

26. It is significant that private higher education institutions are being established in Vietnam and in China. At the same time, Malaysia has rejected proposals for the establishment of private universities.

27. D. Bruce Johnstone, *Sharing the Costs of Higher Education: Student Financial Assistance in the United Kingdom, the Federal Republic of Germany, France, Sweden and the United States* (Washington, D. C.: The College Board, 1986).

28. It is worth noting that agencies, such as the World Bank, have strongly argued against continued expansion of higher education, feeling that scarce educational expenditures could be much more effectively spent on primary and secondary education. See *Education in Sub-Saharan Africa: Policies for Adjustment, Revitalization and Expansion* (Washington, D. C.: The World Bank 1988).

29. Martin Trow, *op. cit.*

30. See Ladislav Cerych and Paul Sabatier, *Great Expectations and Mixed Performance: The Implementation of Higher Education Reforms in Europe* (Trentham, England: Trentham Books, 1986), part 2 for a consideration of access to higher education in Western Europe.

31. Jasbir Sarjit Singh, "Malaysia," in *International Higher Education: An Encyclopedia*, ed. Philip G. Altbach (New York: Garland, 1991), pp. 511-524.

32. There will also be some significant national variations. For example, Britain under Margaret Thatcher's leadership has consistently reduced expenditures for postsecondary education, with significant negative consequences for higher education. See, for example, Sir Claus Moser, "The Robbins Report Twenty-five Years After: and the Future of the Universities," *Oxford Journal of Education* 14 (no. 1, 1988), pp. 5-20.

33. For broader considerations of the reforms of the sixties, see Ladislav Cerych and Paul Sabatier, *Great Expectations and Mixed Performance*, Ulrich Teichler, *Changing Patterns of the Higher Education System* (London: J. Kingsley, 1989). Philip G. Altbach, ed., *University Reform: Comparative Perspectives for the Seventies* (Cambridge, MA: Schenkman, 1974) and Philip G. Altbach, *Perspectives on Comparative Higher Education: Essays on Faculty, Students and Reform* (Buffalo, NY: Comparative Education Center, State University of New York at Buffalo, 1989).

34. For an example of an influential student proposal for higher education reform, see Wolfgang Nitsch et al., *Hochschule in der Demokratie* (Berlin: Luchterhand, 1965).

35. Jan Erik Lane and Mac Murray, "The Significance of Decentralization in Swedish Education," *European Journal of Education* 20 (nos. 2-3, 1985), pp. 163-172.

36. See Alexander Astin et al., *The Power of Protest* (San Francisco: Jossey-Bass, 1975) for an overview of the results of the ferment of the 1960s on American higher education.

37. "The Legacy of Robbins," *European Journal of Education* 14 (no. 1, 1988), pp. 3-112.

38. For a critical viewpoint, see Hans Daalder and Edward Shils, eds., *Universities, Politicians and Bureaucrats: Europe and the United States* (Cambridge, England: Cambridge University Press, 1982).

39. See, for example, "Universities and Industry," *European Journal of Education* 20 (no. 1, 1985), pp. 5-66.

40. Of course, this is not a new concern for higher education. See Thorstein Veblen, *The Higher Learning in America: A Memorandum on the Conduct of Universities by Business Men* (New York: Viking Press, 1918).

41. See Klaus Hufner, "Accountability," in *International Higher Education: An Encyclopedia*, ed. Philip G. Altbach (New York: Garland, 1991), pp. 47-58.

42. Philip G. Altbach, "Academic Freedom in Asia: Learning the Limitations," *Far Eastern Economic Review* (June 16, 1988), pp. 24-5.

43. Edward Shils, *The Academic Ethic* (Chicago: University of Chicago Press, 1983).

44. A classic discussion of the development of the modern university is Joseph Ben-David and Awraham Zloczower, "Universities and Academic Systems in Modern Societies," *European Journal of Sociology* 3 (no. 1, 1962), pp. 45-84.

45. See, for example, Robert Nisbet, *The Degradation of the Academic Dogma: The University in America, 1945-1970* (New York: Basic Books, 1971). Allan Bloom, in his *The Closing of the American Mind* (New York: Simon and Schuster, 1987), echoes many of Nisbet's sentiments.

46. It is significant to note that in those countries that have located much of their research in nonuniversity institutions, such as the Academies of Sciences in the Soviet Union and some Eastern European nations, there has been some rethinking of this organizational model, feeling that universities may be more effective locations for the major research enterprise. See Alexander Vucinich, *Empire of Knowledge: The Academy of Sciences of the USSR (1917-1970)*.

47. See Thomas W. Shaughnessy et al., "Scholarly Communication: The Need for an Agenda for Action—A Symposium," *Journal of Academic Librarianship* 15 (no. 2, 1989), pp. 68-78. See also *Scholarly Communication: The Report of the National Commission* (Baltimore, MD: Johns Hopkins University Press, 1979).

48. These issues are discussed in Philip G. Altbach, *The Knowledge Context, op. cit.* See Irving Louis Horowitz, *Communicating Ideas: The Crisis of Publishing in a Post-Industrial Society* (New York: Oxford University Press, 1986) for a different perspective.

49. For an American perspective, see Howard Bowen and Jack Schuster, *American Professors: A National Resource Imperiled* (New York: Oxford University Press, 1986).

50. Daniel C. Levy, *Higher Education and the State in Latin America: Private Challenges to Public Dominance* (Chicago: University of Chicago Press, 1986). See also Roger L. Geiger, Private Sectors in Higher Education: Structure, *Function and Change in Eight Countries* (Ann Arbor: University of Michigan Press, 1986).

51. Gail P. Kelly, "Women in Higher Education," in *International Higher Education: An Encyclopedia*, ed. Philip G. Altbach (New York: Garland Publishers, 1991), pp. 297-327.

52. A possible exception to this situation are the universities in Britain, where a decade of financial cuts by the Thatcher government has sapped the morale of the universities and has made it difficult for even such distinguished institutions as Oxford and Cambridge to continue top quality research. See Geoffrey Walford, "The Privatization of British Higher Education," *European Journal of Education* 23 (no. 1 and 2,1988), pp. 47-64.

53. *Education in Sub-Saharan Africa, op. cit.*, pp. 68-81.

54. For a survey of student movements, see Philip G. Altbach, ed., *Student Political Activism: An International Reference Handbook* (Westport, CT: Greenwood Press, 1989).

CHAPTER 4

1. Philip H. Coombs. *The World Crisis in Education: The View from the Eighties* (New York: Oxford University Press, 1985); Keith Watson, "Forty Years of Education and Development: From Optimism to Uncertainty," *Educational Review*, 40 (2), 1988: pp. 137-174.

2. Francisco O. Ramirez and John Boli-Bennett, "Global Patterns of Educational Institutionalization," in *Comparative Education*, ed. Philip G. Altbach, Robert F. Arnove, and Gail P. Kelly (New York: Macmillan, 1982).

3. Robert F. Arnove, "Comparative Education and World-Systems Analysis," in *Comparative Education*, p. 456. Wadi Haddad et al., *Education Sector Policy Paper* (Washington, D.C.: World Bank, 1980), p. 21, estimates external aid to Third World educational development at $2.8 billion in 1975, or some 9 percent of total educational expenditures.

4. The most important of these conferences were held in Karachi in 1960, in Addis Ababa in 1961, in Santiago in 1962, and in Tripoli in 1965. Their conclusions were strongly influenced by those of the 1961 Washington Conference on Economic Growth and Investment in Education, sponsored by the Organization of Economic Cooperation and Development.

5. Stephen Heyneman and Daphne Siev White, *The Quality of Education and Economic Development* (Washington, D.C.: World Bank, 1986); Haddad, *Education Sector Policy Paper*; Akilu Habte. "Where the Bank is Going in the Field of Education." *Canadian and International Education*, 12, 1983: pp. 65-74.

6. Details of the Bank's extensive research activities can be found in Peter R. Moock and Robin S. Horn, "Overview of the World Bank's Research on Education," *Canadian and International Education*, 12, 1983: pp. 39-64.

7. See, for example, Thomas Owen Eisemon, *The Consequences of Schooling: A Review of Research on the Outcomes of Primary Schooling in Developing Countries*, Education Development discussion paper 3 (prepared for Harvard University Basic Research and Implementation in Developing Education Systems Project, September 1988).

8. See. for example, Steven J. Klees. "Planning and Policy Analysis in Education: What Can Economics Tell Us?" *Comparative Education Review* 30, November 1986: pp. 574-607; Hans N. Weiler, "Towards a political economy of educational planning," *Prospects* 8 (3), 1978: pp. 247-267.

9. Accounts arguing the value of developmental aid as an important ingredient in foreign policy considerations include two early ones: Edward S. Mason, *Foreign Aid and Foreign Policy* (New York: Harper and Row, 1964); and Joan Nelson. Aid, Influence and Foreign Policy (New York: Macmillan, 1968). Representative critical views can be found in Teresa Hayter, *Aid as Imperialism* (Harmondsworth: Penguin. 1971);

Robert E. Wood, "Foreign Aid and the Capitalist State in Underdeveloped Countries," *Politics and Society* 10 (1980): pp. 1-34; and David Kinley, Arnold Levinson, and Francis Moore Lappe, "The Myth of 'Humanitarian' Foreign Aid," *The Nation*, July 11-18, 1981: pp. 41-43.

10. *The Rockefeller Foundation Directory of Fellowships and Scholarships, 1917-1970* (New York: Rockefeller Foundation. 1970). This $63 million figure is very conservative since it represents only direct grants made by the Foundation itself and excludes those fellowship awards made by organizations supported by the Foundation. The expenditures for student fellowships by many of these organizations, for example, the China Medical Board, were very substantial.

11. The amounts allocated for the foundations' international work had been substantial during the 1950s and 1960s. Figures from a representative year, 1965-66, illustrate the magnitude of their appropriations for Third World work, most of which focused on educational development and expansion. The Rockefeller trustees voted some $19 million for overseas work that year, the Carnegie Corporation some $1.5, while the Ford Foundation appropriations totalled approximately $118 million. Figures drawn from *Rockefeller Foundation Annual Report, 1966*, p 188 and *passim*; *Carnegie Corporation of New York Annual Report, 1966*, pp. 74-89; and *The Ford Foundation Annual Report, 1966*, pp. 68-117.

12. For details: Robert F. Arnove and Edward H. Berman, "Neocolonial Policies of North American Philanthropic Foundations," a paper delivered at the Fifth World Congress of Comparative Education, Paris, July 2-6, 1984.

13. Aimé Damiba, "Educational Planning in Theory and Practice," in *Educational Planning and Social Change*, ed. Hans Weiler (Paris: UNESCO, 1980), p. 73.

14. K. W. Bigelow. "Report on the ATEA 11th Conference in Addis Ababa," 26-31 March, 1972, p. 2. Typescript in Teachers College archives: Bigelow papers.

15. The material on the University of East Africa comes from Kenneth W. Thompson and colleagues, "Higher Education and National Development: One Model for Technical Assistance," in *Education and Development Reconsidered: The Bellagio Conference Papers*, ed. F. Champion Ward (New York: Praeger, 1974), p. 201; that on the University of Ibadan from "University Development, Education for Development Program Review," n.a., October 14, 1975. Rockefeller Foundation: folder 900, Programs and Policies, UNAR-16, p. 33.

16. Robert F. Arnove, "The Ford Foundation and the Transfer of Knowledge: convergence and divergence in the world-system," *Compare*, 13 (1), 1983: pp. 17-18.

17. This discussion is drawn from Joane Nagel and Conrad W. Snyder, Jr., "International Funding of Educational Development: External Agendas and Internal Adaptation—the Case of Liberia," *Comparative Education Review*, 33, February 1989: pp. 3-20.

18. This discussion relies on Kingley Banta, "The Role of International Organi-

zations in Aid: A Case Study of a Teacher Education Programme in Sierra Leone," *International Review of Education*, 34 (4), 1988. pp. 477-493.

19. On the World Bank, see Cheryl Pater, *The World Bank: A Critical Analysis* (New York: Monthly Review Press, 1982); Peter DeWitt, "The IDB and Policy Making in Costa Rica," *The Journal of Developing Areas*, 15 (1980): pp. 67-82; and for a more positive assessment, Robert Ayers, *Banking on the Poor: The World Bank and World Poverty* (Cambridge: MIT Press, 1983). On the foundations see *Philanthropy and Cultural Imperialism: The Foundations at Home and Abroad*, ed. Robert F. Arnove (Boston: G. K. Hall, 1980); and Edward H. Berman, *The Ideology of Philanthropy: the influence of the Carnegie, Ford, and Rockefeller foundations on American foreign policy* (Albany, NY: State University of New York Press, 1983). On the Agency for International Development, see Michael Bujazan et al., "International Agency Assistance to Education in Latin America and the Caribbean, 1970-1984; technical and political decision-making," *Comparative Education*, 23 (2), 1987: pp. 161-171. For general observations, see Martin Carnoy, "International institutions and educational policy: a review of education-sector policy," *Prospects*, 10, (3) 1980: pp. 265-283; and Seth Spaulding, "The impact of international assistance organizations on the development of education," *Prospects*, 11 (4) 1981: pp. 421-433.

20. *Education Sector Policy Paper, 1980* (Washington, D.C.: World Bank, 1980, p. 95.

21. Watson, "Forty Years of Education and Development," provides a helpful chronological overview of Bank programs.

22. Samuel Paul, "Privatization and the Public Sector," *Finance and Development*, 22, December 1985: pp. 42-45; George Psacharopoulos, "The Welfare Effects of Government Intervention in Education," *Contemporary Policy Issues*, 4, July 1986: pp. 51-62.

23. John M. Broder, "World Bank's Benign Image Fading Fast," *Los Angeles Times*, February 2, 1986, 4, pp. 1, 5. Also, Joydeep Mukherji, "World Bank loan policy under fire for adding to misery of very poor," *The Globe and Mail* (Toronto), July 24, 1989, pp. B1, B4; and his "Canada stressing free-market policies in foreign aid programs." *The Globe and Mail*, July 25, 1989. p. B21.

24. Hans N. Weiler. "The Political Economy of Education and Development," *Prospects*, 14 (4) (1984), p. 476. Similar arguments can be found in Henry Levin, "The Identity Crisis of Educational Planning," *Harvard Educational Review*, 51, February 1981: pp. 85-93.

25. The phrase "technocratic strategy" is borrowed from Trent Schroyer, "The Need for Critical Theory," *The Insurgent Sociologist*, 3 (Winter 1973), p. 31. An elaboration of this argument can be found in Berman, *The Ideology of Philanthropy*, ch. 6. Cf. Mathew Zachariah, "Lumps of Clay and Growing Plants: Dominant Metaphors of the Role of Education in the Third World, 1950-1980," *Comparative Education Review*, 29, February 1985: pp. 1-21.

26. Eisemon, *The Consequences of Schooling*, esp. pp. 66-71. A further discussion of the reasons accounting for the failure of so many educational aid projects is the subject of Paul Hurst, "Some Issues in Improving the Quality of Education," *Comparative Education*, 17, June 1981: pp. 185-193.

27. Klees, "Planning and Policy Analysis in Education," esp. pp. 600-607. Cf. Noel McGinn et al., "Educational Planning as Political Process: Two Case Studies from Latin America." *Comparative Education Review*, 23, June 1979: pp. 218-239.

28. Ernst Michanek, "Democracy as a Force for Development and the Role of Swedish Assistance, " *Development Dialogue*, 1, 1985: pp. 56-84.

29. Mathew Zachariah, "People's Movements and Reform of Formal Education: Reflections on Kerala Sastra Sahitya Parishad (KSSP) in India," *Canadian and International Education*, 18 (1) 1989 pp. 3-19. This quotation comes from p. 7.

30. For a discussion of the state's role in the perpetuation of educational dependency in Third World nations, see Martin Carnoy, "Education for Alternate Development," *Comparative Education Review*, 26, June 1982: pp. 160-177.

31. Mathew Zachariah, "KSSP's Improved Chulka Programme," *People's Action*, 1, July 1987

CHAPTER 5

1. G. W. Hegel, *The Philosophy of History* (New York: Dover Publishers, 1956).

2. L. A. Maverick, *China: A Model for Europe* (San Antonio, Texas: Paul Anderson Co., 1946).

3. Joseph Needham, *A History of Science and Civilization in China* (Cambridge Cambridge University Press, 1954-).

4. Evelyn Rawski, *Education and Literacy in Ch'ing China* (Ann Arbor: University of Michigan Press, 1979).

5. Zhu Weizheng, *Coming Out of the Middle Ages: Comparative Reflections on China and the West*, trans. R. Hayhoe (New York: M. E. Sharpe, 1990).

6. Antonio Rosso, OFM, *Apostolic Legations to China the Eighteenth Century* (South Pasadena: Perkins, 1948); E. Ronan, S. J. and B. C. Oh, eds., *East Meets West: The Jesuits in China 1582-1773* (Chicago: Loyola University Press, 1988).

7. Zhu Weizheng, "Han Learning and Western Learning in the 18th Century," in Zhu, *Coming out of the Middle Ages*.

8. Alexander Woodside, "Real and Imagined Continuities in the Chinese Struggle for Literacy," in R. Hayhoe ed., *Education in China's Modernization: Historical and Contemporary Perspectives* (Oxford: Pergamon Press, 1991).

9. Benjamin Elman, *From Philosophy to Philology: Intellectual and Social Aspects of Change in Late Imperial China*, Harvard East Asian Monograph no. 110 (Cambridge: Harvard University Press, 1984).

10. Hiroshi Abe, "Borrowing from Japan: China's First Modern Educational System," in R. Hayhoe and M. Bastid, eds., *China's Education and the Industrialized World*.

11. Teruhisa Horio, *Educational Thought and Ideology in Modern Japan*, trans. Steven Platzer (Tokyo: University of Tokyo Press, 1984).

12. Ruth Hayhoe, "Cultural Tradition and Educational Change: Some Reflections on Nationalist Educational History," in R. Hayhoe ed., *Education in China's Modernization*.

13. The most notable case of this was the famous Southwest United University, which produced many fine scientists over this period, including two who were later to become Nobel prize winning physicists in the United States, C. N. Yang and T. D. Lee.

14. Marianne Bastid, "Servitude or Liberation? The Introduction of Foreign Educational Practices and Systems to China from 1840 to the Present," in R. Hayhoe and M. Bastid, eds., *China's Education and the Industrialized World: Studies in Cultural Transfer* (New York: M. E. Sharpe and Toronto: OISE Press, 1987).

15. Guy Alitto, *The Last Confucian: Liang Shuming and the Chinese Dilemma of Modernity*, 2nd Edition (Berkeley: University of California Press, 1986).

16. P. Seybolt, "The Yenan Revolution in Mass Education," *China Quarterly* no. 48 (1971), pp. 641-669; Wang Hsueh-wen, *Chinese Communist Education: The Yenan Period* (Taiwan: Institute of International Relations, 1981).

17. Alitto, *The Last Confucian*, pp. 321-324.

18. R. Hayhoe, *China's Universities and the Open Door* (Toronto: OISE Press, New York: M. E. Sharpe, 1989). In this volume I have tried to chart curricular change in the eighties and reflect on the contribution of academic exchanges to it.

19. R. Hayhoe, "China's Intellectuals in the World Community," *Higher Education* vol. 17, no. 1 (1988) pp. 121-138.

20. Some of the most provocative writers are women. Those who works are easily available in English translation include Dai Qing, Shen Rong, Zhang Jie, Zhang Kangkang, Zhang Xinxin, and Wang Anyi.

21. Brian Holmes, *Comparative Education: Some Considerations of Method* (London: George Allen and Unwin, 1981).

22. R. Hayhoe, "German, French, Soviet and American University Models and the Evaluation of Chinese Higher Education Policy since 1911," unpublished Ph.D. diss. University of London, 1984.

23. The Popperian term is "piecemeal social engineering."

24. J. Galtung, *The True Worlds: A Transnational Perspective* (New York: Free Press, 1980); Samuel Kim, *The Quest for a Just World Order* (Boulder, Colorado: Westview Press, 1984).

25. J. Galtung, "A Structural Theory of Imperialism," *Journal of Peace Research* 8 (1972): 81-117.

26. R. Hayhoe, *China's Universities and the Open Door* (Toronto: OISE Press, New York: M. E. Sharpe, 1989).

27. Georges Gurvitch, *The Social Framework of Knowledge* (New York: Harper and Row, 1971); Juergen Habermas, *The Theory of Communicative Action*, vols. I & II (Boston: Beacon Press, 1984, 1987).

28. I have tried to make a start at this in two essays, the first using both Gurvitch and Habermas, the Second focusing on Habermas: R. Hayhoe, "Knowledge Categories and Chinese Educational Reform," *Interchange* vol. 19, nos. 3/4 (1988): 92-111; R. Hayhoe, "China's Intellectuals in the World Community," *Higher Education* vol. 17, no. 1 (1988) pp. 121-138.

29. Immanuel Wallerstein, *The Politics of the World Economy: The States, the Movements and the Civilizations* (Cambridge: Cambridge University Press, 1987), pp. 147-185.

30. One of Wallerstein's students has developed a reinterpretation of the history of modern China and Japan in terms of their response to capitalist economic inroads. See Frances Moulder, *Japan, China and the Modern World Economy: Toward a Re-Interpretation of East Asian Development ca. 1600 to ca. 1918*, (Cambridge: Cambridge University Press, 1979).

31. Wallerstein, "The Development of the Concept of Development," in Wallerstein, *The Politics of the World Economy*, pp. 173-185.

CHAPTER 6

1. M. Drachkovitch, *East Central Europe: Yesterday, Today, Tomorrow* (Stanford: Hoover Institute, 1982), pp. 10-18; P. Summerscale, *The East European Predicament: Changing Patterns* (New York: St. Martin, 1982), pp. 58-63.

2. *Europe de l'Est de Francois-Joseph à Gorbatchev* (cadmos Vol XXXIX, special issue): P. Kende and P. Hanak, "Central Europe: Can It be Revitalized?" *Magyar Nemzet* 118 (October 7, 1989), p. 3.

3. T. Rakowska-Harmstone, ed., *Communism in Eastern Europe* (Bloomington: Indiana University Press, 1984) pp. 8-49; I. Volgyes, *Politics in Eastern Europe*

(Chicago: Dorsey, 1986), pp. 3-7; A. Korbonski, "Nationalism, pluralism, and the process of political development in Eastern Europe," *International Political Science Review* 3 (August 1989): pp. 251-62.

4. G. Simon, "Nationalismus und die Grenzen der Sovietunion als Weltmacht," *Politik und ZeitEeschichte* 18 (August 26, 1988): pp. 16-28.

5. E. Bojtar, *The Raid of Europe: The fate of the Baltic countries* (Budapest: Free Forum, 1989).

6. P. G. Altbach, et al, *International Bibliography of Comparative Education* (New York: Free Press, 1981): B. Holmes, ed., *International Handbook of Educational Systems Vol. I: Europe and Canada* (Chichester: Wiley, 1983); O. Anweiler, ed., Staatliche Steuerung u Eigendynamik in Bildungswesen osteuropaischen Staaten (Berlin: Spitz, 1986): G. Kurian, ed., *World Educational Encyclopedia*, (New York: Facts, 1988), vols. 1-3, pp. 165-79, 291-309, 427-446, 540-559, 1006-21, 1042-56, 1294-1321, 1404-27, 1458-61.

7. M. Bernath and F. Schroder, eds., *Biografisches Lexikon zur Geschichte Sudosteuropas* (Munchen: Grotewohl, 1970-81) vol. 1-6: K. Grothausen ed., *Sudosteuropa Handbuch* (Gottingen: Grothausen, 1987), vol. 4.

8. F. Thom, "La violence politique dans les pays de l'est," *Etudes Polemologigues* 2 (1987): pp. 99-143; Z. Golubovic, "Mogucnosti za reforme u socijalistickim drzavama," *Sociologija* 4 (1987: pp. 491-506); S. Larrabee, "Generationswechsel in Osteuropa," *Europaische Rundschau* 2 (1988): pp. 25-42.

9. J. W. Peterson, "Changing leadership patterns in Eastern Europe: 1985-1990," (Conference paper, Valdosta, 1990).

10. F. Argentieri, "Contratto sociale in Ungheria: Una proposta di transizione," *Democrazia e Diritto* 2-3 (1988): pp. 345-57.

11. V. Bova, "Il conflitto tra Stato e societa in Polonia," *Aggiornamenti Sociali* 7-8 (1988): pp. 533-547.

12. P. Artisien, "Albania at the cross-roads," *Journal of Communists Studies* 3 (1988): pp. 231-249.

13. A. Brumberg, "Polen: Die neue Opposition," *Europaische Rundschau* 2 (1988): pp. 77-99.

14. A. Katsenelinbiogen, "Will glasnost bring the reactionaries to power?" *Orbis* 2 (1988): pp. 217-230.

15. A. Vengerov, "Disciplina perestroiki: Protivniki i storonniki," *Sovetskaja Gosudarstvo i Pravo* 8 (1987): pp. 3-12.

16. G. Klein, *The Politics of Ethnicity in Eastern Europe* (Boulder: Westview, 1981), pp. 28-35.

17. F. Heichinger, "About education," *New York Times* 11328 (January 31, 1990): A-3, p. 7.

18. *Regulation of Eight-Year, Secondary and Low-professional Schools: Full-time and part-time* (Tiranan: School Books, 1980), pp. 3-5.

29. P. Sugar, *Ethnic Diversity and Conflict in Eastern Europe* (Santa Barbara: ABC, 1980).

20. Kirchen in Sozialismus: Kirche und Staat in der osteuropaischen sozialistischen Republiken (Frankfurt: Meinecke, 1977)

21. B. Szajkowski, "Muslim people in Eastern Europe: Ethnicity and religion," *Journal of Institute for Muslim Minority Affaires* 1 (1988): pp. 103-118; G. Stricker, "Situation der Christen in der Sovietunion," Osteuropa 6 (1899): pp. 483-99.

22. P. Michel, *La Société Retrouvée: Politique et religion dans l'Europe sovietisee* (Paris: Rayard, 1988).

23. "Human rights campaigner detained by Roumanians," *The Times Higher Educational Supplement* 871 (August 21, 1989): p. 10.

24. P. Maurer, "The emergence of a multinational state: the Yugoslavian case," *Revue de Pays de l'Est* 1 (1987): pp. 105-156.

25. "Eco-movements in Hungary and in the neighboring countries," *Medvetanc* 5 (1987): Special issue.

26. T. Kozma, "Common cores in primary curricula: Experiments in socialist countries," *Zeitschrift fur Internationale Erziehungsforschung* (1987, Special Issue): pp. 101-124.

27. "Molotov-Ribbentrop Pact: The Fiftieth Anniversary," *Edasi* 192 (August 1989): special issue. Tartu: Linnokomitee EKP.

28. "Polish critics scorn Katyn inquiry," *The Times Higher Educational Supplement* 871 (August 19, 1989): p. 10.

29. B. Kiraly et al, *The First War between Socialist States* (New York: Basic Books, 1983).

30. Z. Lauc, "Ustavne promjene i drustveni razvitak u SFRJ," *Politicka Misao* 1 (1988): pp. 62-68.

31. I. T. Berend, "Reform und Ideologie," *Europaische Rundschau* 2 1988): pp. 53-63.

32. Z. Rau, "Some thoughts on civil society in Eastern Europe," *Political Studies* 4 (1987): pp. 573-592.

33. Consiliul de Stat, *Leqea Educatiei si a Invatamintului*, (Bucuresti: Editia Didactica, 1979.), pp. 5-8.

34. "Public education," *Great Soviet Encyclopedia* vol. 24, part 2, pp. 1188-91.

35. *Struktura na sdrzhanieto na professionalna podgatovka na ESPU* (Sofia: Ministerstvo Narodnata Prosveta, 1983).

36. G. Halasz, "The structure of educational policy in Hungary 1960-80," *Comparative Education* 2 (1986): pp. 123-132.

37. H. Buschenfeld, "Die Reform des jugoslawischen Sekundarschulwesens: Idee und Wirklichkeit," *Bildung und Erziehung* 3 (1984): pp. 317-333; Ministry of Public Education, *Education in the People's Republic of Bulgaria* (Geneva: UNESCO BIE, 1981); *L'enseignement et la pedagogie en Roumanie*, (Bucharest: Biblioteque Central de Pedagogie, 1980), pp. 121-123.

38. "Rozvoj ceskoslovenskeho skolstv," *Informacni Zpravodai* 3 (1984): pp. 15-31; Vydavnictva Ministerstvo Skolstva, *Statistiska rocenka skolstva Slovenskei Socialistickei Republiky 1981-85* (Bratislava, 1986), vol. 2, pp. 32-38.

39. *Rocznik Statystyczny Szkolnictva 1981-85* (Warszawa: GUS, 1986); National Commission, *Hungarian Education of the 1980s* (Budapest: UNESCO, 1984), pp. 12-14.

40. T. Kozma, "Wastage in secondary schooling in the Eastern European context," *Journal of Education and Social Change* 3 (1988): pp. 59-80.

41. W. Mitter, *Secondary School Graduation* (Oxford: Pergamon, 1979), pp. 59-80.

42. *Osnovno obrazovanje i vspitanje u SFRK* (Beograd: Republicki Zavod, 1983), pp. 18-22.

43. J. Drewnowski, *Crisis in the East European Economy: The spread of the Polish Disease* (London: Croom Helm, 1982); D. Durasoff, "Conflicts between economic decentralization and political control in the post-Soviet systems," *Social Science Quarterly* 2 (1988): pp. 381-398.

44. O. Sik, "Der real existierende Sozialismus: Theorie und Praxiz," *Basler Zeitung* November 11 (1989): pp. 10-13.

45. K. Gupta, *Marxism and Political Economy of Socialism: Experience of Soviet and East European Economies* (New Delhi: Sterling, 1989).

46. T. Kozma, "Teacher education: Systems, processes, prospects," *European Journal of Teacher Education* 3 (1984): pp. 255-265.

47. D. Howell, "The Hungarian educational act: A study in decentralization," *Comparative Education* 1 (1988): pp. 125-336.

48. T. F. Green, *Predicting the Behavior of the Educational System* (Syracuse: University Press, 1980), pp. 20-29.

49. R. Dahrendorf, "The unusual end of socialism: Turnings and twistings of a traditional movement," *Magyar Naplo* 1 (1989): pp. 11-12; 2: pp. 11-13 .

50. J. Femia, "Ideological obstacles to the political evolution of the communist system," *Studies in Soviet Thought* 4 (1987): pp. 215-232.

CHAPTER 7

*This is a revised and updated version of the chapter, *Educational Expansion and the Drive for Social Equality*, published in the first edition of this book.

1. A vast literature was generated during the 1950s and 1960s regarding the nature of development, its causes and education's presumed role in the process. Space does not permit a detailed analysis of the differing theoretical views advanced, although it should be noted that almost all scholars at the time operated from a consensus or equilibrium rather than conflict model of social change. (See Rolland Paulston, "Social and Educational Change: Conceptual Frameworks," *Comparative Education Review*, 21 (June/October 1977), pp. 370-395.) For a useful review of the general development literature through the mid-1960s, see C. E. Black, *The Dynamics of Modernization* (New York: Harper & Row, 1966), pp. 175-199. For a detailed review and summary of what was then understood to be education's role in social development, see Don Adams and Joseph P. Farrell, *Education and Social Development* (Syracuse: Syracuse University Center for Development Education, 1967).

2. See particularly C. Arnold Anderson, "A Skeptical Note on Education and Mobility," *Education, Economy and Society*. Edited by Halsey and others (New York: The Free Press, 1961), pp. 164-179.

3. Don Adams, "Development Education," *Comparative Education Review*, 21 (June/October 1977), pp. 299-300.

4. Data from the Statistical Division of UNESCO, as compiled at the World Bank. See *Education Sector Policy Paper*, 3d ed. (Washington, D.C.: The World Bank, 1980), pp. 103-106.

5. For classic statements of this "revisionist" view, see Martin Carnoy, *Education as Cultural Imperialism*: McKay, 1974) and S. Bowles and H. Gintis, *Schooling in Capitalist America* (New York: Basic Books, 1976).

6. See, for example, the following work by two of the authors cited in the previous note. Martin Carnoy and H. Gintis, *Schooling and Work in the Democratic State*. (Stanford: Stanford University Press, 1985). See also Daniel P. Liston, *Capitalist Schools: Explanation and Ethics in Radical Studies of Schooling*. (New York: Routledge, 1990).

7. A particularly useful historical analysis of changing conceptions of educational equality is found in James Coleman, "The Concept of Equality of Educational

Opportunity," *Harvard Educational Review*, 38 (Winter, 1968), pp. 7-22.

8. M. Bronfenbrenner, "Equality and Equity," *The Annals*, 409 (September 1973). See also Suzanne Prysor-Jones, "Education and Equality in Developing Countries," *Planning Education for Development*, vol. 1. Edited by R. Davis (Cambridge: Harvard University Center for Studies in Education and Development, 1980), pp. 157-186.

9. For an expansion of this discussion and an application of the "model" to the problem of educational equality over time in a particular developing nation, see Joseph P. Farrell and Ernesto Schiefelbein, *Eight Years of Their Lives: Through Schooling to the Labour Market in Chile.* (Ottawa: International Development Research Centre, 1982).

10. Joseph P. Farrell, "International Lessons for School Effectiveness: The View from the Developing World," *Educational Policy for Effective Schools*, edited by Mark Holmes et al. (New York: Teachers College Press, 1989) pp. 53-70; and Marlaine Lockheed and Adrian Verspoor, *Improving Primary Education in Developing Nations: A Review of Policy Options.* (Washington, D.C.: The World Bank, 1989) table 3.

11. Philip H. Coombs, *The World Crisis in Education: The View from the Eighties.* (New York: Oxford, 1985), p. 84.

12. *Education Sector Policy Paper*, pp. 24-25.

13. *World Charter on Education for All* and *Framework for Action to Meet Basic Learning Needs.* (New York: World Conference on Education for All Secretariat, 1990). The World Conference on Education for All (WCEFA) which was held in Jomtien, Thailand, March 5-9, 1990, sponsored by UNESCO, The World Bank, UNICEF, and the United Nations Development Program, and supported by many other bilateral and private development assistance agencies, brought together more than 1,500 governmental and nongovernmental representatives from almost all nations of the world.

14. Lockheed and Verspoor, p. 31.

15. For an extended analysis of these demand side obstacles, see Mary Jean Bowman, "An Integrated Framework for Analysis of the Spread of Schooling in Less Developed Countries," *Comparative Education Review*, 28 (November, 1984), pp. 563-583.

16. Lockheed and Verspoor, pp. 13-14.

17. For example: Malawi, 28%; Ethiopia, 40%; Mali, 20%; Bangladesh, 20%; India, 38%; Lesotho, 27%; Mozambique, 26%; Pakistan, 34%; Nigeria, 31%. Kenneth King, "Donor Support to Literacy, Adult Basic and Primary Education," *NORRAG News*, no. 7 (March, 1990), p. 52.

18. Ernesto Schiefelbein, "Repeating: An Overlooked Problem of Latin American Education," *Comparative Education Review*, 19 (October 1975), pp. 468-487.

19. Lockheed and Verspoor, p. 14.

20. Data from the Office of Statistics, UNESCO, as distributed at the World Conference on Education for All.

21. *Education Sector Policy Paper*, pp. 108-111.

22. Ernesto Schiefelbein and Joseph P. Farrell, "Women, Schooling and Work in Chile: Evidence from a Longitudinal Study," *Comparative Education Review*, 24 (June 1980, part 2), pp. S160-S179.

23. Lockheed and Verspoor, tables 3 and 13.

24. The Gini coefficient is a widely used measure of the degree to which the observed distribution of something (e.g., years of education) varies from an ideally equal distribution. Its values may range theoretically from zero (perfect equality) to one (perfect inequality). For a simple example of how it is calculated, see Donald R. Snodgrass, "The Distribution of Schooling and the Distribution of Income," *Planning Education for Development*, vol. 1. Edited by R. Davis (Cambridge: Harvard University Center for Studies in Education and Development, 1980), pp. 187-204.

25. *Ibid*, p. 197.

26. That Cuba in 1953 had a relatively low degree of inequality in the distribution of years of schooling is an interesting datum to bear in mind when evaluating the educational accomplishments of the Castro regime since the revolution.

27. J. Finn et al., "Sex Differences in Educational Attainment: A Cross National Perspective," *Harvard Educational Review*, 49 (November 1979), pp. 477-503.

28. Schiefelbein and Farrell, 1982.

29. Stephen P. Heyneman and William Loxley, "The Effects of Primary School Quality on Academic Achievement Across Twenty-Nine High and Low-Income Countries," *American Journal of Sociology*, 88 (May 1983), pp. 1162-94. See also Farrell, 1989.

30. Philip Foster, "Education and Social Differentiation in Less Developed Countries," *Comparative Education Review*, 21 (June/October 1977), pp. 224-25.

31. Farrell, 1989, p. 14.

32. Joseph P. Farrell and Stephen P. Heyneman, eds., *Textbooks in the Developing World: Economic and Educational Choices.* (Washington, D.C.: The World Bank, 1989), pp. 3-5. See also Farrell, 1989 and Lockheed and Verspoor, 1989.

33. Farrell and Heyneman, pp. 3-4; Farrell, 1989.

34. "Symposium: World Bank Report on Education in Sub-Saharan Africa," *Comparative Education Review*, 33 (February, 1989), pp. 93-133. This possibly necessary trade-off was debated further at the World Conference on Education for All. See King, 1990 .

35. Nan Lin and D. Yauger, "The Process of Occupational Status Achievement: A Preliminary Cross-National Comparison," *American Journal of Sociology*, 81 (November 1975), pp. 543-562.

36. Ernesto Schiefelbein and Joseph P. Farrell, "Selectivity and Survival in the Schools of Chile," *Comparative Education Review*, 22 (June 1978), pp. 326-341.

37. Joseph P. Farrell and Ernesto Schiefelbein, "Education and Status Attainment in Chile: A Comparative Challenge to the Wisconsin Model of Status Attainment," *Comparative Education Review*, 29 (November 1985), pp. 490-506.

38. For classic studies among the richest nations see Christopher Jencks et al., *Inequality* (New York: Basic Books, 1972); R. Boudon: *Education, Opportunity and Social Inequality* (New York: Wiley, 1973); and *Education, Inequality and Life Chances* (Paris: OECD, 1975).

39. Joseph Zajda, "Education and Social Stratification in the Soviet Union," *Comparative Education Review*, 16 (March 1980), pp. 3-11.

40. Bob Kuttner, "The Declining Middle," *The Atlantic Monthly* (July 1983), pp. 60-72; Bob Kuttner, *Economic Growth/Economic Justice* (New York: Houghton-Mifflin, 1984).

41. Farrell and Schiefelbein, 1985.

42. See, for example, Paul Willis, *Learning to Labour: How Working Class Kids Get Working Class Jobs.* (Westmead: Saxon House, 1977); J. C; Walker, *Louts and Legends: Male Youth Culture in an Inner-City School.* (Sydney: Allen and Unwin, 1988); B. M. Bullivant, *The Ethnic Encounter in the Secondary School: Ethnocultural Reproduction and Resistance; Theory and Cases.* (Lewes: Falmer Press, 1987); R. W. Connell et al., *Making the Difference: Schools, Families and Social Division.* (Sydney: Allen and Unwin, 1982); J. Anyon, "Social Class and School Knowledge," *Curriculum Inquiry*, 11 (Spring 1981), pp. 3-42; P. D. K. Ramsay, "Fresh Perspectives on the School Transformation-Reproduction Debate: A Response to Anyon from the Antipodes," *Curriculum Inquiry* 13 (Fall 1983), pp. 295-320; R. N. Page, "Games of Chance: The Lower-Track Curriculum in a College-Preparatory High School," and E. Brantlinger, "Low-Income Adolescents' Perceptions of School, Intelligence, and Themselves as Students," *Curriculum Inquiry*, 20 (Fall 1990); Lois Weis, *Working Class Without Work: High School Students in a De-Industrialized Economy* (New York: Routledge, 1990).

43. Ernesto Schiefelbein and Joseph P. Farrell, "Education and Occupational Attainment in Chile: The Effects of Educational Quality, Attainment, and Achievement," *American Journal of Education*, 92 (February 1984), pp. 125-162.

44. Adams, p. 301.

45. Snodgrass, p. 202.

46. Lockheed and Verspoor, table 1.

47. *Ibid*, table 20.

48. Schiefelbein and Farrell, 1978, p. 341.

49. *Ibid.*

CHAPTER 8

*We would like to thank Bob Arnove and Russ Rumberger for helpful comments. An earlier version of this paper was published in *Prospects*, vol. 20, no. 4 (1990).

1. Mary Jean Bowman, "The Human Investment Revolution in Economic Thought," *Sociology of Education* 36 (May 1966): pp. 111-138.

2. Lester Thurow, *Investment in Human Capital* (Belmont, CA: Wadsworth Publishing Company, 1970).

3. Cf. Mark Blaug, *An Introduction to the Economics of Education* (Baltimore: Penguin Books, 1970); H. W. Spiegel, *The Growth of Economic Thought* (Durham, NC: Duke University Press, 1971).

4. The original "marginalists" (Jevons, Wicksteed) were given this name because they based their versions of economic theory on study of the incremental changes in the supply and demand of goods and services—or the changes "at the margin"—that were associated with small shifts in prices.

5. S. E. Roll, *The History of Economic Thought* (London: Faber and Faber, 1983).

6. As will be evident from the discussion of their views, the "institutionalists" received this name because of the importance they gave to historically-developed patterns of economic behavior and their institutional forms.

7. Cf. also R. L. Church, "Economists as Experts: The Rise of an Academic Profession in the United States, 1870-1920," in *The University in Society: Europe, Scotland, and the United States from the 16th to the 20th Century*, ed. Lawrence Stone, (Princeton, NJ: Princeton University Press, 1972).

8. That is, the postulate that wage levels are determined by the productivity of the last worker that it is profitable to hire: an application of neoclassical marginal analysis to the labor market.

9. Robert H. Haveman, and Barbara L. Wolfe, "Schooling and Economic Well-Being: The Role of Nonmarket Effects," *Journal of Human Resources* 14 (March 1984).

10. Steven J. Klees, "Planning and Policy Analysis in Education: What Can Economics Tell Us?" *Comparative Education* 30, 4 (November 1986): pp. 574-607; Steven Klees, "The Economics of Education: A More than Slightly Jaundiced View of Where

We are Now," in *The Prospects for Educational Planning*, ed. Francoise Caillods, (Paris: IIEP, 1989).

11. Milton Friedman, "The Role of Government in Education," in *Economics and the Public Interest*, ed. Robert A. Solo, (New Brunswick, NJ: Rutgers University Press, 1955) pp. 123-44.

12. Glen W. Atkinson, "Political Economy: Public Choice or Collective Action?" *Journal of Economic Issues*, 17, 4 (December 1983): pp. 1057-65; David C. Colander, *Neoclassical Political Economy: The Analysis of Rent-Seeking and DUP Activities* (Cambridge, MA: Ballinger, 1984); Merilee S. Grindle, "The New Political Economy: Positive Economics and Negative Politics," (Development discussion paper no. 311, Harvard Institute for International Development, Cambridge, MA: August 1989).

13. World Bank, *Financing Education in Developing Countries: An Exploration of Policy Options*. (Washington, DC: World Bank, 1986); Emannuel Jimenez, *Pricing Policies in the Social Sectors: Cost Recovery for Education and Health in Developing Countries* (Baltimore: Johns Hopkins, 1987).

14. Steven Klees, "The Need for a Political Economy of Educational Finance," *Comparative Education Review*, 28, 3 (August 1984): pp. 424-440; Klees, "Planning and Policy Analysis in Education: What Can Economics Tell Us"; Klees, "The Economics of Education: *A More than Slightly Jaundiced View of Where We Are Now*; Peter Easton, "The Role of Economic Analysis in Educational Policy Making: Case Study of an Education Sector Assessment in the Republic of Haiti" (Ph.D. diss., Florida State University, 1988).

15. J. Vaizey, *The Economics of Education* (London: Faber and Faber, 1962); Thurow.

16. Samuel Bowles and Herbert Gintis, *Schooling in Capitalist America: Educational Reform and the Contradictions of Economic Life* (New York: Basic Books, 1976); Martin Carnoy and Henry M. Levin, *Schooling and Work in the Democratic State* (Stanford, CA: Stanford University Press, 1985).

17. See Lee S. Friedman, *Microeconomic Policy Analysis* (New York: McGraw, 1984) for a microeconomics textbook that clearly admits these fundamental failings.

18. Steven Klees, "Planning and Policy Analysis in Education"; Klees, "The Economics of Education"; Easton, "The Role of Economic Analysis in Educational Policy Making."

19. "Pareto efficiency" or "optimality" refers to a condition in which all present possibilities for greater production have been exhausted and no one can be made better off without making someone else worse off. This is the condition which perfectly competitive markets are supposed to ensure under neoclassical theory.

20. Steven Klees, "Planning and Policy Analysis in Education"; Klees, "The Economics of Education"; Steven Klees and Sande Milton, "Inferences from Regression

Analysis: The Case of Earnings Functions" (Unpublished paper, Florida State University, 1989).

21. For similar arguments also see, Edward E. Leamer, "Let's Take the Con Out of Econometrics," *American Economic Review* 73, 1 (March 1983): pp. 31-43; Michael C. Lovell, "Data Mining," *Review of Economics and Statistics* 65, 1 (February 1983): pp. 1-12.

22. For supporting arguments, see John K. Smith, "The Problem of Criteria for Judging Interpretive Inquiry," *Educational Evaluation and Policy Analysis* 6, 4 (Winter 1984): pp. 379-392; John K. Smith and Louis Heshusius, "Closing Down the Conversation—The End of the Quantitative-Qualitative Debate," *Educational Researcher* 15, 1 (January 1985): pp. 4-12; J. W. Garrison, "Some Principles of Post-Positivistic Philosophy of Science," *Educational Researcher* 15, (September 1986): pp. 12-78; Hans N. Weiler, "Uncertainty and Power: New Paradigms of Knowing and the Knowledge Base of Educational Planning" (Paper presented at the IIEP Workshop on "The Future of Educational Planning," Paris, November 28-December 2, 1988).

23. Sar A. Levitan and R. Taggert, *The Promise of Greatness: The Social Reforms of the Last Decade and Their Major Achievements* (Cambridge, MA: Harvard University Press, 1976); Eli Ginzberg, *The Skeptical Economist* (Boulder: Westview Press, 1987).

24. Peter Doeringer and Michael J. Piore, *International Labor Markets and Manpower Analysis* (Lexington, MA: Heath Lexington, 1971); Michael J. Piore, "Labor Market Segmentation: To What Paradigm Does It Belong?" *American Economic Review* 73, 2 (May 1983): pp. 249-253.

25. Under the general label of "screening" may be grouped a variety of research efforts undertaken since the late 1960s to contest, broaden or refine the theory of human capital investment. The common denominator of these views lies in the notion that education serves as much to sort or select students according to their economically relevant attributes as it does to instill these characteristics. Cf. Ivar Berg, *Education and Jobs: The Great Training Robbery* (New York: Praeger, 1970); Peter Wiles, "The Correlation Between Education and Earnings: The External-Test-Not-Content Hypothesis (ETNC)," *Higher Education* (March 1974): pp. 43-58; K. J. Arrow, "Higher Education as a Filter," *Journal of Public Economics* (July 1973): pp. 193-216; Michael Spence, "Job Market Signalling," *Quarterly Journal of Economics* (August 1973): pp. 355-374; Peter Easton, "The Screening Debate: Attempts to Specify the Education-Earnings Nexus in Human Capital Theory." (Master's thesis, Florida State University, April 1983).

26. Mark Blaug, "The Empirical Status of Human Capital Theory: A Slightly Jaundiced Survey," *Journal of Economic Literature* (September 1976): pp. 827-856; Mark Blaug, "Where Are We Now in the Economics of Education?" *Economics of Education Review* 4 (January 1985): pp. 17-28.

27. For example, John W. Meyer and W. Richard Scott, *Organizational Environ-

ments: Ritual and Rationality (Beverly Hills, CA: Sage, 1985). There have been recent attempts to reconcile institutionalist and neoclassical views, born out of the incorporation of information theory and the analysis of collective action into the neoclassical framework. This literature has been referred to collectively as "the new institutional economics." (Richard N. Langlois, ed., *Economics as a Process: Essays in the New Institutional Economics* (New York: Cambridge University Press, 1986) and Joseph E. Stiglitz, "The New Development Economics," *World Development* (February 1986): pp. 257-565. "The general hypothesis," as Nabli and Nugent phrase it, "is that institutions are transaction cost-minimizing arrangements which may change and evolve with changes in the nature and sources of transaction costs and the means of minimizing them." Mustapha K. Nabli and Jeffrey B. Nugent, "The New Institutional Economics and Its Applicability to Development," *World Development* (September 1989): p. 1336. Such attempts, however, run counter to the more historical, qualitative, and critical traditions of institutionalist economics.

28. For reviews of the field, see Samuel Bowles and Richard Edwards, eds., *Radical Political Economy, vols. 1-2* (Brookfield, VT: Edward Elgar, 1990).

29. For example, Samuel Bowles and Herbert Gintis, "Education as a Site of Contradictions in the Reproduction of the Capital-Labor Relationship: Second Thoughts on the 'Correspondence Principle'," *Economic and Industrial Democracy* (February 1981): pp. 223-242; Samuel Bowles and Herbert Gintis, *Democracy and Capitalism: Property, Community, and the Contradictions of Modern Social Thought* (New York: Basic Books, 1986); Martin Carnoy and Henry M. Levin, *Schooling and Work in the Democratic State* (Stanford, CA: Stanford University Press, 1985); Mike Cole, ed., *Bowles and Gintis Revisited: Correspondence and Contradiction in Educational Theory* (London: The Falmer Press, 1988).

30. For example, Michael W. Apple and Lois Weis, eds., *Ideology and Practice in Schooling* (Philadelphia, PA: Temple University Press, 1983); Stanley Aronowitz and Henry Giroux, *Education Under Siege: The Conservative, Liberal and Radical Debate Over Schooling* (New York: Bergin & Garvey, 1985); Gail P. Kelly, "Comparative Education and the Problem of Change: An Agenda for the 1980s," *Comparative Education Review* 31 (November 1987): pp. 477-489; Svi Shapiro, *Between Capitalism and Democracy: Educational Policy and the Crisis of the Welfare State* (New York: Bergin & Garvey, 1990).

31. For example, for a review of the Brazilian literature, see Acacia Kuenzer, *Educacao e. Trabalho: O Estado da Questao.* Brasilia: INEP, 1987); Marcos Arruda, Paolo Nosella, Luciola Santos, and Michael Young, "Work and Education: The State of the Art in Brazil and Other Studies" (London: Centre for Vocational Studies, University of London, 1988).

32. William M. Dugger, "Radical Institutionalism: Basic Concepts," *Review of Radical Political Economy* 20, 1 (Spring 1988): pp. 1-20 (p. 8).

33. M. K. Cohen and M. S. Garet, "Reforming Educational Policy with Applied Research," *Harvard Educational Review* 45 (January 1975): pp. 17-44; Martin Rein,

Social Science and Public Policy (New York: Penguin Books, 1976); Martin Rein, *From Policy to Practice* (Armonk, NY: M. E. Sharpe, Inc., 1983); Lee J. Cronbach and Associates, *Toward Reform of Program Evaluation: Aims, Methods and Institutional Arrangements* (San Francisco: Jossey-Bass, 1980); National Research Council, "Research on Education in Developing Countries: Conference Report," (National Academy Press, Washington, DC, 1983).

34. Robert Kuttner, "The Poverty of Economics," *Atlantic Monthly* (February 1985): pp. 74-84 (p. 84).

35. Kuttner, p. 78.

36. Thomas Kuhn, *The Structure of Scientific Revolutions* (2d ed., enlarged), (Chicago: The University of Chicago Press, 1971); P. K. Feyerabend, *Against Method: Outline of an Anarchistic Theory of Knowledge* (London: New Left Books, 1975).

37. D. J. Amy, "Toward a Post-Positivistic Policy Analysis: A Review Article" *Policy Studies Journal* 13 (January 1988): pp. 207-211 (p. 209).

38. Peter Easton, "The Role of Economic Analysis in Educational Policy Making," Klees, "The Economics of Education"; Steven Klees, "Learning from our Mistakes: What do the Debates of the Recent Past Imply for Future Directions in Educational Planning and Policy," (Paper presented at Unesco's International Congress on Planning and Management of Education Development, Mexico City, March 26-30, 1990). For a different, and more "ethnographic" approach to economic research and the analysis of issues like the rate of return to education, see Peter Easton and Simon Fass, "Monetary Consumption Benefits and the Demand for Primary Schooling in Haiti," *Comparative Education Review* 33 (May 1989): pp. 176-193.

39. Steven Klees and George J. Papagiannis, "Education and the Changing World of Work: Implications for Math, Science, and Computer Education Policies," (Center for Policy Studies in Education, Florida State University, April 1989); Henry M. Levin and Russell W. Rumberger, "Educational Requirements for New Technologies: Visions, Possibilities, and Current Realities," *Educational Policy* 1 (March 1987): pp. 333-354; Henry M. Levin and Russell W. Rumberger, "Education, Work, and Employment in Developed Countries: Situation and Future Challenges," *Prospects* 19 (February 1989): pp. 205-224.

40. Henry M. Levin, "The Workplace: Employment and Business Interventions." In *Handbook of Social Intervention*, ed. E. Seidman (Beverly Hills, CA: Sage, 1983); Klees and Papagiannis, "Education and the Changing World of Work."

41. Peter Easton, "Structuring Learning Environments: Lessons from the Organization of Post-Literacy Programs," *International Review of Education* 35 (April 1989): pp. 423-444.

CHAPTER 9

1. For a critique, see Henry Levin, *Public Dollars for Private Schools* (Temple University Press, 1983); Mun Tsang and W. Taoklam, "Comparing the costs of gov-

ernment and private primary education in Thailand" (College of Education, Michigan State University, 1990).

2. Thomas Hobbes, *Leviathan* [1651] (Pelican Books, 1968); John Locke, *On Civil Government* [1692] (Henry Regnery, 1955); J. J. Rousseau, *On the Social Contract with Geneva Manuscript and Political Economy* (St. Martin's Press, 1978).

3. Adam Smith, *The Wealth of Nations* [1776] (Modern Library, 1937).

4. Albert 0. Hirschman, *The Passion and the Interests* (Princeton University Press, 1977), p. 100.

5. *Ibid*, p. 104.

6. See Warren Samuels, *The Classical Theory of Economic Policy* (World Publishing, 1966). The parallel to present-day transformations of state socialist societies in Eastern Europe is striking, and I shall return to a discussion of socialist states in transition later in the essay. The main point to be made here is that the Liberal prescription for change in Eastern Europe is the same as it was in England even though the political conditions are totally different. Whereas Communist bureaucracies dominate their economies with pervasive regulations—hence the facile comparison to the mercantilist state—the groups served by these regulations, at least de jure, are workers and peasants. These mass groups in Eastern Europe (essentially the entire potential voting population), not a small English property-owning class revolting against another property-owning class, have overthrown the state bureaucracy in favor of a new system.

Liberals regard the state as such as inherently corruptible and the free market as incorruptible. But is this as clearly the case when propertyless classes are at least partly served by the state and would not necessarily be the primary beneficiaries of privatization and a free market? In many ways, present-day revolutions in Europe are the eighteenth century turned on its political head. But since Liberal theory views society from the perspective of the individual in the economy (and how the state relates to the economy), it tends to ignore differences in political conditions and to focus on market relations.

7. Charles Murray, *Losing Ground* (Basic Books, 1983).

8. James Smith and Finis Welch, "Black Economic Progress After Myrdal," *Journal of Economic Literature*, 27, June, 1989, pp. 519-564.

9. Adam Smith, *The Theory of Moral Sentiments* [1759] (Clarenden Press, 1976).

10. See, for example, *"Contribution to the Critique of Hegel's Philosophy of Right"* (1844); *The German Ideology* (1845-46); *Manifesto of the Communist Party* (1848); *The Eighteenth Brumaire of Louis Bonaparte* (1852); and *The Civil War in France* (1871). These can be found (at least in part) in Robert C. Tucker, ed., *The Marx-Engels Reader* (W. W. Norton, 1978). In addition, we have Engels' later work, *The Origin of the Family, Private Property, and the State* [1884] (International Publishers, 1968), and Lenin's *The State and Revolution* [1917] (Foreign Language Press, 1965).

11. Marx argued in the *Eighteenth Brumaire* that during "abnormal times" when no class has enough power to exert its control over the state bureaucracy (such as during the reign of Louis Napoleon [1852-70]), the state has much greater autonomy from the dominant bourgeoisie. According to the analysis, the state necessarily still continued to serve bourgeois interests, but without the bourgeoisie having direct control, and as part of policies that also served narrower state interests.

12. Karl Marx and Frederick Engels, *The Manifesto of the Communist Party* (Appleton-Century-Crofts, 1955), pp. 11-12.

13. See V. I. Lenin, *On Youth* (Progress Publishers, 1965). However, Krupskaya, Lenin's wife, was extremely active in the early post-Revolutionary years setting up new schools based on John Dewey's progressive educational model. Nevertheless, these schools never became widespread. See Martin Carnoy and Joel Samoff, *Education and Social Transition in the Third World* (Princeton University Press, 1990).

14. Samuel Bowles and Herbert Gintis, *Schooling in Capitalist America* (Basic Books, 1975).

15. Martin Carnoy, *Education as Cultural Imperialism* (David McKay, 1974).

16. Antonio Gramsci, *Selections from Prison Notebooks* (International Publishers, 1971).

17. For example, Michael Apple, *Ideology and Curriculum* (Routledge and Kegan Paul, 1979); Jean Anyon, "Intersection of Gender and Class: Accommodation and Resistance by Working Class and Affluent Females to Contradictory Sex-Role Ideologies," in Stephen Walker and Len Barton, eds., *Gender, Class and Education* (Falmer Press, 1983), pp. 19-37; Henry Giroux, *Ideology, Culture, and the Process of Schooling* (Temple University Press, 1981); Geoff Whitty, *Sociology and School Knowledge* (Methuen, 1985).

18. See also Samuel Bowles and Herbert Gintis, *Capitalism and Democracy* (Basic Books, 1988).

19. Nicos Poulantzas, *State, Power, Socialism* (New Left Books, 1978).

20. Bowles and Gintis, *Capitalism and Democracy.*

21. Henry M. Levin, "Educational Production Theory and Teacher Inputs," in C. Bidwell and D. Windham, eds., *The Analysis of Educational Productivity: Issues in Macroanalysis* (Ballinger, 1980), pp, 203-231; Martin Carnoy and Jean MacDonell, "School District Restructuring in Santa Fe, New Mexico," *Educational Policy*, 4, no. 1 (1990), pp. 49-64.

22. See Marshall Smith and Jennifer O'Day, "Educational Equality 1966 and Now," School of Education, Stanford University, August, 1990.

23. See, for example, Michel Foucault, *Discipline and Punish* (Vintage Books, 1979).

24. Peter Evans, Dietrich Rueschemeyer, and Theda Skocpol, *Bringing the State Back In* (Cambridge University Press, 1985).

25. *Ibid*, p. 9.

26. See also Bowles and Gintis, *Capitalism and Democracy.*

27. Louis Althusser, *Lenin and Philosophy and Other Essays* (Monthly Review Press, 1971).

28. John Meyer and Richard Scott. *Organizational Environments* (Sage Publications, 1983).

29. John Meyer, Francisco Ramirez, and John Boli-Bennett, "The world educational revolution, 1950-1970," *Sociology of Education*, 50 (1977), pp. 242-258.

30. Pierre Bourdieu and Jean-Claude Passeron, *Reproduction* (Sage, 1977).

31. See, for example, L. S. Gottfredson, "Reconstructing fairness: A matter of social and ethical priorities," *Journal of Vocational Behavior*, 33 (1988), pp. 293-319; Henry M. Levin, "Ability testing for job selection: Are the economic claims justified?" In B. Gifford, ed., *Testing and the allocation of opportunity* (Kluwer Academic Publishers, 1989).

32. Milton and Rose Friedman, *Free to Choose* (Harcourt Brace, 1980).

33. John Chubb and Terry Moe, *Politics, Markets, and America's Schools* (The Brookings Institution, 1990).

34. It is almost axiomatic that European Socialist and Social Democratic governments tend to democratize secondary education and expand university education and conservative governments cut into university spending and shift costs to students and their families.

35. Lenin, *On Youth.*

36. For attempts to do so, see Alec Nove, *The Economics of Feasible Socialism* (George Allen Unwin, 1983), and Carnoy and Samoff, *Education and Transition.*

37. Barry Bosworth and Alice Rivlin, *The Swedish Economy* (The Brookings Institution, 1987).

38. Adam Przeworski and Michael Wallerstein, "The Structure Conflict in Democratic Capitalist Societies," *American Political Science Review*, 76, 2 (1982): pp. 215-238.

CHAPTER 10

1. Proposals for decentralization are catalogued in Donald Winkler, *Decentralization in education: an economic perspective*. Washington: World Bank, Education and

Employment Division, 1988. See also Jon Lauglo and Martin McLean, eds., *The control of education: International perspectives on the centralization-decentralization debate* (London: Heinemann Educational Books, 1985).

2. Carlos Malpica and Shapour Rassekh, eds., *Educational administration and multilevel plan implementation: experiences from developing countries,* Paris: International Institute for Educational Planning, 1983; Polymnia Zagefka Yannakopulos, *Eleven experiences in innovations in decentralization of educational administration and the management of local resources* (Paris: UNESCO, ED-80/WS/120, 1980).

3. Melvin Zimet, *Decentralization and school effectiveness: a case study of the 1969 Decentralization law in New York City* (New York: Columbia University Press, 1973).

4. Carlos Ornelas, "Educational decentralization in Mexico," *Prospects* 18:1 (1987): pp. 105-113.

5. There are a variety of forms of governance of higher education. See Burton R. Clark, The higher education system: *Academic organization in cross-national perspective* (Berkeley: University of California Press, 1983). Recent reforms of governance in French higher education are reported in Guy Neave, "Strategic planning, reform and governance in French higher education, " *Studies in Higher Education* 10 (1985): pp. 7-20.

6. E. Mark Hanson, "Decentralization and regionalization in educational administration: comparisons of Venezuela, Colombia and Spain," *Comparative Education* 25:1 (1989): pp. 41-55.

7. For Brazil see Edi Fracasso, *Organizational planning and policy making in Brazil: the case of the Institutional Program of Faculty Development (PICD)* (Cambridge: Harvard University, unpublished Ed.D. diss., 1984). For Mexico see Noel McGinn and Susan Street, "Higher Education Policies in Mexico" (Austin, TX: University of Texas, Institute of Latin American Studies, Technical Paper Series no. 29, 1980).

8. D. T . Gamage, "The struggle for control of higher education in a developing economy: Sri Lanka," *Comparative Education* 19 (1983): pp. 325-339; and "Vicissitudes in the administration of higher education in a Third World country: Four decades—seven reforms, " *Educational Administration and History* 19 (1987): pp. 47-61. As in Mexico, the government simultaneously attempted to move control over primary schools closer to local communities, and to impose central controls over universities.

Kogan argues that there has been a general shift from local to national control of higher education in industrialized countries: M. Kogan, "Government and the management of higher education: An introductory review," *International Journal of Institutional Management in Higher Education* 12 (1988): pp. 5-15.

9. Francisco O. Ramirez and Richard Rubinson, "Creating members: The polit-

ical incorporation and expansion of public education," in John W. Meyer and Michael Hannan, eds., *National development and the world system* (Chicago: University of Chicago Press, 1979) pp. 72-82.

10. In the eighteen-nineteenth centuries: Francisco O. Ramirez and John Boli, "The political construction of mass schooling: European origins and worldwide institutionalization," *Sociology of Education* 60:1 (1987): pp. 2-17.

11. George Huppert, *Public Schools in Renaissance France* (Urbana: Illinois: University of Illinois Press, 1984) p. 12.

12. Margaret S. Archer, *Social Origins of Educational Systems* (London: Sage, 1979).

13. Alan Crispin, "Finance as a means of control in English education: Recent trends toward centralization," in Jon Lauglo and Martin McLean, *op. cit.*, pp. 119-128.

14. Nicholas Beattie, "Parent participation in French education, 1968-1975," *British Journal of Educational Studies* 26:1 (1978): pp. 40-53.

15. Patricia Broadfoot, "Towards conformity: Educational control and the growth of corporate management in England and France, " in Lauglo and McLean, *op. cit.*, pp. 105-118 . See also Goran Therborn, *What does the ruling class do when it rules?* (London: New Left Books, 1978).

16. Charles T. Kerchner, "Bureaucratic entrepreneurship: The implications of choice for school administration," *Educational Administration Quarterly* 24:4 (1988): pp. 381-392.

17. L. Harmon Zeigler, Harvey J. Tucker, and L. A. Wilson, "How school control was wrested from the people," *Phi Delta Kappan* 58 (1977): pp. 534-539.

18. William C. Webster, *Recent centralizing tendencies in state educational administration* (New York: Columbia University, 1897).

19. Zeigler et al., *op. cit.*, p. 535.

20. Zeigler et al., *op. cit.*, p. 536.

21. See Zimet, *op. cit.*, for an evaluation of the New York experience. Decentralization also failed in rural areas. See G. Williamson McDiarmid, *Governing schools in culturally different communities: effects of decentralization in rural Alaska* (Cambridge, MA: Harvard University. Unpublished doctoral diss., 1984).

22. Emil J. Haller and David H. Monk, "New reform, old reforms, and the consolidation of small rural schools," *Educational Administration Quarterly* 24: 4 (1988): pp. 470-483.

23. Neighborhood school boards have been reinstalled in Chicago, but with a sharply reduced fiscal resource base and inability to attract sufficient numbers of qualified teachers.

24. For one example see Donald C. Hazen, "The politics of schooling in the non-literate Third World: The case of Highland Peru" *History of Education Quarterly* 18:4 (1978): pp. 419-444.
Resistance to centralizing reforms has occurred in many other countries as well. See M. Kazim Bacchus, "The primary school curriculum in a colonial society," *Journal of Curriculum Studies* 6:1 (1974): pp. 15-29; B. Curtis, "Patterns of resistance to public education: England, Ireland and Canada West, 1830-1890," *Comparative Education Review* 32 (1988): pp. 318-333; Gail P. Kelly, "Teachers and the transmission of State knowledge: A case study of Colonial Vietnam," in Philip G. Altbach et al., eds., *Comparative Education* (New York: Macmillan, 1982) pp. 176-194; Donald G. Schilling, "The dynamics of education policy formation: Kenya 1928-1934" *History of Education Quarterly* 20 :1 (1980): pp. 51-76.

25. Donald J. Mabry, *The Mexican University and the State: Student Conflicts, 1910-1971* (College Station, TX: Texas A&M University Press, 1982).

26. This occurred notably in Chile and El Salvador, and more recently in Guatemala.

27. Known as the Consensus of Bogota, the agreement of ministers of education on regionalization is reported in Organization of American States, "La regionalización educativa en América Latina," *La Educación* 87, 88 (1981, 1982): pp. 1-120, pp. 1-143.

28. A detailed bibliography for this reform is provided in Noel McGinn and Susan Street, "Educational decentralization: Weak state or strong state?" *Comparative Education Review* 30:4 (November 1986): pp. 471-490.

29. Susan Street, Organized teachers as policymakers: *Domination and opposition in Mexican public education* (Cambridge: Harvard University, unpublished Ed.D. diss., 1988).

30. Abraham Magendzo, Loreto Egana, and Carmen Luz Latorre, *Privatización de la educación: La educación y los esquemas privatizantes en educación bajo un estado subsidiario (1973-1987)* (Santiago: Programa Interdisciplinario de Investigación Educativa, 1988).

31. Ivan Nuñez, *La descentralización y las reformas educacionales en Chile, 1940-1973* (Santiago: Programa Interdisciplinario de Investigación en Educación, 1989.

32. Parents of Tarahumara Indian children in rural Mexico who wanted their children to remain with them to work the land resented a national program that effectively taught "Mexican" values to their children and drew them into wage labor. Other parents welcomed this opportunity. See Sylvia Schmelkes "Estudio de evaluación aproximativa de las escuelas radiofónicas de la Tarahumara," *Revista del Centro de Estudios Educativos* 2:2 (1972): pp. 11-35.

33. A common method has been provision of programmed guides for teachers. Sivasailam Thiagarajan and Aida L. Pasigna, *Literature Review on the Soft Technologies of Learning* (Cambridge: Harvard Institute for International Development, BRIDGES Research Report Series no. 2, 1988).

34. Mark Bray and Kevin Lillis, eds., *Community financing of education: Issues and policy implications in less developed countries* (London: Pergamon, 1987), pp. 75-93.

35. Reported for Sri Lanka by William K. Cummings, "The decentralization of education: Cambridge" (Harvard Institute for International Development, BRIDGES Project, unpublished paper, 1988).

36. Haim Gaziel, "The emergence of the comprehensive middle school in France: educational policy-making in a centralized system," *Comparative Education* 25:1 (1989): pp. 29-40.

37. *A New Partnership for our Schools* (London: Her Majesty's Stationery Office, 1977).

38. See Paul Hurst, "Decentralization: panacea or red herring?" eds. Jon Lauglo and Martin McLean, *op. cit.*, pp. 79-85; and D. A. Howell, "The Hungarian Education Act of 1985: a study in decentralization," *Comparative Education* 24:1 (1988): pp. 125-136.

CHAPTER 11

*Grateful acknowledgements are due to Gail P. Kelly, Robert F. Arnove, N. V. Varghese, and K. Sujatha for their helpful comments on an earlier version of this chapter. The usual caveats follow.

1. See Tapas Majumdar, *Investment in Education and Social Choice* (Cambridge: Cambridge University Press, 1983).

2. Majumdar, p. 28.

3. George Psacharopoulos and Maureen Woodhall, *Education for Development: An Analysis of Investment Choices* (New York: Oxford, 1985), pp. 130. See also World Bank, *Financing Education in Developing Countries: An Exploration of Policy Options* (Washington, D.C., 1986).

4. Interestingly it may be observed that "public-good qualities of a public service may exist even if they are not documentable." Anita Summers, "Comment," *Journal of Policy Analysis and Management* 6 (1987): pp. 641-643, esp. 643.

5. See E. G. West, *Education and the State* (London: Institute of Economic Affairs, 1970) 2d ed.; and Richard Musgrave, *The Theory of Public Finance* (New York: McGraw Hill, 1959), pp. 13-14. For views on the opposite side, see Milton Friedman, "The Role of Government in Education," in *Capitalism and Freedom* (Chicago: University of Chicago Press, 1962), pp. 85-107. See also Psacharopoulos, "Welfare Effects of Government Intervention in Education," *Contemporary Policy Issues: Economic Analysis for Decision Maker* 4 (July 1986): pp. 51-62.

6. See for a recent review and empirical analysis, Tilak, *Education and its Relation to Economic Growth, Poverty and Income Distribution*, Occasional paper no. 46 (Washington D.C.: World Bank, 1989).

7. J. R. G. Tomilinson, "Public Education, Public Good," *Oxford Review of Education* 12 (1986): pp. 211-222.

8. For example, Daniel Rogers, "The Economic Effects of Various Methods of Educational Finance" (Washington D.C.: World Bank, Economics Department, 1970); and Jean-Pierre Jallade, "The Financing of Education: An Examination of Basic Issues," Staff working paper no. 157 (Washington D.C.: World Bank, 1973).

9. Burton A. Weisbrod, *The Nonprofit Economy* (Cambridge, MA: Harvard University Press, 1988).

10. Nancy Birdsall, "Pragmatism, Robin Hood, and Other Themes: Good Government and Social Well-Being in Developing Countries" (Washington D.C.: World Bank/New York: Rockefeller Foundation, *Draft*, October 1988).

11. Literature on developed countries is also not overwhelming. See *inter alia* Sam Peltzman, "The Effects of Government Subsidies-in-Kind on Private Expenditures: The Case of Higher Education," *Journal of Political Economy* 81 (January/February 1973): pp. 1-27; Ross A. Williams, "Interaction Between Government and Private Outlays: Education in Australia, 1949-50 to 1981-82," Discussion paper no. 79 (Canberra: Centre for Economic Policy Research, Australian National University, 1983); and Walter W. McMahon, "Why Families Invest in Education," in *The Collection and Analysis of Economic and Consumer Behavior Data: In memory of Robert Ferber*, eds. S. Sudman and M. A. Spaeth (Champaign, IL: Bureau of Economic and Business Research & Survey Research Laboratory, University of Illinois, 1984), pp. 75-91.

12. For a methodology to estimate parents' contribution to education, see McMahon, "Potential Resource Recovery in Higher Education in Developing Countries and the Parents' Expected Contribution," *Economics of Education Review* 7 (1988): pp. 135-152.

13. For more empirical details on the household and government investments in education in India, see Tilak, "Family and Government Investments in Education," *International Journal of Educational Development* 11 (1991); and also Tilak, "Trends in Public and Private Finances for Education in India" (Washington D.C.: World Bank, Asia Region-China Country Division, Population and Human Resource Department, 1990) *(mimeograph)*.

14. Tilak, "Costs of Education in India," *International Journal of Educational Development* 8 (1988): pp. 25-42, esp. 28. See also Rati Ram and Theodore W. Schultz, "Life Span, Health, Savings and Productivity," *Economic and Development and Cultural Change* 27 (April 1979): pp. 399-421.

15. Some times it is argued that opportunity costs, if adjusted for unemployment, would be substantially less, or even nil. But unemployment need not necessarily be taken into account as, it is the real value of the input that is estimated as opportunity

costs, and not whether a resource is productively used or not. See Mary Jean Bowman, "Costing of Human Resource Development," in *Economics of Education*, "Costing of Human Resource Development," in *Economics of Education*, eds. E. A. G. Robinson and John Vaizey (London: Macmillan, 1966), p. 425.

16. About half the population is estimated to be below the poverty line.

17. Psacharopoulos and Woodhall, *Education for Development*, p. 131.

18. See Psacharopoulos, "Higher Education Expenditure in OECD Countries," 1980, *mimeograph*, p. 16.

19. See Tilak and N. V. Varghese, "Discriminatory Pricing in Education," Occasional paper no. 8 (New Delhi: National Institute of Educational Planning & Administration, 1985). See also Emmanuel Jimenez, *Pricing Policy in the Social Sectors: Cost Recovery for Education and Health in Developing Countries* (Baltimore: John Hopkins, 1987).

20. This section partly draws from Tilak, "The Political Economy of Education in India," Special studies no. 24 (Buffalo: State University of New York in cooperation with the University of Virginia, 1990).

21. For an account of practices regarding payment of salaries and working conditions of teachers, see Susan Ram "Plight of Teachers of Private Colleges," *Economic and Political Weekly* 13 (23 September 1978): pp. 1619-21.

22. See Henry M. Levin, "Education as a Public and Private Good," *Journal of Policy Analysis and Management* 6 (1987): pp. 628-641, esp. 637.

23. A few examples of such schools are the Delhi Public School, Modern School (Delhi), Doon School (Dehradoon), St. George College (Mussorie), Scindia Schools (Gwalior), and Don Bosco (all over India).

24. *Fourth All-India Educational Survey* (New Delhi: National Council of Educational Research and Training, 1978).

25. R. Gopinathan Nair and D. Ajit, "Parallel Colleges in Kerala: Enrollment, Costs and Employment," *Economic and Political Weekly* 19 (October 20-27, 1984): pp. 1840-47, esp. 1847.

26. V. N. Kothari, "Private Unaided Engineering and Medical Colleges: Consequences of Misguided Policy," *Economic and Political Weekly* 21 (April 5, 1986): pp. 593-596.

27. Lloyd I. Rudolph and Susan H. Rudolph, *In Pursuit of Lakshmi: The Political Economy of the Indian State* (Chicago: University of Chicago Press, 1987), p. 296.

28. Suma Chitnis and C. Suvannathat, "Schooling for the Children of the Urban Poor," in *Basic Needs and the Urban Poor: The Provision of Communal Services*, eds. P. J. Richards and A. M. Thomson (London: Croom Helm, 1984), pp. 189-213, esp. 191.

29. See C. M. Bhatia and V. K. Seth, "Hierarchy in the System of Schools: Political Economy of Education," *Sociological Bulletin*, 24 (March 1975): pp. 13-28; R. P.

Singh, *The Indian Public School* (New Delhi: Sterling, 1972); and Alfred de Souza, *Indian Public Schools: A Sociological Study* (New Delhi: Sterling, 1974). See also Krishna Kumar, "Reproduction or Change? Education and Elites in India," in *Education and the Process of Change*, eds. Ratna Ghosh, and Mathew Zachariah (New Delhi Sage, 1987), pp. 27-41.

30. M. Shatrugna, "Privatising Higher Education," *Economic and Political Weekly* 23 (December 10, 1988): pp. 2624-26, esp. 2624.

31. *The Statesman* (New Delhi, 10 July 1989), p. 4. See also Kothari.

32. Nair and Ajit.

33. Kothari, p. 596.

34. Psacharopoulos and Woodhall, p. 144. Another World Bank study also recognizes that increased private financing at the primary level might obstruct universal coverage of basic education—a socially desirable goal. *Financing Education in Developing Countries*, p. 23.

35. Asim K. Dasgupta, "Income Distribution, Education and Capital Accumulation" (Washington D.C.: World Bank, 1979).

36. While evidence on India is not available on this aspect, the Kenyan evidence indicates that government schools yield returns 50 percent higher than private *(harambee)* schools. See J. Armitage and R. H. Sabot, "Efficiency and Equity Implications of Subsidies of Secondary Education in Kenya," in *The Theory of Taxation for Developing Countries*, eds. David Newbery and Nicholas Stern (New York: Oxford, 1987), pp. 589-614, esp. 601. Also see Psacharopoulos, "Public versus Private Schools in Developing Countries," *International Journal of Educational Development* 7 (1987): pp. 59-67 for related interesting details on Colombia and Tanzania.

37. *Challenge of Education: A Policy Perspective* (New Delhi: Government of India, Ministry of Education, 1985), p. 80.

38. Kothari, p. 596.

39. Tilak, "Family and Government Investments in Education."

40. For example, see M. Thobani, "Charging User Fees for Social Services: Education Malawi," *Comparative Education Review* 2 (August 1984): pp. 402-23.

41. Mark Bray, "Is Free Education in the Third World either Desirable or Possible?" *Journal of Education Policy* 2 (April-June 1987): pp. 119-129.

CHAPTER 12

The authors wish to acknowledge the support of The Spencer Foundation in the preparation of this chapter.

*All discussion of the FRG refers to the pre-1990 territory of the Federal Republic, before unification with the German Democratic Republic (East Germany).

**All discussion of the USSR refers to the period prior to the systemic changes of September 1991.

1. U.S. Department of Education, *Japanese Education Today* (Washington, D.C.: U.S. Government Printing Office, 1987), p. 44.

2. Thomas P. Rohlen, *Japan's High Schools* (Berkeley: University of California Press, 1983), ch. 3, "University Entrance Exams."

3. "A new entrance examination system," *Monthly Journal of Ministry of Education, Science, and Culture*, Tokyo, 1988. Japanese anxiety over the negative personal and social effects of the so-called "examination hell" has been expressed forcefully in reports from the National Council on Educational Reform, see "Summary of Second Report on Education Reform," April 23, 1986.

4. Ministère de l'Education Nationale, *Baccalauréat de l'enseignement du second degré* (Paris: Centre National de Documentation Pedagogique, 1985).

5. *Grund und Strukturdaten* (Bonn: Bundesminister für Bildung und Wissenschaft, 1988).

6. H. von Hentig, *Die Krise des Abiturs und eine Alternative* (Stuttgart: Klett-Cotta, 1980).

7. Friedrich Kuebart, "Schuler leistung—Lehrer leistung. Probleme der Leistungskontrolle im sowjetischen Schulwesen," in B. Dilger, F. Kuebart, and M. P. Schafer, *Vergleichende Bildungsforschung: DDR, Osteuropa und interkulturelle Perspektiven* (Berlin: Berlin Verlag, 1986), pp. 367-369.

8. The topics for the oral examinations at the end of secondary school are published each year by the central education authorities of each Soviet republic. In the Russian Republic the topics are to be found in: *Bilety dlia vypusknykhj ekzamenov za kurs srednei shkoly* (Tickets for the secondary school leaving examinations).

9. L. P. Alekseeva and G. G. Gorodnicheva, "Osnovnie napravleniia sovershenstvovaniia priema v VUZy," *Soderzhanie, formy i metody obucheniia v vysshei i srednei spetsial'noi shkole* (Moskva: Ministerstvo Vysshego i Srednego Spetsial'nogo Obrazovaniia SSSP, 1986), no. 2: pp. 1-43. (Basic procedures in implementing admission to higher education).

10. Jo and Peter Mortimore, *Secondary School Examinations*, Bedford Way Papers 18 (London: Institute of Education, University of London, 1984).

11. Caroline Gipps et al., *The GCSE: An Uncommon Examination*, Bedford Way Papers 29 (London: Institute of Education, University of London, 1986); Michael Kingdon and Gordon Stobart, *GCSE Examined* (London: Falmer, 1988).

12. "Assessment in Swedish Schools" (Stockholm: National Swedish Board of Education, 1985) *mimeograph.*

13. New provisions for admission to higher education will go into effect in 1991. "In the new selection system, marks from the upper secondary school . . . will assume major importance. At least one-third and, at most, two-thirds of the applicants will be admitted on the basis of such marks. Those who do not have sufficiently high marks will have the possibility to sit a proficiency test at the earliest one year after having completed the upper secondary school. This test will count for more in the selection process than experience from working life." "Sweden: Access to Higher Education," *News-Letter/Faits Nouveaux*, 2/88 (Strasbourg: Documentation Centre for Education in Europe, 1988), p. 27.

14. Sixten Marklund, "Education in Sweden: Assessment of Student Achievement and Selection for Higher Education," in Heyneman and Fagerlind, *University Examinations and Standardized Testing*, pp. 89-106.

15. C. T. Hu, "The Historical Background: Examinations and Controls in Pre-Modern China," *Comparative Education* 20 (1984): pp. 7-26.

16. Jonathan Unger, "Severing the Link between School Performance and Careers: the Experience of China's Urban Schools, 1968-1976" *Comparative Education* 20 (1984): pp. 93-102.

17. *A Brief Introduction to Higher Education Enrollment Examinations in China* (Beijing: The State Education Commission of the People's Republic of China, 1986).

18. For example, Lauren B. and Daniel P. Resnick, "Standards, Curriculum, and Performance: A Historical and Comparative Perspective," *The Educational Researcher* 14:4 (April 1985): pp. 5-20.

19. John A. Valentine, *The College Board and the School Curriculum* (New York: College Entrance Examination Board, 1987).

20. For example, The National Commission on Excellence in Education, *A Nation At Risk: The Imperative for Educational Reform* (Washington, D.C.: U.S. Government Printing Office, 1983), pp. 19, 28.

CHAPTER 13

1. The work reported in this chapter relates to a study of teacher education in three countries, funded by the Spencer Foundation of Chicago. It is a revised form of an article published in *Comparative Education Review* 32, no. 2 (May 1988): pp. 142-158, reproduced here by kind permission of the Editors.

2. For a good example of this *genre* see the articles in a special number devoted to Japan of one of the leading journals in comparative education: only one of the con-

tributors elects to make any direct comparative analysis *Comparative Education* 22, no. 1 (1986). An interesting contrast is furnished by a special number of the same journal under the guest editorship of David Phillips significantly titled "Cross-National Attraction in Education" *Comparative Education* 25, no. 1 (1989).

3. See the chapters by Max Eckstein on "The Comparative Mind" and by Harold Noah on "The Use and Abuse of Comparative Education" in Philip G. Altbach and Gail Kelly, eds., *New Approaches to Comparative Education* (Chicago: University of Chicago Press, 1986).

4. Vernon Mallinson, *An Introduction to the Study of Comparative Education* (London: Heinemann, 1975).

5. In the rest of this chapter the term United Kingdom is used for England and Wales. The differences between England and Wales on the one hand and both Scotland and Northern Ireland are indeed considerable, but "the UK" is employed as the less cumbersome term.

6. For an excellent, if elaborate, example of such work see James Lynch and Dudley Plunkett, *Teacher Education and Cultural Change: England, France, West Germany* (London: George Allen and Unwin, 1973).

7. Clifford Geertz, *The Interpretation of Cultures* (New York: Basic Books, 1973), p. 5.

8. Walter P. Metzger, "The Spectre of Professionalism," *Educational Researcher* 7 (August-September 1987): pp. 10-19.

9. The 1988 Education Reform Act has the effect, although not the stated intention, of displacing the concept of client by that of consumer or customer. Harry Judge, "Is there a crisis in British secondary schools?" *Phi Delta Kappan* (June 1989): pp. 813-816. Geoffrey Walford, "The 1988 Education Reform Act for England and Wales: Paths to Privatization," *Educational Policy* 4, no. 2 (June 1990): pp. 127-144.

10. Harry Judge, "Teaching and Professionalism: An Essay in Ambiguity," in *World Yearbook of Education 1980*, ed. Eric Hoyle and Jacquetta Megarry (London: Kogan Page, 1980), pp. 340-342. A modest amount of empirical data supporting the analysis which follows is summarized in R. M. and Helen M. Kelsall, *The School Teacher in England and the United States: The Findings of Empirical Research* (Oxford: Pergamon, 1963), in which chapter 3 is particularly suggestive.

11. Emily Feistritzer, *The Condition of Teaching* (New York: Carnegie Foundation for the Advancement of Teaching, 1983).

12. P. H. J. H. Gosden, *The Evolution of a Profession* (Oxford: Basil Blackwell, 1972), p. 37.

13. *A Nation Prepared: Teachers for the Twenty-First Century* (New York: Carnegie Corporation, 1986), p. 65.

14. Department of Education and Science, *Initial Teacher Training: Approval of Courses* (London: Her Majesty's Stationery Office, 1984 and 1989).

15. For an excellent guide to the 1988 Education Reform Act see Stuart Maclure, *Education Re-Formed* (London: Hodder and Stoughton, 1988). See also B. Salter and J. Tapper, "The DES" in J. Ongar and I. McKay, eds., *Policy Making in Education* (Oxford: Pergamon, 1985).

16. Harry Judge, *American Graduate Schools of Education: A View from Abroad* (New York: The Ford Foundation, 1982), p. 37.

17. Charles Handy and Robert Aitken, *Understanding Schools as Organizations* (Harmondsworth: Penguin Books, 1986), p. 79.

18. Tomorrow's Teachers: A Report of the Holmes Group (East Lansing: The Holmes Group), p. 64. See also footnote 13, and the second report of the Holmes Group *Tomorrow's Schools* (East Lansing: The Holmes Group, 1990).

19. Martin Lawn, ed., *The Politics of Teachers Unions* (London: Croom Helm, 1985).

20. Edgar B. Wesley, *N.E.A., The First Hundred Years: the Building of the Teaching Profession* (New York: Harper and Brothers, 1957). Robert J. Braun, *Teachers and Power: The Story of the American Federation of Teachers* (New York: Simon and Schuster, 1972). Maurice Berube, *Teacher Politics: the Influence of Unions* (New York: Greenwood Press, 1988).

21. Maurice Kogan, *The Politics of Educational Change* (London: Fontana, 1978), p. 79.

22. Bruce S. Cooper, *Collective Bargaining, Strikes and Financial Costs in Public Education: A Comparative Review* (Eugene, Oreg: ERIC Clearinghouse, 1982).

23. Frank Musgrove and Philip H. Taylor, *Society and the Teacher's Role* (London: Routledge and Kegan Paul, 1969), p. 7.

24. Tony Becher and Stuart Maclure, *The Politics of Curriculum Change* (London: Hutchinson, 1978), p. 41.

25. Raymond E. Callahan, *Education and the Cult of Efficiency*, (Chicago: University of Chicago Press, 1962), p. 244. David Tyack and Elisabeth Hansot, *Managers of Virtue: Public School Leadership in America, 1820-1980* (New York: Basic Books, 1982), p. 218.

26. John Mann, "Who killed the Schools Council?" in *Life and Death of the Schools Council*, ed. Maurice Plaskow (Lewes: The Falmer Press, 1985), pp. 179-193.

27. Gary Sykes, "Contradictions, Ironies and Promises Unfulfilled," *Phi Delta Kappan* (October 1983): pp. 87-93.

28. Arthur E. Wise, *Legislated Learning: the Bureaucratization of the American*

Classroom (Berkeley: University of California Press, 1979).

29. Linda M. McNeil, *Contradictions of Control: School Structure and School Knowledge* (New York: Routledge and Kegan Paul, 1986).

30. Dan C. Lortie, *Schoolteacher: A Sociological Study* (Chicago: University of Chicago Press, 1986). Philip Jackson, *Life in Classrooms* (New York: Holt, Reinhart and Wilson, 1968) and more recently, *The Practice of Teaching* (New York: Teachers College Press, 1986).

31. Thomas J. Peters and Robert H. Waterman, Jr., *In Search of Excellence* (New York: Warner Books, 1982), p. 201.

32. H. C. Dent, *The Training of Teachers in England and Wales, 1800-1975* (London: Hodder and Stoughton, 1977), p. 33.

CHAPTER 14

1. See Ramesh Mishra, *The Welfare State in Crisis* (Brighton, England: Harvester-Wheatsheaf, 1984).

2. Quoted in Joseph A. Pechman, ed., *Setting National Priorities: Agenda for the 1980s* (Washington, D.C.: The Brookings Institution, 1980), p. 208.

3. See Joan Higgins, *The Poverty Business: Britain and America* (Oxford, England: Basil Blackwell, Martin Robertson, 1978).

4. C. B. Cox and A. E. Dyson, eds., *Fight for Education: A black paper* (London: The Critical Quarterly Society, March 1969); C. B. Cox and A. E. Dyson, eds., *Black Paper Two: The crisis in education* (London: The Critical Quarterly Society, 1969); C. B. Cox and A. E. Dyson, eds., *Black Paper Three: Goodbye Mr. Short* (London: The Critical Quarterly Society 1970); C. B. Cox and Rhodes Boyson, eds., *Black Paper 1975: The Fight for Education* (London: J. M. Dent and Sons Ltd., 1975); C. B. Cox and Rhodes Boyson, eds., *Black Paper 1977* (London: Maurice Temple Smith Ltd).

5. See C. B. Cox and Rhodes Boyson, eds., *Black Paper 1975: The Fight for Education* (London: J. M. Dent & Sons Ltd, 1975) p. 1.

6. Stuart Hall, "The Great Moving Right show" *Marxism Today*, 1979.

7. Miriam E. David, *The State, the Family and Education* (London: Routledge and Kegan Paul, 1980).

8. Centre of Contemporary Cultural Studies, *Unpopular Education: Schooling and Social Democracy in England since 1944* (London: Hutchinson, 1981) p. 221.

9. *Ibid.*, p. 222.

10. *Ibid.*

11. Jeanne Gregory, *Sex, Race and the Law: Legislating for Equality* (London: Sage, 1987).

12. See V. Burke and V. Burke, *Nixon's Good Deed* (NY: Columbia University Press, 1974).

13. J. H. Bunzel, ed., *Challenge to American Schools: The Case for Standards and Values* (NY and Oxford: Oxford University Press, 1985) p. 51.

14. See *ibid.*, and Gillian Peele, *Revival or Reaction: The Right in America* (Oxford, England: Oxford University Press, 1986).

15. David Bull and Caroline Glendenning, "Access to 'Free' Education: Erosion by Statute and Stealth," in David Bull and Paul Wilding, eds., *Thatcherism and the Poor* (London: Child Poverty Action Group, April 1983), pp. 53-58.

16. See Miriam David, *The State, the Family and Education.*

17. This has also been noted by Roger Dale, 1989, *The State and Education Policy* (Milton Keynes: The Open University Press, 1989) in both chapters 6 and 7, the latter of which looks at the background to Thatcherism.

18. See, in particular, J. Fitz, T. Edwards, and G. Whitty, "Beneficiaries, Benefits and Costs: An Investigation of the Assisted Places Scheme," *Research Papers in Education*, 1, 3, October, 1986.

19. Miriam David, "Education," in Mike McCarthy, ed., *The New Politics of Welfare* (London: Macmillan: 1989), pp. 154-177.

20. Stuart Hall, "Education in Crisis" in J. Donald and Ann Marie Wolpe, eds., *Is There Anyone Here from Education?* (London: Pluto Press, 1983) p. 1.

21. Roger Scruton, A. Ellis-Jones, and D. O'Keeffe, *Education and Indoctrination* (Harrow, Middlesex: Education Research Centre, 1985).

22. David, "Education."

23. Roger Dale, "The Thatcherite Project in Education: The Case of City Technology Colleges" *Critical Social Policy* issue 27, (Winter 1989/90), pp. 4-19.

24. The Swann Report, *Education for All*, The Report of the Committee of Inquiry into the Education of Children from Ethnic Minority Groups, CMND 9543, (London: HMSO, 1985).

25. See Philip Altbach's introduction in Philip Altbach, Gail Kelly, and Lois Weis, eds., *Excellence in Education* (Buffalo: Prometheus Books, 1985), p. 17.

26. *Ibid.*, p. 18.

27. See Kelly, *ibid.*, p. 31.

28. See Altbach, *ibid.*, p. 20.

29. See Kelly, *ibid.*, pp. 39-40.

30. Robert B. Hawkins, "Strategy for Revitalizing Public Education" in John Bunzel, ed., *Challenge to America's Schools*, (NY and Oxford: Oxford University Press, 1985), p. 46.

31. Margaret Goertz, "Education Politics for a New Century: introduction and overview" in Douglas Mitchell and Margaret Goertz, eds., *Education Politics for a New Century: The Twentieth Anniversary Politics of Education Yearbook*; a special issue of the *Journal of Education Policy*, vol. 4, no. 5 (London and NY: Taylor & Francis, 1989) p. 5.

32. *Ibid.*

33. E. L. Useem, 1986, *Low Tech Education in a High Tech World* p. 61 and 104, quoted in Carol A. Ray and Rosalyn A. Mickelson, "Business Leaders and the Politics of School Reform" in Douglas Mitchell and Margaret Goertz, eds., *Education Politics*, p. 121.

34. Ray and Mickelson in "Business Leaders," p. 122.

35. See, for example, Miriam David, "Moral and Maternal: The Family in the Right" in Ruth Levitas, ed., *The Ideology of the New Right*, (London: Polity Press, 1986); and Miriam David, "Teaching Family Matters," *British Journal of Sociology of Education*, 1986, vol. 7, no. 1, pp. 35-57.

36. *Ibid.*

37. David L. Clark and Terry A. Astuto, "The Disjunction of Federal Education Policy and Educational Needs in the 1990s" in Douglas Mitchell and Margaret Goertz, eds., *Education Politics*, p. 16.

38. Clark and Astuto, *ibid.*, p. 19.

39. See, for example, Madeleine Arnot "Consultation or Legitimation? Race and Gender Politics and the Making of the National Curriculum" in *Critical Social Policy*, issue 27, (Winter 1989-90), pp. 20-39.

40. Roxanne Bradshaw, "On the Future of Education in America" in Harvey Holtz et al., eds., *Education and the American Dream: Conservatives, Liberals and Radicals Debate the Future of Education* (Granby, MA: Bergin and Garvey, 1989) p. 201.

41. *Ibid.*, p. 226.

42. See, for example, Roger Dale, "Thacherite Project," and the special issue of *Critical Social Policy*, issue 27, (Winter 1989-90), entitled *Education in the 1990s*. Together the articles make a powerful critique of the effects of Conservative education policy in the 1990s.

CHAPTER 15

1. For details on the condition of primary education in the developing societies, see Marlaine E. Lockheed and Adrian Verspoor, *Improving Primary Education in Developing Countries* (Washington, D.C.: The World Bank, 1990).

2. Henry M. Levin, *Educational Reform for Disadvantaged Students: An Emerging Crisis* (West Haven, CT: NEA Professional Library,1986). Aaron M. Pallas, Gary Natriello, and Edward L. McDill, "The Changing Nature of the Disadvantaged Population: Current Dimensions and Future Trends," *Educational Researcher* 5 (June-July, 1989), pp. 16-22.

3. Prominent examples of this literature include Ivan Illich, *Deschooling Society* (New York: Harper and Row, 1971) and Martin Carnoy, ed., *Schooling in a Corporate Society* (New York: David McKay Co., Inc., 1972).

4. John E. Coons and Stephen D. Sugarman, *Education By Choice* (Berkeley, CA: University of California Press, 1978).

5. Ron Edmonds, "Effective Schools for the Urban Poor," *Educational Leadership*, vol. 37, no. 1 (1979), pp. 15-24. Wilbur Brookover and Larry Lezotte, *Changes in School Characteristics Coincident with Changes in Student Achievement* (East Lansing, Michigan: College of Urban Development, 1979).

6. Ron Edmonds, "Effective Schools for the Urban Poor."

7. U.S. General Accounting Office of the U.S. Congress, *Effective Schools Programs: Their Extent and Characteristics* (Washington, D.C.: U.S. Printing Office, 1989).

8. Marshall Smith and Stuart Purkey, "Effective Schools: A Review," *Elementary School Journal*, vol. 83, (1987), pp. 427-452.

9. Mark K. Felton, *The Effective Schools Movement: A Review of Its Research and Implementation*, unpublished senior thesis, Honors Program in Education (Stanford University, June 1990).

10. John F. Witte and Daniel E. Walsh, "A Systematic Test of the Effective Schools Model," *Educational Evaluation and Policy Analysis*, vol. 12, no. 2 (Summer 1990), pp. 188-212.

11. Michael Rutter et al., *Fifteen Thousand Hours* (Cam,bridge, MA: Harvard University Press, 1979).

12. Peter Mortimore et al., *School Matters* (Berkeley: University of California Press, 1988).

13. Rutter et al., *Fifteen Thousand Hours*, pp. 184-204.

14. See James P. Comer, *School Power* (New York: The Free Press, 1980); James

Comer, "New Haven's School—Community Connection," *Educational Leadership*, vol. 44, no. 6 (March 1987), pp. 13-18.

15. James Comer, "The Yale-New Haven Primary Prevention Project: A Follow-up Study," *Journal of the American Academy of Child Psychiatry*, vol. 24, no. 2 (1986), p. 155.

16. James Comer, "New Haven's School—Community Connection."

17. James Comer, "The Yale-New Haven Primary Prevention Project: A Follow-up Study," p. 157. Questions, however, have been raised about the comparability of the student groups.

18. For details on accelerated schools, see Henry M. Levin, *Accelerated Schools for At-Risk Students*, CPRE Research Report Series RR-010 (New Brunswick, NJ: Center for Policy Research in Education, Rutgers University, 1988) and "Accelerated Schools for Disadvantaged Students," *Educational Leadership* 6 (March 1987), pp. 19-21.

19. The underlying approach is found in Theodore Sizer, *Horace's Compromise* (Boston: Houghton Mifflin Co., 1984) . For details on implementation see Holly Houston, "Restructuring Secondary Schools," in Anne Lieberman, ed., *Building a Professional Culture in Schools* (New York: Teachers College Press, 1988), pp. 109-128.

20. Details on Impact can be found in William Cummings, *Low-Cost Primary Education: Implementing an Innovation in Six Nations* (Ottawa: International Development Research Centre, 1986).

21. For a comprehensive description of the CIEPs and their evolution, see Ana C. Leonardos, "CIEP: A Democratic School Model for Educating Economically Disadvantaged Students in Brazil," paper presented at World Bank Conference on "Effective Schools for Students from Impoverished or Economically Disadvantaged Backgrounds," Washington, D.C. (September 27-28, 1989). Revised 1990 for publication in a World Bank volume to be edited by Henry M. Levin and Marlaine Lockheed.

22. The best overall summary of the New School is found in Vicky Colbert, Clemencia Chiappe, and Jairo Arboleda, "The New School Program: More and Better Primary Education for Children in Rural Areas," Revision of a paper prepared for World Bank Conference on "Effective Schools for Students from Impoverished or Economically Disadvantaged Backgrounds, " Washington, D.C., (September 27-28, 1989). Revised 1990 for publication in a World Bank volume to be edited by Henry M. Levin and Marlaine Lockheed.

23. Nicholas Bennett, "How Can Schooling Improve the Lives of the Poorest? The Need for Radical Reform," Paper prepared for World Bank Conference on "Effective Schools for Students from Impoverished or Economically Disadvantaged Backgrounds," (September 27-28, 1989), Washington, D.C.

24. See Mun Tsang and Christopher Wheeler, "Local Initiatives and Their Impli-

cations for a Multilevel Approach to School Improvement in Thailand," Paper prepared for World Bank Conference on "Effective Schools for Students from Impoverished or Economically Disadvantaged Backgrounds," (September 27-28, 1989), Washington, D.C. Revised 1990 for publication in a World Bank volume.

25. Douglas M. Windham, "The Cost of Effective Schools," In P. Veeder, ed., *Fundamental Studies in Educational Research*, (Amsterdam: Swetz and Zeitlinger), forthcoming.

26. For a different interpretation of the research on effective schools as it applies to developing societies that is more closely aligned with the checklist strategy, see Elchanan Cohn and Richard A. Rossmiller, "Research on Effective Schools: Implications for Less Developed Countries," *Comparative Education Review*, vol. 31, no. 3 (August 1987), pp. 377-399. Also see the new journal which began publishing in 1990: *School Effectiveness and School Improvement*, published by Sets & Zeitlinger, Lisse, Heereweg 347, 2161 CA, Lisse, The Netherlands.

CHAPTER 16

This essay is largely based on a paper originally prepared for the Organization for Economic Cooperation and Development (OECD).

*Reprinted with permission from *Comparative Education Review* 31 (February 1987): 29-46.

1. T. N. Postlethwaite and A. Lewy, eds., *Annotated Bibliography of IEA Publications*, 1962-1978 (Stockholm: IEA, University of Stockholm, 1979).

2. John Schwille and Leigh Burstein, "The Necessity of Tradeoffs and Coalition Building in Cross-national Research: A Response to the Article by Theisen, Achola and Boakari, 'Underachievement of Achievement Studies'" (paper prepared for the Annual Meeting of the Comparative and International Education Society, Stanford University, Stanford, CA, April 1985), p. 9.

3. Torsten Husén, ed., *International Study of Achievement in Mathematics: A Comparison of Twelve Countries* (New York: Wiley, 1967), vols. 1-2.

4. Torsten Husén, "International Impact of Evaluation," in *Educational Evaluation: New Roles, New Means*, 68th Yearbook of the National Society for the Study of Education (Chicago: University of Chicago Press, 1969), pp. 335-349.

5. B. H. Choppin, "The Introduction of New Science Curricula in England and Wales," *Comparative Education Review* 18 (June 1974): pp. 196-206; Torsten Husén, Ingemar Fagerlind, and Robert Liljefors, "Sex Differences in Science Achievements and Attitudes," *Comparative Education Review* 18 (June 1974): pp. 292-304; T. N. Postlethwaite, ed., *Comparative Education Review*, vol. 18 (June 1974), special issue on IEA publications through 1973.

6. A. C. Purves and D. Levine, eds., *Educational Policy and International Assessment* (Berkeley, CA: McCutchan, 1975).

7. Torsten Husén and Maurice Kogan, eds., *Educational Research and Policy: How Do They Relate?* (Oxford: Pergamon, 1984).

8. Sixten Marklund, "The IEA Project: An Unfinished Audit," Report no. 64 (Stockholm: University of Stockholm, Institute of International Education, 1983).

9. NCES, International Education Statistics, Summary of Discussions, Education Indicators Conference, April 11-12, 1985 (Washington, D.C.: U.S. Department of Education, National Center for Education Statistics, 1985).

10. A. H. Passow, H. J. Noah, M. A. Eckstein, and J. R. Mallea, *The National Case Study: An Empirical Comparative Study of Twenty-one Systems* (New York: Wiley, 1973).

11. Hellmut Becker, "The Case of Germany: Experiences from the Education Council," in Husen and Kogan, eds.

12. Husén and Kogan, eds.; C. B. Cox and A. E. Dyson, eds., *Black Paper Two: The Crisis in Education* (London: Critical Quarterly Society, October 1960).

13. D. E. Super, ed., *Toward a Cross-national Model of Educational Achievement in a National Economy* (New York: Teachers College Press, 1969).

14. W. Shultze, *Die Leistungen im naturwissenschaftlichen Unterricht in der Bundesrepublik im internationalen Vergleich* (Achievements in Science in the Federal Republic in an International Perspective), (Frankfurt: Deutsches Institut fur Internationale Padagogische Forschung, 1974).

15. J. Karvonen, "School Democracy and Social Attitudes of Students and Teachers in Finnish Schools," *Comparative Education Review* 18 (June 1974): pp. 207-216.

16. J. V. Torney, A. N. Oppenheim, and R. F. Farnen, *Civic Education in Ten Countries: An Empirical Study* (New York: Wiley, 1976).

17. R. M. Wolf, "The Two Cultures," in *The IEA Six-Subject Survey: An Empirical Study of Education in Twenty-one Countries*, ed. D. A. Walker (New York: Wiley, 1976), pp. 241-258.

18. Torsten Husén, *Talent, Equality and Meritorcracy* (The Hague: Martinus Nijhoff, 1974).

19. G. De Landsheere et al., "High Achievers in Belgium," *Comparative Education Review* 18 (June 1974): pp. 188-195.

20. Ian Dunlop, *The Teaching of English in Swedish Schools: Studies in Methods of Instruction and Outcomes* (Stockholm: Almqvist & Wiksell, 1975).

21. *Ibid.*

22. Malcolm J. Rosier, "Factors Associated with Learning Science in Australian Secondary Schools," *Comparative Education Review* 18 (June 1974): pp. 180-187.

23. J. B. Carroll, *The Teaching of French as a Foreign Language in Eight Countries* (New York: Wiley, 1975), and "A Model of School Learning, " *Teachers College Record* 64 (1963): pp. 723-733.

24. Carroll, *The Teaching of French as a Foreign Language in Eight Countries.*

25. Otto Neurath, "Protokollsatze," *Erkenntris* 3 (1932-33): pp. 42-95; cf. Karl Popper, *Unended Quest: An Intellectual Autobiography* (La Salle, IL: Open Court, 1976); and Stig Lindholm, *Paradigms, Science and Reality: On Dialectics, Hermeneutics and Positivism in the Social Sciences* (Stockholm: University of Stockholm, Institute of Education, 1981).

26. Thomas Kuhn, *The Structure of Scientific Revolutions* (Chicago: University of Chicago Press, 1962).

27. Arthur W. Foshay, ed., *Educational Achievement of Thirteen-Years-Olds in Twelve Countries* (Hamburg: Unesco Institute for Education, 1962).

28. Lorin Anderson, "The Classroom Environment Study: Teaching for Learning" (in this issue). See also D. W. Ryan and L. W. Anderson, "Rethinking Research on Teaching: Lessons Learned from an International Study," *Evaluation in Education*, vol. 8, no. 2 (1985).

29. Marklund, n. 8 above.

CHAPTER 17

1. See, for example, Nelly Stromquist, "Women and Illiteracy: The Interplay of Gender Subordination and Poverty," *Comparative Education Review* 34 (no. 1, 1990): pp. 95-111.

2. All the enrollment statistics cited here are from UNESCO, *UNESCO Statistical Yearbook* (Paris: UNESCO, 1988).

3. *Ibid.*, table 3.7.

4. *Ibid.*, table 2.4, pp. 2-17.

5. See Gail P. Kelly, "Women and Higher Education," in Philip G. Altbach, ed., *International Encyclopedia of Higher Education* (New York: Garland). In press.

6. Statistics on women in higher education here are taken from *UNESCO Statistical Yearbook*, 1988.

7. *Ibid.*

8. *Ibid.*

9. Inga Elqvist-Saltzman, "Educational Reforms—Women's Life Patterns: A Swedish Case," *Higher Education* 17 (no. 5, 1988): pp. 479-490.

10. Lyn Yates, "Australia" in Gail P. Kelly, ed., *International Handbook of Women's Education* (Westport, CT: Greenwood Press, 1989), pp. 213-242.

11. Maxine S. Seller, "The United States," in Gail P. Kelly, ed., *International Handbook of Women's Education* (Westport, CT: Greenwood Press, 1989) pp. 515-546.

12. Hildur Ve and Nina Fjelde, "Public-Private Tendencies within Higher Education in Norway from a Woman's Perspective" in Gail P. Kelly and Sheila S. Slaughter, eds., *Women's Higher Education in Comparative Perspective* (Amsterdam: Kluwer Academic Publishers, 1990).

13. Margaret Sutherland, "Women in Higher Education: Effects of Crises and Change, " *Higher Education* 17 (no. 5, 1988): pp. 479-490; Kathryn M. Moore, "Women' s Access and Opportunity in Higher Education Toward the Twenty-First Century," *Comparative Education* 23 (no. 1, 1987): pp. 23-34.

14. E. A. Cebotarev, "Women, Work and Employment: Some Attainments of the International Women's Decade" in Aisla Thompson, ed., *The Decade for Women* (Toronto: Canadian Congress for Learning Opportunities, 1985) p. 70.

15. *Ibid.*

16. See, for example, Audrey Chapman Smock, *Women's Education in Developing Countries: Opportunities and Outcomes* (New York: Praeger, 1981); Rounaq Johan and Hanna Papanek, eds., *Women and Development: Perspectives from South and Southeast Asia* (Dacca: Institute of Law and International Affairs, 1979).

17. Gavin W. Jones, "Economic Growth and Changing Female Employment Structure in the Cities of Southeast and East Asia" in Gavin W. Jones, ed., *Women in the Urban and Industrial Workforce; Southeast and East Asia* (Canberra: Australian National University, Development Studies Centre, monograph no. 33, 1984) pp. 17-60; Cynthia B. Lloyd, ed., *Sex Discrimination and the Division of Labor* (New York: Columbia University Press, 1975).

18. *Ibid.* See also E. Schiefelbein and J. P. Farrell, "Women, Schooling and Work in Chile: Evidence from a Longitudinal Study," *Comparative Education Review* 24 (part 2, June 1989): pp. S160-S179 .

19. Gail W. Lapidus, *Women in Soviet Society* (Berkeley: University of California Press, 1980); Francine D. Blau and Carol L. Jusenius, "Economic Approaches to Sex Segregation in the Labour Market: An Appraisal," *Signs* (1976): pp. 181-199.

20. Smock, *op. cit.*; Claire Robertson, *Sharing the Same Bowl: A Socioeconomic History of Women and Class in Accra. Ghana* (Bloomington, Indiana: Indiana University Press, 1984).

21. Jones, *op. cit.*

22. See Earl L. Sullivan, "Women and Work in Egypt, " in Earl L. Sullivan and Korima Korayen, eds., *Cairo Papers in Social Sciences* (monograph 4, December 1981), pp. 1-44; Nermin Abadan-Unat, *Women in the Developing World: Evidence from Turkey* (Denver: University of Denver School of International Studies, monograph series in World Affairs no. 22, 1986); Eve Howard-Merriman, "Egypt" in Gail P. Kelly, ed., *International Handbook of Women's Education* (Westport, CT: Greenwood Press, 1989), pp. 433-454.

23. Susan McCrae Vander Voet, "The United Nations Decade for Women: The Search for Women's Equality in Education and Employment" in Aisla Thomson, ed., *Decade for Women* (Toronto: Canadian Congress for Learning Opportunities, 1985), pp. 78-79.

24. Cebotarev, *op. cit.*

25. Vander Voet, *op. cit.*, p. 85.

CHAPTER 18

*This article is based on our "Introduction" to our co-edited book, *National Literacy Campaigns: Historical and Comparative Perspectives* (New York: Plenum, 1987), pp. 1-28, and "National Literacy Campaigns: Historical and Comparative Lessons," *Phi Delta Kappan* 69 (November 1987): pp. 202-206.

1. Agneta Lind and Anton Johnston, *Adult Literacy in the Third World: A Review of Objectives and Strategies* (Stockholm: Institute of International Education, University of Stockholm and Swedish International Development Authority, 1986), p. 12.

2. Leslie Limage, "Adult Literacy Policy in Industrialized Countries, " *Comparative Education Review* 30 (February 1986), p. 50, and Jonathan Kozol, *Illiterate America* (Garden City, NY: Anchor Press/Doubleday, 1985).

3. Nelly Stromquist, "Women and Illiteracy: The Interplay of Gender Subordination and Poverty," *Comparative Education Review* 34 (February 1990), p. 99.

4. Gabriel Cárceles, "World Literacy Prospects at the Turn of the Century: Is the Objective of Literacy for All by the Year 2000 Statistically Plausible," *Comparative Education Review* 34 (February 1990), p. 10.

5. Shirley Heath, "Language and Literacy, " paper presented at Workshop on Literacy at Interagency Commission for the World Conference on Education for All, New York, June 1989; cited in Stromquist, "Women and Illiteracy, p. 96.

6. Baba Haidara, "Tendencias Negativas: Combatir el Analfabetismo en África," *El País* (Madrid), "Temas de Nuestra Epoca," January 18, 1990, p. 9.

7. Cárceles, "World Literacy Prospects," p. 2.

8. G. Carron and A. Bordia, *Issues in Planning and Implementing Literacy Programmes* (Paris: Unesco/IIEP, 1985), p. 18.

9. The chapters in our edited collection, *National Literacy Campaigns* examine Reformation Germany, early modern Sweden and Scotland, the nineteenth-century United States, nineteenth- and early twentieth-century Russia and the Soviet Union, pre-Revolutionary and Revolutionary China, and a variety of Third World countries in the post-World War II period (Tanzania, Cuba, Nicaragua, and India). There also is a chapter on the UNESCO-sponsored Experimental World Literacy Program and the piece by Limage on recent adult literacy efforts in the United Kingdom, France, and the United States.

10. H. S. Bhola, *Campaigning for Literacy: A Critical Analysis of Some Selected Literacy Campaigns of the 20th Century, with a Memorandum to Decision Makers* (Paris: UNESCO/International Council for Adult Education, 1982), p. 211.

11. Peter Kenez, "Liquidating Illiteracy in Revolutionary Russia," *Russian History* 9 (1982), pp. 180-181, cited in Ben Eklof, "Russian Literacy Campaigns," in Arnove and Graff, *Literacy Campaigns*, p. 131.

12. Roger Pethybridge, *The Social Prelude to Stalinism* (London: Macmillan, 1974), p. 152.

13. Eklof, "Russian Campaigns," p. 131.

14. Lind and Johnston, *Adult Literacy*, p. 18.

15. *Ibid.*, pp. 123-131. On the literacy campaign in China, see Evelyn Sakakida Rawski, *Education and Popular Literacy in Ch'ing China* (Ann Arbor: University of Michigan Press, 1979); and Charles W. Hayford, "Literacy Movements in Modern China," in Arnove and Graff, *Literacy Campaigns*, pp. 99-122.

16. Edward Stevens, "The Anatomy of Mass Literacy in Nineteenth-Century United States," in Arnove and Graff, *Literacy Campaigns*, pp. 99-122.

17. Bhola *Campaigning*, pp. 85-90.

18. *Ibid.*, p. 98.

19. Limage, "Industrialized Countries."

20. International Council for Adult Education, *World of Literacy* (Ottawa, Ontario: IDRC, 1979), p. 12; cited in Lind and Johnston, *Adult Literacy*, p. 85.

21. Eklof, "Russian Campaigns," p. 144.

22. Arthur Gillette, "The Experimental World Literacy Program: A Unique International Effort Revisited," in Arnove and Graff, *Literacy Campaigns*, p. 215.

23. A. Noor, "Managing Adult Literacy Training," *Prospects* 12 , no. 2 (1982), p. 179; cited in Lind and Johnston, *Adult Literacy* p. 85.

24. Yussaf Kassam and Bud Hall, "Tanzania's National Literacy Campaign: A Journey of Imagination, Energy, and Commitment," unpublished paper, International Council for Adult Education, Toronto, 1985; and Jeff Unsicker, "Tanzania's Literacy Campaign in Historical-Structural Perspective," in Arnove and Graff, *Literacy Campaigns*, pp. 173-196.

25. Stromquist, "Women and Illiteracy," p. 95.

26. Shozo Jizawa, "El Tamaño del Desafío: Analfabetismo en Asia y el Pacífico," *El País* (Madrid), "Temas de Nuestra Epoca," January 18, 1990, p. 8.

27. Haidara, "Tendencias Negativas," p. 9.

28. The exception is Cuba, which claims that its 1961 campaign reduced the rate of illiteracy from 24% to 4%. See Marvin Leiner, "The 1961 National Cuban Literacy Campaign," in Arnove and Graff, *Literacy Campaigns*, pp. 173-196.

29. Gerald Strauss, *Luther's House of Learning: Indoctrination of the Young in the German Reformation* (Baltimore: Johns Hopkins University Press, 1978); and Richard Gawthrop, "Literacy Drives in Preindustrial Germany," in Arnove and Graff, *Literacy Campaigns*, pp. 31-33.

30. Lind and Johnston, *Adult Literacy*, p. 3.

31. Juan Carlos Tedesco, "La Década Perdida: Analfabetismo, Democracia y Desarrollo en América Latina," *El País* (Madrid), "Temas de Nuestra Epoca," January 18, 1990, p. 6.

32. Haidara, "Tendencias Negativas," p. 9.

33. See, for example, Robert F. Arnove, *Education and Revolution in Nicaragua* (New York: Praeger, 1986), esp. ch. 3.

34. See, for example, E. D. Hirsch, Jr., *Cultural Literacy* (New York: Houghton Mifflin, 1987).

35. See Peter Easton and Stephen Klees chapter in this book; and Harry Braverman, *Labor and Monopoly Capital* (New York: Monthly Review Press, 1976); Samuel Bowles et al., *Beyond the Wasteland* (New York: Anchor Press/Doubleday, 1984); on the process of deskilling in the profession of education, see Michael Apple, *Teachers and Texts: A Political Economy of Class and Gender Relations in Education* (New York: Routledge & Kegan Paul, 1986).

36. Paul Kelly and David Wallace, "A Technology of the Intellect? Reflections on Literacy and Ideology," *Writing Instructor* 5, no. 3 (1986), p. 142; cited in Louie Crew, "Using and Abusing Literacy: Nine Vignettes, *Comparative Education Review* 34 (February 1990), p. 88.

37. Kathleen Rockhill, "Gender, Language and the Politics of Literacy," *British Journal of Sociology of Education* 8, no. 2 (1987).

38. See, for example, Daniel A. Wagner, "Literacy Assessment in the Third World: An Overview and Proposed Scheme for Survey Use," *Comparative Education Review* 34 (February 1990): pp. 61-84; and Harvey J. Graff, "Whither the History of Literacy? The Future of the Past," *Communication* 11 (1988): pp. 5-22.

39. On the problems of national planning, see Henry M. Levin, "The Identity Crisis of Educational Planning," *Harvard Educational Review* 51 (February 1981): pp. 85-93; and on the difficulties of determining literacy outcomes, see Harvey J. Graff, *The Legacies of Literacy: Continuities and Contradictions in Western Culture and Society* (Bloomington: Indiana University Press, 1987).

40. John C. Cairns, in "Introduction" to Audrey Thomas, "Adult Illiteracy in Canada—A Challenge," occasional paper no. 42 (Ottawa, Ontario: Canadian Commission for UNESCO, 1983), p. 8.

Contributors

Philip G. Altbach is professor and director of the Comparative Education Center, State University of New York at Buffalo. He is North American Editor of *Higher Education* and author of *Higher Education in the Third World, The Knowledge Context* and other books. He served for ten years as editor of the *Comparative Education Review*.

Robert F. Arnove is professor and head of the History, Philosophy, and Comparative Education Program at Indiana University, Bloomington. He has written extensively on the politics of educational reform movements. He co-edited the Februrary 1990 special issues of the *Comparative Education Review* on adult literacy.

Edward H. Berman is professor and chair of the Foundations of Education Department at the University of Louisville. He has published extensively on missionary education in Africa and the influence of philanthropic foundations on education in the United States and abroad.

John Boli is a comparative political sociologist living in Sweden. He is the author of *New Citizens for a New Society: The Institutional Origins of Mass Schooling in Sweden* and the coauthor of *Institutional Structure: Constituting State, Society and the Individual.*

Martin Carnoy is professor of the education and economics at Stanford University. He has written extensively on the state and education and economic development, the political economy of the United States, and the role of the state in social change. He is currently at work on a book that traces minorities' changing economic role in the U.S. economy during the past fifty years.

Miriam David is Professor and Chair of the Department of Sociology at West Bank Polytechnic in London. She has published books and numerous articles on parents, children, and the state.

Peter Easton is Assistant Professor of Social Foundations of Education at Florida State University. He is an economist and directs an AID project on basic education in Haiti.

Max A. Eckstein is professor of education at Queens College, City University of New York. He is co-author of *Toward a Science of Comparative Education*. Dr. Eckstein is a past president of the Comparative and International Education Society.

Joseph P. Farrell is professor in the Department of Adult Education of the Ontario Institute for Studies in Adult Education and is director of OISE's recently established Comparative, International, and Development Education Centre. A past president of the Comparative and International Education, he has written extensively on education and social change.

Harvey J. Graff is professor in the School of Arts and Humanities, University of Texas at Dallas. He has published extensively on the history of literacy.

Ruth Hayhoe is professor in the Higher Education Group, Ontario Institute for studies in Education, Toronto. She is currently the Cultural Attache at the Canadian Embassy in Beijing, China. Dr. Hayhoe has written extensively on education in China.

Torsten Husén is professor emeritus at the University of Stockholm. He was chairman of the International Evaluation of Educational Achievement (IEA) from 1962 to 1978. He has published numerous articles and books on the IEA and the theme of equality of educational opportunity.

Harry Judge is director/emeritus of the Department of Educational Studies at Oxford University. He is currently professor in the College of Education at Michigan State University.

Gail P. Kelly was professor and chair of the Department of Educational Organization, Administration, and Policy at the State University of New York at Buffalo. She wrote extensively about the education of women and about Comparative Education as a field of study. She was a past president of the Comparative and International Education Society.

Steven Klees is a Professor in the Social Foundations of Education at Florida State University. He has published numerous articles on economics of education and on educational technology in Latin America.

Tamas Kozma is co-director of the Hungarian Institute for Educational Research, Budapest. He has written extensively on education in Eastern Europe and has published in *Prospects* and other journals. Most recently, he was Fulbright Visiting Professor at Syracuse University.

Henry M. Levin is professor of education and affiliated professor in economics and director of the Center for Educational Research at Stanford University. He is the director of the nation-wide Accelerated School Program for At-Risk Students. He has written on the economics of education, workplace democracy, and innovative educational programs for at-risk students.

Noel F. McGinn is professor in the Harvard Graduate School of Education. He is Director of Project BRIDGES and its successor Project ABLE. His scholarship has focused on the politics of education in Latin America.

Harold J. Noah is professor in the Department of Educational Organization, Administration, and Policy, State University of New York at Buffalo. He was formerly Gardner Cowles Professor at Teachers College, Columbia University. He was editor of the *Comparative Education Review* and a president of the Comparative and International Education Society.

Francisco O. Ramirez is Professor of Education and (by courtesy) Sociology at Stanford University. He is the co-author of *Institutional Structure: Constituting State, Society, and the Individual* and the editor of *Rethinking the Nineteenth Century: Contradictions and Movements*.

Jandhyala B. G. Tilak is on the staff of the National Institute of Educational Planning and Administration, New Delhi, India. He has been on the staff of the World Bank and a visiting professor at the University of Virginia. He has written extensively on the economics of education.

Index